Managing Sport

Contemporary sport is shaped by wider society. Today those managing sport must be aware of the broader social and cultural context within which it exists if their effectiveness is to be established and their careers defined. This book is the first of its kind to contextualize the wider social and cultural environment of sport management and explain the key issues and practical implications of this for those working, or intending to find employment, in the field.

Written by a team of leading international experts on sport management, the book explores important topics, such as:

- corporate social responsibility in sport;
- race equality;
- gender equity;
- sport and violence;
- globalization and labour migration;
- populations with individual needs;
- doping in sport;
- social capital;
- social exclusion.

As part of a comprehensive coverage of these and many other social issues, readers are reminded of the fundamental requirement to appreciate properly the cultural sensitivies of the managerial environment in which they intend to operate.

Each issue is examined from the perspective of the manager or sport practitioner, and each chapter includes a range of useful features, such as case studies and self-test questions, to encourage readers to think critically about the role of sport in society and about their own professional practice. This is the first sports management textbook to be based on the thesis that a more socially aware manager is a more effective manager, and thus should be regarded as essential reading for all sport management students.

David Hassan is Senior Lecturer within the Ulster Sports Academy at the University of Ulster, Northern Ireland. His research expertise concerns the relationship between sport and national identity, the politics of sport and sport governance.

Jim Lusted is Senior Lecturer in the sociology of sport at the University of Northampton, UK. His research focuses on the implementation of equity policies into grassroots sport.

Foundations of Sport Management

Series Editors:
David Hassan, University of Ulster at Jordanstown, UK
Allan Edwards, Griffith University, Australia

Foundations of Sport Management is a discipline-defining series of texts on core and cutting-edge topics in sport management. Featuring some of the best-known and most influential sport management scholars from around the world, each volume represents an authoritative, engaging and self-contained introduction to a key functional area or issue within contemporary sport management. Packed with useful features to aid teaching and learning, the series aims to bridge the gap between management theory and practice and to encourage critical thinking and reflection among students, academics and practitioners.

Also available in this series

Managing Sport Business: An Introduction
David Hassan and Linda Trenberth

Managing Sport: Social and Cultural Perspectives
David Hassan and Jim Lusted

Managing Sport

Social and cultural perspectives

Edited by David Hassan and
Jim Lusted

Routledge
Taylor & Francis Group

LONDON AND NEW YORK

First published 2013
by Routledge
2 Park Square, Milton Park, Abingdon, Oxon OX14 4RN

Simultaneously published in the USA and Canada
by Routledge
711 Third Avenue, New York, NY 10017

Routledge is an imprint of the Taylor & Francis Group, an informa business

British Library Cataloguing in Publication Data
A catalogue record for this book is available from the British Library

Library of Congress Cataloging in Publication Data
Managing sport: social and cultural perspectives / edited by David Hassan and
Jim Lusted.
p. cm.—(Foundations of sport management)
1. Sports—Management. 2. Sports administration.
3. Sports—Sociological aspects.
I. Hassan, David. II. Lusted, Jim.
GV713.M362 2012
796.068—dc23
2012017245

ISBN: 978–0–415–57215–6 (hbk)
ISBN: 978–0–415–57216–3 (pbk)
ISBN: 978–0–203–85657–4 (ebk)

Typeset in Perpetua and Bell Gothic
by Swales & Willis Ltd, Exeter, Devon

Contents

List of figures

List of tables

List of boxes

List of case studies

About the authors

Jack Anderson is a Senior Lecturer in Law at Queen's University, Belfast. His primary research interest is the relationship between sport and the law and in 2010 he published *Modern Sports Law* (Oxford: Hart). He is a qualified arbitrator, being a Fellow of the Chartered Institute of Arbitrators (FCIArb), and is a member of a number of sports dispute resolution tribunals, including Sports Resolutions UK and Just Sport Ireland.

Simone Baglioni is a Lecturer in Politics at Glasgow Caledonian University (GCU). He holds a PhD in Political Science from the University of Geneva. Before joining GCU he worked as a researcher and lecturer in various universities (Florence, Geneva, Neuchâtel and Bocconi University in Milan). From 2006 until the end of 2008 he was a Marie Curie Research Fellow in the EU-funded comparative research, Sport and Social Capital in Europe, where he was responsible for an Italian case study. Simone has investigated civil society organizations that are active across various fields, including sport, and is interested in the relationship between social class reproduction and sport as well as in the 'dark sides' of social capital in sport.

Jodi Baker is an Assistant Clinical Professor in Athletic Training and the Director of the Athletic Training Education Program at the University of the Pacific, California. On completion of her first degree and athletic training certification she spent ten years as a clinical athletic trainer providing medical care to athletes in a variety of settings, including clinics, high schools and universities. She also has 4 years of experience in athletic training education and is responsible for the administration of an accredited athletic training education programme. Her research interests include disordered eating and eating disorder education for athletic training students as well as the effects of these conditions on collegiate athletes. Another area of interest includes appropriate and effective methods of educating athletic training students in general medical and orthopaedic medical conditions.

Urmilla Bob is an Associate Professor in the Discipline of Geography (School of Environmental Sciences) at the University of KwaZulu-Natal, Durban. She completed her Masters and her PhD in geography at West Virginia University in the USA. She conducts research on urban and rural development issues, sustainable land use and natural resource management as well as the socioeconomic impacts of tourism (specifically ecotourism and sport events). Professor Bob has published in these fields in both nationally and internationally recognized academic books and journals. She has been involved in collaborative research with national and international organizations and has attended several conferences and workshops worldwide.

Michelle Brassell has extensive management consultancy experience in supporting and advising a range of businesses on corporate social responsibility (CSR), including the sport sector. She helped develop the CSR strategies ad activities of European football clubs on behalf of the G-14 European football body. She created the Clubs that Count programme, a CSR scheme for sports clubs, and has taught CSR to business management postgraduate students at the University of Lyon, France. She is currently working as a consultant with a range of organizations on CSR-related agendas.

Todd Davenport is an Assistant Professor in the Department of Physical Therapy at the Thomas J. Long School of Pharmacy and Health Sciences of University of the Pacific, California. While working toward his first degree, he spent 1,200 hours working in an athletic medicine environment. Since completing his clinical training, Dr Davenport has achieved recognition as a board-certified specialist in Orthopaedic Physical Therapy by the American Board of Physical Therapy Specialties. His research interests broadly include the identification of best practices in diagnosis, treatment and prevention of disability related to musculoskeletal pathology. His current research explores which interventions are optimal for individuals with long-standing symptoms, such as chronic fatigue and foot pain, as well as the psychological implications of wellness and disability. In addition to his academic responsibilities, Dr Davenport continues to use his experience and training for clinical consulting for patient care, including the care and prevention of athletic injuries.

Sandra Dowling is a social anthropologist who has been working in research in the field of intellectual and developmental disabilities for the past 12 years. She is a member of the management team for the Regional Research Collaborating Centre with Special Olympics Europe Eurasia at the University of Ulster and Research Manager on a series of programme and practice evaluations in collaboration with Special Olympics. During time at the University of London and King's College London her research focused on the social and psychological well-being of people with intellectual disabilities. She is interested in inclusive research techniques and methodological development. She has published and presented her research widely.

Spencer Harris is currently Assistant Professor in the Department of Human Performance and Physical Education at Adams State College in Colorado, USA. His previous experience includes 16 years in community sports development, working as a Sport Development Manager at Crawley Borough Council; as Head of Performance for Sport England East; and spending a year in Arua, Uganda as a Project Coordinator for Right to Play. In addition, he worked as a Senior Lecturer in Sports Development at the University of Hertfordshire from 2008 to 2011. Spencer's publications include work on voluntary sport and sport policy. He is currently in the final year of his PhD, which is focused on analysing the relationship between national governing bodies of sport and county sport partnerships in the implementation of increased participation in community sport.

David Hassan (co-editor) is a Senior Lecturer at the University of Ulster Jordanstown. He is the Deputy Executive Academic Editor of *Sport in Society*, an international, peer-reviewed journal published by Taylor & Francis. He is also Series Editor (with Dr A.

Edwards) of *Foundations in Sport Management*, a new Routledge collection. He has published extensively on the social, historical and political aspects of sport and has received numerous awards for the excellence of his scholarship over the last decade.

Chris Janssen is Graduate Assistant in the Department of Sport Sciences at the University of the Pacific in California. He has a BA in Sport Sciences – Sport Management from Pacific. He has worked in intercollegiate athletics and private industry where he was a top salesperson. Chris enjoys working out, travelling and meeting new people.

Lara Killick is an Assistant Professor in Sociology of Sport and Sport Pedagogy at the University of the Pacific, California. On completion of her first degree, she spent 5 years in the sports management and coaching industry engaged with projects designed to promote social inclusion through sport. She also has over ten years' experience coaching cricket, field hockey and health-related fitness programmes in the UK, Australia and New Zealand. Dr Killick's research interests include young people's embodied understandings of the sport–health–risk nexus, development of epistemic devices around sporting pain and injury and media representations of the (injured) body and sport. These connect with broader concerns related to the construction of gendered athletic identities, the role of achievement in sport in physical education and power relations within the school environment. Her most recent work has focused on the governance and commercial potential of the UK netball Superleague, social and cultural determinants of health and the use of emergent technology within teacher education programmes.

Paul Kitchin is Lecturer in Sport Management at the University of Ulster, where he teaches sport strategy, finance, marketing and policy. Paul is currently on the editorial boards of the *International Journal of Sports Marketing and Sponsorship* and the *International Journal of Sport Management and Marketing*. Paul has experience working with UK third-sector sporting organizations in the provision of research, planning and consultancy services. A graduate of the University of Tasmania and Deakin University, he is currently completing his PhD at Loughborough University, investigating the development of self identity in young people with disabilities through sporting participation.

Jim Lusted (co-editor) is a Senior Lecturer in the sociology of sport at the University of Northampton, UK. He completed a PhD in 2009 in collaboration with the English Football Association (FA), investigating issues around the implementation of their equity policies into the grassroots level of the game. He has published articles relating to race equality policies in local sport in a number of journals, including *Managing Leisure* and *Soccer and Society*. He is also a licensed tutor for the FA's Equality Workshop which he delivers to local football stakeholders across England.

Nicole Matuska graduated from Northwestern University with a journalism degree. Upon receiving a Fulbright scholarship, she travelled to Morocco to do research on the role of women in modern Moroccan society through the lens of sports. She produced several photo projects, academic publications and a 20-minute documentary on women's football in Morocco. Nicole continued working with various local grassroots organizations using sport as a tool for social change. Living in Casablanca, Morocco, Nicole is currently the

Learn Manager at Women Win, a non-profit organization based in Amsterdam that uses sports as a way for girls around the world to access their rights relating to gender-based violence, sexual and reproductive health and rights, and economic empowerment.

Roy McConkey is Professor of Learning Disability at the University of Ulster, Northern Ireland. A psychologist by training, he has been involved in research and development in the field of intellectual disability for over 40 years. He has written numerous books and peer-reviewed journal articles and has undertaken consultancies for various United Nations and international agencies in over 20 countries throughout the world.

Sabine Menke is Director of Youth, Unified Sports and Research, Special Olympics Europe/Eurasia. She holds a Masters in Sport Sciences from the German Sport University Cologne. She has completed a postgraduate Executive Master in Sport Organization Management at the University of Lyon, France, in cooperation with the International Olympic Committee.

Dino Numerato is a research fellow at University of West Bohemia in Pilsen, Department of Sociology (Czech Republic) and Bocconi University (Milan, Italy). He is also an external lecturer in the Sociology of Sport at Masaryk University (Brno, Czech Republic), where he received his PhD in Sociology in 2006. His research interests are in the sociology of sport, sport governance, sport policy and its transformation in the post-communist Czech Republic. He has also been working on the nexus between sport and the media and the relationship between sport and politics, with a particular focus on sport-based resistance. He has published articles in journals such as *Sociology*, the *International Review for the Sociology of Sport*, *Sport in Society*, the *International Journal of Sport Communication* and *International Journal of Sport Policy and Politics*.

Ian O'Boyle is a Lecturer in Sport Management within the School of Sport and Exercise at Massey University in New Zealand. He is a graduate of University College Dublin (Ireland) and University of Ulster (UK). Ian has previously taught at Stranmillis University College in Northern Ireland and at Northern Regional College also in Northern Ireland. Ian's primary research interest lies in the area of performance management within organizational sport management; he is also involved in research projects relating to sport governance and various other sport management-related topics.

Sean O'Connor has 30 years' experience in the marketing and management of international sport. In the early 1980s he pioneered the communication of the successful Marlboro motorsport programme in the Middle East and later World Rally Championship (WRC). He was the co-founder and promoter of Rally Ireland, which generated the highest TV figures on its debut in the WRC series. He has lectured at Dublin Institute of Technology, where he was awarded an MPhil in 2005; he holds an MA for Dublin City University in Political Communication and received his PhD from the University of Ulster in December 2011. He is a Director of the Automobile and Touring Club of the UAE.

Jimmy O'Gorman is a Senior Lecturer in Sports Development at Edge Hill University. He was awarded his PhD in 2010 from Loughborough University, having worked with the

Football Association to analyse the processes and practices engaged by volunteers in the implementation of the Charter Standard scheme. Jimmy has presented at several European and international conferences on the processes and theory of sport policy implementation with particular reference to grassroots sports clubs and volunteers, and has an emerging publishing record in this area. Jimmy also holds a UEFA B certificate in coaching football, and is an active coach at grassroots and university level.

H. Thomas R. Persson is a Senior Lecturer and Researcher at the Department of Sport Sciences and the Department of the Individual and Society at Malmö University (Malmö, Sweden). His research interests lie in the areas of sport and leisure governance, policy and social integration. His work includes studies of governance, corporate social responsibility (CSR), social capital and sport; state-governed body-governed recreational physical activity in the third age; social integration and sport participation; governance of municipal-run leisure activities; ethnic discrimination in the area of employment; and national integration policies. Persson has published (on sport) in the *International Journal on Sport Policy and Politics*, *International Review for the Sociology of Sport*, *Entertainment and Sports Law Journal*, *Idrottsforskning* and on Idrottsforum.org. He has co-edited a special issue of the *International Journal on Sport Policy and Politics* focusing on the governance of sport from a Scandinavian perspective.

David Reid is Lecturer in Sports Coaching at the University of Ulster where he teaches sports coaching and physical education as well as athletics coach education. David has several years' experience working in performance sport, specifically in the sport of athletics in the UK and Ireland. A graduate of the University of Ulster, he is currently completing his PhD at the University of Ulster, investigating the education of talented athletes in anti-doping, as well as anti-doping policies and procedures.

Pete Schroeder is an Associate Professor of Sport Management and chair of the Department of Sports Sciences at the University of the Pacific in California. He earned his doctorate from the University of Missouri in Leadership and Policy Analysis and a BSc in Exercise Science at Truman State University. He has conducted award-winning research on organizational culture in university and college sport and has published research in *Sport, Education and Society*, *Journal of Sport Behavior*, *Journal of College Student Development* and *Journal of Issues in Intercollegiate Athletics*. In addition, he has presented research on international labour migration and sport management pedagogy. He is a member of the College Sport Research Institute and has consulted for multiple university athletic departments and teams. During his free time, he enjoys travelling, skiing and playing basketball.

Sally Shaw is a Senior Lecturer in Sport Management at the University of Otago, Dunedin, New Zealand. Using critical approaches, her research focus includes gender equity in sport organizations, and organizational governance. She has published widely in these areas in international journals, and is on the review boards of the *Journal of Sport Management* and *Sport Management Review*. She has recently been a mentor for the New Zealand Olympic Committee's Women in Governance programme.

XV

Kamilla Swart is an Associate Professor in the Faculty of Business and heads the Centre for Tourism Research in Africa, Cape Peninsula University of Technology, Cape Town. Her research interests include sport and event tourism, with a specific focus on the 2010 FIFA World Cup and event policies, strategies and evaluations. Professor Swart has published on varied topics relating to the bidding and impacts of sport tourism events in South Africa (*Politikon, Urban Forum, The Sociological Review*, among others) and has published in several books. She was instrumental in developing the 2010 FIFA World Cup Research Agenda and served as the City of Cape Town's Research Coordinator for 2010.

Richard Tacon is a final-year doctoral student at the Department of Management, Birkbeck, University of London. His doctoral research looks at how social capital develops within voluntary sports organizations and at how realist evaluation can be used to inform social policy. His other research examines governance and corporate social responsibility in non-profit organizations. He recently co-authored a report on governance within national governing bodies of sport in the UK and a report on corporate social responsibility in European football. Previously, Richard worked at the Central Council of Physical Recreation (now the Sport and Recreation Alliance), the umbrella organization for the governing and representative bodies of sport and recreation in the UK.

Dag Tuastad holds a doctoral degree in Anthropology and is an Associate Professor of Middle Eastern Studies at the University of Oslo. His main research has been on Palestinian politics, including studies on the role of kinship in Palestinian politics, Hamas' concept of a long-term ceasefire, and the democratization process in the Palestine Liberation Organization. He is currently working as a Researcher at the Center for Islamic and Middle East Studies at the University of Oslo on the research project The New Middle East; Emerging Political and Ideological Trends.

Preface

The collection of chapters in this book provides what we believe to be a long overdue attempt to deal with some of the key contemporary social and cultural issues that directly impact upon sport and leisure management. The management of sport across the world is a rapidly evolving maelstrom; it has become a very sophisticated complex commercial business at one end of the sport continuum but remains a continually evolving process with many different challenges at the other, more 'local' level. Similarly, the truly global nature of sport means all kinds of local cultural specificities increasingly need to be considered by sport managers working across different national settings. Amid these changes, the influence of social issues like gender relations, social responsibility or violence in sport – to name just a few – remains a constant feature. How those managing sport are thought to respond to controversies that can emerge from issues like these, however, is rarely discussed. The challenges facing sport managers today are overwhelmingly social and cultural in nature, and yet much of the current literature on sport management fails to engage fully with the wider sociocultural context in which sports take place. Sport management texts have been dominated by rather narrow functional approaches – often drawn from experts in the fields of business studies and economics – that all too frequently ignore the broader social and cultural sources that appear to lend themselves to many of the areas that are traditionally covered in the sport management syllabus. One might take the topic of marketing in sport as an illustrative example: the study of customer need and demand is likely to be enhanced with a broader understanding of the ways in which a social and cultural setting can shape, limit and even determine the actions of individuals.

This overwhelmingly managerialist approach to sport management probably reflects the much wider trend for disciplines to remain largely exclusive and insular, rarely delving into other fields for otherwise potentially fruitful sources of explanatory concepts and theories. The same could no doubt be said of texts that cover sociocultural issues in sport that are drawn heavily from those working exclusively in the fields of sociology and cultural studies. Although this disciplinary myopia may characterize previous scholarship in the field of sport, we have reason to be optimistic and excited about the future in this respect. The study of sport is certainly better placed than most others to engage in an interdisciplinary approach, as most sport departments and degree programmes will testify. We would like to think that the reader will be able to identify multiple signs of this disciplinary flexibility and collaboration in the articles contained in this book. These chapters can be seen, at various times, to be informed by theories and concepts traditionally housed in the fields of sociology, cultural studies, critical management studies, philosophy, history, geography, political studies, policy studies and business studies, to name but a few.

We believe that the articles in this book offer a fresh and stimulating look at sport management issues – an approach that reflects much of the contemporary teaching in this field. In recent years we have witnessed a growing convergence between the fields of sport management and sport studies (including the sociology of sport, the politics of sport and sport history) in degree programmes across the globe. Indeed, our collection might be best seen as a response to such changes in teaching and curricula, providing a range of articles that offer a more critical appraisal of sport management issues than exists in other texts. This interdisciplinary approach is also intended to prepare students and practitioners better for management careers in the sport and leisure industries. Moreover, an awareness of the sociocultural conditions which shape these industries is not only likely to facilitate a better understanding of key sport management issues today but also to help practitioners to find more creative and effective solutions to the problems they will face throughout their careers.

The book is not, however, simply designed for sport management scholars and practitioners. Those with an interest in sociocultural issues in sport can be rightly criticized for failing to engage fully with the field of management studies in their analysis of some popular areas of inquiry such as social inequality and inclusion/exclusion. This book is also aimed at students and scholars who may have less familiarity with key management concepts and theories as applied to their particular fields of study. The articles should be of relevance and interest to students from a wide range of subjects, both within leisure programmes (not just management but also relevant studies, sciences and education courses) and beyond – indeed, any scholarly activity that has as its aim a fuller, more rounded study of sport and its wider significance to our everyday lives. Put simply, we necessarily limit our understanding of sport if we fail to appreciate the ways in which it is managed, the organizations responsible for managing it and the everyday concerns of those who are tasked with the act of management.

Another feature of the book is the scope that the various chapters cover in their totality. Sport management studies continue to be overwhelmingly concerned with the professional, elite level of sport and the global, multinational corporations associated with this level. While some of the chapters contained herein cover such familiar terrain, many others focus on sport at its most basic, grassroots level, where recreational sport is played and where volunteers continue to dominate. We can also claim to have a truly global collection, from all corners of the world, including the UK, USA, mainland Europe, New Zealand and, perhaps uniquely, the Middle East. We hope this variety not only offers 'something for everyone', but also reflects the increasingly globalized nature of sport, the variety of sociocultural contexts in which it takes place, and the increasing diversity of what is considered to be 'sport' – and legitimate academic study in this field – in contemporary societies and universities across the world.

THE COLLECTION

Ian O'Boyle focuses on the issues of strategic and performance management in sport organizations. He points to the quite wide-ranging changes in remit and purpose of many sports organizations in recent years that have put pressure on them to be increasingly professionalized and more transparent and accountable. These changes lend themselves to a strategic approach to the management of sport, and the use of performance management systems and tools. Both these issues are critically surveyed in Chapter 1.

Nicole Matuska takes the reader to Casablanca, Morocco, for her fascinating overview of the ways in which the use of urban space for recreational sport can facilitate both social inclusion and exclusion. She concentrates on the experiences of working-class females in Casablanca and their difficulties in accessing sport facilities while leisure space in the city has become increasingly privatized and costly. In her analysis (Chapter 2), Matuska also explores the ways in which gender relations and religious practice can impact on women's participation in football in Morocco.

David Reid and *Paul Kitchin* explore the issue of doping in sport – always high on the agenda of those managing elite sport. They provide a useful critical summary of the various ways in which the key doping agencies for international sport have attempted to manage the doping problem, while also briefly exploring the often inconsistent coverage that the topic receives in the media of various parts of the world. Chapter 3 concludes with a survey of some of the recommendations that have been made, particularly by athletes themselves, to deal with doping in the future.

Ever wondered why violence in sport is often treated differently than in other places? In Chapter 4 *Jack Anderson* presents an intriguing account of the extent to which criminal law can apply to acts of violence in sport, particularly in the UK. With the use of relevant case studies, he explores the reasons why, in the main, the courts show little appetite for applying laws such as grievous bodily harm for on-the-field violent incidents that might otherwise be considered as such. Anderson explores the extent to which one can say an athlete 'consents' to potential acts of violence when playing sports that have obvious risk of intense physical contact.

Politicians in the UK have taken an increased interest in sport in recent years. *Spencer Harris* provides an authoritative overview of this changing stance by the UK government to sport, with particular focus on the development of sport at the grassroots, recreational level (Chapter 5). He provides detail of the various initiatives created by successive politicians to attempt to increase the participation base of sport in the UK, before providing a critical overview of the implementation process associated with Sport England's ambition to increase participation by one million by 2012.

In Chapter 6 *Jim Lusted* explores the various ways in which race equality policies are 'sold' to sports organizations, particularly at the local level in the UK. He presents a model that suggests such policies tend to be adopted for moral, political/legal or business reasons. In reviewing each 'case' for race equality, he assesses the limitations of each and suggests that, far from there being an antiracist consensus in UK sport, race equality policies can be the source of a number of controversies that make their implementation particularly challenging.

Sandra Dowling, Sabine Menke, Roy McConkey and David Hassan offer a critical analysis of the Unified Sports programme, offered by Special Olympics Europe-Eurasia, in Chapter 7. The programme aims to encourage the social inclusion of disabled people, specifically those with an intellectual disability. The particular challenges associated with sport provision for this group are surveyed, at governmental, policy and grassroots levels. The authors suggest that the programme offers numerous benefits to participants, and identify several examples of good practice that might be applied to future programmes of this kind. They also point to the wider sociocultural limitations that a scheme like this inevitably faces in its attempts to embed social inclusion into local communities.

Those of us who have played sport will probably all have picked up an injury and suffered some pain on our fields of play. *Lara Killick, Todd Davenport* and *Jodi Baker* provide a fascinating examination of pain and injury in sport in Chapter 8. This topic has overwhelmingly been the subject of physiological and psychological study, but in this chapter the authors offer a sociocultural approach to the ways in which pain and injury are dealt with in sports organizations. They point to a number of tensions between health and performance outcomes in sport – pressure to 'play through pain' – and also the obligations placed on sports organizations when players suffer injuries. The message here is that sport managers can reproduce quite damaging messages about how athletes should cope with pain and injury in sport.

Pete Schroeder and *Chris Janssen* contribute a useful chapter on the impact of labour migration on the management of sport (Chapter 9). They detail the consequences for the movement of labour as a result of the increasing globalization of sport, before raising some of the issues that can emerge as athletes move to other parts of the world to pursue their sport careers. Such migration patterns can have implications for 'donor' and 'host' nations, which are explored here, noting the challenges these may bring to sport managers.

Dag Tuastad takes us to the Middle East in his absorbing chapter that details the ways in which football clubs and contests can come to represent wider ethnonational relations and tensions in a region (Chapter 10). He uses the tensions between two teams, Wihdat, drawn from a Palastinian refugee camp, and Faisali, representing 'original' Jordanians, to explore the contrasting patterns of nationalist inclusion and exclusion that can be identified through the actions of the supporters of these teams. This is a fascinating account of the role of football in a national setting almost completely absent in standard texts on sport management.

Why do there continue to be so few women in the highest positions in sport across the world? This is the question that *Sally Shaw* attempts to address in her insightful chapter on gender equity in sport organizations (Chapter 11). Shaw draws upon her own research, conducted in New Zealand, to explore the contrasting attempts to increase the numbers of women in sport administration. Drawing upon different feminist approaches, she examines the long-term impact that both liberal and radical policies have, specifically in relation to changing the organizational cultures that historically tend to privilege men in sport, particularly in positions of power.

Social capital has become something of a contemporary buzzword in sport in recent years. *Richard Tacon* takes the reader through the key approaches to social capital, surveying the main 'schools of thought' in this field of study (Chapter 12). It is generally understood that sport is well placed to develop social capital, however defined, and yet Tacon suggests the evidence for this remains thin. In particular, how social capital is 'created' through sport remains an area of contention, and sport managers should be wary in their assumptions about sport's power to build communities in the way we often think it can.

Sport has always been characterized by quite astounding levels of voluntary commitment and duty, particularly at the grassroots level. Managing volunteers can be very challenging. *Jimmy O'Gorman* takes us through some of the changes that have occurred in sports volunteering in the UK in recent years (Chapter 13). He particularly points to the ways in which attempts to modernize grassroots sport have placed a range of pressures on traditional sport volunteers. The English Football Association's Charter Standard scheme for grassroots clubs is one element of this modernization, and O'Gorman identifies the various ways in which voluntary sports clubs and volunteers have engaged with the scheme – supportive, indifferent and resistant.

Sean O'Connor and David Hassan return to the Middle East to explore the consumption patterns related to sport in the United Arab Emirates (UAE) in Chapter 14. They make the point that, although this region is often seen as ripe for the expansion and consumption of sport, we know very little about the sporting interests and habits of nations like the UAE. Using research the authors were involved in collecting, they offer an overview of the interest in sport in this region, highlighting the popularity of motor sport, particularly Formula One. This has particular resonance given the recent decision that Qatar will host the Football World Cup in 2022. It is suggested that bringing global sport events to the Middle East can help internationalize the outlook of local spectators and consumers of sport.

On this theme, Kamilla Swart and Urmilla Bob provide a critical analysis of the long-term impact of hosting sporting mega-events in Chapter 15. In particular, they focus on the ways in which such impact has been measured previously, pointing out some of the important limitations in the current and historic approaches to evaluating the legacy of mega-events. Perhaps we shouldn't be surprised with the authors' view that the positive consequences of hosting mega-event are always overemphasized, while any negative outcomes are rarely considered by governments and local organizers. That said, the chapter reminds us to adopt a more sceptical approach to 'impact' studies than we may have done in the past.

In Chapter 16 Michelle Brassell discusses another of the more common buzzwords in contemporary sport management – corporate social responsibility (CSR). An excellent survey of the origins and development of CSR in sport is provided in Brassell's chapter, before she examines the varied uptake and engagement with CSR across the diverse range of organizations that manage sport around the world – at local, national and transnational levels. The chapter identifies good practice in CSR before providing a critique of the limitations of CSR in helping sport businesses meet their wider social obligations.

There seems no lack of media interest associated with corruption in sport governance – often at the very highest levels of power. Dino Numerato, Simone Baglioni and H. Thomas R. Persson take the reader over to the 'dark side' in their discussion of the corruptive elements of global sports governance (Chapter 17). Drawing upon their own data collected in a range of national and sporting settings, they point to practices and procedures that can bring about situations like conflicts of interest, financial irregularities, misuses of power and social exclusion. This entertaining chapter reminds us again of the need to take a critical approach in our studies of sport management in order to understand better the current state of the sports we enjoy.

The chapters that follow give us reason to feel excited and optimistic about the future of sport management as an academic discipline. The overall tone of this book points the way to a more critical approach to understanding and ultimately finding solutions to the contemporary issues facing sport and leisure management scholars and practitioners. There are, of course, likely to be several oversights and omissions within the collection that the editors must acknowledge. The book is not, for example, meant as an exhaustive overview of all the issues facing sport management today (there wouldn't be a bookcase large enough to store the book) and we are obviously not able to cover every national setting in our discussion of the chosen topics. The editors acknowledge any oversights that might have been made in this respect, and in any anomalies in the final versions of all chapters. Warm thanks must be paid to the contributing authors for their patience, diligence and understanding throughout the formation of the book.

Chapter 1

Managing organizational performance in sport

Ian O'Boyle

TOPICS

The modern sport organization • Strategic management in sport • Performance management in sport • The future for performance management in sport

---

OBJECTIVES

By the end of this chapter, you will be able to:

- Understand issues facing the modern sport organization;
- Define the various areas of performance relating to sport management;
- Discuss how performance can be measured in different settings;
- Understand how external factors can impact upon performance management in sport;
- Describe the future for performance management within sport organizations.

KEY TERMS

Governance – the process of granting power, verifying performance, managing, leading and/or administrating within an organization.

Non-profit organization (NPOs) – an organization that may earn a profit at year end, but in order to retain its non-profit status must reinvest this within the organization. Unlike publicly owned organizations, NPOs do not have shareholders who receive a dividend at the close of the financial year.

Sport – an athletic activity requiring skill or physical prowess and often of a competitive nature. Examples include various codes of athletics, rugby and football.

Stakeholder – a person, group or organization that has a direct or indirect stake in an organization because it can affect or be affected by the organization's actions, objectives and policies.

Transparency – in the social context, acts which generally imply openness, communication and accountability.

OVERVIEW

The modern sport organization's administration and management require increasingly specific industrial knowledge. To sustain the existence of their non-profit status (where appropriate), managers must be equipped with the necessary skills to lead these organizations into the future, deploying an ever more professional approach, one that might not typically have been evident heretofore. As such, leaders must familiarize themselves with the various management techniques required to perform well within the modern sports environment, which often requires an adaptation of existing approaches applied within traditional business environments.

Nowadays sport organizations have evolved to perform a role in education, healthcare, economic development and the labour market alongside promoting various social concerns and initiatives. The way in which these organizations are managed therefore requires a degree of adaptation from what might be regarded as being more traditional forms of organizational management. The principles, methods and conditions that exist within any given sport organization must be analysed before executives decide upon the most appropriate managerial style to be utilized within their particular organization. Management must ultimately address two key issues when establishing their future business principles and practices: (1) the nature of performance that the organization is seeking to achieve; and (2) how this performance is going to be attained, retained and enhanced into the future.

At present sport organizations are being confronted with an operating environment that has witnessed substantial change over recent years, mostly regarding issues of competitiveness and professionalism. As a result, many organizations have progressed from simply fulfilling an administrative function to adopting a promotional-led, ongoing strategic and performance-driven approach to their activities. Chappelet and Bayle (2005) argue that this strategic and performance management style is crucial for organizations to define projects with which they are involved, to structure them in a way that will allow them to achieve successful outcomes, and, most importantly, to evaluate such projects once they have been completed in order to draw useful conclusions concerning the continuation of such programmes of work or the establishment of new directions and policies (Chappelet and Bayle 2005).

It is evident that organizations must clearly define their strategic plans and objectives before any performance management system can be properly established. Management itself can be considered as being a cyclical process, consisting of subprocesses that interrelate with each other on a number of different levels (Fischer and Ostwald

2005). In practice, performance management will be impacted upon in direct relation to the strategic direction and objectives operating within a particular sport organization. It has been clear up until now that strategic and performance management approaches, such as those outlined above, have been most commonly applied in traditional business settings. Yet it is clear that they can also provide significant benefits for many other institutions as well, such as schools, churches, community meetings, health settings, governmental agencies, political environments and, of course, sports organizations (Diaz-Martin *et al.* 2000).

Like most organizations, those concerned with the delivery of sporting opportunities are predominantly concerned with the effective delivery of their central mission, typically increasing the numbers of people through their doors and scoping further opportunities for revenue generation. Potentially they may end up turning over a profit at the close of the financial year but these extra finances must be reinvested within the organization in order to retain its non-profit status (again, if appropriate). Sport organizations can be compared with businesses in other sectors by comparing their members and stakeholders to clients and shareholders typically present within established, traditional business institutions. Sport organizations can take the form of associations, foundations, cooperatives, trusts, societies and even corporations and companies (Kotler and Andreasen 1991: 10).

CASE STUDY: SPORT AND RECREATION NEW ZEALAND (SPARC)

SPARC is the Crown entity responsible for sport and physical recreation in New Zealand. The organization was established on 1 January 2003 under the Sport and Recreation New Zealand Act (2002). SPARC provides leadership in research and the development and implementation of policies that recognize the importance of sport and physical recreation in New Zealand. This involves working with other government agencies to increase participation and strengthen the sport and physical recreation sector, and ensuring these agencies understand the potential that sport and physical recreation offer as a means of achieving their own objectives and outcomes.

SPARC's delivery model is based on partnering with key organizations in the sport and recreation sector (primarily national-level sport and recreation organizations and regional sports trusts) to help achieve their desired outcomes.

These partner organizations deliver sport and physical recreation to New Zealanders from grassroots to high-performance levels. SPARC is not primarily a delivery agency, but is responsible for setting direction and providing investment and resources to the sector. SPARC works to:

- **invest** – target investment to organizations that are the most capable and ready to deliver on desired outcomes.
- **lead** – provide clear and strong leadership and work in the best interests of the sport and recreation sector through advocacy, policy development and research, and coordination of the sector to be stronger and more effective.
- **enable** – build the capability of partners by providing staff, resources, research and examples of good practice across the sector – for example, in coaching, governance and management systems, research and monitoring (SPARC 2011).

3

The organization is a prime example of an entity that has recognized the increased demands that are being placed on modern sport organizations in relation to competitiveness and a call for greater transparency. In response to this, SPARC has formed a leadership team that has a passion and appreciation for sport in New Zealand but also contains individuals who possess an indepth corporate knowledge of how to manage such an organization effectively in the modern environment. This corporate knowledge has led to increased efficiency and positive results for the organization, particularly within the field of performance management.

SPARC conducts formal performance appraisal processes with individual members of staff every 6 months. Individuals' performance within the organization is based on the expectations of their line manager and the details of their position as outlined within their personal job description. SPARC realizes that performance within an organization begins at an individual level and a formal performance appraisal process ensures individual employee performance can be directly related to the strategic and performance goals of SPARC. Even the current chief executive officer (CEO) of SPARC, Peter Miskimmin, is subject to this formal performance appraisal process. The CEO is responsible to the board and his performance is analysed every 6 months in keeping with all other staff members.

Aside from individual performance evaluation processes, SPARC has also adopted a form of Balanced Scorecard in order to assess the performance of the organization as a whole. The scorecard is essentially based on the ongoing strategic plans of SPARC and successes and failures can be clearly established through the implementation of this performance management tool.

STRATEGIC MANAGEMENT IN SPORT

As indicated, thus far the majority of sporting bodies remain as non-profit organizations (NPOs). Whilst arguably the private (sports) sector as a whole failed to adopt the concept of strategic planning fully until the late 1990s, the public sector and particularly NPOs did see the value in creating strategic plans throughout this period, if not before, and were generally more receptive to these new and emerging initiatives. In explaining this, Nutt and Backoff (1992) stress 'the importance of strategy in the public and non-profit sectors' due to 'turbulent conditions that were forcing change' over this timeframe (Nutt and Backoff 1992: 1–2). Joyce states: 'the formal system of strategic management in the public sector has emerged ... and is based on strategic planning principles' (Joyce 2000: 3). Crozier (1991) concurs, claiming in the early 1990s that within the public sector 'a reform can only develop based on the vision of a different future and by affirming some strong directions,' hence by 'drawing up a strategy, a choice of priorities depending upon reasonable reflection regarding resources, constraints and objectives' could emerge. As implied, therefore, prior to the 1990s, the term 'strategy' was largely absent from the management of sport organizations. However, equally it became increasingly apparent that if these entities were to succeed in an increasingly competitive environment, they could no longer look past the importance of strategic management in order to prove responsive to the unpredictable and fast-moving environment in which they then operated (Ramanantsoa and Thiery-Basle 1989: 23).

The majority of literature dealing with this issue expounds the argument that strategic management in sport organizations differs from that utilized within the wider commercial sector (Nutt and Backoff 1992: 22). It is argued that a primary cause of any such difference between these two sectors is that NPOs have a higher level of public responsibility when compared with traditional commercial organizations. A good example of this divergence occurred in 1999 when the International Olympic Committee became embroiled in a bribe scandal and a large degree of public interest was generated in its affairs, itself emanating from many parts of the world. It could be argued that a similar scandal within a private company would not have given rise to the same amount of public scrutiny and media attention, albeit there have been some examples in recent times (specifically the worldwide financial crisis of 2008 involving some of the world's leading financial institutions) when this quite clearly has been the case (Bozeman 1987). Due to the impact that NPOs are considered to have upon the general public, it is imperative that the issues of accountability and transparency remain high on the agenda of senior management. Sport organizations must exercise concern regarding their many stakeholders whilst, in contrast, traditional businesses can identify clients and shareholders as being their highest priority, since their main goal is to achieve profits. NPOs must also operate with a satisfactory degree of efficiency, effectiveness and overall performance and generally with proper regard for their various stakeholders, such as volunteer groups, fans and communities. These organizations promote a vision that is often idealistic and which consequently may never be fully realized. A substantial degree of volunteerism exists within the non-profit sector, and elected officials often are part of this reality; yet these are the individuals who, in principle, decide on the strategy to be followed by the organization in question. Nevertheless, 'Their motivations and opinions may be different from those of the salaried managers who are responsible for carrying out the strategy but who often also draw it up' (Chappelet and Bayle 2005: 6).

Even though there are clear differences in the strategic management of these two types of organization, it does not necessarily prevent the application of the concepts and tools of strategic management to NPOs in general on a local, regional or even national level. It does however require an intelligent and skilled management team: one that can take these major differences into account and ensure that the application of such practices proves not to be counterproductive to the overall aspirations of the organization, which may not always be financial in nature.

PERFORMANCE MANAGEMENT IN SPORT

Only very limited research has been carried out to date examining how sport organizations view the issue of performance management or even recording if they use models such as the Performance Prism (Neely 2002), Balanced Scorecard (Kaplan and Norton 1996) or European Foundation for Quality Management (EFQM) models (Wongrassamee et al. 2003) to assist them in achieving their strategic goals or managing performance effectively. These models have been proven to be successful in the traditional business environment and, given that many sport organizations increasingly share a great deal in common with other industrial sectors, it is imperative that research be undertaken to examine this issue critically in more detail.

As an NPO, most sport organizations may be described as entities whose main goal is not utility maximization but the execution of their core mission (Chappelet and Bayle 2005). This

5

is why the question of performance management is of critical importance in such cases, again perhaps even more so than organizations trading within a traditional business environment. Many commentators (Miller 1997; Mahony and Howard 2001) on the business of sport suggest that management teams working in this industry are limited by their ability to transfer knowledge of conceptual business practices to the sporting realm. Indeed, it remains one of the greatest challenges for sport organizations to ensure that their current and future managers have the necessary skills to lead their organizations in the early part of the twenty-first century (Chappelet and Bayle 2005).

Before any performance management system can be applied within a sport organization, senior management must fully adopt principles that are based on improving overall organizational performance (Bond 1999). They must be seen to endorse the new system at all levels within the organization along with ensuring a consistent relationship with other pre-existing initiatives operating within the organization, such as cross-functional integration, and focus on the accountability of teams rather than individuals operating within the organization. Lyons (2006) claims an organization must focus on its strategies and vision as opposed to the daily internal operations of the organization. Strategic objectives must be directed by management to ensure that all employees are aware of how their own job description fits in with the strategies and performance goals of the organization as a whole. He goes on to claim that teams themselves are the 'owners' of the performance management system and are accountable for all aspects of that system. Management should allow teams to dictate which measures will assist them in the implementation of their roles most effectively. Management must not assume that they are aware what is best for the teams as in doing so they may remove ownership of the system from employees and thereby revert to a 'command and control' style of management, in turn leaving others comparatively powerless (Moffat 2000).

An integral part of the performance management system within both traditional and non-profit entities is the setting of key targets. Performance targeting (Walsh 2000) retains the ability to make positive contributions to any management environment. It is important that organizations make proper use of performance targets as this technique can in fact have a number of limitations and, if not implemented properly, result in adverse effects upon overall performance. Research has shown that, if such processes are not carefully designed and implemented, employees can become solely focused on short-term targets and lose sight of the long-term objectives and aims of the organization (Walsh 2000; Hood 2003). Indeed, this has proven to be one of the major pitfalls when establishing performance targets to date, including within sports organizations.

Walsh (2000) argues performance targets are created in order to focus attention upon particular processes and outcomes relating to a given organization and also to align the behaviour and actions of individuals to the overall goals and objectives of the organization, along with the expectations of stakeholders. The case often arises where unintended consequences relating to performance targets adversely impact upon the overall performance of the organization, requiring constant monitoring and a robust review of the current processes (Van de Walle and Roberts 2008). The most common example of this, as stated above, occurs when individuals become solely focused on targets that are established only for themselves and lose sight of the overall mission of the organization in its entirety (Maleyeff 2003).

MEASUREMENT: THE BALANCED SCORECARD

Kaplan and Norton (1992) developed the concept of the Balanced Scorecard, a performance management model that has been used as an effective strategic planning and management tool throughout many organizations over the last two decades. It has provided senior management teams with an effective method of monitoring actions and processes undertaken by employees and allowed them to keep a record of these actions and their consequences in an efficient manner. Although initially only adopted across western nations, it has now spread throughout the global business world and has been integrated into many non-English-speaking countries in recent years. Indeed, since 2000, use of the Balanced Scorecard and its derivatives, such as the Performance Prism (Neely 2002), and other similar approaches to management, including Results-Based Management, have become commonplace in a range of markets. Kurtzman (1997) has published research confirming that almost 70 percent of companies responding to a questionnaire were in fact measuring performance in a way that was extremely similar in style to that of the Balanced Scorecard. This method of performance management has been implemented by traditional businesses and corporations, some government agencies and a small number of other NPOs.

Standardized Balanced Scorecards are relatively easy to implement and can have a positive impact on a sports organization. However, using one organization's Balanced Scorecard and attempting to apply it to another organization can prove very difficult and indeed research has suggested that one of the major benefits of the scorecard lies with the use of a bespoke design process (Kurtzman 1997). Specifically, problems can arise if the Balanced Scorecard is established by consultants who may not have had intimate operational knowledge of a specific organization.

The unique aspect of the Balanced Scorecard, which represents a new development in the measurement initiatives adopted by for-profit organizations, combines financial and non-financial aspects of businesses to offer a more detailed view of how an organization has been truly performing within its operating environment. In addition, utility and clarity were further enhanced as Kaplan and Norton (1992) suggested that measures within an organization should be condensed and grouped together so they could be easily displayed within a four-box model. Aside from this new approach to measurement within an organization, the original definitions of the Balanced Scorecard model and its deployment remained sparse. From its initial inception, however, it became clear that the selection of measures, relating to both the filtering and clustering process, would prove to be the key activities that management would deploy in the implementation of this tool. The measures that were to be selected, according to Kaplan and Norton (1992), should be synonymous with issues and initiatives that were relevant to the organization's strategic plans and a simple process of requiring information concerning attitudinal issues would aid in determining which measures should be associated with each perspective (Kaplan and Norton 1992).

A major issue that became apparent after the publication of Kaplan and Norton's initial book, *The Balanced Scorecard* (Kaplan and Norton 1996b), was that the model did not address the managerial issue concerning the development of long-term sustainable strategies. Following on from this initial publication, a second book, *The Strategy-focused Organisation*

(Kaplan and Norton 2000), echoed research previously conducted in this area (Olve *et al.* 1999) relating to the visual documentation of the links associated with the measurement and development of a so-called strategy map (Kaplan and Norton 2000). This important evolution of the model inspired a number of very similar variants, improved the model's utility and propelled it into mainstream industries that recognized the value of adopting just such a performance measurement technique. Modern versions of the Balanced Scorecard can be closely associated with this type of model and thus initial samples of the model have become mostly redundant. Modern Balanced Scorecards have also evolved to be more flexible and 'user-friendly' and can be applied to almost every type of organization, in both for-profit and not-for-profit sectors.

As indicated, Kaplan and Norton's (1992) initial design was laid out as a simple 'four-box' model that could help organizations ensure they were getting the best results from all their available resources. The model suggested that financial measures should not be the only perspective to be analysed. They proposed three other markers in addition to the traditional financial insight: (1) learning and growth; (2) internal business processes; and (3) customer; the last marker was chosen to represent the major stakeholders within any organization (Mooraj *et al.* 1999). Research in the field of Balanced Scorecards is now vast and some authors have argued in favour of the renaming of these perspectives, along with the addition of new perspectives within the model. These arguments have come about following recognition that dissimilar but equivalent perspectives would potentially result from using a different set of measures. A crucial aspect in the adoption of this model for users is that they have the confidence that those aspects that are selected and measured are relevant to them, otherwise any results that are achieved may be regarded as being insignificant or erroneous. As indicated, this has been the predominant reason why first-generation Balanced Scorecards ultimately became redundant in the majority of cases (Olve *et al.* 1999; Kaplan and Norton 2000; Niven 2006).

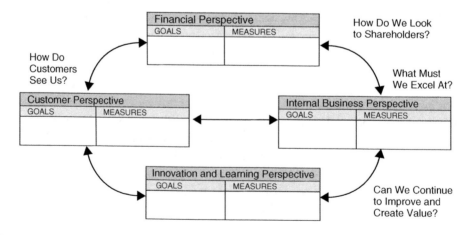

Figure 1.1 *First-generation scorecard (source: Cobbold and Lawrie 2002).*

Again, despite its huge popularity and widespread fascination as a concept, literature relating to the design of the first-generation Balanced Scorecards remains limited. The small amount of literature that does exist (Butler *et al.* 1997), alongside related organizational experiences (Ahn 2001), generally supports the model but also details weaknesses in its initial design phase and suggests improvements that then subsequently became incorporated into future Balanced Scorecard designs (Epstein and Manzoni 1997; Eagleson and Waldersee 2000; Kennerley and Neely 2000).

Since its initial inception in the early 1990s, many variants and alternatives of the Balanced Scorecard's 'four-box' approach have become popular within the performance management literature. Many of these variants serve little purpose and have limited utility. They are often proposed by academics in order to propel other agendas, notably those associated with environmental or 'green' issues (Brignall 2002) or private consultants who develop comparable approaches in order to increase profits from book sales or conference appearances (Bourne *et al.* 2003). Many of these related models are unquestionably similar and research (Cobbold and Lawrie 2002) has attempted to establish a pattern highlighting these similarities, in turn noting three distinct types of variation. These models can be conceptualized as 'generations' and part of the evolving process of this performance measurement model (Cobbold and Lawrie 2002). The original Kaplan and Norton design, along with other models that propose the simplistic 'four-box' approach, is often classed as constituting the first-generation Balanced Scorecard. The emergence of concepts, including the Performance Prism (Neely et al. 2002) and the Performance Driver model (Olve *et al.* 1999), heralded the emergence of so-called second-generation Balanced Scorecards. More modern incarnations, which incorporate a paragraph relating to the long-term vision of the organization, called 'destination statements' within the model, have now predictably become known as third-generation Balanced Scorecard models (Cobbold and Lawrie 2002).

CASE STUDY: SPARC – ORGANIZATIONAL DEVELOPMENT TOOL (ODT)

In keeping with SPARC's refocused emphasis on adopting a performance management approach to its operations, it developed a tool that assisted the organization in managing its ongoing strategic and performance objectives. The ODT has been implemented successfully within SPARC and as a result the organization has also encouraged many other sporting bodies throughout New Zealand to adopt the ODT.

The ODT is a practical and comprehensive process designed by experts as part of SPARC's focus on developing increasingly successful and sustainable sport and recreation organizations at national, regional and club level in New Zealand.

The ODT supports the development of successful and sustainable sport and recreation organizations by:

- providing a comprehensive Warrant of Fitness to help identify priority areas for improvement;
- establishing a single national standard framework for development and capability work;
- providing a simple way of measuring improvements;
- creating a shared centre of good practice resources.

The ODT offers a comprehensive review of capability and performance that:

- identifies areas of strength and opportunity;
- includes a built-in good practice database;
- provides clear direction for improvement;
- generates quality assessment reports.

One standard approach across all sector organizations provides:

- a network of trained facilitators;
- improved consistency and comparability of results;
- flexibility for wide application with open questions;
- an easy way to monitor and evaluate performance and improvement.

Trained facilitators help organizations work through the tool and produce an assessment report. The tool is supported by a five-step development process as shown in Figure 1.2:

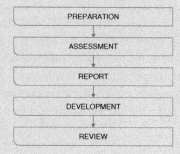

PREPARATION

ASSESSMENT

REPORT

DEVELOPMENT

REVIEW

Figure 1.2 *Five-step development process.*

As indicated, the tool is offered in three different versions, supporting national sport organizations, regional sport organizations and clubs. All are based on the six-module framework outlined in Figure 1.3. This ensures every facet of an organization is assessed.

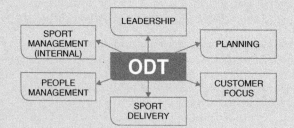

LEADERSHIP

SPORT MANAGEMENT (INTERNAL)

PLANNING

ODT

PEOPLE MANAGEMENT

CUSTOMER FOCUS

SPORT DELIVERY

Figure 1.3 *Six-module framework of the organizational development tool (ODT).*

Assessments are led by trained facilitators. A network of facilitators is located within SPARC, regional sports trusts and some national sport organizations (SPARC, 2011).

We found this to be a wonderful tool to assess where we were at and identify areas we needed to address in our planning (Anne Taylor, Chair, Bowls Waikato).

The whole process has added significant value to our organization (Dave Beeche, CEO, Triathlon NZ).

Second-generation scorecards

One of the major criticisms of the 'first-generation' Balanced Scorecard was that, whilst it seemed like a solid idea in theory, when implemented in practice, a number of difficulties arose that led to some practitioners abandoning the model on account of its lack of utility and overall vagueness. Throughout the 1990s, new design methods began to emerge, some from Kaplan and Norton (1992) and others from independent consultants with similar theories and thought processes. These new designs incorporated the strategy map, which consisted of a set of objectives strategically placed within the model in order to assist an organization further in maintaining its focus and long-term vision. Under this new design approach, Balanced Scorecards began to consider strategic aims alongside the pre-existing four perspectives and as a result were able visually to 'connect the dots' concerning the organization's objectives and those aspects of the business that were to be measured as part of this new approach.

Kaplan and Norton (1992) argued that for an organization to be successful in financial terms, it must analyse the ways in which it appears to its shareholders. Second-generation scorecards did not adopt this approach and instead created a process of associating a limited amount of performance measures to be placed alongside each perspective within the model. Strategic objectives now became a key priority within the model and were used to capture the essence of the organization's strategic operations associated with each performance aspect. The aspects of the organization that were to be measured were then carefully selected in order to ensure they coincided with these prioritized strategic objectives (Kaplan and Norton 1993). Although initially not considered as a major redesign of the pre-existing model, strategic objectives proved to be an integral readjustment to the Balanced Scorecard as these objectives were now directly derived from the organization's strategic plans. The strategy map element of the revised model emerges as management select those aspects of the organization's operating model it feels to be the most important to measure; then the 'cause-and-effect' relationship between these aims can be defined through the establishment of links between them. The model can subsequently be derived to portray the strategic performance of an organization by combining strategic objectives, the selected measures and the visual assistance of the strategy map. This innovation within the Balanced Scorecard model allows management greater ease of use and provides a justification for choosing the selected measures.

These changes in the design and evolution of the Balanced Scorecard were recorded in Kaplan and Norton's seminal (2000) book *The Strategy-focused Organisation*. They claimed that the Balanced Scorecard model had by then evolved from a simple performance management tool to become a core competency that should be applied within all organizations. Alongside their belief that the Balanced Scorecard could assist an organization with the implementation of its strategic objectives, Kaplan and Norton (1996) argued that this model should be at the heart of all strategic and performance management activities present within any organization.

From 1996 onwards, second-generation Balanced Scorecards became popular throughout all sectors and industries and established themselves as the leading performance measurement tool available to organizations. A number of criticisms remained but they have proved, as a result of practical application, to be still more successful when compared with the original Kaplan and Norton models of some years previous.

Third-generation scorecards

Just before the dawn of the new millennium, further evolution of the Balanced Scorecard concept took place. This emerged in response to the deficiencies apparent within the second-generation scorecard design that failed to acknowledge that opportunities to intervene in the strategic process must be available in order to anchor objectives within real and current management operations. Another major weakness of the second-generation designs was that they ignored the need to 'roll forward' and assess the impact that strategic objectives would have on any particular organization in the future. As a result a further element was added to the mix within the Balanced Scorecard design: this became known as the destination statement. This concept consisted of little more than a brief paragraph detailing what the 'strategic success' or 'end-date' of the strategic plans would look like. Initial destination statements were constructed, with specific timelines associated with them (e.g. 'in four years' time') and detailing those objectives that needed to be achieved in a specific time period. Through the application of this new instrument, organizations could now assess how targets were being met on an annual basis and if the strategic vision of the organization was in fact on its way to being realized. Management quickly began to understand that if a destination statement was to be incorporated within a Balanced Scorecard model, the selection of strategic objectives and measurement of strategic operations would become a more straightforward exercise for the organization by allocating targets and measures that could be selected to view and track the progress of strategy.

Organizations quickly began to realize that, through the implementation of a destination statement, senior management and individuals within the workplace were able to relate their roles directly to this statement without constantly making reference to strategic goals that had been set out by the organization but which remained somewhat abstract in nature. As a result, the approach taken around the design of the model was 'reversed', with destination statements attracting the initial attention of the designers as opposed to the final element of the design phase. It was further uncovered through its practical application that establishing a destination statement initially made the selection of strategic objectives and achieving consensus amongst management and teams within the organization a more efficient process in a development generally welcomed by all.

For a sport organization to have the ability to make rational decisions relating to its operations and to set targets for strategic objectives, it must develop and be able to articulate exactly what the organization is seeking to achieve (Senge 1990; Kotter 1995). Through the application of a destination statement a sport organization can define exactly the way it will aim to look within an established timeframe in an easily accessible and understood manner (Olve *et al.* 1999; Shulver *et al.* 2000).

SUMMARY

As the modern sport organization continues to evolve in terms of its professionalism, accountability and transparency, it is crucial that the management of these organizations recognizes the importance of implementing an adequate performance management system throughout its entire operation. The gap of industrial knowledge between the for-profit and not-for-profit sectors appears to be slowly closing; however management within sport organizations must continue to familiarize themselves with the best practice of successful systems and business initiatives within the traditional business environment. This knowledge is almost completely transferable to sport management and will increase the strategic, performance and overall organizational success of these unique entities.

Looking to the future, it is imperative that the Balanced Scorecard becomes a model that is synonymous with performance management within sport organizations, and management within this sector must remain conscious of the inevitability of further evolution of the current models. Strategy maps have proven to be successful under practical application and these instruments, in keeping with destination statements, should be used alongside the adoption of the Balanced Scorecard model in the sport management sector. Sport organizations should adopt the approach of other organizations that have begun to use the Balanced Scorecard in order to guide and monitor the overall performance of their strategies and assist supervisory boards in strategic decision-making. It is important that the measurement of data required in order to satisfy demands of the model can be executed efficiently and annual reports within a sport organization should begin to focus more on the application and results of the organization in relation to the effective utility of the Balanced Scorecard. Sport organizations must accept that information technology and Balanced Scorecard software are now playing key roles in the operations of all modern-day organizations and understand the importance of adopting a performance management culture, which is being reinforced throughout all industries as its importance becomes fully accepted.

The theory surrounding management control and the practical applications of the Balanced Scorecard have begun to align along a similar pathway. This is a positive indicator that supports the argument that latter-day Balanced Scorecard designs are indeed more useful compared with the prototype model, initially proposed by Kaplan and Norton (1992), because they are more likely to impact positively upon a sport organization. However, although modern Balanced Scorecard models have shown significant improvements and greater scope for utility, the evolution process is far from complete. The model can become much more attractive and credible if financial values for pre- and post-case scenarios are incorporated within the framework. Another key criterion for the adoption of the Balanced Scorecard within sport organizations is the ability to demonstrate added value through its adoption. When a sport organization does adopt the Balanced Scorecard model, it can be implemented throughout each department and can be used as a successful strategic planning and performance management tool (Shulver et al. 2000).

REVIEW QUESTIONS

1   What are the major challenges facing the modern sport organization?
2   The Balanced Scorecard has proved to be an effective performance management tool that can positively impact upon the modern sport organization. Provide a brief description of the evolution of this performance management model and some of the challenges that have emerged throughout the course of this process.

3   In New Zealand, SPARC has offered a good example to other sport organizations by adopting various performance management practices and systems. Describe the Organizational Development Tool (ODT) and its benefits for the organization that chooses to adopt it.

FURTHER READING

Bacal, R. (1999). *Performance Management.* New York: McGraw-Hill.

Covell, D. (2007). *Managing Sports Organizations: Responsibility for Performance.* Amsterdam: Elsevier/Butterworth-Heinemann.

Masteralexis, L., Barr, C. and Hums, M. (2009). *Principles and Practice of Sport Management.* Sudbury, MA: Jones and Bartlett.

Taylor, T., Doherty, A. and McGraw, P. (2008). *Managing People in Sport Organizations: A strategic human resource management perspective.* Oxford, UK: Butterworth-Heinemann.

WEBSITES

Balanced Scorecard Institute:

www.balancedscorecard.org

Sport and Recreation New Zealand:

www.sparc.org.nz

Sport Business:

www.sportbusiness.com

REFERENCES

Ahn, H. (2001). "Applying the Balanced Scorecard Concept: An Experience Report." *Long Range Planning* 34(4): 441–461.

Bond, T.C. (1999). "The Role of Performance Measurement in Continuous Improvement." *International Journal of Operations and Production Management* 19(12): 1318.

Bourne, M., Franco, M. and Wilkes, J. (2003). "Corporate Performance Management." *Measuring Business Excellence* 7.3: 15–21.

Bozeman, B. (1987). *All Organizations are Public: Bridging public and private organizational theories.* San Francisco: Jossey-Bass

Brignall, S. (2002). "The Unbalanced Scorecard: A Social and Environmental Critique." *Proceedings of the 3rd International Conference on Performance Measurement and Management* (PMA 2002), Boston, MA, July.

Butler A., Letza, S.R. and Neale, B. (1997). "Linking the Balanced Scorecard to Strategy." *Long Range Planning* 30(2): 242–253.

Chappelet, J.-L. and Bayle, E. (2005). *Strategic and Performance Management of Olympic Sport Organisations.* Champaign, IL: Human Kinetics.

Cobbold, I. and Lawrie, G. (2002). "The Development of the Balanced Scorecard as a Strategic Management Tool." Performance Measurement Association. Conference paper, Boston, MA.

Crozier, M. (1991). *Etat Moderne, Etat Modeste, Stratégies pour un autre changement.* Paris: Seuil.

Diaz-Martin, A., Iglesias, V., Vázquez, R. and Ruiz, A.V. (2000). "The Use of Quality Expectations to Segment a Service Market." *Journal of Services Marketing* 14(2): 132–146.

Eagleson, G.K. and Waldersee, R. (2000). "Monitoring the Strategically Important: Assessing and improving strategic tracking systems." Performance Measurement – Past, Present and Future. 2nd International Conference on Performance Measurement, Cambridge, UK.

Epstein, M.J. and Manzoni, J.-F. (1997). "The Balanced Scorecard and Tableau de Bord: Translating Strategy into Action." *Management Accounting (USA)* 79(2): 28–37.

Fischer, G. and Ostwald, J. (2001). "Knowledge Management: Problems, Promises, Realities, and Challenges." *IEEE Intelligent Systems* 16(1): 60–72.

Hood, C. (2003). "Control, Bargains, and Cheating: The Politics of Public-service Reform." *Journal of Public Administration Research and Theory* 12(3): 307–321.

Joyce, P. (2000). *Strategy in the Public Sector: A guide to effective change management.* Chichester: Wiley.

Kaplan, R.S. and Norton, D.P. (1992). "The Balanced Scorecard: Measures that Drive Performance." *Harvard Business Review* 70(1): 71–80.

Kaplan, R.S. and Norton, D.P. (1993). "Putting the Balanced Scorecard to Work." *Harvard Business Review* 71(5): 2–16.

Kaplan, R.S. and Norton, D.P. (1996). *The Balanced Scorecard: Translating strategy into action.* Boston, MA: Harvard Business School Press.

Kaplan, R.S. and Norton, D.P. (2000). *The Strategy-focused Organization: How Balanced Scorecard companies thrive in the new business environment.* Boston, MA: Harvard Business School.

Kaplan, R.S. and Norton, D.P. (2004). *Strategy Maps: Converting intangible assets into tangible outcomes.* Boston, MA: Harvard Business School Press.

Kennerley, M. and Neely, A.D. (2000). "Performance Measurement Frameworks – A Review." Proceedings of the 2nd International Conference on Performance Measurement and Management (PMA 2000), Cambridge, July.

Kotler, P. and Andreasen, A.R. (1991). *Strategic Marketing for Nonprofit Organisations,* 4th edn. Englewood Cliffs, NJ: Prentice Hall.

Kotter, J.P. (1995). "Leading Change: Why Transformation Efforts Fail." *Harvard Business Review OnPoint* (March-April): 1–10.

Kurtzman, J. (1997). "Is Your Company Off Course? Now You Can Find Out Why." *Fortune* 135(3): 128–130.

Lyons, P. (2006). "Team Member Involvement in Team Leader Training and Performance." *Team Performance Management* 12(4):102–114.

Mahony, D. and Howard, D. (2001). "Sport Business in the Next Decade: A General Overview of Expected Trends." *Journal of Sport Management* 15: 275–296.

Maleyeff, J. (2003). "Benchmarking Performance Indices: Pitfalls and Solutions." *Benchmarking: An International Journal* 10(1): 9–28.

Miller, L.K. (1997). *Sport Business Management.* Gaithersburg, MD: Aspen Publication.

Moffat, J. (2000). "Representing the Command and Control Process in Simulation Models of Conflict." *Journal of the Operational Research Society* 51(4): 431–438.

Mooraj, S., Oton, D. and Hostettler, D. (1999). "The Balanced Scorecard: A Necessary Good or an Unnecessary Evil?" *European Management Journal* 17(5): 481–491.

Neely, A, ed. (2002). *Business Performance Measurement: Theory and practice.* Cambridge: Cambridge University Press.

Neely, A.D., Adams, C. and Kennerley, M. (2002). *The Performance Prism: The scorecard for measuring and managing business success.* London: Financial Times/Prentice Hall.

Niven, P.R. (2006). *Balanced Scorecard. Step-by-step. Maximizing Performance and Maintaining Results.* Hoboken, NJ: Wiley.

Nutt, P.C. and Backoff, R.W. (1992). *Strategic Management of Public and Third Sector Organisations.* San Francisco, CA: Jossey-Bass.

15

Olve, N., Roy, J. and Wetter, M. (1999). *Performance Drivers: A practical guide to using the Balanced Scorecard*. New York: Wiley.

Ramanantsoa, B. and Thiery-Basle, C. (1989). *Organisations and Sport Federations, Sociology and Management*. Paris: PUF.

Senge, P. (1990) *The Fifth Discipline*. Garden City, NY: Doubleday Currency.

Shulver, M., Lawrie, G. and Andersen, H. (2000). "A Process for Developing Strategically Relevant Measures of Intellectual Capital." Proceedings of the 2nd International Conference on Performance Measurement and Management (PMA 2000), Cambridge, July.

SPARC. (2011). Organisational Development Tool. http://www.sportnz.org.nz/en-nz/our-partners/Developing-Capabilities/Organisational-Development-Tool

Van de Walle, S. and Roberts, A. (2008). "Performance Information in the Public Sector: How is it Used?" Houndmills: Palgrave, pp. 211–226.

Walsh, P. (2000). "Targets and How to Assess Performance Against Them." *Benchmarking: An International Journal* 7(3): 183–199.

Wongrassamee, S., Simmons J.E.L. and Gardiner, P.D. (2003). "Performance Measurement Tools: The Balanced Scorecard and the EFQM Excellence Model." *Measuring Business Excellence* 7(1): 14–29.

Chapter 2

Urban space, culture and sports in the Middle East

A case study of Casablanca, Morocco

Nicole Matuska

TOPICS

Management of urban space • Public policy and sports development • Civil society and sports development • Cultural attitudes and sports exclusion • Football and sports exclusion

---

OBJECTIVES

By the end of this chapter, you will be able to:

- Review current research on sports and social exclusion;
- Consider how sports can be a tool for social inclusion (as well as social exclusion);
- Explain how the interactions between urban space, public policy, civil society and cultural attitudes affect sports and development and social exclusion/inclusion;
- Highlight how women and youth are most affected by sports and social exclusion;
- Use women's football to examine the process of exclusion from sport in Morocco and the parts of the Middle East more generally.

KEY TERMS

Cultural attitudes – social beliefs and perspectives that come from within specific communities, based on religion, social life or commonly held traditions and beliefs.

> **Open public urban space space** – land in an urban area (typically a city) not owned by a private citizen or private company; everyone has access to it without the payment of a fee, e.g. public parks.
>
> **Social exclusion** – access or lack thereof to four basic social systems: democracy, welfare, work and family/community. It is the idea that a citizen is excluded from some combination of wealth, income, employment, education, political representation and social or economic support.
>
> **Sports and/for development** – use of sport as a tool for community or personal development and peace.

OVERVIEW

This chapter is about how sports can be used as a tool for both social inclusion as well as social exclusion. In order to illuminate these points a case study, located within the city of Casablanca, Morocco, will be utilized, although in a lot of instances the same issues are relevant across a range of other cities within the Middle East. The chapter will focus on the interaction of urban space management, public policy, civil society and cultural attitudes and their effect on sports and development within underdeveloped urban areas. It will also focus on one of the most socially excluded groups, economically disadvantaged (poor) women, and how it is the most targeted group in sports and development yet at the same time often the most excluded. The chapter will conclude with a discussion around association football's role in sports and social exclusion for women and young girls and what the future holds for women's access to sport in the Middle East.

One aspect of sport management that is often overlooked is the organization of urban space, particularly within a city that is growing and expanding at an almost uncontrollable rate. This is certainly true in the Middle East, where rural populations increasingly flock to urban centres for work and enhanced opportunities generally. Of course, one thing many cities in North Africa, the Middle East and particularly the Gulf states do well is the management of elite sports. Urban space is quickly allocated for first-class stadiums, expensive private gyms and Olympic training facilities. However, the management of sport for the masses seems to take something of a 'back seat' and this is where the problem of using urban space arises. Faced with increasing populations, a need for housing and construction booms amid decreasing land area, these cities often overlook the importance of allocating enough open space to the public for the expressed purposes of sport and recreation. Without allocation of urban land as public open space, then even association football, often referred to as 'the global game' due to its apparent ability to be played almost anywhere with little equipment, may become more and more difficult to sustain because one of its only requirements, a semi-flat open piece of land, is itself becoming increasingly difficult to preserve.

CASE STUDY: WOMEN'S FOOTBALL IN CASABLANCA, MOROCCO

Tucked away in the middle of one of Casablanca's last green spaces, next to a disused cathedral and right around the corner from the city hall, is an old stadium named Casablancaise. It is hard to describe it except in a way that makes it seem like it is falling down and in ruins. Not many people notice it as they pass by on some of the busiest boulevards in the city. Indeed, not many people know it still exists, or of its grand history as one of Morocco's most splendid athletic fields until a lack of proper management or interest left it in its current desperate state. However, there are many things that make the stadium worth writing about and bringing to the attention of a wider audience.

On any given day, at any given hour, the simple dirt track and interior field blanketed in weeds fill up with all types of people. There is usually an exercise group of older men and women who come around 6 a.m. and do some stretching, light walking and running. You can see women, completely covered from head to toe and wearing the niqab, doing laps as young teenage boys run past them finishing a set of sprints. You see youth track teams, male and female running groups and healthy-minded Casablanca residents stretching and doing lunges on the concrete steps of what was once seating for the stadium. It is free. Anyone can walk inside, past a sleeping security guard and his dog.

The most remarkable characteristic is, however, that the stadium is one of the last of its kind, outliving others throughout the cities, which have long ago closed their doors to public recreation. The story of the stadium Casablancaise is a great example of the inclusionary power of sports. Unfortunately, it is also an example of the fast decline of sports spaces that are free to use and are open to the general public in the city.

The early 2000s saw an increase in high-cost elite gyms and recreation areas catering to a quickly growing upper class with high levels of disposable income in most large cities throughout Morocco. At the same time, space became more and more limited within cities as urban development and private developers grabbed any open land for a chance to make handsome profits during the construction boom. This is most evident in Casablanca, the country's economic capital and its largest city with a population of just over three million people, a large portion being rural migrants looking for work. As land and open space become scarce, recreation and leisure, especially for those who can't pay for it, become ever-more inaccessible. Sport has, all of a sudden, become a tool of exclusion, rather than inclusion.

Looking deeper, you quickly notice that open public space, or the lack thereof, is one of many interwoven barriers blocking access to sports activities in Casablanca, even though the national dialogue seems to be dominated by the idea that we are in a changing era where access to sports is available to all. However, this national dialogue (in which grassroots non-governmental organizations, medical professionals, government agencies and athlete celebrities are all participating) fails to address the issue that sports can actually be exclusionary if not approached correctly and that the groups mostly excluded, even while being those that are in fact often the most targeted, are youth and women.

The government and civil society have recently begun efforts to increase sports and recreation opportunities at the non-elite level and particularly in low-income neighbourhoods. However Casablanca remains largely unaffected by many of these increased efforts. Due to a mix of misguided public sports development policy, private and public land development, a rapidly widening gap between rich and poor and lingering cultural and social attitudes not addressed by those invested in sports development programmes, youth and women are most of the time excluded from having the opportunity to play sports and this, it is argued, is a form of social exclusion with significant social implications.

DEFINING SOCIAL EXCLUSION IN CONTEMPORARY RESEARCH

Lately, sport as a development tool has become quite popular with international organizations and associations. Groups like Right to Play, Laureus Sports for Good Foundation, Grassroots Football and so forth are using sports to reach aid to orphans, women, child soldiers, the poor, refugees and many other marginalized groups within society. This has naturally led to a body of research on how sport can be a tool for inclusion, which is something we are used to, and conversely, how sport can also be a tool of exclusion, which is not always as evident. Although this existent research mostly focuses on Europe (specifically the UK) and Australia, many of the key points can also be applied to other parts of the world.

According to Michael F Collins, who has worked extensively with the British government on sports policy issues, social exclusion is the access (or lack thereof) to four basic social systems: democracy, welfare, work and family/community (Collins 2008: 78). It is the idea that a citizen is excluded from some sort of combination of wealth, income, employment, education, political representation, and social or economic support. These citizens typically tend to be adolescents, elderly people, low-income families, ethnic minorities, those with disabilities, the long-term unemployed or homeless people (Velija 2009: 1). Different people can fall into more than one category or experience more than one form of exclusion.

Collins (2008) often refers to the idea of social capital, or personal social capital, which is the ability to take part fully in all aspects of society, including culture and sport. Others simply refer to this as citizenship. According to Collins, an individual person's allocation of social capital often depends on his or her social, economic environment, psychological milieu where they grew up and associated values or meanings (Collins 2008: 80).

Researchers in this field make the connection that sports, leisure and culture are important parts of citizenship or of an individual's life within his or her community or society, much the same as a person's ability to find work, take part in social activities or have access to healthcare and education. It should not be limited to social class, age, gender and income. Its effect on a person's emotional and psychological state, health, happiness and ability to integrate has been researched thoroughly. In fact, sport is often used as a tool to tackle social exclusion in other sectors. However, the idea that sport within a certain cultural or political context or environment can actually be a tool for exclusion is often overlooked, or at least rarely discussed. Therefore, looking at social exclusion through the lens of sports development, one must analyse and critique the policies and programmes in place that address or influence access to sports and recreation (Velija 2009: 2). In other words, one must also examine cultural attitudes and their influence on these policies and programmes.

The proposal contained within this chapter is informed by the idea that sport and exercise themselves are not intrinsically exclusive. Many sports require little or no equipment and some, such as running or walking, require nothing but an open space. The problem develops in the management and allocation of space, people's relationship with each other and their own bodies and cultural and social attitudes within a community. Basically, humans make sport and physical activity exclusive. Football, an integral part of sports culture in Morocco and still arguably the most popular sport across all social classes, cannot be ignored in this analysis.

Before addressing the emergence and place of football and its role in sports development in Morocco, the chapter needs first to address the barriers and obstacles that exist for sports participation in general, for populations from low-income areas and then how these barriers and obstacles are exaggerated when gender becomes a complicating factor. It is only within this context that football's role in social inclusion and/or exclusion can be fully evaluated.

The case study central to this chapter considers the city of Casablanca, specifically a neighbourhood called Sidi Moumen. This neighbourhood, with a population of over 350,000, is located on the extreme outskirts of the city and was one of Morocco's first slum towns with still some of the largest informal settlements in the country. The result of rural migration to large cities for work, Sidi Moumen has grown quickly over the years but the delivery of basic healthcare, education and employment services regrettably has failed to keep pace. The unemployment rate in this neighbourhood alone is 32 per cent, whilst the illiteracy rate stands at 64 per cent, 10 points higher than the rest of Casablanca (Mazria-Katz 2009). This neighbourhood was also home to all 14 suicide bombers who attacked western and Jewish targets in the Casablanca city centre on 16 May 2003, killing 45 people. The area became notorious for recruiting youth into fundamentalist Islamic groups such as Salfia Jihadi, believed by some to be linked to Al Qaeda (Crumley 2003).

Casablanca is a unique city within Morocco because of its high density of low-class neighbourhoods, its embrace of the construction boom and its role as Morocco's economic hub. Although the issues discussed here regarding sports and exclusion are applicable to most urban centres in Morocco, they are particularly concentrated in Casablanca. Later in this chapter there will be an attempt to apply certain conclusions to the broader region of the Middle East generally, drawing upon similar cultural attitudes, sports pastimes and space/urban landscapes.

URBAN SPACE: AN OXYMORON

When driving through Sidi Moumen, the first thing you notice is people, everywhere. Then the dusty tan ground and the concrete; then fruit and vegetable sellers, cars, donkeys and horses pulling carts, cafés and mechanic garages. Open or empty space simply doesn't exist. The few patches of open space that do are usually turned into a garbage dump or a place to park vehicles. As a neighbourhood with over 350,000 residents, there is not even a single public park.

Open green space is something that any city in the world battles to retain; however, it is even harder to make it a priority in developing cities, let alone some of their poorest neighbourhoods. Kathleen Day, an American Rotary Scholar undertaking research on the allotment of urban open space in the city, tells a story of sitting with several Casablanca urban planners and asking about the priority of open space in city planning. 'A few of the urban planners just laughed,' said Day. 'I could just imagine them saying in their heads, poor naive American. You instantly could tell it wasn't a priority.' According to the Urban Agency of Casablanca, the government organization in charge of urban planning and data collection in the city, in 2008 there was just less than 1 metre squared of green space for each resident of the city. The population of Casablanca in 2008 was just under 3 million people and the calculation includes a non-accessible closed-off 'zoo' along the beach that went out of business and two forested areas outside of the city that are difficult to access if you don't have a car (SDAU 2008: 11).

As one resident from Rabat, Morocco's administrative capital with several large parks and tree-lined boulevards, said about the city, 'Casablanca is the economic capital. No, there is nothing in Casa[blanca] but pollution, no space, just stress.' It's appropriate to talk about open space because this is the most natural place to start with when discussing access to sports. Many people interviewed for this chapter, particularly those in their 40s and 50s, recall a time in the city of Casablanca, particularly in lower-income areas, when there was always an empty patch of grass or concrete slab within walking distance for kids. Hassan Manyani, a former journalist with Radio Mars, one of Morocco's most listened-to sports stations, feels the same way.

'There was always an empty space with goals or just an empty space nearby,' said Manyani. 'You could find it in every district. We could go play, or watch a neighbourhood match. We were active youth and it wasn't hard to be active. You could just step outside and there were opportunities and spaces to be active.'

The reason for this decline in open space is in fact a result of a combination of factors. Residents and community organizers say that land, because of the construction boom in the 1990s, became very expensive in Casablanca. Everyone wanted to build; it was profitable to construct apartments or storefronts. Those who had land sold it. Anything empty was seen as just a wasted opportunity to make money. The government profited from this as well, selling off land to private developers or rezoning land to profit as much as possible. Unfortunately, there was no regulation concerning public land allotted for recreation.

This situation can be found throughout many of Casablanca's low-income areas. Even upper-class areas, with their palm tree-lined streets, green grass lawns and boulevard islands, face a shortage of space. However, the difference is their proximity and access to one of Casablanca's only open public spaces, the Corniche, or the coastal boardwalk and the beach itself.

The Corniche, a 3-km-long sidewalk lined with cafés, restaurants, snack stands and views of the beach and Atlantic ocean, is theoretically open to all. No one can stop you from walking on the pavement, or going to the beach. There is no entrance fee and it is maintained by taxpayer money. At any time during the day, you see people walking, running, jogging, playing football and riding bicycles in this area. However, a closer look at the economic and social demographics of those who frequent the Corniche (whether it is just walking or for the specific purpose of doing sport) will usually reveal middle- and upper-class families and lower-class young males. There is a large absence of lower-class women and young girls. There are many reasons for this, which will be detailed shortly; purely in terms of space and distance, it takes 10 minutes by car to get to the Corniche from some of the most affluent areas in Casablanca while it takes over 1 hour by bus to get there from Sidi Moumen and many similarly poor suburbs of Casablanca.

Another reason the beach and Corniche boardwalk are becoming less and less 'open to the public' is the privatization of the coast in Casablanca. Three large development projects are simultaneously underway: Africa's largest mall, a private residential resort park and the

Casablanca marina. All three have taken large swathes of public beach and essentially made them accessible only to those who can pay. According to urban researchers Day and Nabil Scally, whose organization Bahri (My Beach) is also lobbying the city of Casablanca to keep beaches public, the beach is normally zoned as public, forbidden to be sold to private developers. However, there is a loophole that allows land to be rezoned fairly easily (SDAU: 2008). In cash-strapped Casablanca, rezoning land becomes very attractive.

This lack of public space extends to free public fields and stadiums as well. Casablancaise was mentioned briefly in the introduction to this chapter. The stadium is used at all hours of the day, from 5 a.m. until the sun sets (there are no lights) by all types of people. The large numbers of people who train there is a testament to the need of sport spaces in the city. After years of reporting on sports issues for Radio Mars, journalist Manyani has noticed a trend: 'The problem is the way space is allocated and the way sports structures are placed throughout the city.' Manyani continues that most stadiums these days are reserved for elite teams and regional league matches. Very few options exist for 'pick-up' football games and spontaneous neighbourhood matches or for people to jog around a track in an enclosed space away from the exhaust fuel of cars.

Community organizer Hassan Aadak said:

> There used to be a neighbourhood field near the youth cultural centre where I work. It wasn't anything special, just a dirt clearing with goals at either end that neighbourhood teams would use for games and practices. We would use it for our kids at the cultural centre on Sundays. The city decided to build the headquarters for the new tramway there and basically took away the field. When the neighbourhood complained, they said we could use a field 10 minutes away by bus or car. We had no way to transport our kids to another field, which was already most likely full.

The implications of a lack of available open space or public stadiums for the lower class, youth and women are enormous. What it says is that sports, or simple recreational activities, which should be on some level free and open to all, are quickly becoming available only to those who can pay for often expensive gym memberships or who belong to an elite sports club. Sport is beginning to exclude already socially excluded groups.

PUBLIC POLICY AND CIVIL SOCIETY

The 1970s was the birth of the Dar Chabab (youth centre) run by the Ministry of Youth and Sports. These centres were stationed in most districts throughout the country and accessible to all young people. One could find sports fields, classrooms, ping-pong tables, board games, coaches and language classes. In the 1990s, these centres started closing and, according to Manyani, it was due to mismanagement, lazy directors or lack of funding. Various Dar Chababs visited throughout the city of Casablanca for this research are notorious for being closed during most of the day and staffed by very unsupportive and unenthusiastic directors.

The Ministry has begun a new ambitious project – a sophisticated alternative to the Dar Chababs called Centre Socio-*Sportif* de Proximité (CSP). According to the Ministry, the goal is to have 1,000 such facilities by the end of 2016. With already 24 operational throughout the country, these centres are placed in low-income areas and offer a mix of equipped gyms, multiple sports fields, training and education venues and day care for mothers. Some have been relatively successful: there are stories of women participating in aerobics classes in extremely rural areas, and very conservative women forming running and training groups in areas not normally known for encouraging women's sport. However, Casablanca, one of the largest urban centres, has only one CSP within city limits.

Some are weary of the financial commitment needed to manage these expensive centres, which already are charging small membership fees that could perhaps prove limiting to the most poor.

'The Dar Chababs were not managed well,' said radio journalist Manyani. 'The ministry is making another risk with these centres [CSPs] in terms of being able to manage them financially and administratively.' However the Ministry seems optimistic. Najat Bentalha, who leads the women's sports promotion team at the Division of Sports Promotion at the Ministry of Youth and Sports, states that the CSP project is running on course despite a few obstacles. Bentalha said:

> Our largest problem right now is human resources. Who will be the administrative staff for these centres? We are looking for solutions, one of them being training unemployed youth to work as coaches and trainers and directors at these centres, paid by the government.

However, one must be careful not to associate simply building structures or dedicating sports spaces in low-income neighbourhoods with automatic success. To do this is surely to fail in creating policy and programmes that truly make sports inclusive rather than exclusive. Many criticize or point out that the new Ministry CSPs are great but that their outreach, especially to women and youth, is severely lacking. This is where we look to civil society.

'I think we need around 10 years to see the fruits of the Ministry's programmes, that is when we will see their impacts,' said Naoufal Uariachi. Uariachi is founder and director of the Uariachi Hoops Camps, an organization that holds basketball and leadership camps throughout the country. He is part of that growing civil society that is stepping in and filling some of the gaps existing in current policies and programmes aimed at increasing sports opportunities for youth. He remembers as a young boy in Tangier trying to play basketball in a public lot and being beaten by a stick by the guard. 'We need to support and encourage the youth to play, foster a sense of playing for fun and not the importance of elite competition.' Uariachi says he is trying to drag young children away from the internet cafés and their homes and back out on to the sports field.

Meryem Hajji works at the US Embassy as Youth and Sports Coordinator in the Public Affairs Department. She has worked with Uariachi as well as other civil society leaders, developing youth through sport. Hajji points out: 'Playing sports is a state of mind. To encourage women in low-income areas to go to the gym, you have to know their problems in life, their current priorities – you have to help them with these other issues.'

SOCIAL/CULTURAL ATTITUDES

Beyond the problem of a lack of space, stadiums or comprehensive government policy, a large amount of social and cultural issues must be addressed in order to make sports socially inclusive, particularly for women and young girls.

Firstly, it should be pointed out that very little statistical data exists on women's leisure time and sports participation in the Middle East and particularly North Africa and Morocco. Most of this research is based around interviews with women in Sidi Moumen and throughout Casablanca, associations and organizations working in sports development and observations and research carried out in other parts of Africa and the Middle East.

The obvious solution to a lack of open urban space and public sports stadiums is to convert land into recreational areas. It is a basic question of urban planning. However, for some groups, merely freeing up space would not solve the problem. Public policy and civil society programmes aimed at simply increasing space/infrastructure either exclude certain groups even further or their situation of exclusion stays the same. A host of social and cultural attitudes embedded in sports culture cause sport to become an exclusive experience for women and young girls. Aitchison points out that studies done in Western countries (the USA and Europe) and Iran show that, although material constraints in non-participation of sports for women, such as time, money, facilities and transport, are usually ranked the same, the cultural restraints are largely different. In the West, non-participation often has to do with personal or sociological issues related to individual self-confidence, self-esteem, body image and friendship networks. In the Middle East, intrapersonal restraints related to social institutions, including family, education and religion, remain more prevalent (Aitchison 2007: 85).

BARRIER OF OPEN SPACES

One of the first obstacles due to cultural or social barriers for women and young girls in low-income areas is their inability to practise sports or exercise in just any open space. Although it is common to see women and teenage girls running, jogging or walking along the Corniche, the public beach boardwalk along the coast, this is not an option in the slums of Sidi Moumen. As one woman put it, 'You can't just put on a jogging suit and walk around the neighbourhood. People would think you are crazy, make funny comments about you or tell you "shame on you".' Since these women tend to be more conservative or low-income neighbourhoods tend to be more conservative in general (Sidi Moumen being a good example), it is often inappropriate, especially for older and/or married women, to practise sports in open fields. These include simple activities such as aerobics or light stretching. What they need is either an enclosed stadium or a women's-only gym. Both are extremely rare, if they exist at all.

Imane Majid, a staff member with the Moroccan Sports and Development Association for over 5 years, says that this is a huge factor that excludes most lower-class and middle-class women from doing sport.

> People here in Morocco, when trying to decide what to build, want to make money so they don't think about a low-cost sports gym. In places like Sidi Moumen, they think

25

cafés, cheap snack food restaurants, apartment buildings, but the idea of creating inexpensive sports facilities targeting women, even if it would bring in a little money, isn't there. There is no thought about giving back to the community.

This translates into few opportunities for women who want to exercise or participate in sports, whether it is simply walking laps on a track or in a garden/park, or doing aerobics in comfortable clothes and taking off the veil in an all-women's environment.

ATTITUDES TOWARDS LEISURE ACTIVITIES

The above obstacle overlaps with another social barrier, which is attitudes toward leisure time or leisure activities. As Bentalha from the Ministry of Youth and Sports observed, women from these low-income neighbourhoods view sports as excessive and an activity for the elite with money and time.

Majid, of the Moroccan Sports and Development Association, echoes the same sentiment. 'If a woman was searching for a gym in an area of Sidi Moumen, others would say "shame on you". You are spending money on yourself, on something frivolous when you could be spending that money on your kids or the house.'

This is of course assuming time exists in the first place for women to partake in sport or physical activity. Percentage of leisure time for the poor is generally very low, but women who are in this category have even less time. Little research exists directly related to Moroccan women or North African women and leisure time; however, research on Africa in general points out the reality of the situation for women in lower-income social classes. According to Shaw, in her chapter in the book *Leisure in Urban Africa*, women surveyed in Botswana and Nigeria state that their leisure time is severely restricted because of their roles and responsibilities in the house (Shaw 2003: 67). According to Arab-Moghaddam *et al.* (2007: 109), the largest restraints on leisure activities for women married with children with no or little education are expectations in the home and no personal income. The same is true in Morocco and neighbourhoods like Sidi Moumen. Women generally have all the domestic responsibilities of cooking, cleaning, raising children and taking them to school. In addition to this, many women sew or do some sort of extra activity in order to bring a supplementary income into the household, which is usually put towards domestic expenses and not kept for personal expenses.

SPORT AND HEALTH

This cultural attitude ties directly into the reason people participate in sport to begin with. Although the link between sports and health is recognized among women in lower-class neighbourhoods, it is usually overlooked by a more dominant narrative, which is that sports are for boys to release energy and for the rich to maintain slim figures.

Uariachi, Director of the basketball and leadership camps observed:

> I think women in the past in Morocco were more active. They would move, walk a long distance to the market and clean an entire house. Now you see a similar thing happening

with women that is happening with children, which is that there is TV on all the time and more women are staying in the home more often, particularly younger generations of women. If you go into the rural areas, you still see women extremely active. But in the city, not so much. However, habits are changing with more education, teaching the idea that sport is necessary for health.

Bentalha observes that sport is becoming 'stylish' in Morocco. She sees groups of women getting together on weekends, forming walking groups and integrating sports into their morning activities. However, this is usually only true of the upper and middle classes. Sports' connection to health has not yet become important enough for lower-class women to sacrifice their limited financial resources and their time in its pursuit.

SPORT AND SCHOOL

Yet another obstacle that affects access to sport, particularly children and young girls, is the school versus sports debate. According to interviews with teachers and students at various local grammar schools in Sidi Moumen, sports activities in schools have decreased over the past 10 years, leaving children with less time to engage in some sort of physical activity at school (Figure 2.1).

'Kids at our youth centre are spending less and less time playing sports at school, a lot less then when I was their age,' said community organizer Aadak. 'We added a sports programme on Sunday morning to compensate for that.'

Bahia Elyahmidia, a women's football coach as well as a member of the Football Federation's Women's Committee, is witnessing the same phenomenon.

Figure 2.1 *Youth centre sport programs compensate for decline in school sport*

> The school system here in Morocco does absolutely nothing to promote sports partici-
> pation. We used to have mandatory physical activity sessions on Wednesday and Friday
> afternoons every week, but now they have even taken that away. The school day is filled
> with classes and exams. If there is a time set aside for sports it is usually Friday afternoon
> or Saturday morning but those are also the times set aside for exams. If a child chooses to
> participate in sports, he or she will miss and fail the exams.

Many people interviewed shared the same perspective that, in Morocco, school and sports are
in conflict and not activities that can somehow unfold simultaneously. This points to a state of
mind among many families in Morocco, which is that a student must choose either sports or
education, that sport interferes with studies and thereby decreases the student's chances of success. This is particularly the case with young girls. Through the author's work at a youth centre
in Sidi Moumen, she observed such goings on as well as talked to volunteers, who similarly support these observations. They point out that young girls between the ages of 7 and 14 years will
often come to Sunday-morning sports activities without any problems whatsoever. However, as
soon as they reach high school and especially during their last 2 years, in which they must study
intensively for the high-school exit exam, the girls' participation drops off dramatically when
compared with that of the boys. When asked why this was the case, the volunteers and some of
the young girls themselves say that their parents will not let them play sports at all because they
must concentrate on their high-school exams. The pressure to succeed, particularly for young
women in low-income areas who would have little opportunity without a high-school degree, is
so great that sport, even once a week as a leisure or healthy activity, becomes an obstacle.

MASCULINE SPORTS AND FEMININE SPORTS

Lastly, there is still the subtle attitude in Morocco that certain sports are 'masculine' and certain sports are 'feminine': this is by no means a phenomenon exclusive to this region.

According to authors Kay and Jeanes, and similarly argued by many feminists and non-
feminist sport researchers, sports have no intrinsic male or female value; rather this tag is
socially constructed. The authors argue that these 'prevailing cultural definitions of femininity
limit sports participation' (Kay and Jeanes 2008: 130–154). In Morocco, this is no exception,
particularly among the lower and more conservative classes. Feminine sports include games
such as handball, track and field and, increasingly, basketball. Sports falling under the 'for
boys' category are usually those requiring more heightened levels of contact such as karate,
kickboxing, judo, rugby and, most famously, association football.

FOOTBALL AS A TOOL FOR SOCIAL INCLUSION

It is at this point that this chapter will consider the role of football in women's access to sport.
Football is important in this analysis because, as the most popular and easily accessible sport in
the country, it has the greatest potential to reach girls and women and increase their opportunities in sport participation (Figure 2.2). However, as the most popular and most accessible
sport, it is in fact doing the exact opposite.

Figure 2.2 *Football has the greatest potential to reach Moroccan girls and women*

Women's football and its development in Morocco and the Middle East

It can virtually go unsaid that football in the Middle East is mostly a game for young boys and men. However, women have been slowly, and with great difficulty, entering the playing fields across the Middle East.

Sahar El-Hawari, a pioneer of women's football in Egypt, organized the first unofficial women's Arab tournaments in 1997 and 2001. The Arab Football Federation organized the first official Women's Arab Cup in Egypt in 2006 (*Al Ahram Weekly* 2006). Even a Palestinian women's team participated in the tournament (*Al Ahram Weekly* 2006). Jordan's women's national team has been successful in Asian tournaments since the late 1990s. More and more media attention has been placed on struggling women's programmes in areas such as Palestine, Turkey and the Kurdish regions of Iraq (El-Nasrawy 2009). Not to be outdone, football in Morocco has also come a long way. In 2008, a national league was established (Siraj 2007), whilst today, the league consists of 24 teams. There are also local neighbourhood teams that play in regional tournaments, school championships or at youth centres (first-league men's teams are now required by the Fédération Royale Marocaine de Football (Royal Football Federation) to have a women's team).

It is only natural that women want a part of one of the region's most popular sports. As argued in the article 'The Development of Women's Football in Morocco,' long gone are the days in which institutions, governments and public policy forbade women from playing football. Nonetheless, what remains are more subtle forms of denying access or excluding women from a game played on the streets all over the country, particularly the dirt streets of Sidi Moumen. One of these is a lingering unconscious cultural attitude that football is a 'masculine' game (Matuska 2010).

Saida Salah, a 38-year-old physical education teacher in Sidi Moumen who began playing football in the early 1990s, says that, although football for women has changed a lot over the years, there is still little support for girls who play because it is still considered a boy's game, in other words aggressive and rough. Girls are seen differently when they play football. They are considered less feminine and more masculine, which is generally considered undesirable.

Adil Faras, a coach of one of Morocco's more successful first-division women's teams in Sidi Moumen, often gives his young players a lecture on how to retain feminine characteristics while playing football. His advice typically draws attention to small cultural things, such as keeping their hair long and not cutting it to resemble a boy's haircut, wearing trousers rather than shorts, not using bad words on the field and not fighting with other girls. However, as many of the girls observe, some of the best female players in the country have short hair and are very 'masculine' in their behavior on and off the field.

On the level of public policy, not much is done to erase the 'football is for boys' mindset. There are hardly any women coaches or training programmes for women to become coaches themselves. There is a lack of women in decision-making positions within federations and sports organizations. There is a women's football committee within the Royal Football Federation; however, according to Bahia Elyahmidia, who is a member of the committee, they are rarely heard or listened to when it comes to forming policies surrounding football and the management of leagues. There are very few government programmes that target women's and young girls' participation in football, even though it is the most popular and easily accessible sport. Sport schools, free sports programmes for low-income children under 12 years old throughout the country run by the Ministry of Youth and Sports, offer basketball, football, handball and running. However, football is only open to boys.

This cultural resistance is sending young women mixed signals. In order to participate they must adopt a certain 'tomboyish' attitude to fit in, to be able to play and be taken seriously on the field of play. However, beyond the sports field, they are berated for being masculine, called derogatory names, and even considered girls who actually want to be boys. These girls are basically told that if you want to play, you must act like a boy but if you act like a boy, you will be shunned in your community and perhaps you will even undermine your chances of marriage.

This lack of enthusiasm to promote the game to women within Morocco has an impact. First, organized teams are few, if they exist at all, in neighbourhoods throughout Moroccan cities. An organized team environment is often necessary for young girls who want to play. Their parents or the community at large requires a safe field, with an adult coach present at all times. The idea of playing on the streets, joining 'pick-up' games or playing in empty fields with boys is often not welcome or allowed. Second, the first-division national league, an offshoot of the requirement that every Moroccan professional male team must have a female equivalent, is underfunded and disorganized. Little effort has been made by the federation or the clubs to develop young female players at an early age. Also, little effort is made to retain older players, either as coaches or managers. Third, space is already limited for male neighbourhood teams. A women's team finds it extremely difficult to get playing time at all, and sometimes the girls must choose between missing school and playing football because that is the only time they can secure the field.

Faras, the coach of Sidi Moumen's first-division women's team, said:

> It is impossible to get field space. We compete for time with a couple of local third-division boys' teams and about five neighbourhood boys' teams. There is just never any time and, if there is, it is during school hours. I can't ask the girls to practise during school.

Fourth, there is a lack of female role models in the world of football. Not many women in Morocco have heard of the American Mia Hamm or Marta from Brazil and nationally, there are no signs of any women assuming that role. The very first generation of women who began playing football in Morocco are now in their 30s and 40s; however, they are not encouraged to stay in Morocco to be trained as coaches or develop the younger generation of women players. One of the most famous players, Nadia Madiq, who everyone refers to as Tigana after a famous player for France, played with the national team until her mid-30s and then left for the United Arab Emirates for a job after being unable to find work in Morocco. Many younger girls know her name; however, not many know what she is doing now or where she has seemingly disappeared to.

Lastly, there are no active efforts to target women once they reach their 30s or get married. The idea still exists that, although it is fine for a young girl to play football, once she is in her 20s and getting ready for marriage, or is married, it is inappropriate for her to do so. When a group of married women at the cultural centre where the author was employed were asked about the question of playing football, they all sniggered and then laughed hysterically. 'Could you imagine us kicking a football,' they said? 'It is crazy. Where?'

These lapses at the policy level, combined with a civil society still hesitant to embrace football for women, have caused a sort of recurring cycle within the women's football world. Young girls not yet reaching puberty are allowed to play and run around with the boys. Once they reach their early teens, they must either join an organized team or stop playing altogether. Once they reach the age of marriage and the end of their high-school years, they must concentrate on their studies and once they get married, they must stop all together. Women's teams and the institution of women's football are consistently young, with very few older players, mentors and coaches. The cycle begins again, with young girls left to play and, as they grow up, the opportunity for them to do so disappears.

Access

Thus it all comes down in the end to access. To deny access or fail to tackle the cultural restraints surrounding women's participation in football is to create a sports environment within the country that is exclusionary towards women. Of course, not every girl wants to play football and thus alongside football all types of sports and physical activity should be encouraged. However football – being so prevalent and easily accessible for low-income communities – seems like the most logical sport to use to encourage women's participation in sport.

Open public spaces, parks and free public stadiums like Casablancaise are quickly disappearing. Women in low-income areas have little time or money to spend on recreation. The government and civil society are struggling to address issues related to access to sports in these neighbourhoods. Therefore, not to encourage women's access to the one game that can be played anywhere at any time is actively to exclude them from the most popular and most accessible form of recreation available to boys and men. Football is a form of social exclusion for women in Casablanca and this exclusion from football prevents many opportunities to engage women and young girls in healthy recreation and leisure activities.

SUMMARY

This chapter focused on the ideas of sports and social exclusion affecting the urban poor, particularly the youth and women of Casablanca, Morocco. Three factors seem to affect these two groups the most: (1) lack of open urban space; (2) public policy concerning access to sports for youth and women formulated by the Ministry of Youth and Sports; and (3) prevailing cultural attitudes. These include ideas of masculinity and femininity, sport as an activity for the elite, the importance of schooling over leisure and traditional gender roles within the home. The chapter concluded with a focus on women's football and how, in order to promote sports access for women and young girls in low-income areas with very little resources or space, cultural ideas and hesitation among policy-makers that make football less accessible to girls must be addressed.

REVIEW QUESTIONS

1   How can sport be a tool for social inclusion as well as social exclusion?
2   What are civil society's role and the government's role in promoting sport access and battling social exclusion through sport?
3   Why is football important in the battle to make sport accessible to all groups, specifically women?

FURTHER READING

Coalter, F. (2007). *A Wider Social Role for Sport: Who's keeping the score?* New York: Taylor and Francis.
Collins, M. (2009). *Examining Sports Development.* New York: Taylor and Francis.
Hylton, K. and Bramham, P. (2007). *Sports Development: Policy, Process and Practice.* New York: Taylor and Francis.

WEBSITES

International Platform for Sports and Development:
   www.sportanddev.org
Sport for Development and Peace: United Nations:
   www.un.org/wcm/content/site/sport
UK Sport International:
   www.uksport.gov.uk/uk-sport-international

REFERENCES

Aitchison, C.C. (2007). "Marking Difference of Making a Difference: Constructing Places, Policies and Knowledge of Inclusion, Exclusion and Social Justice in Leisure, Sport and Tourism," in Atelievic, I., Pritchard, A. and Morgan, N. (eds) *The Critical Turn in Tourism Studies: Innovative research methodologies*. Harlow: Elsevier, p. 85.

Al Ahram Weekly (2006) "It's Official." http://weekly.ahram.org.eg/2006/791/sp2.htm.

Arab-Moghaddam, N., Henderson K. and Sheikholeslami, R. (2007). "Women's Leisure and Constraints to Participation: Iranian Perspectives." *Journal of Leisure Research* 39(1): 109–126.

Collins, M.F. (2008). "Social Exclusion from Sport and Leisure," in Houlihan, B. (ed.) *Sport and Society: A student introduction*, 2nd edn. New York: Sage Publications, p. 78.

Crumley, B. (2003). "Carnage in Casablanca." *Time Magazine* May 18. http://www.time.com/time/magazine/article/0,9171,452784,00.html (accessed 18 June 2012).

El-Nasrawy, J. (2009) "Kurdish Women Seek Football Freedom." http://news.bbc.co.uk/2/hi/middle_east/7999867.stm.

Kay, T. and Jeanes, R. (2008). "Women Sport and Gender Inequity," in Houlihan, B. (ed.) *Sport and Society: A student introduction*, 2nd edn. New York: Sage Publications, pp. 130–154.

Matuska, N. (2010). "The Development of Women's Football in Morocco," in *Middle East Institute Viewpoints: Sports and the Middle East*. Washington, DC: Middle East Institute, May pp. 35–37.

Mazria-Katz, M. (2009). What Chicago can learn from Morocco's ghettos. *Time Magazine* July 19. http://www.time.com/time/world/article/0,8599,1910565,00.html (accessed 18 June 2012).

(SDAU) Schéma Directeur d'Aménagement Urbain du Grand Casablanca. (2008) Casablanca: Royaume du Maroc Ministère de l'Intérieur Agence urbaine de Casablanca.

Shaw, S. (2003). "Feminist Approaches to the Study of Leisure: Incorporating gender into the analysis of leisure in Africa," in Zeleza, T. and Veney, C.R. (eds) *Leisure in Urban Africa*. Trenton: Africa World Press, p. 67.

Siraj, M. (2007). http://www.yabiladi.com/article-sport-573.html, 2007 (accessed 18 June 2012).

Velija, P. (2009). *Resource Guide to Social Exclusion and Sport*. London: The Higher Education Academy, Hospitality, Leisure, Sport and Tourism Network, p. 2.

Chapter 3

The management of anti-doping

An ongoing challenge for sport

David Reid and Paul Kitchin

TOPICS

WADA, the BALCO scandal and the Whereabouts System • The organizational and cultural context of doping • Drug testers: using science to compete against science • Media attitudes to drug use • Recommendations for dealing with doping in sport

---

OBJECTIVES

By the end of this chapter, you will be able to:

1 Understand the challenges faced by those trying to police doping in sport;
2 Understand the complexity of the network of athletes, coaches and pharmacists who use doping;
3 Identify how scientific developments compete in doping;
4 View possible changes to policy and procedures to eradicate doping.

TERMS

Athlete Whereabouts System – a policy implemented by WADA (q.v.) for athletes to provide consistent updates as to their location to enable the facilitation of random testing.

BALCO scandal – a doping scandal involving numerous athletes (at the time including Olympic gold medallist Marion Jones and baseball star Barry Bonds) and the Bay Area Laboratory Cooperative.

Doping – the use of doping substances that lead to performance enhancement.

Gene doping – the development of genes and genetic technology to improve athletic performance.

Performance-enhancing drugs – chemical substances, developed predominantly in laboratories, which are used to improve athletic performance.

Therapeutic use exemptions (TUEs) – a certificate provided by a doctor to allow athletes to use a chemical substance contained on the WADA list of prohibited substances and methods for health reasons.

World Anti-Doping Agency (WADA) – an international agency, established in 1999, that is responsible for developing research into, and testing systems for, doping and the monitoring of the World Anti-Doping Code. Its mission is to work 'towards a vision of a world where all athletes compete in a doping-free sporting environment' (WADA 2012a).

CASE STUDY: ATHLETES' PERSPECTIVES ON DOPING

In my view, people who take drugs are just cheating themselves and their sport. Sport is about passion, determination to be the best, training, effort and dedication. What is the point of having a dream that involves personal physical achievement and then taking some drug to make it happen? It seems to me there isn't one. Over the years the drug testing protocol has become much more watertight, making it increasingly difficult for athletes to cheat. Yet we know there are pharmacists and doctors working hard to keep one step ahead of the system, to produce performance enhancing drugs that will be undetectable. As a result, it's an accepted part of an athlete's life to be subjected to random drug testing, whether after a race or when the tester arrives on your doorstep without warning.

(Holmes, 2005: 107)

Yesterday on the way out for the ride I was stopped by the anti-doping guys. The ITU [International Triathlon Union] have started a process they call a 'biological passport', whereby they want to have an ongoing profile of our bloods. This is great news, we all welcome what can keep our sport clean. The blood test and associated paperwork took no more than 10 minutes and off we went on our ride!

(Morrison, 2011).

OVERVIEW

In recent years the punitive 'law and order approach' (Waddington 2000) to dealing with doping in sport has not been working in the way many had expected. This approach seeks to develop testing regimes designed to identify athletes who are taking performance-enhancing substances. If caught taking drugs, athletes face suspension in the first instance and expulsion from their sport upon the second violation of the anti-doping guidelines. However, issues over the use of performance-enhancing substances still pervade sport; recent instances include the scandal at the 2006 Tour de France, or the positive tests of Jamaican sprinter Steve Mullings (his second occurrence) in 2011. Both these examples, which are in no way indicative of the scale of the problem, highlight that there are still many athletes competing in high-profile sport who are willing to take risks and try to outwit the system. The personal memoirs of cyclist Paul Kimmage (2007) and sprinter Dwain Chambers (2009) point to the ever-present moral dilemma of knowing the professional and social risks of taking performance-enhancing substances, but both felt there was no other way to succeed in their chosen disciplines.

This chapter will provide an overview of the industry of doping and the ever-more fruitless attempts, it seems, to address its exponential growth. A critical examination of the organizational–cultural context of doping will establish the foundations for further discussion. Following this, the authors will review the structure, function and key policies of the World Anti-Doping Agency (WADA), which establishes international doping policy and procedures. The battle to prevent – or even eradicate – doping in sport is fought not just against athletes and their coaches but also against the advance of science itself. The challenge science presents for policy-makers is therefore also discussed during the course of this work. International media outlets have had mixed responses to the issue of drugs in sport, ranging from a somewhat blasé approach to one that gives rise to 'moral panic'; however as attitudes are changing amongst a more informed public, so too are media viewpoints. This chapter will then critically examine the efforts of WADA to ensure that the 2012 Summer Olympic and Paralympics Games are the toughest yet for any parties who believe they can cheat the system. The chapter will then conclude with a focus upon how individuals from the field of sport management might best deal with the situation of drug use in sport in the time ahead.

THE WORLD ANTI-DOPING AGENCY

WADA is the peak agency involved in campaigning to eradicate doping from sport. Formed in 1999, WADA operates in partnership with sporting organizations and national governments to develop research, testing and monitoring of their World Anti-Doping Code (WADA 2012a). This code provides the policy framework for the implementation of anti-doping activities.

Since its formation, WADA has attempted to develop an approach to doping that is comprehensive and partnership-led. It relies on partnerships with its stakeholders in order to pursue its key mission. WADA's core priorities are:

- monitoring their partner's compliance with the Code;
- cooperating with law enforcements agencies such as Interpol;
- research to identify and detect doping substances;
- the coordination and development of anti-doping efforts;
- the development of education programmes and outreach work (WADA 2012b).

In their efforts to confront doping in sport, WADA has been accused of compromising the human rights of athletes by implementing the Whereabouts System, to be discussed later in this chapter. However, research has shown that in certain countries athletes concerned about preventing the advance of science that facilitates doping admit that better detection measures such as these may in fact be required (Vidar Hanstad and Loland 2009).

DOPING IN SPORT AS A MANAGERIAL CONUNDRUM

Since the 1980s athletes have undergone drug-testing procedures aimed at identifying athletes who wish to cheat their way to success. Initially this was carried out at regular competitions on athletes who performed well in a defined event, i.e. they secured first, second or third place or on athletes who had just won a team sport competition final. More recently, testing has expanded to include athletes 'out of competition' at their homes and training venues. The rationale for this shift in the venue for drug testing was an attempt to combat the rise in the use of masking agents, which were used to prevent the detection of performance-enhancing substances or the practice of clearing the body of doping substances before competition begins. Similarly, the level of testing has expanded whereby all manner of athletes, including Paralympic, Masters (35 years old and over) and other professional team sport participants competing at all performance levels are also tested. In fact, there have been a number of failed drugs tests across the levels of competition, highlighting that performance-enhancing drug use is not exclusive to so-called elite sports.

The use of performance-enhancing substances is not a common occurrence. The modern difference is that contemporary doping systems rely on the practice of science to ensure their 'positive' effects. This contrasts with the use of supposed performance-enhancing substances that were believed to aid athletes, such as the intake of brandy for Tour de France cyclists in the 1940s and 1950s. In Olympic sport the emergence of scientific-led doping was heavily linked to quests for 'sportive nationalism.' Certain nations within the former Soviet bloc of countries believed that in order to demonstrate the success of their society, achievement at the Summer and Winter Olympic Games was paramount. The rise of East Germany as a sporting nation coincided with the application of scientific principles to athletic training, and according to former athletes from the region, that application extended to the taking of performance-enhancing substances. Sportive nationalism is still prevalent today, as was witnessed at the Commonwealth Games in India in 2010. India had a very successful games; however, the gloss was taken away from the performances when several of their athletes failed drugs tests (BBC online 1/7/2011).

Lynn Davies (2011) believed that the Seoul 1988 Olympic and Paralympic Games was when sport lost its innocence and its battle with cheating athletes. He was of course referring to the sprinter Ben Johnson, who was disqualified for the use of steroids; however this was merely a tipping point concerning the public awareness of doping in sport. A decade later, attention would be drawn to the Tour de France, when an entire team, Festina, was disqualified for doping infractions. An experienced team assistant (*soigneur*) Willy Voet was caught by customs agents with 250 batches of steroids and 400 ampoules of erythropoietin (EPO) in his car. From a management perspective the individuals are not necessarily the main focus but it is developing an understanding of what culture exists within an organization that would make the consideration of doping acceptable. Cycling has been tainted with drug-related issues ever since this affair; however, a cultural aspect of the sport has always considered performance enhancement to be a plausible strategy for gaining advantage. Waddington and Smith (2008: 155) mention: 'in some respects the situation in cycling may be rather special and as a consequence, it may be the case that in cycling these

37

networks are more organised and systemised – in a word they are more institutionalised – than in most other sports'.

The scale of the problem in cycling during this era was depicted by Paul Kimmage in his account of professional cycling, entitled *Rough Ride*. Kimmage (2007) outlined that the elite cyclists had a law of *omerta* (silence) and that riders were discouraged from breaking this law and 'spitting in the soup'. When he finally succumbed to taking performance-enhancing drugs, Kimmage said he felt accepted, and like 'one of the boys'. This outlines the socialization that was occurring in cycling throughout this era with regard to drugs and the institutionalized nature of the ethos. The group mentality was so strong that if anyone challenged this dominant ideology they faced internal sanctions. Where an athlete goes against this ethos, such as in the case of young cyclist Christophe Bassons, who refused to take performance-enhancing drugs despite the majority of his team doing so, it is often difficult for that athlete to retain his position within the team. His disapproval was forthright on cycling's drug problem, yet ultimately he left the sport citing the pressure he was put under by his peers within the peleton (Walsh 2007). Kimmage (2007) describes other riders in his hotel hanging upside down from door-frames to keep the blood moving in their bodies amid often bizarre practices designed to evade detection. Sudden deaths on tour in 2000, as well as soaring sales of aspirin (to thin the blood) suggested that some cyclists felt that not much had changed following the Festina affair. These considerations regarding the institutionalization of doping are important for policy-making and the future management of organizations. To alter a culture of doping within an organization would require a considerable amount of organizational change and institutionalized practices are often buried deep within the fibre of the organization itself (Zucker 1987).

The extent of the cycling problem helped facilitate the emergence of WADA in 1999 in a move thought to herald a decline in doping in sport. WADA attempted to regulate the use of performance-enhancing substances by getting international and national federations to sign up to the WADA Code. Nevertheless, their investigations into doping in sport have resulted in further issues being highlighted and have not yet, arguably, documented the scale of this global sporting problem. One of WADA's methods to decrease doping is to inform athletes better about various substances that exist counter to its code surrounding banned drugs. To do this they publish the WADA list of prohibited substances. However this document is reasonably abstruse (see further reading). The list is updated regularly from developments in research on performance enhancement or from the testing of new drugs that will breach the Code; analysis by the general public is difficult. Therapeutic use exemptions (TUEs) have been developed in order to allow some athletes to use substances that relate to a pre-existing medical condition and are approved by a doctor. A common example of this is the approved use of an inhaler for an athlete who is asthmatic. Unfortunately this process can be open to manipulation by athletes seeking to gain an advantage, while difficulties are exacerbated as the issue is often poorly explained in related media reports.

Since 2003 WADA has attempted to implement the Athlete Whereabouts System, in which athletes are obliged to account for their whereabouts for 1 hour of every day. This reporting system is to ensure that a strict regime of in-competition and out-of-competition testing can be facilitated. To implement the policy athletes are required to provide their specific location so that doping testers can ensure that all athletes receive random testing.

Vidar Hanstad and Loland (2009) state that the aim of the rule is to increase the detection of dopers and also to act as a deterrent for athletes considering doping. The measure has been criticized as tantamount to athlete surveillance and a potential breach of an athlete's human rights. Arguments which posit that 'if you have nothing to hide you have nothing to fear' do not consider a principle of natural justice as being that one is assumed innocent until proven guilty. Nevertheless the policy has experienced significant obstacles since its implementation and is by no means perfect in its current form.

DIFFICULTIES IMPLEMENTING THE WHEREABOUTS SYSTEM

Three strikes

Although the Whereabouts System was designed to ensure that athletes could not avoid the drug testers and hence being caught if engaged in doping, in practice it has caused much confusion. A couple of cases highlight these difficulties. In 2006, the Athens Olympic 400m champion Christine Ohuruogu was missed by drug testers on three occasions. This failure to meet with the testers, despite notification of her whereabouts, resulted in her receiving a 1-year ban from the sport.

> Christine was the first track-and-field athlete to be caught under the 'three strikes' rule and, while the regulations and penalties were available to all, she did not expect such harsh punishment. She says: 'I swear if you went and spoke to any athlete you'd find they had one or two missed tests. I just happened to be the first one who missed three and if it hadn't been me it would have been someone else. I truly believe that. I feel like the system was designed not to catch cheats, but caught [sic] a person with bad time-management.' Certainly, the recent admission by IAAF [International Association of Athletics Federations] general secretary Pierre Weiss that there have been as many as 1,000 missed tests worldwide in the past year puts Christine's situation in perspective.
>
> (*The Guardian* 2007)

Indian cricket

While cricket might be seen merely as a Commonwealth sport in many parts of the world, it remains the number-one sport in India. As the chief financier of world cricket (estimates put the contribution of Indian cricket to world cricket's funds at 70–80 per cent: Mehta 2007) the national governing body, the Board for Control of Cricket in India (BCCI) supported their players who refused to sign an agreement to abide by the Code, citing security issues within the proposal. The influence of the BCCI on world cricket persuaded the International Cricket Council (the world's governing body) to implement a two-tiered structure around the issue. The structure originally placed national cricketers on the second tier of the whereabouts system, which relaxed some of the reporting requirements associated with it. Nevertheless, as the sport is played between nations there are technically speaking no international athletes in cricket. Hence there is no pool of players at the top tier for WADA to test. This simply highlights the complications of implementing international policy across diverse sports.

Operational issues still hamper the efforts of WADA to implement its code and test athletes. The Bay Area Laboratory Cooperative (BALCO) case is highlighted in greater detail later in this chapter, but if coach Trevor Graham had not handed in a needle containing a designer steroid, which sparked off the investigation in the first place, the drugs and the evidence pointing to the extensive list of dopers may never have bee found. Hence only being able to test for what they know exists remains a major scientific conundrum for WADA. Following the investigations by the US government and WADA it was discovered that Victor Conte was the head of BALCO and responsible for the supply of drugs to a network of sports. After serving a prison sentence, Conte has been very contrite and forthcoming about the procedures that occurred in his lab. In an open letter to British 100m runner Dwain Chambers, Conte wrote:

> We are now in the 21st century; science has progressed by leaps and bounds. The anti-doping agencies have a database with most drugs known to be used in sport. As a scientist, I understand how things work in the world of drug testing and this enabled me to develop undetectable drug programmes … It is also important to know that there is a rather large list of performance-enhancing drugs that are undetectable by the testers.
>
> (cited in Chambers 2009: 65)

Furthermore, organizational issues serve to complicate matters. The Chairman of the British Olympic Association (BOA) Colin Moynihan has stated that he is less than impressed with WADA's role over the last decade, labelling the organization 'toothless' and pointing out: 'never have sanctions on hard-line cheats been so weak since the end of the cold-war. Marion Jones and countless others have flourished during the WADA era' (Moynihan 2011). This hard-line BOA approach and dissatisfaction with WADA's work have resulted in the organizations being embroiled in ever-more fractious levels of confrontation. In the lead-up to the London 2012 Olympic and Paralympic Games, the BOA has undergone challenge from WADA at the Court for Arbitration for Sport concerning the lifetime Olympic bans it issues to athletes caught doping. WADA argues that the UK has signed up to the Code, which enforces a 2-year ban for a doping offence, and that the BOA's lifetime ban is incompatible. The BOA claims that it sought clarification concerning the rights of clean athletes who are denied selection by an athlete on illegal enhancements. And what is worse, the cheat, possibly with a lifelong benefit of a course of growth hormones and other drugs, is able to compete once more in a future Games (Moynihan 2011). Arguably the BOA's stance could gather momentum for a broader change. It is difficult for WADA to justify why it focuses on the BOA stance whilst certain sports and nations also breach aspects of the Code without any such retribution.

In addition to this some continue to have doubts over the integrity of certain national sports federations: 'in Spain and some other countries, political protection of elite athletes is a serious obstacle to WADA and its allies' (Hoberman 2011: 12). In other countries there have been debates over the importance of high-profile athletes when providing good role models for young people. This has resulted in attention being diverted away from performance-enhancing substances towards ensuring that illicit-drug use by athletes is avoided. The following case study focuses on the Australian experience.

CASE STUDY: DETERMINING THE REGULATION OF ILLICIT-DRUG USE IN AUSTRALIAN SPORT

The regulation of drugs in sport has been a pressing issue in Australian sport since the dramatic increase in doping exemplified by Eastern European nations in the second half of the twentieth century. Doping struck at the heart of Australia's sporting success as, before the significant investment in Australian sport over the course of the 1980s, Australia relied on its most gifted athletes rising to the top of its sporting pyramid. Australia's apex was, until this time, very competitive internationally but poor national management systems and the rise of scientific doping saw this success significantly curtailed, resulting in a country with a proud competitive history at the Olympics claiming only three medals overall at the Montreal Olympics of 1976.

The investment in Australia's sporting system allowed it to achieve a sustained competitive advantage over other nations of similar populations and sporting resources. While this advantage is not sustainable indefinitely, it has given rise to an advanced and well-organized system of sport production. Australian sport and its followers, particularly the media, adopted a punitive approach to drugs in sport. When the Chinese swimming team were found with drugs in their possession at the airport and four tested positive for masking agents at the 1998 Fédération Internationale de Natation (FINA) World Championships in Perth they were essentially driven from the country by a hostile national populous.

The Olympic Games were held as sacrosanct and an anti-doping policy was established to ensure the 'pure performance' of Australian athletes competing in the Summer and Winter Olympic Games. However a significant number of illicit-drug use incidents continued to plague other high-profile sports in Australia, such as Australian Rules Football and the National Rugby League, causing much consternation amongst Australian sport policy makers.

Australian academics Stewart *et al.* (2011) investigated the efforts of the sporting hierarchy to implement drug regulations across all Australian sporting organizations, not just those relevant at Olympic and World Championship levels. To inform their analysis they used aspects of Pierre Bourdieu's (1977) practice theory in order to explain how a dominant ideology about the role of drugs in sport came to define legitimacy in the 'drugs-in-sport field of play'. In short, practice theory examines the relationships between different agents in a field of competition. This competition was the right to determine how illicit-drug use would be dealt with when pertinent issues came to the fore. In their analysis there was a coalition of dominant stakeholders (the Australian government through the Australian Sports Anti-Doping Agency, national governing bodies and the Australian Sports Commission), who collectively possessed large amounts of capital, which ensured that their values (moral and social arguments on drugs in sport) dominated how the issue was to be viewed, understood and debated. This capital manifests itself through economic resources, their status in the field and a network of linkages between various stakeholders within sport (economic, symbolic and social capitals). These views contrasted with other stakeholders and their opinions on how to deal with illicit-drug use. This smaller coalition was able to provide evidence to show that zero-tolerance policies had few health benefits, disavowing health arguments about illicit-drug use. Eventually the moral/social ideology (which viewed drug use as a threat to both the sport's integrity and at the same time the elevated position of athletes as role models – despite a lack evidence to prove either) became the dominant discourse and established itself as influential over policy-making. Hence in this case the authors demonstrated how certain ideologies outperformed competing values, despite the evidence base their opponents possessed.

COMPETING AGAINST SCIENCE

> There is a scientist in Pittsburgh ... who has succeeded in increasing muscle mass of mice by up to 35% using genetic engineering. Half the letters he receives are from athletes who say 'try it out on me' .... When Sweeney answers that he works with animals and has no idea how a human body would respond to this kind of intervention they write back and say: 'that's okay, do it on me anyway.' The world of people who dope is a sick world.
>
> (Spiegel Online International 2008)

The BALCO scandal

Before 2002 few people in the field of sport had heard of a drug called THG, also known in certain circles as 'The Clear'. However, following one of the highest-profile doping scandals in world sport, the careers and reputations of many elite athletes were tarnished forever. Tetrahydrogestrinone (THG) and four other substances (human growth hormone, modafinil, testosterone cream and EPO) had been used by Victor Conte and others at the BALCO in California to enhance athletic performance illegally. The regimented use of these substances would allow athletes to avoid detection from doping testers. The US Anti-Doping Agency was tipped off by the coach of Marion Jones and Tim Montgomery to the existence of THG. From the sample of THG provided, scientists were able to develop a test to show categorically that it had been taken by as-yet unnamed athletes. From this test a number of athletes were subsequently exposed, such as Jones (who would later serve a prison sentence for perjury) and Montgomery, alongside other successful US athletes. Dwain Chambers, the British sprinter and captain of the British athletics team at the 2003 World Championships, also returned a positive test for the substance in 2003. Outside the field of athletics BALCO was providing substances for National Football League (NFL) footballers, cyclists, boxers and baseball players such as Barry Bonds.

Following the scandal a number of changes occurred throughout the sports involved. Once again WADA developed its testing regime to identify the presence of THG in cheating athletes. The subsequent media attention of Bonds' inclusion in the investigation forced baseball's administrators to implement policies to reduce doping in the sport, which would bring it into line with other sporting organizations. Jones and other medal winners were retrospectively stripped of their ill-gotten gains by the International Olympic Committee (IOC) and other sporting organizations. The chief instigator of the scandal, Victor Conte, was sentenced to a prison sentence for selling illegal steroids but has since completed his term of imprisonment and has now started a new company selling *legal* performance enhancements.

As the BALCO scandal has demonstrated, technological and pharmacological developments have meant the availability of performance-enhancing products has increased in a marked fashion over the last two decades (Waddington and Smith 2008). The emergence of 'high-street' shops such as Holland & Barrett in the UK has facilitated the increasing prevalence of vitamin supplementation into everyday life, not just for athletes but also for anyone interested in exercise improvement. Journalist David Walsh (2007) detailed how cyclists knew exactly where to go, and in which countries, to get items like EPO over the counter. We do not argue that all practitioners are involved in the supply and development of dubious substances. Sports nutrition and medicine are highly specialized and professional areas comprised of many highly ethical service providers working internationally with sports teams and government agencies.

Technology has continually developed to increase sporting performance. One only has to look at the battle between Speedo and its competitors over the development of swimsuits and swimsuit material to increase swimmers' times as a case in point. Off-season design changes to Formula One cars consistently demonstrate the impact that technological advancement can have on performance. But add to this advanced design work on performance-enhancing drugs and such evolutionary practices assume a more sinister dimension. The BALCO case accentuated the centrality of the relationship between elite-evel athletes and practitioners of sports medicine (Waddington and Smith 2008) and highlights the issue for doping control. Victor Conte outlined how he used their expertise in order to develop performance-enhancing drugs that were undetectable and supplied many of the world's top sportspeople until they were arrested. 'The increasing use of illicit drugs has been associated with the emergence, in both the world of sport and the world of medicine, of those who may be described as innovators or entrepreneurs' (Waddington and Smith 2008: 81).

> Despite the claims of organisations such as the IOC and within Britain, the Sports Council (now UK Sport), there is in fact among informed analysts widespread recognition that positive test results are an extremely poor – indeed almost worthless – indication of the extent of drug use in sport, for it is widely acknowledged that those who provide positive tests simply represent the tip of a large iceberg.
>
> (Waddington and Smith 2008: 119)

A new challenge for WADA arises because of a change in scientific methods that shift the focus amongst those who would wish to cheat the system away from chemistry in the direction of biology. Gene doping has long been discussed as a possible future path that athletes may take to avoid detection:

> genetic manipulation has created faster, larger, stronger and more enduring animals. [the idea that] athletes deliberately altering their genetic make-up to gain an edge in performance raises profound ethical issues [and testing strategies] as [they] may be undetectable by current tests.
>
> (Schneider and Rupert 2009: 163)

The lure of performance enhancement remains because by 'transforming mere mortals into supermen, sport becomes a test of, say, chemistry, rather than human talent and ability' (Carr 2008: 204). However the debate could suggest that we consider how developments in chemistry are different from developments in other areas of science. Apart from the secrecy involved, how different is doping to other technologies such as unequal access to government-funded training facilities and advanced equipment? Possibly the ban should be lifted as some of the 'legal' practices that are allowed under the guidelines also push the boundaries. For example, was Tiger Woods' laser eye surgery natural, or were Paula Radcliffe's multiple

43

altitude camps each year permissible? Indeed, are sports drinks or protein powders and recovery shakes actually natural aids to performance? Controversially, Petersen and Kristensen (2009) debate whether we should end the ban on drugs in sport to level the playing field. However, 'to claim no athlete will be in a competitive inferior situation is pure speculation' (p. 93), and concomitantly, this is also to assume that all athletes would begin to take performance-enhancing drugs if they became legalized – a situation that is very unlikely to materialize.

> Any attempt here to draw a compelling line seems arbitrary and indicative of spurious essentialism. But even if we could make a clear distinction here, it doesn't follow that artificial performance enhancers should be prohibited simply because they are artificial. The distinction would only matter if artificial performance enhancers gave an athlete an advantage we don't feel they should have, but we can't derive this solely from the fact that a performance enhancer is artificial.
>
> (Petersen and Kristensen 2009: 194)

Morgan (2009) argues that media and public opinion is swaying towards a view that performance-enhancing drugs are required and now morally acceptable when maintaining current levels of performance – albeit not yet by the sports industry. At the same time there are many commentators who disagree that this is the case, and it seems that further investigation is needed to establish public opinion at this stage.

MEDIA ATTITUDES TO DRUG USE

The majority of the popular media sees drug failures as a major issue and reacts angrily, often with 'moral panic'. However attitudes in some countries seem to lack consistency. Fighting a global issue could arguably depend on the support of international media; however there tends to be a laissez-faire attitude to drug failures in much of, for example, the popular media in the USA. Brian Cushing still claimed the Associated Press NFL defensive Rookie of the Year award for 2010 despite testing positive for performance-enhancing substances (Wilner 2010). Similarly, Waddington and Smith (2008) point to the case of baseball player Mark McGwire breaking the home run record and the *San Francisco Chronicle* not once mentioning his admittance of having taken steroids earlier in his career.

However, in other countries the treatment of athletes is significantly different. Former Irish pro cyclist Paul Kimmage (2007) described popular Irish talk show host Gay Byrne's interrogation of him as personifying the public reaction, or indeed overreaction, to these issues. Byrne did not want to know his story; he had already made up his mind in advance:

> Ireland's favourite broadcaster wasn't pleased. He had a look on his face I would see many times over the next few weeks. A look that said, 'how dare you cast a shadow on our fairytale?' A look that said, 'How dare you poison our dreams?' He expected me to stand before the good people of Ireland and reassure them that only losers like myself got tangled up in the drugs web and that the sports heroes were clean.
>
> (Kimmage 2007: 7)

Byrne's approach could be seen to fall into a sense of 'moral panic.' Arguably a new attitude would be helpful if we are to address the problem effectively. 'The idea that performance-enhancing drugs should be outlawed because they possess certain morally objectionable features, that they are harmful, coercive etc, has little or no currency in critical circles today' (Morgan 2009: 163).

Some commentators see that the organizational attempts to maintain the ban on drugs on medical grounds is overly paternalistic (Waddington and Smith 2008). Brown (2009) suggested that 'little evidence has been adduced to establish these dangers, particularly in comparison to the dangers of the sports themselves' (p. 127). However, there are more anecdotal examples of athletes who have had serious ill health as a result of a performance-enhancing drugs programme. There has been much speculation linking world sprint record holder Florence Griffith-Joyner's death to her taking performance-enhancing drugs during her athletic career. Many years after the ultimately tragic case of Joyner, Dwain Chambers was part of one of the most sophisticated drug programmes in history. However he also describes the abdominal pains that were symptomatic of his drug use: 'and yet again, as I lay on a cold bathroom floor doubled up in pain, I realized I wasn't looking after myself. How could I be? Someone who looks after himself, watches what he eats, doesn't drink or smoke, and yes … stays away from drugs' (Chambers 2009: 128).

DOPERS BEWARE!

Managers of international sporting events and federations have used 'threat' tactics to persuade dopers to stay away from their events. The Chairman of the London Olympic Organizing Committee for the Olympic Games Lord Sebastian Coe challenged the dopers, stating: 'what I can say to athletes coming to London is that we have the technology in place that is in excess of any technology that you will have encountered anywhere in the world. You come to London and you try that, we will get you' (cited in *The Age* 2011). Professor David Cowan (BBC News 2011), who is in charge of anti-doping for the Olympics, has announced that new tests for blood doping would be carried out at the Games. In addition an improved test for human growth hormone plus one that tests for gene doping were also in development.

Whilst these claims are broadly welcomed it is interesting to see why the organizers would inform potential cheats of their intended actions. Is it to protect the image of the 2012 Games, that is, to try and avoid the potentially hazardous public relations issues of a drug scandal? We raise these questions as previous experience has also shone a light upon this dilemma. In the summer of 2010 the IAAF announced the following: 'The IAAF will collect blood samples from ALL athletes taking part in the IAAF World Championships in Daegu in an unprecedented anti-doping programme' (IAAF 2011) in close proximity to the championships. This announcement of the extent of testing was welcomed by most within the anti-doping community; however, again the timing of the announcement was queried by some of the world's best track and field athletes. Many athletes took to social networking sites such as Facebook and Twitter to question the timing of the announcement and requested that the general public pay close attention to any resultant withdrawals that may have been linked to this announcement.

High-profile annual sporting competitions and mega-events are very valuable commodities for a host of stakeholders. One sceptical approach might be to view doping-control messages as more important in protecting the image of the event by encouraging drop-outs rather than risk leaving a tarnished image due to doping failures. BALCO's Victor Conte is now working with a number of boxers and his view of the organization of that sport is dim: 'I don't believe they want to know how rampant the use of drugs really is. Testing in boxing is completely and totally inept' (BBC Sport 2010). However, from an entertainment point of view, no one wants to watch a sport where the winner is retrospectively disqualified months later, robbing the viewer of the spectacle and the true champion of his or her moment on the podium.

Houlihan (2002) suggests that three factors have necessitated a review of doping policy: 'first the failure of the policy to produce movements in the selected measures of performance; second the emergence of new dimensions to the target problem; and third a redefinition of the problem' (Houlihan 2002: 120). Houlihan goes further, to suggest that in order to solve the issue WADA and its partners need to agree their 'end-game'. He suggests that they need to decide what they want from their policies: do they want the complete elimination of all doping in all sports, in certain sports, or only in some sports at certain levels, or even do they want simply to contain the extent of drug use?

POSSIBLE RECOMMENDATIONS FROM SPORT'S STAKEHOLDERS

This penultimate section addresses three suggested solutions from the various stakeholders involved in the debate concerning anti-doping measures. These suggestions involve athletes counselling other athletes on the personal and professional risks to doping; the implementation of harsher periods of suspension for offenders; and, perhaps more radically, alterations to the management of sport.

Athletes as counsellors

Recently WADA appointed the former cyclist and convicted doper David Millar to its Athletes Commission. This commission meets regularly to discuss anti-doping issues and it is perceived that his personal experience can inform policy and athlete actions by the sharing of his knowledge and insights. Similarly, Dwain Chambers has suggested using ex-offenders to help address the issue:

> There is no person better placed to help them improve drugs detection and increase the deterrents than someone in my position. I flouted their detection methods for more than a year and a half. In the real world professional security companies employ ex-burglars in order to make their security systems as watertight as possible. Reformed bank robbers and pickpockets assist the police. I feel that I am in the same position.
>
> (Chambers 2009: 164)

Harsher periods of suspension

The threat of lifetime bans from sport is one strategy that sport's stakeholders could follow. While the finality of the lifetime ban seems severe, the former athlete Roger Black (2011) claimed that the balance was too much in favour of dopers (and their supporters) and not enough in favour of clean athletes. He argued for a lifetime ban which would also imply that, ultimately, some innocent athletes would have to suffer. Nevertheless this proposal would be, to a larger extent, protecting clean athletes worldwide. Caution however is urged by those with personal experience:

> There's a place for lifetime bans in sport, but I'd like to think that what I've been through is a shining example of the worth of second chances. Every case needs to be judged on its own merits. I don't think every athlete should be treated the same way. Imagine you have a 16-year-old who's been given something by their coach and goes positive and receives a lifetime ban, that doesn't seem fair. But maybe, if you have a 34-year-old multi-millionaire who lives in Monte Carlo, with a team of medical staff, who goes positive, maybe they should get a lifetime ban for a first offence. But those two cases are so different that they can't be judged the same.
>
> (BBC Sport 2011)

Changing the governance of the sport

Given the testing capabilities that are now in use, some of sport's stakeholders have queried some more controversial ways of managing the issues. In 1999 the unified German Athletics Federation suggested erasing all sports records and starting at year zero in order to rehabilitate the tarnished image of sport in the country. Many of its records are dubious in their legitimacy and currently almost unattainable with the current testing regime. The Federation took this to the council of the IAAF but were unsuccessful in this somewhat radical plan. Renaldo Nehemiah (former sprint hurdler) made an interesting suggestion in order to battle the use of performance-enhancing drugs. Nehemiah suggested that shifting from a focus on times to a focus on the result on the day would alleviate the need for clocks (cited in *New York Times* 2004). However, given the conservative nature of many sporting organizations and the myriad number of stakeholders, agreement on these points, for the meantime at least, remains unlikely.

SUMMARY

This chapter has sought to provide the reader with an overview of the industry of doping. It is clear that WADA has an extremely difficult job attempting to police drug-taking in sport. While the organization has a very functional structure it does not consider the wider stakeholders who could pressure its workings that should also be considered. The problem for WADA is that it is an organization that by its very remit is fighting a battle on many fronts, which include research on doping and testing for doping, ongoing compliance issues with sporting federations and athletes, and, at times, an unsupportive media. This has ensured that WADA and its partners have had to spend time and resources prompting the veracity of its testing systems rather than benefitting from the opportunity to work on changing stakeholder attitudes within sport.

REVIEW QUESTIONS

1   Is WADA's mission possible?
2   Has WADA been successful in dealing with the issue of doping in sport? In what way has it or has it not been successful?
3   What do you think of the suggestion of using former drugs cheats to educate athletes about doping in sport?

FURTHER READING

Athletes must avoid any substances from the Prohibited List outlined by WADA.
World Anti-Doping Agency. (2008). "World Anti-Doping Code: The 2008 Prohibited List." Online at: http://www.wada-ama.org/rtecontent/document/2008_List_En.pdf.
To represent the complexity the relationship has with the many stakeholders of sport, WADA has presented an organizational chart, available at: http://www.wada-ama.org/Documents/About_WADA/Strategy/WADA_GlobalAntiDopingOrganizationChart_200901_EN.pdf.
Waddington, I. (2000). *Sport, Health and Drugs: A critical sociological perspective*. London: Routledge.

WEBSITES

AFL players say 'no' to drugs:
    www.afl.com.au/Portals/0/afl_docs/AFLPlayersSayNoToDrugs.pdf
Wikipedia:
    en.wikipedia.org/wiki/Use_of_performance-enhancing_drugs_in_sport
World Anti-Doping Agency:
    www.wada-ama.org/en

REFERENCES

BBC News (2011). "New Tests Promise Toughest Olympics for Cheats." http://www.bbc.co.uk/news/science-environment-14890564 (accessed 10 October 2011).
BBC Online (1/7/2011) "India: Six Indians Fail Doping Test." http://www.bbc.co.uk/news/world-south-asia-13986366 (accessed 10 October 2011).
BBC Sport (2010). "Boxing: Victor Conte Slams Professional Boxing's Drug Testing." http://news.bbc.co.uk/sport1/hi/boxing/8485892.stm (accessed 28 January 2010).

BBC Sport. (2011). "Cycling: David Millar Will Not Challenge BOA Lifetime Ban." http://news.bbc.co.uk/sport1/hi/cycling/15922346.stm (accessed 28 November 2011).

Black, R. (2011). Interview. BBC Radio FiveLive Morning Drive programme, 21 November.

Bourdieu, P. (1977). *Outline of a Theory of Practice.* Cambridge: Polity Press.

Brown, W.M. (2009). "The Case for Perfection." *Journal of the Philosophy of Sport* 36(2): 127–139.

Carr, C.L. (2008). "Fairness and Enhancement in Sport." *Journal of Philosophy of Sport* 35(2): 193–207.

Chambers, D. (2009). *Race Against Me, My Story.* Spain: Libros International

Davies, L. (2011). Presentation to Athletics Northern Ireland General Council, Belfast, 19 October 2011.

Hoberman, J. (2011). Macro-Sociological Obstacles to Doping Control. Presented at the conference on 'Anti-doping- Rational Policy or Moral Panic?' International Conference at Aarhus University, Aarhus, Denmark, 18 August.

Holmes, K. (2005). *Black, White and Gold.* London: Virgin Books.

Houlihan, B. (2002). *Dying to Win.* Germany: Council Of Europe Publishing.

IAAF (2011). "Blood Tests for All Athletes in Daegu in Unprecedented Anti-Doping Programme." http://www.iaaf.org/news/newsid=61097.html (accessed 10 October 2011)

Kimmage, P. (2007). *Rough Ride.* London: Random House.

Mehta, N. (2007). The great Indian news trick: satellite television, cricketisation and Indianisation. Paper presented at One-Day Seminar on International Cricket at the University of London, 2 March 2007.

Merti, S. (2010). "Canadian IOC Member Dick Pound Calls Doped Athletes 'Sociopathic Cheats'." *The Canadian Press,* cp.org February 9, 2010 (cited in Hoberman, J., 2011).

Morgan, W.J. (2009). "Athletic Perfection, Performance-Enhancing Drugs, and the Treatment-Enhancement Distinction." *Journal of the Philosophy of Sport* 36(2): 162–181.

Morrison, A. (2011). "Aileen's Blog." http://blog.aileenmorrison.com/#category0 (accessed 1 October 2011).

Moynihan, C. (2011). British Olympic Association Interview. Associated Press, 18 November.

New York Times. (2004). "Track and Field: Track Hears a Call To Wipe Out Records." http://www.nytimes.com/2004/07/18/sports/track-and-field-track-hears-a-call-to-wipe-out-records.html?pagewanted=all&src=pm (accessed 18 October 2011)

Petersen, T.S. and Kristensen, J.K. (2009). "Should All Athletes Be Allowed to Use All Kinds of Performance Enhancing Drugs? A Critical Note on Claudio M. Tamburrini." *Journal of Philosophy of Sport* 36(1): 88–99..

Schneider, A.J. and Rupert, J.L. (2009). "Constructing Winners: The Science and Ethics of Genetically Manipulating Athletes." *Journal of Philosophy of Sport* 36(2): 182–206.

Sky Sports News (2011) Edwin Moses interview. 16 November. http://www.skysports.com/video/inline/0,,12606_4171150,00.html (accessed 16 November 2011).

Spiegel Online International. (2008). Interview with former anti-doping czar. http://www.spiegel.de/international/world/0,1518,593937-2,00.html (accessed 19 October 2011).

Spiegel Online Sport, Germany (2008) "Doping is Organized Along Mafia Lines. Interview with Richard Pound." http://www.spiegel.de/international/world/0,1518,593937-2,00.html (accessed 19 October 2011).

Stewart, B., Adair, D. and Smith, A.C.T. (2011). Drivers of illicit drug-use regulation in Australian sport. *Sport Management Review* 14: 237–245.

The Age, Australia. (2011). "We'll Catch Drug Cheats, Says Coe." http://www.theage.com.au/sport/well-catch-drug-cheats-says-coe-20110727-1i08m.html (accessed 10 October 2011).

The Guardian. (2007). "Run! Christine run!" http://www.guardian.co.uk/sport/2007/nov/25/athletics.features (accessed 19 October 2011)

Vidar Hanstad, D. and Loland, S. (2009). "Elite Athletes' Duty to Provide Information on Their

Whereabouts: Justifiable Anti-doping Work or an Indefensible Surveillance Regime?" *European Journal of Sport Science* 9: 3–10.

WADA (2012a). About WADA. http://www.wada-ama.org/en/About-WADA/ (accessed 12 January, 2012).

WADA (2012b). Priorities. http://www.wada-ama.org/en/About-WADA/History-Mission-Priorities-and-Strategic-Plan/Priorities/ (accessed 12 January, 2012).

Waddington, I. (2000). *Sport, Health and Drugs: A critical sociological perspective.* London: Routledge.

Waddington I. and Smith, A. (2008). *An Introduction to Drugs in Sport: Addicted to winning?* 2nd edn. Oxon: Routledge.

Walsh, D. (2007). *From Lance to Landis.* New York: Ballantine Books.

Wilner, B. (2010). "Brian Cushing Wins Rookie of the Year Revoting Despite Drug Suspension." http://www.huffingtonpost.com/2010/05/12/brian-cushing-wins-rookie_n_573878.html (accessed 28 September, 2011).

Zucker, L. (1987). "Institutional Theories of Organizations." *Annual Review of Sociology*, 13: 443–464.

Chapter 4

Sanctioned aggression or criminal sanction?

Violence, contact sports and the law

Jack Anderson

TOPICS

Examples of violent and ill-disciplined play in sport • Sports-related offences in criminal law • Reckless disregard and the defence of consent • The criminal law as a last resort

---

OBJECTIVES

By the end of this chapter, you will be able to:

1 Provide an insight into why contact sports are deemed an exception to the ordinary law of criminal assault;
2 Ascertain the practical implementation of this exception by the police and the criminal courts;
3 Assess the safe level of risk that a participant in a contact sport may assume;
4 Offer an analysis of whether the criminal law is a useful means of combating violence in sport or should be used only as a last resort.

KEY TERMS

Contact sports – any sport in which the participants necessarily come into bodily contact with one another. The contact in question can range from physically invasive sports, such as rugby and American football, which are, in effect, collision sports; to limited-contact sports, such as association football and hockey.

> **Law** – in the context of this chapter, means the criminal law, which is that branch of law concerned with prosecutions brought by the police against persons deemed to have committed wrongs of such a serious nature that they should be punished by the state in criminal proceedings, and which occasionally can result in the culprit having to serve a jail sentence.
>
> **Unacceptably violent play** – the manner in which this phrase is defined in, and sanctioned by, the playing rules and culture of a particular contact sport is often the key determinative factor in the police's decision whether to instigate criminal proceedings against a player alleged to have inflicted serious injury on an opponent.

OVERVIEW

This chapter considers the law's role, if any, in policing and sanctioning unacceptably violent play in contact sports. The most problematical phrase and the one that is central to this chapter is that of 'unacceptably violent play' during the course of a sporting contest. The manner in which this phrase is understood remains the key consideration in the authorities' decision whether to instigate action against a player alleged to have inflicted injury upon an opponent. Finally, for now, although the principal focus will be on the attitude of the criminal law in the UK to sports violence, reference will also be made, where appropriate, to the law in Canada, the USA, Australia and New Zealand.

INTRODUCTION AND KEY CASE STUDIES OF VIOLENT PLAY IN SPORT

One of the most dramatic moments in the history of the FIFA World Cup occurred near the end of the 2006 final in Berlin. With the game tensely poised and heading towards penalties, France's Zinedine Zidane exchanged words with an Italian defender, Marco Materazzi. Evidently provoked and clearly incensed, Zidane headbutted the Italian in the chest, knocking him to the ground. The ignominy of being sent off in his last competitive game was compounded for Zidane when Italy went on to win the game on penalties. It was a truly shocking moment in sport, played out before a global TV audience of millions, and one that was exhaustively analysed in its immediate aftermath. One of the points that were not raised in that post-match analysis was the question as to whether Zidane should have been cautioned by the German police. Before this question can be dismissed as being fanciful, it has to be asked, what if such a clash had taken place outside a nightclub as patrons spilled out on to the streets in the early hours of the morning? What if, taunted by another, a man rushed across the street and headbutted the victim to the ground and did so in full view of a police officer and numerous witnesses, including CCTV cameras? Is there not a high likelihood that the culprit would be arrested and charged with a criminal, assault-based offence? In short, should it not be the case that to strike another without legal justification is a crime, whether it takes place in the street, in the family home or on the football pitch?

The Zidane incident raises many questions (such as the role of provocation as the source of violence on the sports field) which are returned to in the body of this chapter. For now, it must be noted that the Zidane–Materazzi clash was very much of an 'off-the-ball' nature, meaning an incident that occurs while the ball and play are elsewhere. An interesting and controversial 'on-the-ball' incident involving violent play, again in association football, took place in April 2001 during the course of a game between Manchester United and Manchester City when United's Roy Keane kicked out at City's Alf-Inge Haaland. The tackle injured Haaland's knee and saw Keane receive a red card, for which he eventually received a four-match playing ban. Although at first instance there is no doubt that the tackle was an aggressive and dangerous one, it could, arguably, be dismissed as not being entirely unique or unusual in the context of both the game (a heated local derby) and the player in question (in his top-flight career Keane accrued over a dozen red cards). Nevertheless, the fallout from the incident revealed that Keane's tackle was not as rash as might have at first appeared and subsequently it necessitated a further investigation by the football authorities and some concern that 'it was time for the law to become involved' (James 2002: 73).

There was, in the vernacular of the game, a 'history' between the players, stemming from an incident in 1997 when Haaland accused Keane, wrongly as it happened, of feigning injury and thus there was a revenge element to Keane's subsequent tackle (both tackles can be viewed at www.youtube.com/watch?v=p_st29mlQwU). Moreover, Keane's autobiography, published in 2002, left readers in no doubt as to what had motivated the Irishman:

> I'd waited almost 180 minutes for Alfie, three years if you looked at it another way. Now he had the ball on the far touchline. Alfie was taking the piss. I'd waited long enough. I fucking hit him hard. The ball was there (I think). Take that you cunt. And don't ever stand over me again sneering about fake injuries ... I didn't wait for [the referee] to show the [red] card. I turned and walked to the dressing room.
>
> (Keane and Dunphy 2002: 230)

By admitting that he had set out to hurt Haaland deliberately and that he had intended to harm him, irrespective of where the ball was, Keane was, in effect, confessing to an assault on an opponent. In short, the above paragraph from Keane's autobiography pushed the incident away from the sports field and into the realm of criminality. As it happened, the Greater Manchester Police did not pursue the matter and in October 2002, Keane was charged by the Football Association's Disciplinary Committee with 'bringing the game into disrepute' and was fined £150,000 and banned for a further five matches. Again, the Keane incident raises a number of questions as to when the criminal law should, if ever, venture 'beyond the touchline' to police violent play and particularly where one of the key challenges to mounting a successful prosecution – proving that the culprit intended or meant to commit the crime – was, in this case, not at issue given the culprit's written confession. Similarly, it could be argued that the Keane incident was more properly dealt with by the football authorities – by way of lengthy suspension and a meaningful fine – and that instead of pursuing sports stars, police time is better served pursing 'real' crime.

53

Keane's tackle injured Haaland's right knee. Haaland never played a full game again and was forced to retire prematurely from football in 2003. Although there were rumours that he was considering suing Keane and Manchester United for compensation, the reality was that Haaland's career ended because of a pre-existing injury in his left knee, which would not respond to surgery. Nevertheless, the type and seriousness of injury that a player suffers are factors in assessing whether criminal charges might be brought against the injuring player and especially so if the tackle is beyond not just the rules of the game, but also the game's playing culture or ethos, that is, beyond what could reasonably be expected to occur, and out of all proportion to what normally does occur, during the course of a game. In terms of the technical language of the criminal law, these principles on the playing culture of sport have been translated to mean that where a player shows 'reckless disregard' for the safety of an opponent, criminal charges can be considered. What follows is as attempt to break down and assess the various constituent parts of the criminal law's approach to violence in sport into something that can be understood by those who play and administer sport.

Before those legal technicalities are addressed, three final introductory points are noteworthy. The first is to keep in mind, as this chapter progresses, whether a late, poorly executed tackle resulting in a horrendous, career-threatening injury could ever give rise to criminal charges. These types of incident reveal the kernel of this issue, which is how to distinguish between injury resulting from 'hard' play and injury resulting frrom a criminal assault. In recent times, the most arresting images in this regard are probably those injuries sustained by the Arsenal players, Eduardo (against Birmingham in a Premier League game in February 2008 whereby he suffered a fractured left tibula and dislocated ankle as a result of a tackle by Martin Taylor) and Aaron Ramsey (against Stoke City in a Premier League game in February 2010 whereby he suffered a double-leg break as a result of a tackle by Ryan Shawcross). In this, it is of interest that in the aftermath of the Eduardo tackle, Sepp Blatter, the President of FIFA, football's world governing authority, called for lifetime bans and criminal prosecutions of footballers guilty of dangerous tackling (Anderson 2008a: 751).

The second point to note is that this chapter reviews the applicability of the criminal law of assault to incidents of violent play on the sports field and asks when is it appropriate, if ever, for criminal liability to attach to the perpetrator of an injury inflicted upon an opponent in the course of a game? The chapter does not dwell so much on the wider issue as to why sports participants such as footballers commit egregious acts of aggression on the sports field. Nevertheless, in attempting to show how the criminal law distinguishes between 'sanctioned aggression' and 'unsanctioned aggression' in contact sports, the social, cultural, moral and psychological rationales for violently ill-disciplined play are not underestimated and are taken to include: the attribution of such misbehaviour to poor refereeing and coaching standards in the sport at issue; or a 'win at all costs' mentality; or 'heat of the moment' reactions; or the tactical use of intimidation in sport; or the view that gratuitous violence in some sport is sometimes reflective of a general societal rise in interpersonal violence (Smith 1983; Bredemier 1985; Kerr 2005; Guilbert 2006; Russell 2008).

The third and final introductory point is that what follows concentrates on non-fatal assaults on the sports field. Nevertheless, it is worth keeping in mind that if death results from a sports-related assault, the culprit could be charged with manslaughter or possibly murder, depending on the defendant's intent. Homicide charges arising out of sports-related violent play are extremely rare but they are not unknown (Anderson 2010: 180). In July 2009, at the Old Bailey criminal court in London, a Sunday-league footballer who killed an opponent with a single punch was sentenced to 28 months' imprisonment (*Forwood* 2010). Although violence-related fatalities on the playing field are highly unusual, the buildup that led to the tragic blow here is, arguably, not all that infrequent in games that are sometimes dismissed euphemistically as 'ill-tempered' or 'tempestuous' in nature. In this light (and also because it gives a portrayal of many of the characteristics and features of incidents recounted in the case law mentioned subsequently in this chapter), the factual background to *Forwood* is worth recounting briefly.

The culprit, 21-year-old Darren Forwood, was playing for Kingshill Town in a match against their close rivals Old Greenfordians in a Division One game of the Hayes and District Sunday Football League in West London. Kingshill Town started well and raced into a 3–0 lead but they eventually lost 4–3. The game had been a physical encounter – Forwood had been booked for a bad tackle – and an Old Greenfordians player, Stephen Ritchie, who was in his forties, had been sent off. When the final whistle blew a number of players rushed up against Ritchie amid (unsubstantiated) claims that he had gestured provocatively towards the losers. A protective cordon of teammates surrounded Ritchie but Forwood circumvented it and attacked Ritchie from behind with a swinging blow of his fist on to the head area. The blow was of such force that it threw Ritchie off his feet and ruptured the arteries in his neck, leading to his death. Noting both that Ritchie was utterly defenceless at the time of attack and the need to deal severely with such 'mindless violence', the judge passed the jail sentence on Forwood. Thankfully, incidents such as the jailing of Forwood are extraordinary in sport but the next question to assess is whether the same can be said of non-fatal assaults.

SPORTS-RELATED OFFENCES IN CRIMINAL LAW

The robust spontaneity and physicality of contact sports (and their accompanying conventions, ethos or spirit) are not easily translated from the playing field to the courtroom. Indeed, when the basic offences in the law of criminal assault in the UK are outlined (Ormerod 2009: 735–789 on non-fatal offences against the person), and the guidance given by the Crown Prosecution Service (CPS) as to the appropriate charge a culprit should face for the assault of another is reviewed (the CPS charging standard for offences against the person is available online at www.cps.gov.uk/legal/l_to_o/offences_against_the_person), it is difficult at first to understand why contact sports have not already been prohibited in law. For instance, the most basic assault offence is that of 'common' assault and battery, which is taken to mean any act by which the culprit intentionally inflicts unlawful personal violence upon the victim (battery) or causes the victim to fear the infliction of such violence (assault). The 'violence' in question can equate to no more than a slap or a push and the CPS charging standard advises that a common assault charge is appropriate where the sustained injuries amount to any of the following: grazes, scratches, abrasions, minor bruising or swelling, reddening of the skin, superficial cuts or a 'black eye'. A person found guilty of a common assault is typically fined, with the maximum penalty set at £5,000.

Those who play contact sports such as rugby will realise that the above list summarizes many of the injuries they see when the look around the dressing room after virtually any competitive game! So why do criminal charges and fines not follow? Furthermore, where the sustained injuries are of a more serious nature, one of three aggravated assaults outlined in the Offences Against the Person Act 1861 (OAPA 1861) come into play. The first of these, in ascending order of gravity, can be found in section 47 of the OAPA 1861. A section 47 offence is committed where the culprit assaults another so as to cause actual bodily harm. The CPS charging standard advises that examples of bodily harm include: loss or breaking of teeth; temporary loss of consciousness; extensive or multiple bruising; displaced broken nose; minor fractures; and minor cuts requiring stitching or other medical treatment. A person found guilty of a section 47 offence is usually fined but can also face imprisonment to a maximum of six months. Again, section 47-type injuries would not be unknown to the contact sports competitor.

Finally, the OAPA 1861 has two grievous bodily harm (GBH) offences. Under section 20, a person commits an offence when he or she unlawfully and maliciously wounds another or inflicts GBH upon that person. GBH means serious bodily harm and examples of such harm include: injury resulting in permanent disability; long-term concussion; minor permanent visible disfigurement such as broken limbs, bones or a fractured skull; compound fractures of the cheek, jaw, ribs or bones; injuries causing substantial loss of blood, usually necessitating transfusion; injuries resulting in lengthy treatment or incapacity. A jail sentence, of up to a maximum of 5 years, can attach to a section 20 conviction. Section 18 of the OAPA 1861 is also a GBH-type offence – wounding or causing GBH with intent – but it can carry a maximum penalty of life imprisonment. The distinction between sections 20 and 18 is based on intent – was there a purposeful, premeditated motivation to the attack? In the context of sport, it is interesting to note that, under section 18, a specific intent can include a repeated or planned attack; the making of prior threats; or kicking a prostrate and defenceless victim in the head.

Given the above, how then do contact sports manage largely to remain outside the grasp of the criminal law? At its narrowest, the answer is twofold. First, there are a number of sociocultural factors at issue, which can be identified in, and are common to, jurisdictions around the world such as Australia (Healy 2005: 132–140); Canada (Tracey 2006); Ireland (McCutcheon 1994); New Zealand (Farugia 1997); the UK (Livings 2006); and the USA (Standen 2009). The principal one is that police and prosecution services are often overwhelmed by 'street' crime, or what might generally be perceived as real or serious crime, and thus pursuing a sports star for an alleged assault is not seen as a priority or an initiative that is likely to prove popular with the general public. Moreover, ultimately in most criminal cases a jury will decide upon the culprit's guilt and again convincing a jury 'beyond a reasonable doubt' that the culprit intended to harm the opponent (as opposed to an accidental or instinctive 'agony of the moment' reaction) is extremely difficult. Police and prosecution services in many countries have also learned that such prosecutions have proved extremely unpopular within sports communities which often, and quite rightly in some cases, point to the fact that their own internal disciplinary mechanisms have adequately punished the culprit in question through either a lengthy playing ban or a fine or both. Similarly, victims may feel uncomfortable with the police's involvement in the sense that if their club or sport has provided them with adequate insurance cover or the culprit has made them an informal offer of compensation to cover associated medical or dental costs, victims may well be satisfied with this and not wish to draw any further adverse publicity to the matter to the detriment of their sport.

There are positive and negatives aspects to the above analysis. On the positive side, there is little doubt that a speedy, consistent and fair internal disciplinary scheme in a sport is the most effective deterrent against unnecessarily violent play, as opposed to the more distant and unpredictable applicability of the criminal law. Such matters are clearly better dealt with 'in-house' because that is where the expertise lies and it is where long-term preventive measures, such as rule changes, can be implemented in a coherent way in order to ensure that such ill discipline will not occur again in the future. The negatives relate to what can be called the 'misguided machoism' portrayed by the attitude of 'what happens on the field stays on the field', which often is no more than an excuse for an escalating, retaliatory cycle of violence (Anderson 2010: 177–178). Finally, these broad sociocultural aspects notwithstanding, the principal reason that the criminal law's reach rarely strays 'beyond the touchline' is because if it can be shown that the victim consented to the risk of bodily harm, then that 'consent' can be used as a full defence to a charge of assault.

RECKLESS DISREGARD AND CONSENT

At present, it appears that the law in the UK and other similar jurisdictions such as Australia, Canada, Ireland, New Zealand and the USA is that if the injuring sports player's violent act is seen to have been within the bounds of what one might reasonably foresee as a physical hazard of the game then that culprit, notwithstanding the severity of injury inflicted on the victim, will not face criminal charges. This is because, on participating in a contact sport, a participant is taken to have assumed the risk, or consented to a level, of injury commensurate to the ordinary physical perils inherent in the normal playing of that game. Put simply, the courts recognise that when players take to the rugby or football pitch, a likelihood of injury (and sometimes even the risk of serious harm, such as spinal injuries in rugby) arises but that players agree impliedly to take that risk on board in playing the sport in question. Consequently, it is evident that not every foul or unwanted physical contact in a sport is a crime. In this, there is a strong, underlying policy concern, averred to by the criminal courts in the UK for well over a century, that involvement in sport is a healthy and socially beneficial pastime and thus on the grounds of its 'social utility', participation in sport, even in physically invasive sport, should be protected from the normal reach of the criminal law of assault. Bluntly, if there was a risk that every time one took to the pitch one could be arrested by the police or sued by an opponent for injuries arising during the course of that game, then evidently contact sports would soon be rendered uninsurable and unviable.

That perspective does not however permit contact sports participants to act with impunity and again the case law from the UK and other countries illustrates that where the inflicted injury is in deliberate or reckless disregard of the safety of another, and is outside the level of physicality that is incidental to the norms of a properly conducted game, the criminal law's threshold of consent-based toleration will be exhausted. Two case examples arising from English club rugby called *Moss* (2000) and *Garfield* (2008) illustrate that the criminal law's and the courts' patience with, and toleration of, violence in sport is not exhaustive. Both cases ended up in the Court of Appeal, which is second only to the UK Supreme Court in terms of primacy in the UK's courts system.

In *Moss*, the culprit was said to have punched an opponent in the face, fracturing his eye socket. He was found guilty of a section 20 OAPA offence and sentenced to 8 months' imprisonment. Mr Moss appealed the case. He did not disagree with the guilty verdict but argued that the sentence was overly harsh and he asked the Court of Appeal to take into account that he had no previous convictions and that he had offered to pay compensation to the victim. He also presented independent expert evidence suggesting that he was truly remorseful for what he had done and that the risk of reoffending was extremely low. Finally, Moss showed the court a number of 'glowing' character references from those within the local sports community, many of whom pointed out that Moss, a married man with dependent children, also maintained a small family business, and that both his family and business would suffer greatly in his absence. The appeal was rejected. The Court of Appeal noted that all of these mitigating factors had already been taken into account at the initial trial. Furthermore, the Court of Appeal held, at paragraph 11 of the judgment, that the reason the sentence was neither inappropriate nor excessive was because rugby:

> was not a licence for thuggery and was a game covered by strict rules; the offence involved an assault off the ball and after play had moved on; serious injury had been inflicted; the offence was so serious that only a [jail] sentence could be justified.

In *Garfield*, the culprit was accused of stamping on an opponent's head in a ruck during the course of a rugby game, resulting in a deep 10-cm-long, stud-like laceration to the victim's head. The culprit argued that the stamp was accidental and unavoidable and that in a 'hard rucking' situation it was not always possible to judge or control where one's studs might land. That excuse was not accepted and Garfield was found guilty of a section 20 OAPA offence and sentenced to 15 months' imprisonment. Again, the culprit did not disagree with the guilty verdict but argued that the sentence was overly harsh and, in particular, he asked the Court of Appeal to take into account that, given his genuine remorse and previous good standing in the community, a sentence involving supervised community work would have been the more appropriate sanction. In fact, and as Garfield reminded the court, his character references 'went well beyond the merely positive' and included the fact that in saving a colleague from injury, he himself sustained a serious injury that prevented him from ever playing rugby again. The appeal was, however, rejected, with the Court of Appeal observing that, the strong mitigating plea notwithstanding, the culprit had recklessly and without due care stamped with his steel studs on the head of a defenceless man in a manner that was wholly unacceptable and inexcusable.

There are at least two interesting points to be taken from *Moss* and *Garfield*. The first is that the second most senior court in England takes a very hard line on violence in contact sport and the fact that a culprit is genuinely sorry for his 'out of character' actions should not necessarily deter the courts from imposing a jail sentence for sports-related 'thuggery'. The second is slightly more problematical: *Moss* and *Garfield* were fairly clearcut cases – there was little doubt that the culprits were criminally careless about the safety of their opponent and, in both instances, their appeals were confined to pleas against the length of sentence and not the sentence itself. Cases are not always so straightforward – think, for instance, about 'fifty–fifty' challenges in football – and the question must be asked how the criminal courts, in the context of fast-moving, multiple-collision sports such as rugby and football, draw the line between intentional violence and the type of conduct that is not intentional but may still be quite reckless in its disregard for the safety of an opponent. The answer seems to lie in the approach taken by the English Court of Appeal in a case called *Barnes* (2005).

Barnes resulted from an incident that occurred during the course of an amateur football match when the culprit tackled an opponent with such force that the victim sustained a serious leg injury. The allegation was that the tackle was a recklessly late and high or 'over-the-top' type of tackle, and of a kind that one could neither reasonably expect nor reasonably accept to happen during the course of a Sunday-league game. Barnes was found guilty of a section 20 OAPA offence and received a 240-hour community punishment order and had to pay compensation in the sum of £2,609 to the victim. He appealed on a technicality relating to the fact that the trial judge had misdirected the jury, which means that Barnes claimed that the trial judge had not explained the disputed point of law properly to the jury, rendering the conviction and guilty verdict 'unsafe' (Pendlebury 2006). The appeal was successful and the Court of Appeal went on to summarize what the law should be with regard to the reckless causing of injury by a sports participant to another during the course of a contact sport.

The Court of Appeal in *Barnes* held that reckless disregard for the safety of an opponent would have to be judged according to a number of objective criteria. These criteria would, according to the Court, better enable a jury to decide whether a tackle was, in the context of the game and its rules and its conditions, simply an instinctive reaction, error or misjudgement in the heat of the game; or whether it was, in contrast, so violent and so outside the norms of the sport in question that it should be considered criminal in nature. The objective criteria, which a jury can consider in a sports violence trial, are as follows:

- the type of sport in question;
- the safety rules, level and conditions under which the game in question was played;
- the 'playing culture' or 'spirit' of the game, recognising that in highly competitive contact sport conduct outside the rules should be expected to occur 'in the heat of the moment' but might not reach the required level of criminality;
- the nature of the injuring act and its surrounding circumstances, recognizing that injury inflicted 'off the ball' is more likely to breach the boundaries of implied sporting consent;
- the extent of force employed;
- the degree of risk of injury, including the probability of serious harm;
- the state of mind of the defendant.

THE CRIMINAL LAW AS A LAST RESORT

The *Barnes* criteria can be seen to good effect in the jailing of another Sunday-league footballer at Warwick Crown Court in March 2010 (*Chapman* 2010). The case attracted an amount of publicity given that, unlike previous cases, which mainly involved punches and/or off-the-ball acts, this case's sole concern was with the nature of the tackle made by the culprit on the opposing player. Accordingly, Chapman was deemed, somewhat inaccurately, to have made legal history by becoming the first footballer to be jailed for an on-field tackle. The culprit was playing for Long Lawford in a game against the Wheeltappers club in the Rugby and District Sunday Football League in Warwickshire. As the game was coming to an end, and with Wheeltappers winning 3–1, their left back was 'shepherding' a ball over the line. Clearly frustrated at what he perceived to be time-wasting, and having been criticized earlier by his teammates for showing a lack of effort, the culprit raised his foot in a stamping motion and with his studs snapped the tibia and fibula bones of the victim's right leg. The noise was such that the other players thought at first that what had cracked were the victim's shin pads, not bones. The tackle was of such severity that at hospital a long incision had to be made in the victim's leg to relieve the swelling and later the victim underwent extensive reconstructive surgery, including skin grafts, and the insertion of a metal rod and four permanent bolts in the shattered leg.

In his defence against a charge of aggravated GBH assault, Chapman's defence lawyer pointed to the Ryan Shawcross tackle on Arsenal's Aaron Ramsey, which had occurred the week prior to the trial. In this, the defence lawyer argued that what had occurred took place in the spur of the moment and that the regrettable injuries, for which the culprit showed very early remorse, had more to do with the angle of the tackle rather than the force applied. The trial judge rejected this comparison out of hand and, pointing to the fact that the referee had considered the tackle a callous, premeditated act with intent to cause injury, the trial judge jailed Chapman for 6 months. Moreover, in concluding his judgement, the trial judge alerted the sporting public to the fact that a football match is never an excuse for 'wanton violence'.

As a result of the tackle, the victim claimed that he now suffered a permanent limp which meant that not only would he never play football again but it also hindered his capacity to work and support his family. The trial judge noted that in such circumstances, and as the 'blameless' victim of a crime, the injured player could apply for compensation under the government-run criminal injuries compensation scheme (www.cica.gov.uk). There is also the strong possibility that in this case the victim will go on to sue the culprit directly and separately for compensation relating to the injuries, associated medical costs and loss of earnings. Personal injury actions taken by one player against another have occurred from time to time over the past number of decades and particularly in the instance, as here, where an amateur player, who is either poorly insured or not insured at all against recreational sporting injuries, is forced to miss work for a considerable period of time. In contrast, full-time professional players tend to be insured by their clubs and have their own private insurance, which will more than adequately cover any associated losses (Anderson 2008b). The only exception in the professional game is where the tackle in question is so bad that it brings the injured player's career to a premature end. In 2008, for example, a former Manchester United trainee, Ben Collett, was awarded £4.5 million in damages by the English High Court (mainly for loss of future earnings as a player with a bright future in the Premier League) as a result of a 'career-ending' tackle received in a reserve game against Middlesbrough when aged 18 (Anderson 2010: 242).

Reflecting on the Chapman case, it must be reiterated that in the vast majority of cases excessively violent play on the sports field will be dealt with adequately by on-field penalties or playing suspensions. The reach of the criminal law is likely to remain confined to the most exceptional of circumstances involving egregious, gratuitous violence. That is not to say the sports bodies should dismiss the threat of criminal sanction lightly. In fact the opposite should be the case, and the shadow of the criminal law should be used as a pretext for sports governing bodies to ensure that their internal disciplinary proceedings are consistently strict in the face of the insidious and corrosive practice that is unacceptably violent play in sport. In sum, if sport does not deal with thuggery on the playing fields; then the courts will.

SUMMARY

For anyone who has taken part in competitive contact sport such as rugby or football, the risks of injury, hurt and pain are all 'part of the game'. Players train, not just to enhance their skills with the ball, but also to develop the strength and conditioning to withstand the 'hits' and tackles that are an integral and attractive aspect of such games, for both players and spectators alike. The criminal law, and the courts that implement it, recognise that a balance must be struck between the risk of injury and the social and health benefits of sporting activity. That balance is very much tilted towards the latter and, moreover, in participating in a regulated contact sport, participants are taken to assume a level of risk of injury broadly in line with what can reasonably and typically be expected to happen during the course of the sport in question. Accordingly, and even though they may both result in serious injury to the victim, what may be seen as an inexcusably dangerous and criminal act on the street may, on the sports pitch, be explained as nothing more than the instinctive, reflexive, if unfortunate, actions of a player acting in the heat of the moment.

Nevertheless, no particular part of society, even one as popular and socially beneficial as sport, is permitted to exist outside the law. In short, although it presents a unique factual context of analysis for the ordinary law of assault, contact sport is not a criminal law-free zone. Admittedly, only a handful of players have ever had their misconduct on the playing field considered by a criminal court and yet cases such as *Forwood* and *Chapman* should demonstrate to all players that from now on when they cross the white line they should give due respect not just to the rules of the game but also to the laws of the land.

REVIEW QUESTIONS

A case study on professional boxing

Taking into consideration the criminal law's view of violence in sports such as rugby and association football, have a class debate on the legal status of professional boxing. In your discussion, consider both sides of the debate, laid out as follows, and also consider any application the debate may have for the future legal status of mixed martial arts such as ultimate or cage fighting.

Note also: Anderson, J. (2007). *The Legality of Boxing: A punch drunk love?* London: Birkbeck Law Press.

First, consider the argument made for the prohibition of boxing by organizations such as the British Medical Association which argues that:

- Unlike other sports, the basic intent of boxing is to produce bodily harm in the opponent.
- Boxing can result in death and produces an alarming incidence of chronic brain injury.
- Although a number of other sporting activities involve physical risks, boxing is deemed a special case justifying the strictest attention because the nature of the sport implies that extra points are given for brain damage.
- The physical exploitation of boxers in the ring is aggravated by the fact that many of them are financially exploited out of the ring.
- Professional boxing is little more than 'human cockfighting' and as such is 'morally repugnant'.

Second, consider the arguments made in support of boxing, including:

- Boxers know the risks when they enter the ring but train specifically for them and in any event choose of their own free will to box.
- The number of injuries and death are far lower than in many other sports such as mountaineering or motor sports, for example, and yet no one is calling for those pursuits to be banned.
- Prohibiting boxing in law will simply force it underground and make the situation, in terms of the safety of participants, even worse.
- Instead of trying to abolish the sport, every effort should be made to ensure that the sport is properly regulated to the highest health and safety standards.
- Those who seek to ban boxing are middle-class 'do-gooders' who forget that professional boxing has for many decades presented opportunities to otherwise socially disadvantaged athletes and in many deprived communities the 'social good' that boxing clubs do clearly outweighs the associated risk of participating in the sport.

FURTHER READING

The following texts are considered leaders in the field of sports law. Each text has at least one chapter dedicated to the topic of criminal violence in sport.

Beloff, M., Kerr, T. and Demetriou, M. (1999). *Sports Law*. Oxford: Hart, chapter 5.
Cox, N. and Schuster, A. (2004). *Sport and the Law*. Dublin: FirstLaw, chapter 4.
Gardiner, S., O'Leary, J., Welch, R., Boyes, S. and Naidoo, U. (2006) *Sports Law*, 3rd edn. London: Cavendish, chapter 15.
Grayson, E. (2000). *Sport and the Law*, 3rd edn. London: Butterworths, chapter 6.
Greenfield, S. and Osborn, G., eds (2000) *Law and Sport in Contemporary Society*. London: Frank Cass, chapter 6.

Hartley, H. (2009). *Sport, Physical Recreation and the Law*. London: Routledge, chapter 4.

James, M. (2010). *Sports Law*. Basingstoke: Palgrave, chapter 6.

Lewis, A. and Taylor, J. (2008). *Sport: Law and Practice*, 2nd edn. London: Tottel Publishing, chapter D6.

Thorpe, D., Buti, A., Davies, C., Fridman, S. and Johnson, P. (2009). *Sports Law*. Melbourne: Oxford University Press, chapter 4.

Weiler, P. and Roberts, G. (2004). *Sports and the Law: Text, cases and problems*, 3rd edn. Westport, CT: Thomson West, chapter 13.

WEBSITES

British Association for Sport and Law:

   www.britishsportslaw.org

World Sports Law Report:

   www.deloitte.com/view/en_GB/uk/industries/sportsbusinessgroup

REFERENCES

Anderson, J. (2008a). "No Licence for Thuggery: Violence, Sport and the Criminal Law." *Criminal Law Review* 751–783.

Anderson, J. (2008b). "Personal Injury Liability in Sport: Emerging Trends." *Tort Law Review* 16(2): 95–119.

Anderson, J. (2010). *Modern Sports Law*. Oxford: Hart.

Barnes, Regina v. (2005). *Criminal Appeal Reports (Sentencing)* 1: 507.

Bredemier, B. (1985). "Moral Reasoning and the Perceived Legitimacy of Intentionally Injurious Sports Act." *Journal of Sport Psychology* 7(2): 110–124.

Chapman, Regina v. (2010). Warwick Crown Court 4 March: online report by the *Daily Telegraph*. http://www.telegraph.co.uk/news/uknews/crime/7369009/Footballer-first-to-be-jailed-for-on-field-tackle.html.

Farugia. P. (1997) "The Consent Defence: Sports Violence, Sadomasochism and the Criminal Law." *Auckland University Law Review* 8(2): 472–502.

Forwood, Regina v. (2010) Unreported Central Criminal Court (Old Bailey, London) 6 July: online report by the *Guardian* at http://www.guardian.co.uk/uk/2009/jul/06/sunday-league-player-jailed-killing (accessed 20 August 2010).

Garfield, Regina v. (2008). *Criminal Appeal Reports (Sentencing)* 2: 364.

Gilbert, S. (2006). "Violence in Sports and Among Sportsmen: A Single or Two-Track Issue?" *Aggressive Behaviour* 32(3): 231–240.

Healy, D. (2005). *Sport and the Law*, 3rd edn. Sydney: UNSW Press.

James, M. (2002). "The Trouble with Roy Keane." *Entertainment Law* 1(3): 72–92.

Keane, R. and Dunphy, E. (2002). *Keane: The Autobiography*. London: Michael Joseph.

Kerr, J. (2005). *Rethinking Aggression and Violence in Sport*. London: Routledge.

Livings, B. (2006). "Legitimate Sport or Criminal Assault? What are the Roles of the Rules and the Rule-makers in Determining Criminal Liability for Violence on the Sports Field?" *Journal of Criminal Law* 70(6): 495–508.

McCutcheon, P. (1994). "Sports Violence, Consent and the Criminal Law." *Northern Ireland Legal Quarterly* 45(3): 267–284.

Moss, Regina v. [2000] *Criminal Appeal Reports (Sentencing)* 1: 307.

Ormerod, D. (2009). *Smith and Hogan's Criminal Law: Cases and materials.* Oxford: Oxford University Press.

Pendlebury, A. (2006) "Perceptions of Playing Culture in Sport: The Problem of Diverse Opinion in the Light of *Barnes." Entertainment and Sports Law Journal* 4(2).

Russell, G. (2008). *Aggression in the Sports World: A social psychological perspective.* New York: Oxford University Press.

Smith, M. (1983). *Violence in Sport.* Toronto: Butterworths.

Standen, J. (2009). "The Manly Sports: The Problematic Use of Criminal Law to Regulate Sports Violence." *Journal of Criminal Law and Criminology* 99(3): 619–642.

Tracey, O. (2006). "From Hockey Gloves to Handcuffs: The Need for Criminal Sanctions in Professional Ice Hockey." *Hastings Communication and Entertainment Law Journal* 28(2): 309–331.

Chapter 5

Reviewing the role of UK central government in sports development

Spencer Harris

TOPICS

Central government intervention in sport • The policy process with a particular emphasis on policy implementation • The challenges associated with implementing the community sport element of the 2012 Summer Olympic Games Legacy Plan for the UK government

OBJECTIVES

By the end of this chapter you will be able to:

- Understand the changing nature of central government's involvement in sport;
- Be familiar with the range of central government policies, strategies and programmes for sport in the postwar era;
- Analyse the progress and challenges associated with the community sport policy process;
- Critically examine the aspiration (of the UK government) to increase sports participation by one million people within its jurisdiction.

KEY TERMS

Central government – the nationally elected government (of the UK in this chapter).
Community sport policy – primarily concerned with adult (16+) participation in sport, with the overall aim of increasing the number of adults participating in sport on three occasions per week for a minimum of 30 minutes per occasion.
National sport policy or policy objectives – the stated policy intentions of government and related agencies with regard to school, community and elite sport.

Olympic and Paralympic legacy – This refers specifically to the plan to deliver longer-term results or impacts associated with hosting the 2012 Olympic and Paralympic Games by the UK authorities.

Policy implementation or implementation – carrying out particular activities for the purpose of achieving policy objectives.

OVERVIEW

This chapter provides a summary of the relationship between central government and sport with a specific focus on the evolution of sports development policy in England and the UK more broadly. It will assess the changing relationship between central government and sports development, emphasizing the core role of central government in the evolution of sports development policies, and provide a case study of the community sport policy area from 2008 to 2012, exploring progress against the stated intentions of government and identifying key issues and challenges relating to community sport policy. The broader subject of government involvement in sports development and a deeper analysis of the relationship between politics, policy and sport is beyond the scope of this chapter but has been usefully provided elsewhere (Houlihan 1991, 1997; Henry 1993; Houlihan and White 2002; Coalter 2007; Bloyce and Smith 2010). The chapter focuses on central government sports policy in England; specifically, the stated policy intentions and the range of organizations responsible for these objectives, rather than Goldsmith's broader understanding of policy as 'all actions of governments' (Goldsmith 1980: 22, cited in Henry 1993).

Understanding the role of the state in sport and, more specifically, the involvement of central government in the evolution of sports development is an important issue not least because it: (1) allows an understanding of the changes in the government's involvement in sport and the broader political, social and economic conditions that shape this involvement; (2) provides greater awareness of how the decisions taken by central government direct resources at the national, regional and local level and directly impact the creation of strategies, programmes and jobs; (3) enables analysis of both the intended and unintended consequences of government involvement in sport, and assesses whether government involvement in sports delivers what it promises; and (4) helps students and practitioners to understand better the realities of the policy process for sport as a highly political, often intensely personal process where microdynamics often surpass logic and rational thought (Talbot 2011).

CASE STUDY: SPORTS DEVELOPMENT POLICY IN THE UK – INCREASING PARTICIPATION BY ONE MILLION BY 2012

Increasing adult participation in sport throughout the UK, otherwise known as community sport, forms a central part of the 2012 Olympic and Paralympic Legacy Plan. But there are some important questions about the community sport policy area that require proper consideration by academics and practitioners alike. For example, what role does central government perform in advocating that adults play sport on a regular basis[1]? And even if they continue with this approach, how do government departments such as the Department of Culture, Media and Sport and national-level organizations such as Sport England and national governing bodies (NGBs) of sport extend their reach to the community level to implement activities that will help to get one million more adults playing sport?

The process of delivering the community sport aspiration is led by Sport England, working closely with 46 NGBs. In total, £480 million of funding has been invested in NGBs for the purpose of increasing adult participation in sport. The amount allocated to each NGB varies according to the target for growth in participation in a particular sport, as well as targets for sustaining participation and developing the talent pool generally. Each of these targets is included within a 3-year sport-specific whole-sport plan.

The aggregated total for NGB growth in participation is 500,000. The means that 50% of the increase in adult participation is expected to be delivered by NGBs. The remaining 500,000 participants have been allocated to alternative methods of delivery, specifically higher education (300,000), third-sector organizations (100,000), and commercial partner activities (150,000), providing a relatively small planning contingency of 50,000 (Sport England 2008a).

Whilst policies of this type may help to enhance the perceived importance of sport, the problems associated with following through and delivering what was promised require careful consideration. As Pressman and Wildavsky (1973) portrayed in their seminal work, *Implementation,* that which is planned in a nation's capital, by the nation's leaders, is not necessarily what ends up being offered in the local communities up and down the country. The network of organizations involved, the relationships between these organizations, their respective priorities, resources, capacity and decisions, and ultimately their ability either to deliver directly or delegate delivery of policy at the local level, requires careful consideration. All of this assumes that we know the 'magic formula', that is, what works in getting more adults to play more sport. Clearly, as the information in this chapter demonstrates, this is not the case. It is likely, therefore, that community sport faces an uncertain future. The final participation statistics from Active People in 2012 will tell us how far short we are from the aspiration of one million additional participants in sport in the UK, but the longer implications for community sport as both a policy concern and a political priority remain considerably less clear.

THE SHIFTING SANDS OF CENTRAL GOVERNMENT SPORTS POLICY

The development of sport policy in the UK, particularly over the past decade, provides a vivid example of the vulnerability of sport to the 'whim and caprice of governments and individual ministers' (Houlihan and White 2002: 206). The last 10 years have seen significant government interest and involvement in sport. New policy objectives for school, community and elite sport were set and, following this, sport became exposed to a new public-sector performance management culture, whereby far-reaching targets for improvements in sports participation and performance were established.

The UK government has historically had a patchy but nonetheless long tradition of intervening in sporting matters. This can be traced right back to the Tudor period (1485–1603), when numerous 'statutes defined the opportunities for recreation and their proper use'

(Brailsford 1991: 33). Governments have also played an important role in controlling access to sports and pastimes, in particular the playing of sports on the sabbath (Brailsford 1991), and through specific legislation which 'reflected the exercise of power to preserve class privilege' (Houlihan 1997: 61). In Victorian Britain, government involvement in sport and recreation was stimulated by the rational recreation movement, which placed great value on the role of sport and recreation in the 'creation of a healthy, moral and orderly workforce' (Houlihan 1991: 136). In the twentieth century and up to the late 1950s, the government had a marginal interest in sport that was limited to improving military preparation and addressing poor standards of health in urban areas (Houlihan 1997). The 1960s is generally considered the point when the UK government started to accept that sport was a 'legitimate governmental responsibility' (Houlihan 1991: 27), when sport shifted from being an area of marginal political interest to one where government accepted a more central role in sports policy (Hargreaves 1985). Much of this attention was in response to the Central Council of Physical Recreation (CCPR)-commissioned Wolfenden committee report on sport. This report contained 57 recommendations, largely focusing on the promotion and development of sport for its own sake, and with a particular focus on developing the facility base, increasing participation in sport and reducing the number of young people who drop out of sport once compulsory education is complete (Houlihan and White 2002).

During the latter part of the 1960s, the advisory Council adopted a Sport for All policy that reflected the broad welfare-state discourse of the government at the time (Houlihan and White 2002). Perhaps the most significant impact of the Sport for All policy on sports participation was the rapid development of public-sector leisure facilities during the 1970s, including pools, sports halls and multi-use leisure complexes (Houlihan and White 2002). This was primarily led by the need to cater for the demands of the 'new leisure age' (Sillitoe 1969; Blackie *et al.* 1979; Veal 1982, cited in Coalter 2007) and made possible by the combination of Sports Council grants and local government reorganization which led to larger local authorities with greater spending power.

The 1980s were dominated by promoting participation amongst specific population or target groups, specifically groups that were perceived to 'constitute social problems' (Houlihan and White 2002: 34). The Action Sports programme was a 'conventional policy esponse' to the urban riots of 1981 (Houlihan and White 2002: 35). This was a targeted, interventionist community development scheme that sought to improve accessibility by reaching out into local communities, employing leaders with appropriate skills and street credibility, and delivering a broad range of mainstream and alternative sports activities, thereby offering a different approach to the range of public-sector leisure facilities that had been developed. In this respect, Active Sports has widely been reported as the forerunner or catalyst to what is now commonly referred to as sports development (Coalter 2007).

Whilst the rhetoric of sport as a welfare instrument and tool to engage the disenchanted may be ideologically potent, it actually 'remained politically weak and relatively marginal to core public policy developments' (Coalter 2007: 11). Evidence of the marginal position of sport as welfare includes the funding strategy of the Sports Council at the time, which shows the largest single sum being allocated to elite sport (Coalter *et al.* 1988). The actual degree of UK government interest was variable in the 1980s, depending on the Minister of Sport and his/her particular enthusiasm for sport. Margaret Thatcher, the British Prime Minister at the time, generally had little time for sport (Bloyce and Smith 2010), and the government's involvement in what it considered a marginal policy matter did not fit well with the neoliberal politics of thatcherism. In addition, interagency tensions, particularly between the Sports Council and the CCPR, added to the instability, with a growing perception that sport was poorly organized, divided and 'bedevilled by the lack of a coherent voice' (Green and Houlihan 2005: 54).

Towards the end of the 1980s, under a second-term Conservative government, Coalter *et al.* (1988: 188) observe that 'sport occupied an uneasy place between ideologies of the market and ideologies of welfare', with policies being modified to reflect the government's political ideology and the economic reality of the time. A striking example of the balance between market and welfare ideologies was the introduction of compulsory competitive tendering (CCT) in sport in 1992. Under CCT, local authorities retained ownership of the facility, but the management of the facility and its services were subject to a process of tendering. This process involved a number of different contractors preparing bids to manage the facilities and services, with the overall aim being a reduction in operating costs (Coalter 2007). The implications for sports development were mixed, as the local-authority sports development service was not subject to CCT, but their reliance on facilities that did come under CCT invariably caused difficulties (Houlihan and White 2002).

Despite the uncertainty brought about by CCT, the Sports Council focused efforts on the new continuum approach to sports development (Figure 5.1). This approach served to bring a 'conceptual coherence' to sports development (Houlihan and White 2002: 41),

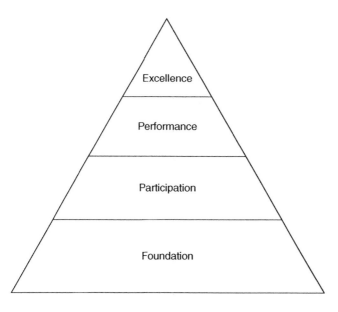

Figure 5.1 *The pyramid sports development continuum (source: Sports Council 1990).*

showing the logic of a joined-up approach where mass participation feeds and benefits elite sport and elite sport, via role models, benefits mass participation. In addition, the English Sports Council continued to attempt to build the national sports development infrastructure through targeted grants to local authority leisure departments. Despite the focus on local government and an attempt to align more closely with the equity concerns of local government, central government generally maintained a distance, a general neglect and lack of interest, more a reflection of general indifference than the fact that the majority of local councils were controlled by a Labour administration (Houlihan and White 2002). However, this was set to change fairly radically after John Major replaced Margaret Thatcher as the Conservative leader and led the party to victory at the 1992 general election. Major's approach to sport, in stark contrast to Thatcher, was generally enthusiastic, a result of his personal interest in sport and it fitting neatly with his 'more traditional view of Conservatism' (Coalter 2007: 14).

During Major's leadership, the British government was involved in three significant developments which brought about a period of sustained investment and more active government involvement in sport (Bloyce and Smith 2010). The first of these was the creation of the Department of National Heritage (DNH) in 1992, which eventually led to the reorganization of the Sports Council, with the formation of an English Sports Council responsible for mass participation (alongside similar home-country Sports Councils in Wales, Scotland and Northern Ireland), and a UK Sports Council responsible for elite sports development (Houlihan and White 2002).

The second major development, and a catalyst for more direct government involvement in sport, was the establishment of the National Lottery in 1994, representing what Henry (2001: 92)refers to as a 'masterstroke of leisure policy'. With the National Lottery, the government could leverage greater financial opportunity for good causes such as sport, art and heritage without any increase in tax-related subsidy (Coalter 2007). Bloyce and Smith (2010: 46) point to both the 'enabling and constraining' features of lottery funding:

> On the one hand, the various organisations involved in running, developing and promoting sports now had greater access to money that was previously unavailable. But, on the other hand, this simultaneously helped to constrain their activities through the growing accountability that was associated with the increasing autonomy that the National Lottery monies helped give them.

Indeed, following the launch of the National Lottery and the apparent growing government interest in sport, the Conservative party published the second government sports strategy, Sport: Raising the Game (Department of National Heritage, 1995). The traditional focus of one-nation Conservatism prioritized school and elite sport, primarily for their intrinsic benefits, their ability to harness the true competitive nature of sport and their capacity to reflect Major's one-nation ideology (Houlihan and White 2002; Coalter 2007). The strategy all but ignored local community sport, in particular the impetus that had grown around sports equity and recognition of the critical role of local authorities, not only as sports facility providers, but also as the guardians of a growing network of professional sports development officers.

A New Labour government was elected in 1997, and its particular approach to sport ushered in a whole raft of changes – the implications of which will be explored more closely in the case study at the end of this chapter. Led by a new Third Way ideology and a commitment to reform and modernize the machinery of government, this new politics was reported as 'a modernised version of social democracy' and a progressive means to 'modernise government, strengthen civil society and address issues of social exclusion' (Roberts 2009: 111), particularly when compared to the left–right positions of traditional politics in the UK (Coalter 2007: 15). In this respect the Third Way is positioned between the opposing commitments to heavy state intervention and anti-individualism, and 'Thatcherite neoliberal, free-market policies and extreme individualism' (Coalter 2007: 15).

The New Labour government immediately replaced the DNH with the Department for Culture, Media and Sport (DCMS). The English Sports Council (branded Sport England) responded quickly and used the opportunity to develop a joined-up package of programmes, referred to commonly as the 'Big Picture' (Figure 5.2). The Big Picture involved four interconnected programme areas, active schools, after communities, active sports and world class, and the initiatives developed within each area were shaped by the key tenets broadly associated with the Third Way politics of the new government, and the party's manifesto for sport, produced in 1996 (Bloyce and Smith 2010).

During the latter part of the 1990s, central government was directly involved in sport, pursuing a range of innovations that moved sport from the margins of government policy to the centre stage (Houlihan and White 2002). This differed from previous government approaches inasmuch as such governments tended to delegate responsibility to quangos, whereas the DCMS was more visible, clearly involved in leading specific policies, strategies and programmes that would shape the growth of sports development

The new government's sports strategy, A Sporting Future for All (Department of Culture, Media and Sport 2000) emphasized school and elite sport, and endorsed the important role of local authorities as both facility provider and sports development enabler (Green 2008). Indeed, local authorities were identified as a lead agency in the quest to break down

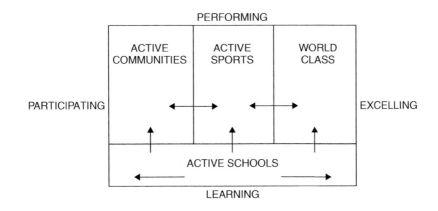

Figure 5.2 *The Big Picture (source: Sports Council 1998).*

barriers and work toward fair access in sports participation (Department of Culture, Media and Sport 2000). However, the aspirations of the Sporting Future for All were short-lived, with the DCMS and the government's Strategy Unit publishing a new vision entitled Game Plan: A Strategy for Delivering Government's Sport and Physical Activity Objectives (Department of Culture, Media and Sport 2002). This strategy provided the government rationale for investing in sport, including focusing on physical activity with the objective of encouraging 70 percent of the UK population to be reasonably active by 2020 (Department of Culture, Media and Sport, 2002). The strategy maintained a focus on school and youth sports development as well as high-performance sport. The strategy presented a twin-track approach to mass participation and elite performance, compared to models in Australia, the USA and Finland, which the DCMS argued were either more laissez-faire or one-dimensional (Figure 5.3).

The strategy also identified poor coordination between grassroots and high-performance sport, with specific criticism levied at the lack of robust talent identification mechanisms, and a tendency to undertrain and overcompete amongst the young (Department of Culture, Media and Sport, 2002). The government strongly advocated the use of Balyi's Long-term Athlete Development (LTAD) framework (Balyi 1999), encouraging NGBs and other agencies to work together to deliver a coordinated series of services in line with the key stages of the LTAD (Figure 5.4).

The range of innovations developed in the late 1990s/early 2000s represented a fundamental shift from the welfare approach of developing sport in communities to the development of communities through sport (Houlihan and White 2002; Coalter 2007), and serves to demonstrate New Labour's view of sport, and in particular the party's view of its value in promoting active citizenship, or what Coalter (2007: 18) refers to as the 'systematic attempt to use sport as an economy of remedies to a variety of social problems'.

In 2005, in addition to the news that London was to host the 2012 Summer Olympic and Paralympic Games, four developments significantly influenced the British government's

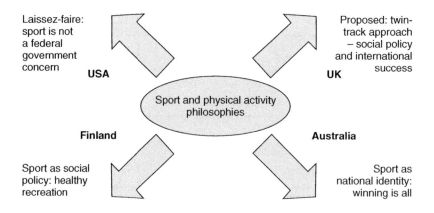

Figure 5.3 *International sport and physical activity philosophies (source: Department of Culture, Media and Sport 2002).*

72

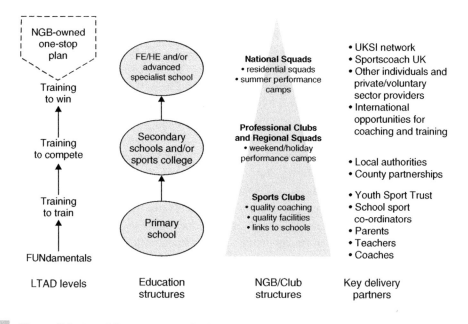

Figure 5.4 *Key delivery partners for implementing Long-term Athlete Development (LTAD) plans. NGB, national governing body; FE, further education; HE, higher education; UKSI, UK Sports Institute (source: Department of Culture, Media and Sport 2002.)*

involvement in sport. First, the Carter Review, a government-commissioned review of efforts and resources in national sport, set out five key recommendations for sport: (1) the development of robust measurement and monitoring systems; (2) the promotion of the personal benefits of sport and physical activity; (3) the improvement of the delivery of sport; (4) the creation of a single access point and brand for sport in England; and (5) the provision of targeted incentives for commercial investors via a new National Sports Foundation (Carter 2005). Sport England immediately responded to this with the creation of the single system, or what was later referred to as the delivery system for sport (Figure 5.5). The delivery system

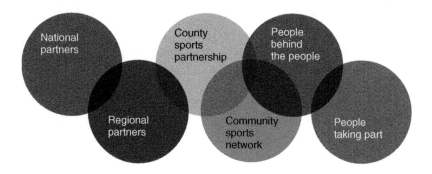

Figure 5.5 *The delivery system for sport (source: Sport England 2005).*

73

for sport sought to clearly articulate the relationship and flow of responsibilities between the national, regional, subregional and local agencies involved in planning, delivering and evaluating sport, thereby clarifying who does what and galvanising a collective approach to increasing participation in PE, sport, and active recreation (Sport England 2007).

The second development followed the government's spending review in 2004 and included sport in the renewed list of Public Service Agreements (PSAs). The agreements were introduced by New Labour in 1998 in an attempt to performance-manage the local delivery of nationally agreed policies systematically. Local authorities were required to develop and implement plans in order to meet agreed targets. Sport was included in the PSA framework in 2004–2005 with two specific agreements/targets being established: (1) 85 per cent of 5–16-year-olds in at least 2 hours of PE and school sport (PSA 1), led by the Youth Sport Trust; and (2) a 3 per cent increase in adult participation in sport and active recreation (PSA 3), led by Sport England. However, these agreements were only selected as a priority in a small number of local authorities.

The most dramatic shift in sports policy during this era followed the change in Prime Minister in 2007, and the subsequent Cabinet reshuffle in June 2007. In taking up his new appointment as Secretary of State for Culture, Media and Sport, James Purnell repositioned DCMS so that it would focus on 'pure sport' and 'sport for its own sake', as opposed to the instrumental use of sport for other means (Department of Culture, Media and Sport, 2008). Further, Purnell was clear in the separation of the vision for his department (the DCMS) and that of the wider government. He stated that the DCMS would fund the creation of a world-leading sports development system, involving high-quality PE and school sport, high levels of community sports participation and enhanced elite performances with record medal wins at major events (Purnell, 2007). In contrast, the 'spill-over benefits', the wider education, crime reduction or health promotion-related benefits attributed to sport, would require funding from other relevant government departments (Purnell, 2007). Further still, Purnell was committed to ensuring that NGBs were the central driving force of sports policy, with bodies such as UK Sport and Sport England directly investing in NGBs to deliver improved levels of mass participation and enhanced performance in international competition.

Playing to Win, the British government's most recent sport policy, shaped three distinct emerging policy areas for sport in England: PE and school sport (5–19 years), community sport (16+), and high-performance or elite sport (Department of Culture, Media and Sport 2008). Focusing on these three, the government set about simplifying sporting structures in England, aiming to show that they were capable of addressing Jowell's assertion that such structures were a 'nightmare' (Moynihan 2010), and Carter's (2005) view that sporting structures were 'unfathomably complex'. Figure 5.6 provides an overview of what was referred to as the 'landscape for sport', a simplified structure of sport which sought to 'improve focus at every level of sport policy (school, community and elite), and better knit the three delivery bodies together' (Department of Culture, Media and Sport 2008: 6). Thus, the government view was a new, simplified structure for sport.

The fourth development, reflecting New Labour's systematic attempt to modernize local government, was the development of the Comprehensive Performance Assessment. This provided local councils and citizens with an independent judgement of the council's leadership and its ability to improve services for local people (Audit Commission 2006). Included

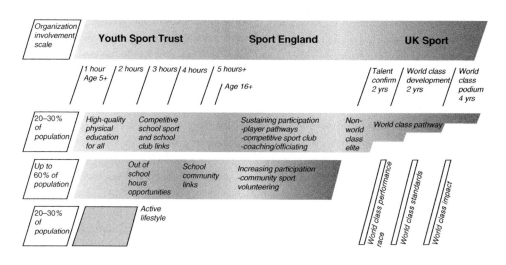

Figure 5.6 *The landscape for sport (source: Department of Culture, Media and Sport 2008).*

were a range of performance indicators, measuring and reporting on the performance of local council services, including sport. The government created Local Area Agreements (LAAs) to supersede the PSAs between central and local government. Central to the LAA was the Local Performance Framework for Local Authorities, which involved a total of 198 performance indicators, many reflecting the new phase of PSAs which would run from 2008 to 2011. This was a notable development in that it attempted to reshape the way in which central and local government worked together, joining up national and local public service priorities, using an evidence-based approach to policy formulation which required local authorities to select national indicators that were most important to the local community, and agreeing any specific local priorities that required action. Two of the indicators were directly focused on sports participation, namely the PE and school sport 5-hour offer (national indicator 57) and the target to increase participation in community sport (national indicator 8). It is estimated that 75 local authorities selected the NI8 indicator (Sport England 2008a), with delivery planning and implementation largely a collective effort shared between local authorities, County Sports Partnerships (CSPs) and other local partners.

The political change resulting from the UK general election in May 2010 had a dramatic effect on the government's involvement in and relationship with sport. The overall Conservative party vision for sport was clearly set out in the party's policy document published in 2009 and was the dominant position adopted by the Liberal–Conservative coalition that assumed power at that time, hardly surprising given the dominance of Tory ministers in the DCMS. The vision emphasized a balanced approach, viewing 'sport as both an end in itself and a means to achieve a better society' (Conservative Party 2010: 4). Similarly, the overarching priority noted in the Conservative policy for sport was suitably broad, encompassing both the aspiration to increase the numbers of people playing sport, as well as highlighting the other opportunities that sport can provide (Conservative Party 2010).

75

Whilst it was possible to observe some level of continuity in the British government's policy objectives for sport, particularly in relation to the community sport policy system, there was considerable change in other areas, made conspicuous by the way in which policy was changed, and the contradiction between the changes and the stated intentions or policies of government departments. Nowhere was this more notable than in the policy for PE and school sport. In October 2010, Michael Gove, the Secretary of State for Education, announced that the previous policy and strategy directing PE and school sport, the PE and Sport Strategy for Young People, was 'neither affordable nor likely to be the best way to help schools achieve their potential in improving competitive sport' (Department for Education 2010). Driven, as noted in official documents, by the desire to decentralize power and incentivize competition, Gove announced that the Education Department would no longer pursue the aims or aspirations of the PE and school sport strategy, including the plan to deliver 5 hours of PE and school sport, nor would it continue specifically to commit funding for school sport partnerships, or provide a dedicated grant to specialist sports colleges (Department for Education 2010). In its place the Education Department planned to implement a framework of district, county and national school sport competitions and planned to provide funding to allow PE teachers to spend one day a week outside the classroom to allow competitions to be planned and organized (Department for Education 2010).

These changes, in Gove's opinion, would remove the top-down targets and erase the excessive bureaucracy and box-ticking associated with the PE and sport strategy for young people, and would emphasize and enhance the prospects of competitive team sports. It is too early to tell the impact of this decision; Grix (2007) criticized the change as being rushed and ill informed, pointing out that the decision contradicts the number-one legacy promise of the 2012 Games. Notably, the substantial changes to school sport were seen to be driven primarily by ideology or perhaps austerity, rather than any notion of improving school sport, or improving the nation's chances of meeting the highly publicized aspirations of the 2012 Games legacy.

At the time of writing, the community sport policy area as a whole has been left relatively unscathed by the change in political leadership in the UK, with the exception of changes in funding resulting from austerity measures, addressed in more detail below. The government has remained committed to the idea of an NGB-led delivery system, with increased levels of adult sports participation being directed by the whole-sport plans of 46 NGBs, with subregional support provided by CSPs throughout England. The apparent opposition of the coalition government to performance targets resulted in the legacy aspiration of two million more people involved in frequent physical activity being discarded, and the British Secretary of State for Culture, Media and Sport announcing that he would replace the target of one million more adults participating in sport with a 'more meaningful' national measure (Gibson 2011).

The most recent policy development worthy of attention is the much-maligned Big Society. The brainchild of Prime Minister David Cameron, the Big Society is not simply about a reduction in the size of the state, although Cameron (2009) makes several references to big government and the rapid expansion of the state under New Labour, but more about 'the potential for social renewal' (Cameron 2009), built on the idea that progress is achieved through local action and is the responsibility of every citizen. As a vision statement, the Big Society was presented as the antidote to the inefficiency, state dependency and lack of responsibility generally associated with an overinflated state. At the core of the Big Society ideal was the redistribution of power from the state to society, from the centre to the local level (Conservative Party 2010), to connect with community activists, encourage mass community engagement and, in doing so, galvanize community-based collective action (Cameron 2009).

ANALYSING THE COMMUNITY SPORT POLICY PROCESS

The whistle-stop tour of the changing relationship between central government and sports development provided thus far in this chapter highlights the implications of political change and the major policies and strategies that have directed and shaped sports development practice to the point that sport in the UK can be seen as 'an established feature in the machinery of government' (Houlihan 2005: 163). It has also touched on some of the key tensions that perennially challenge sports development, including the dualistic notion of sport for sport/sport for good, the tension between mass participation and elite sport, the prioritization of youth sports development over other forms, the focus on physical activity over sport, the reduction of sports development (i.e. player, coach, club, volunteer, competition, facility development) to the mere promotion of sports participation and, notably, the short-term nature of sports policy set against the needs of long-term behaviour change. This chapter concludes with a deeper analysis of the community sport policy process and, in light of the above, an examination of progress against the sport-specific goals for community sport. To assess the challenges associated with the implementation of community sport policy, van Meter and van Horn's (1975) policy implementation framework will be applied. By outlining this particular case study, students should be able to identify and add to the range of challenges affecting the community sport policy process, as well as utilize a similar analytical approach to critique the implementation of other aspects of government sports policies in the UK and elsewhere.

INCREASING PARTICIPATION BY ONE MILLION BY 2012

The case study at the start of the chapter outlines Sport England's vision of increasing the numbers of people regularly participating in sport by one million by 2012. The Sport England strategy was published in summer 2008, with the Active People survey producing baseline data for participation rates in 46 sports in the same year. The survey is repeated annually, and 2012 data will be used to assess whether sports participation targets have been achieved. Analysis of the Active People data from 2010 provides the opportunity for a midterm assessment of progress on a sport-by-sport basis. Table 5.1 provides further information, including a list of sports, the initial 2008 baseline, the 2012 target and the actual reported participation rates in 2010.

Table 5.1 reveals a disappointing picture and poor return on investment, although it should be stressed that this is a midway analysis, and 2 years remain for targets to be met. With considerable sums invested in NGBs to deliver increased participation, some sports have actually regressed, with fewer participants in 2010 than in 2008. The likely cause of this outcome extends beyond the rational or overly simplistic accusation of poor NGB leadership

Table 5.1. *Review of actual versus target participation by sport (source: Sport England 2009).*

Sport	Actual participation (2008)	Target for 2012	Growth required to meet target	Actual participation (2010)	Difference (2008–2010)
Athletics	1,612,000	1,750,000	138,000	1,826,700	214,700
Badminton	535,700	605,700	70,000	535,000	−700
Basketball	186,100	224,000	37,900	184,300	−1,800
Bowls		no published data			
Boxing	106,800	131,800	25,000	117,400	10,600
Canoeing		no published data			
Cricket	204,900	277,449	72,549	206,600	1,700
Cycling	1,767,200	1,892,200	125,000	1,880,800	113,600
Equestrian		no published data			
Fencing		no published data			
Football	2,144,700	2,294,700	150,000	2,146,100	1,400
Golf	948,000	1,023,000	75,000	894,200	−53,800
Gymnastics	89,200	94,300	5,100	62,100	−27,100
Hockey		no published data			
Mountaineering	86,100	103,700	17,600	81,400	−4,700
Netball	118,900	138,500	19,600	125,100	6,200
Rounders	25,900	39,680	13,780	18,600	−7,300
Rowing	55,000	65,000	10,000	49,000	−6,000
Rugby league	88,000	139,628	51,628	73,300	−14,700
Rugby union	230,300	371,612	141,312	203,200	−27,100
Sailing	89,900	111,280	21,380	80,000	−9,900
Skiing	120,700	127,700	7,000	110,400	−10,300
Squash	293,900	349,185	55,285	290,500	−3,400
Swimming	3,244,400	3,514,400	270,000	3,162,400	−82,000
Table tennis	75,700	92,200	16,500	85,600	9,900
Tennis	487,000	637,000	150,000	517,700	30,700
Volleyball	48,400	58,500	10,100	40,300	−8,100

or unrealistic target-setting in the first place, although this may provide a partial explanation in some sports. What the outcome does demand is a more thorough analysis of issues and challenges which have affected the implementation of the policy. van Meter and van Horn's (1975) implementation model provides the opportunity to illuminate some of the critical issues which have challenged implementation of the community sport policy and thus it is worth briefly summarizing this model.

A MODEL OF IMPLEMENTATION (VAN METER AND VAN HORN 1975)

The conceptual model of implementation developed by van Meter and van Horn (1975) identified six interrelated variables that influence the policy implementation process, and there-

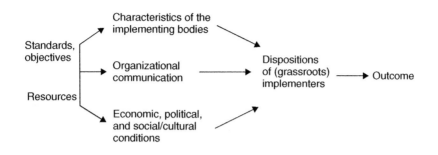

Figure 5.7 *Implementation model (source: van Meter and van Horn 1975, adapted by Kjellberg and Reitan 1995).*

fore can be seen as instrumental in determining the success or failure of policy (van Meter and van Horn 1975). The conceptual model begins with a consideration of: (1) policy objectives and (2) resources, and then progresses into a group of three filtering variables (Skille 2008), consisting of (3) the characteristics of implementing bodies; (4) intergovernmental/organizational communication; and (5) the economic, political and social/cultural conditions. The conceptual model then analyses the final link in the chain: (6) the disposition of grassroots implementers, which then directly affects overall policy outcome (Figure 5.7).

Whilst the model was primarily developed for use in the public sector (Skille 2008), it is argued that the model provides sufficient attention to variables that are highly relevant to all sectors, although further analysis of the varying values, beliefs and norms of different sectors involved in the implementation of community sport policy should be central to the analysis as these have the potential to enable or constrain policy implementation.

CHALLENGES ASSOCIATED WITH THE IMPLEMENTATION OF COMMUNITY SPORT POLICY

The analysis presented here will give detailed attention to policy objectives, resources and the disposition of grassroots implementers with a summary analysis of the three filtering variables – the characteristics of implementing bodies, organizational communication, and the economic, political and social/cultural conditions that influence policy implementation.

Policy objectives

There are two important considerations in relation to establishing policy objectives: (1) the amount of change required to previous policy goals and delivery mechanisms; and (2) the level of consensus on the policy (van Meter and van Horn 1975). Effective policy implementation is far more likely when marginal change has occurred and goal consensus is high (van Meter and van Horn 1975). With regard to change, it would be difficult to argue that increasing participation in sport represents a dramatic change in policy. Indeed, increased participation has been a regular feature of sports development, certainly in the UK since the

79

1990s. However, when we analyse the policy in more detail it is possible to observe dramatic change, particularly in the focus on adults (aged 16 and over), the precise definition of regular moderate-intensity participation in sport, the method of measuring participation and, most significantly, the NGB-led strategy. These issues represent a relatively major shift in policy environment, and expecting effective policy implementation amid such change is unrealistic.

Policy consensus largely remains a research question. That said, there is no doubting the challenge associated with changing the behaviour of one million more adults so that they engage in at least three 30-minute sessions of sport per week. The particular issue here is not so much about the one million more participants, but the frequency of participation, and, in particular, whether this frequency is realistic for people who would generally not be classified as sports enthusiasts. This is an issue of concern for implementing agents, as well as government departments and new ministers who do not wish to be associated with failure in reaching established targets. Given the ambitious nature of the target, it was widely reported at the time of writing that the policy objective and target would be revised and changed to a measure of moderate-intensity participation in sport, for at least 30 minutes, at least once a week. If this happens, the more realistic objective of once a week rather than three times a week would be a welcome relief from what has been seen by a range of agencies involved in community sport as an unrealistic policy objective.

Resources

The level of funding invested in community sport in the UK exceeds £450 million, and whilst it might be naive to argue against the need for even more funding, significantly more funding has been invested into community sport today than has ever been the case previously. That said, there is still a debate as to whether this amount is reasonable in the context of changing the behaviour of one million adults to commit to regular sports participation. Of more concern are recent austerity measures across the UK public sector and the potential implications of these measures on the local authority-led sports development services. Dismantling sports development provision at the local level would dramatically reduce the sports development workforce, resulting in fewer opportunities to engage in community sport as well as less capacity-building resource to help support and develop voluntary sports clubs (VSCs), social enterprises and small-scale commercial operators, although some might argue that this function could easily be met, or is already met, by CSPs.

Other resource-related issues which require consideration in the community sports policy process include facilities and more subtle human capacity issues such as knowledge, skills and authority, which van Meter and van Horn (1975) argue are important considerations for effective policy implementation. A recent report into the state of sports facilities in the UK concluded that no or little additional spending on facilities was required to sustain significant increases in participation, with local authorities advised to rationalize facility provision and more schools encouraged to be proactive in opening up their facilities to wider community use outside school times (CCPR 2010). Conversely, Sport England (2008b) has stressed the need for major investment in the facilities infrastructure, stating that £10 billion of investment is required to refurbish local-authority facilities in order to keep them open and fit for purpose. In addition to the challenge of maintaining a good-quality, affordable built environment, another challenge for the implementation of community sport is maximizing the use of alternative settings for sport, in particular the natural environment, including parks, open spaces and cycle ways. As England Athletics has found, improving awareness of, access to and use of resources such as these can bring substantial success in facilitating significant increases in participation in athletics – this increase was largely a result of more people jogging rather than more people taking part in formalized, club-based athletics.

Knowledge and skills include issues such as the evidence base – in particular, an understanding of what works – which activities, in which conditions will help to grow adult participation in sport (Coalter, 2007). In addition, the skills, not to mention capacity, of the sports development workforce to undertake robust evaluation of interventions, thereby helping to address the aforementioned issue, and the skills and knowledge to contribute to, and shape, other forms of evidence which are commonly used in the development of future policy are key resource issues (Coalter 2007; Piggin *et al.* 2009). This latter point is an issue which brings us full circle, back to the point at which the workforce have, in many cases, a limited capacity to contribute to shaping realistic policy goals for sport from the outset. In addition, authority, or the lack of it, has been shown to be a problematic issue in sport. For example, Taylor *et al.* (2003), Nichols *et al.* (2005), Harris *et al.* (2009) and Collins (2010) have all referred to the complexity of NGB–VSC relations, stressing the independence and autonomy of VSCs. In most cases NGBs rely on the good will and cooperation of VSCs as they are not able to govern or manage VSC efforts, although this is being blurred by the increasingly purposive stance being taken by government, national sport organizations (e.g. Sport England) and NGBs (Kendall 2000), the development of priority or focus club initiatives by NGBs such as the Rugby Football Union, Lawn Tennis Association and the English Cricket Board, and the conditions attached to lottery funding. On this latter issue, Garrett (2004) found that VSCs successful in securing lottery funding had developed various strategies for addressing the conditions applied to funding, with many developing a resistant or indifferent attitude toward conditions of award. This is an issue which the lottery distributor had, in theory, the authority to enforce, but seemingly lacked the capacity, skills or commitment to lottery funding to achieve the organizations' objectives from the outset. Sport England has recently been addressing this issue with funding awards being clawed back from NGBs of sport (e.g. rugby union, rugby league, cricket and basketball) that are failing to hit agreed participation targets. However, given the size of the initial target, and the difference between this and actual performance, the amount reclaimed can be best described as modest (Table 5.2).

Table 5.2. *Amount reclaimed from national governing bodies (source: www.sportengland.org)*

Sport	Target for 2012	Actual performance against baseline (2010)	Investment for period 2008–2011	Reclaimed amount
Basketball	37,900	−1800	£8,200,000	£1,200,000
Golf	75,000	−53,800	£12,851,500	£107,023
Rugby union	141,312	−27,100	£31,219,004	£1,078,000
Rugby league	51,628	−14,700	£29,408,341	£956,188

CHARACTERISTICS, COMMUNICATION AND ECONOMIC, POLITICAL AND SOCIAL/CULTURAL CONDITIONS

A summary analysis of the filtering variables that affect the implementation process is provided in Table 5.3. This presents a brief explanation of each variable and a summary analysis

Table 5.3. *Summary analysis of filtering variables*

Variable	Description of variable	Challenges for community sport
Characteristics of the implementing bodies	The nature of the organizations involved in the policy process, including issues such as organizational viability and quality of human resources, as well as knowledge and power	Power tends to be dominated by government departments. Sport is seen as a policy-taker rather than a policy-maker (Houlihan and White 2002). Policy delivery is, however, in the hands of grassroots implementers. Government and other partners have limited means to enforce policy delivery
		The complex system for delivering community sport involves myriad agencies who compete for resources
		Do NGBs have the capacity or organizational reach to deliver increased participation in sport?
		Knowledge, particularly in relation to what mechanisms/processes work in what situations, is exceptionally limited
Organizational communication	The quality of communications between central government and other partners	Communication in sport requires consideration of national, regional, subregional and local levels, as well as cross-organization communication across public, private and voluntary sector organisations. Communication between all partners needs to be improved, for example, to improve awareness of policy goals, to secure commitment from various partners in the delivery of policy, to coordinate planning and delivery of policy and to enhance the evaluation of policy implementation
Economic, political and social/cultural conditions	The economic, political and social/cultural conditions of the society in which a policy is situated	Recent economic austerity measures are likely to result in fewer direct opportunities for community sport; the economic environment is also likely to see consumer spending fall and/or see consumers seeking alternative, cheaper means of staying active (i.e. jogging, cycling). The political environment in which policy is developed and delivered rarely stays stable for long enough to allow for sustained behaviour change in sport to occur.

Variable	Description of variable	Challenges for community sport
		Myriad social/cultural issues challenge the implementation of community sport. These include age, sex, education, parental socialization and social class, all of which are inextricably linked with sport. Two prominent social issues are: (1) the ageing population and in particular the potential effect of more people living sedentary lives; and (2) the clear association between inequality and a range of policy concerns, including physical activity levels and sports participation, whereby equal societies almost always do better (Wilkinson and Pickett 2009; Veal 2010). Until policy addresses fundamental concerns such as inequality, secondary concerns such as community sport are likely to experience marginal change

NGBs, national governing bodies.

of each in relation to community sport, bringing the ideological context into sharp relief, not least the varying values, beliefs and norms of the different agents involved in community sport policy implementation.

THE DISPOSITION OF (GRASSROOTS) POLICY IMPLEMENTERS

The final variable in van Meter and van Horn's (1975) implementation model is the disposition of implementers; that is, the attitude or behaviour of implementers towards policy goals and consideration of the way in which the attitudes or behaviour of implementing agents affect policy performance. Of particular importance is a consideration of the grassroots implementers' cognition of policy (van Meter and van Horn 1975) – in other words their understanding and comprehension of policy, and their direction of response to it. This latter issue considers alternative priorities that the implementing agent may have, and the overall level of commitment of the implementing agent to the policy.

Clearly, in order to analyse the disposition of grassroots implementers of policy, it is important to identify exactly who these are. Whilst this should be a relatively straightforward task, the lack of DCMS, Sport England or NGB literature relating to the implementers of community sport policy is notable by its absence. Indeed, the more direct source of information in this respect is the Sport England strategy, whereby targets are allocated to specific sectors, as detailed earlier in the chapter. This points to VSCs, CSPs, higher education and local authorities as the primary grassroots implementers of community sports policy.

Table 5.4 provides an analysis of the disposition of each of the grassroots implementers of community sports policy using van Meter and van Horn's (1975) implementation model. It is important to note the diversity of each implementer inasmuch as each one represents a range

83

Table 5.4. *The disposition of grassroots implementers of community sport policy*

Agent	Cognition of policy	Response to policy
National governing bodies (NGBs) (×46)	The 46 NGBs involved in the whole sport plan process should have a clearer understanding of the objectives for community sport. Different sports have different structures, particularly locally, with some of these wholly reliant on voluntary effort. There is the potential for some regional associations to have a confused or outdated view of policy	In 2008, a small number of NGBs lobbied central government for greater involvement in the community sport policy process and a greater share of lottery funding to deliver the policy. The challenge in terms of how NGBs respond to policy is: (1) balancing resources and workload committed to the dichotomous goals of participation and performance; and (2) ensuring that a comprehensive delivery system is in place to deliver the NGB whole sport plan at the local level
Voluntary sports clubs (VSCs) (×106,000)	Research suggests that VSCs remain unclear about the policy goals for community sport. Many VSCs remain unaware, or hold an outdated view, of policy (Harris et al. 2009; May et al. in press)	Given the number and distribution of VSCs across England and the targets set to VSCs within the Sport England strategy, the response of VSCs to community sport policy is an important matter. Research has shown that many clubs lack the ability or willingness to act as policy deliverers (Taylor et al. 2003; Nichols et al. 2005; Harris et al. 2009; May et al. in press). Many voluntary entities prioritize internal matters ahead of external concerns such as policy implementation. Larger, more formally managed clubs are more likely to respond positively to community sports policy (Taylor et al. 2007, Harris et al. 2009, May et al. in press)
County sports partnerships (CSPs) (×49)	Community sport policy has formed a key part of the agreement between CSPs and Sport England since 2008. The core team representing each CSP should therefore have a clear understanding of the policy objectives for community sport	CSPs' response to community sport policy is generally supportive, being actively engaged in strategies and programmes that attempt to sustain and grow participation in sport. However, many CSPs share a wide range of priorities, of which community sport forms a part, and the ability and in particular capacity of CSPs to respond to the community sport policy challenge is questionable
Local authorities	Local authorities' understanding of community sport policy is likely	Some local authorities will invest heavily in sports development, others not at all.

Agent	Cognition of policy	Response to policy
(×353)	to be inconsistent. This depends on the authorities' general position towards sports development, whether they offer a sports development service and whether the local authority has previously committed to Local Area Agreement targets	This is shaped by the political make-up of the council, its core values/priorities, the presence of a high-profile champion for sport within the council, their historical relationship with sports development, and, more recently, their financial position. Many local authorities will develop physical activity programmes or schemes that aim to create a healthier community
Higher education institutions (HEIs) (×130)	HEIs are likely to vary in their understanding of community sport policy. Some HEIs will be aware of policy objectives while others may have little or no understanding as the capacity for sport is limited or attention wholly focused on performance sport	HEIs have not been a traditional partner in the implementation of community sport. Significant funding through the Active Universities programme is likely to secure greater commitment from the 40 HEIs successful in securing funding through this programme. The response to policy amongst other HEIs is likely to be one of general indifference, whereby HEIs pursue their own sports-related objectives

of agencies, and each agency employs or relies upon individual agents to work collectively to implement policy. Table 5.4 therefore presents a general position or tendency across each implementing agent.

SUMMARY

This case study has applied van Meter and van Horn's (1975) model of implementation to identify the critical issues that lie between policy intentions and performance for community sport. This is not intended as a definitive account, but it presents a range of issues which restrict, challenge or prevent effective policy implementation. In terms of policy and resources, the critical issues include the nature of policy change, the realism of policy goals, the consensus amongst partners to work collectively to achieve policy goals, the potential budget cuts in the public sector and workforce reduction resulting from the 2010 comprehensive spending review austerity measures, and the lack of knowledge, particularly in relation to understanding what it is that works – which activities, which mechanisms, in which contexts work to increase participation in sport (Coalter 2007). With regard to characteristics, communication and economic, political and social/cultural conditions, the major challenges include power relations between partners, particularly between those who make policy (policy-makers), those who accept it (policy-takers) and those who are expected to deliver what has been agreed. There are also challenges associated with communication across levels (national, regional, subregional and local) and different sectors. The economic, political and social/cultural conditions also offer a number of challenges to the policy community, not least the evidence that addressing inequality helps to deliver effective results in other policy areas, such as sports participation (Wilkinson and Pickett 2009, Veal 2010). Finally, the disposition of grassroots implementers is vital in understanding the awareness and commitment of implementing agents to the policy objectives. The challenge of ensuring that implementing agents are aware and committed to delivering community sport is critical in the link between policy intentions and policy performance. Clearly in this regard there is more work to do, particularly in relation to assessing the size and capability of formal VSCs, developing alternative forms of NGB-led delivery, and in the post-LAA world of local government, securing local government commitment to policy implementation.

In conclusion, as Foster *et al.* (2005) have previously argued, creating well-meaning policies is all well and good, but it is absolutely essential to ensure that these policies are rooted in the realities of people's lives. This case study argues that the community sport policy objective is beset by a range of constraints and is simply not realistic, as it does not reflect the reality of sports participants, potential sports participants or the range of implementing agents expected to deliver policy.

NOTE

1   Regular basis means three separate occasions, each lasting a minimum of 30 minutes, every week.

REVIEW QUESTIONS

1   Summarize the changing nature of UK central government's involvement in sports development between 1980 and 2011.
2   Identify the key events led by the UK central government that contributed to the evolution of sports development policy and practice.
3   Define and discuss the differences between 'sport for sport' and 'sport for good', as referred to during this chapter.
4   Evaluate the opportunities and challenges attached to central government intervention in sport throughout the UK.
5   Discuss how economic, political and social/cultural conditions affect the implementation of policy in a setting of your choice.
6   Using van Meter and van Horn's (1975) model of implementation, review the policy for PE and school sport, performance sport or international sport for development.

FURTHER READING

Bloyce, D. and Smith, A. (2010). *Sport Policy and Development: An introduction*. London: Routledge.
Coalter, F. (2007). *A Wider Social Role for Sport: Who's keeping the score?* London: Routledge.
Houlihan, B. and White, A. (2002). *The Politics of Sports Development*. London: Routledge.

WEBSITES

County Sports Partnerships:
www.cspnetwork.org
Department for Culture, Media and Sport:
www.culture.gov.uk
London 2012:
www.london2012.com
Sport England: Active People Diagnostic:
www.ipsos-archway.com/apd/login.aspx
Sport England:
www.sportengland.org

REFERENCES

Audit Commission. (2006). *Briefing on the Audit Commission's Comprehensive Performance Assessment Framework.* London: Audit Commission.

Balyi, I. (1999) "Long-term Planning of Athlete Development, Multiple Periodisation, Modeling and Normative Data." *FHS* 4: 7–9

Blackie, J., Coppock, T. and Duffield, B. (1979). *The Leisure Planning Process.* London: Social Sciences Research Centre/Sports Council.

Bloyce, D. and Smith, A. (2010). *Sport Policy and Development: An introduction.* London: Routledge.

Brailsford, D. (1991). *Sport, Time and Society: The British at play.* London: Routledge.

Cameron, D. (2009). *The Big Society.* Hugo Young speech, November 10, 2009.

Carter, P. (2005). *Review of National Sport Effort and Resources.* London: DCMS.

CCPR. (2010). *Facilities Inquiry: Report and recommendations.* London: CCPR.

Coalter, F. (2007). *A Wider Social Role for Sport: Who's keeping the score?* London: Routledge.

Coalter, F., Long, J. and Duffield, B. (1988). *Recreational Welfare: The rationale for public sector investment in leisure.* Aldershot: Gower/Avebury.

Collins, M. (2010). *Examining Sports Development.* London: Routledge.

Conservative Party. (2010). *Extending Opportunities: A Conservative policy paper on sport.* London: Conservative Party.

Department for Education. (2010). "A New Approach for School Sports – Decentralising Power, Incentivising Competition, Trusting Teachers." Press release (online) issued 20 December 2010. Available from: http://www.education.gov.uk/inthenews/inthenews/a0071098/a-new-approach-for-school-sports-decentralising-power-incentivising-competition-trusting-teachers (accessed 21 May, 2011).

Department of Culture, Media and Sport. (2000). *A Sporting Future for All.* London: DCMS.

Department of Culture, Media and Sport. (2002). *Game Plan: A strategy for delivering government's sport and physical activity objectives.* London: DCMS.

Department of Culture, Media and Sport. (2008). *Playing to Win: A new era for sport.* London: DCMS.

Department of National Heritage. (1995). *Sport: Raising the Game.* London: DNH.

Foster, C., Hillsdon, M., Cavillo, N., Allender, S. and Cowburn, G. (2005). *Understanding Participation in Sport: A systematic review.* London: Sport England.

Garrett, R. (2004). "The Response of Voluntary Sports Clubs to Sport England's Lottery Funding: Cases of Compliance, Change and Resistance." *Managing Leisure* 9: 13–29.

Gibson, O. (2011). "Jeremy Hunt Admits London 2012 Legacy Targets will be Scrapped." *The Guardian*, Tuesday 29 March 2011.

Green, M. (2008) "Non-governmental Organisations in Sports Development," in Girginov, V. (ed.) *Management of Sports Development.* Oxford: Butterworth-Heinemann.

Green, M. and Houlihan, B. (2005). *Elite Sport Development: Policy learning and political priorities.* London: Routledge.

Grix, J. (2007). "Cuts to School Sport Partnerships: A Case of Ideology over Reason?" Weblog. Available from: http://www.birmingham.ac.uk/news/thebirminghambrief/items/school-sports-partnerships-03Nov.aspx (accessed 21 May, 2011).

Hargreaves, J. (1985). "From Social Democracy to Authoritarian Populism: State Intervention in Sport and Physical Recreation in Contemporary Britain." *Leisure Studies* 4.

Harris, S., Mori, K. and Collins, M. (2009). "Great Expectations: Voluntary Sports Clubs and their Role in Delivering National Policy for English Sport." *Voluntas* 20(4).

Henry, I. (1993). *The Politics of Leisure Policy.* Basingstoke: Macmillan.

Henry, I. (2001). *The Politics of Leisure Policy,* 2nd edn. Basingstoke: Macmillan.

Houlihan, B. (1991). *The Government and Politics of Sport.* London: Routledge.

Houlihan, B. (1997). *Sport, Policy and Politics: A comparative analysis.* London: Routledge.

Houlihan, B. (2005). "Public Sector Policy: Developing a Framework for Analysis." *International Review for the Sociology of Sport* 40(2): 163–185.

Houlihan, B. and White, A. (2002). *The Politics of Sports Development.* London: Routledge.

Kendall, J. (2000). "The Mainstreaming of the Third Sector into Public Policy in England in the late 1990s: Whys and Wherefores." *Policy & Politics* (28)4: 541–562.

Kjellberg, F. and Reitan, M. (1995). *Studiet av Offentlig Politikk – En innføring.* Oslo: TANO.

May, T. and Harris, S. (2011). "Size Matters: A Review of VSCs as Implementers of Central Government Sports Policy" (in press).

May, T., Harris, S. and Collins, M. (2012). Implementing Community Sports Policy: understanding the variety of voluntary club types (in press).

Moynihan, C. (2010). Interview with Inside the Games publication. http://insidethegames.biz/sub-domains/dev1/httpdocs/latest/10310-exclusive-moynihan-wants-central-role-for-boa-in-new-british-sport-structure.

Nichols, G., Taylor, P., James, M., Holmes, K., King, L. and Garrett, R. (2005). "Pressures on the UK Voluntary Sport Sector." *Voluntas: International Journal of Voluntary and Nonprofit Organisations* 16(1): 33–49.

Piggin, J., Jackson, S. and Lewis, M. (2009). "Knowledge, Power and Politics: Contesting 'Evidence-based' National Sport Policy." *International Review for the Sociology of Sport* 44: 87–101.

Pressman, J.L. and Wildavsky, A. (1973). *Implementation.* Berkeley, CA: University of California Press.

Purnell, J. (2007). *World Class Community Sport.* School Sport Partnership Conference, 28 November 2007.

Roberts, K. (2009). *Key Concepts in Sociology.* Basingstoke: Palgrave Macmillan.

Sillitoe, K. (1969). *Planning Leisure.* London: HMSO.

Skille, E.Å. (*2008*). "Understanding Sport *Clubs* as Sport *Policy Implementers.*" *International Review for the Sociology of Sport* 43(2): 181–200.

Sport England. (2005). *A Framework for Sport.* London: Sport England.

Sport England. (2007a). *Sport England Policy Statement: The delivery system for sport in England.* London: Sport England.

Sport England. (2008a). *Sport England Strategy 2008–11.* London: Sport England.

Sport England. (2008b). *Developing Sustainable Sports Facilities: A toolkit for the development of a sustainable community sports hub*. London: Sport England.

Sport England. (2009). *Active People Dataset*. London: Sport England.

Talbot, M. (2011). *Power Plays in Sport and PE. Sport in Times of Austerity*. Birmingham: University of Birmingham, 18 March, 2011.

Taylor, P., Nichols, G., Holmes, K., James, M., Gratton, C., Garrett, R., Kokolakakis, T., Mulder, C. and King, L. (2003). *Sports Volunteering in England 2002: A report for Sport England*. London: Sport England.

Van Meter, D. and Van Horn, C. (1975). "The Policy Implementation Process: A Conceptual Framework." *Administration and Society* 6: 445–488.

Veal, A. (1982). *Planning for Leisure: Alternative Approaches*. Papers in Leisure Studies, 5. London: Polytechnic of North London.

Veal, A. (2010). *Leisure and the Spirit Level*. Leisure Studies Association annual conference: Diversity and Equality in Leisure, Sport and Tourism, Leeds Metropolitan University, July, 2010.

Wilkinson, R. and Pickett, K. (2009). *The Spirit Level: Why equality is better for everyone*. London: Penguin.

Chapter 6

Selling race equality to sports organizations

Challenges and limitations

Jim Lusted

TOPICS

Tackling racism in and through sport • Race equality policies in sport • Policy reception and implementation in sport organizations

---

OBJECTIVES

By the end of this chapter you should be able to:
- Appreciate the different reasons why sport organizations promote race equality;
- Critically reflect on the limitations of race equality policies in sport;
- Identify some of the controversies associated with race equality activities in sport;
- Problematize the antiracist consensus in sport.

KEY TERMS

Amateurism – an ideological project connected to the formation of modern, organized sports in Victorian Britain; led by the emerging middle classes who placed specific set of morals and values on sport participation, including sport for sport's sake, fair play and against all forms of professionalization of sport.

Fairness – related to debates around social justice; how we ensure that people get what they deserve in life, particularly around the fair allocation of resources and opportunities to individuals in a society. In a sporting sense, fairness is often associated with amateurism and playing by the rules.

Policy implementation – the process in which a set of policy statements and aims becomes adopted into organizational practice and procedures.

Race equality – policies and practices that aim to reduce the inequalities associated with ideas of 'race' and ethnicity, tackle racial discrimination and promote opportunities for people from ethnic minority backgrounds.

Sports equity – a movement emerging in the mid-1990s that advocates a more radical approach to tackling inequalities in sport, including the use of positive action and focusing particularly on institutional change.

OVERVIEW

We often hear claims made about sport's special status as a meritocratic 'level playing field', where sporting success is seen to be directly related to talent, and where discrimination and social inequalities can be dissolved through the cohesive power of sport. This is perhaps particularly relevant when it comes to ideas of 'race'[1] and racism (Long 2000; St Louis 2004), where sport is often regarded as having some 'inherent property that makes it a possible instrument of integration' (Jarvie and Reid 1997: 211). These types of egalitarian ideologies that are embedded in sporting structures and cultures – in the UK at least – might suggest sport organizations would warmly embrace the principles of race equality. Indeed, high-profile and well-supported antiracism campaigns such as Kick It Out in English football point to something of a general consensus within British sport around the need to challenge racism and tackle inequalities associated with ideas of 'race' – both in sport itself (in terms of the diversity of its participants and representatives), and in wider society through sport (in contributing to wider community development, social inclusion and cohesion). There are a number of reasons why we should treat this antiracist 'consensus' in sport sceptically, not least because the evidence around ethnic minority participation in sport in the UK and beyond indicates that ideas of 'race' have both a long-standing and ongoing mediating influence on people's involvement in sport – not only in terms of actual participation, but representation in the whole raft of positions in sport, be it officials, coaches, managers, volunteers, board members or administrators (Long *et al.*, 2009).

While there are obvious examples of ethnic minority achievement in sports across the world, the broader trends indicate the continued presence of racialized inequalities in sport. In this chapter I want to try to address some of the reasons why race equality policies in UK sport seem to have limited impact since their formation. Elsewhere (Lusted 2009, 2011; Lusted and O'Gorman 2010) I have focused particularly on the structural and cultural conditions of English grassroots football governance organizations that, I have suggested, do not lend themselves easily to embracing what are relatively 'new' race equality policies. I will take a slightly different approach here by exploring the ways in which these policies have been 'sold' to sports organizations – particularly national and local governing bodies. What factors have encouraged the formation of such policies at this particular moment? Why do sport organizations feel it necessary to engage with race equality when, for the majority of their histories, there is little evidence of any formal commitment to such ideals? It is important to understand the various mechanisms that have caused the rather sudden uptake of race equality policies among sport organizations because they can help indicate the underlying motivation behind such policy formation. As I will show, the mechanisms behind the adoption of race equality policies can differ quite considerably and are likely to help us predict the extent to which organizations will meaningfully engage with such policy aims and embed their principles into sport. Moreover, the chapter should be of interest to sport managers who are increasingly tasked with implementing race equality policies and initiatives – often with a range of targets associated with future funding contracts. A better understanding of the underlying motivation of an organization in adopting race equality policies might help sport managers to implement changes that go further than the very basic rhetorical commitment to race equality that characterizes many sport organizations in the UK.

CASE STUDY: RACE EQUALITY AT THE ENGLISH FOOTBALL ASSOCIATION

In 2002, the Board of the English Football Association (FA) granted approval of the Ethics and Sports Equity Strategy, a document that marked the first formal commitment from English football's governing body to promote social equality. Many of the statements related to the often-ignored grassroots level of the game, which is solely controlled by the English FA through its local governance arms, County Football Associations. The document contained a number of statements in relation to the need to make football fairer and more accessible to underrepresented groups, with people from ethnic minority backgrounds providing much of the focus for the strategy. The document reads very similarly to Sport England's own Equity Strategy, which it published in the same year (Sport England 2002), and represented a new movement in tackling inequalities that became termed 'sports equity'. This policy change in UK sport came with some fairly radical proposals – first, to recognize that sporting cultures and organizations needed to acknowledge their own complicity in perpetuating inequalities, and second, to undertake a range of positive action interventions, including the redistribution of resources and power to reflect the diversity of current participants and local populations more broadly. In its equity strategy, the FA made a range of unprecedented statements about the state of English football with regard to race equality, notably the lack of ethnic diversity of its membership – particularly at decision-making level – and in non-playing positions in the game such as coaching and refereeing. It also pointed to failures in protecting those who face overt racist discrimination and abuse in the game.

Fast forward some 10 years, and the picture of progress in tackling inequalities and widening participation in English football looks rather mixed. The employment of women and girls football development officers across regional County Football Associations has helped the game become the fastest-growing female sport in the UK, while a similar focus on disability football has seen provision in this area rise dramatically. For race equality, however, little progress appears to have been made within the football organizations themselves, particularly the diversity of those in positions of power. UK Minister for Sport Hugh Robertson MP recently claimed that football was the 'worst governed sport' in the UK (*The Guardian* 2011a), pointing to the lack of diversity among decision-makers as a key factor: 'Every single one of the directors is white, male and late middle-aged, and there is nobody ... from the ethnic (sic) communities' (*The Mail Online* 2011). It can be difficult to see just how policies such as the FA's Ethics and Sports Equity Strategy (The Football Association 2004) have contributed to increasing opportunities for ethnic minorities and promoting positive change in relation to race equality in sport since their inceptions.

'SELLING' RACE EQUALITY PRINCIPLES TO SPORT: A 'NEW' IDEA?

The title of this chapter may indicate to the reader that, far from race equality being a central concern of sport in the UK, research evidence suggests that a fair amount of 'convincing' is needed to prompt sports organizations to engage with the race equality agenda (Long *et al.* 2005). This may seem counterintuitive given the at least rhetorical consensus about tackling racism in sport that is regularly articulated. If, however, the commitment to race equality was so deeply embedded in UK sport, we might expect to see race equality policies and procedures well established in broader sport policy over a long period of time. In fact, a brief glance at the history of UK sport policy displays a general absence of concern around race equality; in the public sector, the Sport for All movement advocated widening access to sport provided by local authorities from the mid-1970s, but had marginal impact in increasing ethnic minority involvement and its focus was regularly influenced by changing political concerns of the day (Carrington and McDonald 2008). Most UK sports organizations – including Sport England (formerly Sports Council), national governing bodies, professional clubs and right down to local sports clubs – have only begun to adopt formal race equality policies and initiatives in the last 10 years or so. In English football – perhaps the most progressive of sports with regard to race equality – the Kick It Out campaign was only formed in 1993, initially without the official support of many of the football authorities, and at least some 20 years after a time when racist chanting in the professional game was endemic (Garland and Rowe 2001). The Sports Council created its first formal race equality document shortly after, in 1994, recommending that 'sports organisations inspect their own procedures and practices, and develop proactive policies to ensure equity within their own structures' (Carrington and McDonald 2008: 238). Some five years later, the organization Sporting Equals was formed to assist Sport England in its race equality activities, which included establishing a Race Equality Charter in 1999 and a Standard in 2000 (Sporting Equals 2001) for sport organizations – notably national governing bodies – to adopt. The governing body of English football, the FA, adopted its first formal equality policy as late as 2002 (The Football Association 2004a, b). It seems that sports organizations have continually needed to be 'prodded' to engage with race equality. Finally, when such policies have been established, their reception has been rather mixed. The albeit small pool of research we have on race equality policies in sport all points to a general scepticism and sometimes even open hostility to the types of formal race equality interventions that have begun to be implemented in recent years, be it in local-authority sport provision (Horne 1995; Swinney and Horne 2005), in response to Sporting Equals' Charter and Standard (Spracklen *et al.* 2006) or in the local reception of national governing body equality policies (Lusted 2009, 2011).

The need to convince organizations to embrace race equality – and to provide some kind of justification or case for its necessity – is not limited to the field of sport. In her discussion of equal opportunities in business management, Dickens (1999) identifies three key cases that are made for organizations to consider equality as a core concern of their company: the business case, legal regulation and social regulation. From a social policy perspective, Bagilhole (2009) identifies the cases made for adopting equal opportunities and diversity policies in public-sector organizations are drawn from moral, economic/business and social cohesion concerns. These models relate specifically to the private and public sectors so may not fit perfectly with the predominantly voluntary sector that characterizes British sport; a slightly adapted model, however, can be useful in assessing the main ways that race equality has been sold to the particular setting under scrutiny here. The adapted model is as follows; firstly, the *moral* case, which refers to race equality being seen as both a desirable and necessary underpinning value for a sport. Secondly, the *political/legal* case, which relates to race equality policies being seen as needed in sport in order to comply with relevant legislation and wider political policy. Finally, the *business* case, which is centred on the notion that promoting race equality can increase the efficiency and revenue of a sport and its particular organizations. I will spend the rest of the chapter detailing each of these cases and the controversies that can arise from them. In addition, I will explore the potential consequences they may have in relation to the meaningful commitment of sports organizations to the principles of race equality, and the likely chances of each case contributing to long-term change with regard to tackling racialized inequalities both in and through sport. Where appropriate, I will draw upon evidence and examples from my own research into grassroots English football and the engagement of County Football Associations (the local governance bodies) with equality policies.

The moral case for race equality

Perhaps the most obvious case to be made to sports organizations to embrace race equality is that it is simply the *right* thing to do – a sort of moral or social obligation that those involved in the organization of sport might be reasonably expected to comply with. I have already mentioned the broad antiracist consensus that exists in sport in the UK and particularly in English football where attempts to challenge racism enjoy a relatively high media profile (Back *et al.* 2001; Garland and Rowe 2001; Burdsey 2007) and the (at least rhetorical) support from players, fans, managers and clubs. There are two aspects of British sport that we might reasonably expect to help view race equality as a moral or social obligation. Firstly, attempts to connect sport with debates around morality and moral obligation are both long-standing and quite deep-rooted. Sport has been described as a kind of 'moral laboratory' for wider debates about society and ethics (McFee 2004); the idea of sport as a moral educator – a place where we learn to identify right from wrong – has a long history, rooted in the Victorian British public schools that are credited with forming modern sport as we know it (Brailsford 1991; Dunning 1999). Sport is often regarded as a place where one can learn 'life lessons' about treating others, playing by the rules and learning the values of fairness, meritocracy and justice, values that underpinned the wider amateurist movement in Victorian Britain (Holt 1989). These amateurist ideas of fairness and fair play continue to inform the practice of sports organizations, particularly local governance organizations (Lusted 2009, 2011). Egalitarian claims in sport can imply that any form of *unfair* activity – like overt racial discrimination perhaps – is unlikely to be tolerated and goes against the spirit of the game. In my own research at County Football Associations, I found that many people felt that social equality (of some sort) was a basic requirement for the game (Lusted 2009, 2011): a component of the core values, culture and practices of the organization or what Shaw (2007) calls its 'deep structure'. When positioned alongside these egalitarian ideals associated with sport, race equality can be sold as simply an extension of, or complement to, the existing guiding values of those who work or volunteer in sport. Recent responses to the allegations of racist abuse between players in the English Premier League point to the overwhelming view that such overt discrimination is not in the spirit of the game and should be punished accordingly (*The Guardian* 2011b).

Secondly, and similarly, sport is seen to be loaded with a whole range of social obligations or functions, often with exaggerated or mythologized benefits (Coalter 2007). One of the reasons why sport attracts so much voluntary commitment and devotion is precisely because of these social obligations that people feel are part of sport's role – a kind of social altruism (Coleman 2002), and sport provides the vehicle for people to 'give something back' or 'help the community'. So, alongside a moral commitment to promoting values like fairness and justice that might be seen to connect with ideas of race equality, sport is often seen by its proponents as a site to provide a range of social duties like encouraging social cohesion, inclusion, tolerance and community development – all functions that might reasonably chime with basic race equality principles.

A glance at the policy documents associated with race equality show that attempts have indeed been made to call upon these moral and social obligations that exist in sport and to connect them to the mission of race equality. Take the FA's Ethics and Sports Equity Strategy's opening statement, for example:

> sports equity is about fairness. It's about football for all … It's about making sure everyone has a chance to be involved in football, regardless of ability, race or religion … It's about using the power of football to build a better future.
>
> (The Football Association 2004a: 3)

The statement calls to both the rhetoric of 'fairness' that is so familiar to sport cultures, and also the social role that sport plays in contributing to progressive social change ('a better future').

Given the previous comments made about both the sceptical and even hostile reception of race equality, and the relatively slow pace of change in relation to ethnic minority representation in all levels and areas of sport, clearly this attempt to connect race equality to sport's interpretations of its long-standing moral and social obligations has some limitations. Sport managers charged with promoting race equality in their organizations and wider sport should be cautious in making explicit connections between their race equality objectives and these long-standing ideas of fairness in sport, however. Some of the resistance that might face the implementation of race equality initiatives can be traced to the very values that remain core components of organizational cultures in sport, such as fairness. Ideologies such as the 'level playing field' and 'fair play' are seen as more than just moral metaphors drawn from sport; they are also a description of sport's own egalitarian credentials, particularly in relation to ideas of 'race' and ethnicity (St Louis 2004). One of the big stumbling blocks here is that, rather than embracing *new* race equality policies, connecting race equality with existing ideologies of fairness in sport can lead to the sense that sport is *already* fair and equal towards ethnic minorities in the way it is being governed or organized. The logical outcome of this organizational culture is that little more needs to be done with regard to promoting race

95

equality (Lusted 2011). In this sense, the problem of racism is regarded as having already been solved, or is already being suitably dealt with through current policy, procedure and practice, and so no new policy interventions are required. Long (2000) refers to this approach to racism in sport as the 'sporting innocence' where there is a generally held view that sport is inherently fair and that there is no problem with racism or racialized inequalities; by deny-ing the existence of racism there is little appetite in local sport organizations to embrace fully – and resource – race equality activities (St Louis 2004; Spracklen *et al.* 2006; Lusted 2009). Moreover, sport organizations can point to the strong values of fairness embedded in their organizations as evidence that the current conditions are in little need of reform.

Secondly, the amateurist interpretation of fairness that continues to inform decision-mak-ing at County Football Associations (Lusted 2011) is a particularly narrow understanding of social equality and does not particularly map well on to the types of race equality policies that have emerged from the sports equity movement that I described earlier. In fact, one can identify a number of important clashes between these two interpretations of what race equal-ity actually is and how it should be achieved. County Football Association council members – locally elected and voluntary representatives of various parts of local football – with whom I spoke, for example, tended to adopt what Baker *et al.* (2009) call a basic or formal approach to equality, one that views equality as based around everyone having the same basic human rights, and that equality can be achieved by protecting these rights through various laws. This formal approach to race equality in sport is one that advocates the same rights to participate for all, achieved primarily by tackling any violation of these basic rights, such as racial abuse from player to player during a match. A more liberal and even radical approach to equality – one that characterizes many of the nationally led race equality policies such as the FA's Ethics and Sports Equity Strategy – proposes that activities should be created that encourage more of what Baker *et al.* (2009) term an 'equality of condition' position. Here, race equality is measured by the diversity of ethnic representation across all levels and all aspects of sport rather than simply the existence (or tackling) of overt racial discrimination. These competing interpretations of what equality 'is' and what the best way is to achieve it are the source of many of the disputes around the implementation of race equality in local sports organizations such as County Football Associations (Lusted 2011). As a result, the sport manager is likely to come up against a rather complex picture of acceptance and resistance to various elements of race equality activities – depending on their nature – if the moral case for race equality is made to local sport organizations.

The political/legal case for race equality

Calls to embrace race equality on moral grounds might be described as a 'soft' sell, or at least one that might chime best with (at least the perceived) existing practice and culture of sports organizations. In contrast, a 'harder' case for adopting a race equality policy can be made on the basis of needing to comply with changes in political policies, agendas and associated legis-lation. This has the potential for race equality to be perceived as a threat – often financial – and one that will result in some form of 'punishment' should an organization not wish to adopt race equality, either through possible litigation or the loss of future public funding. And while there may be a much longer ideological history of morality and fairness in sporting cultures, the need to comply with UK law and political agendas is a much more recent phenomenon, which represents the sea-change that has occurred in UK sport more broadly in recent years (Houlihan and White 2002; Houlihan and Green 2009), moving from a largely voluntary status at the grassroots level, to an increasingly professionalized public service as a result of being the recipient of substantial government funding (Robinson and Palmer 2011). Prior to 2000, there is little indication that local sport organizations needed to pay much direct attention to changes in government political agendas or antidiscrimination legislation. Although there is some evidence of government interest in sport prior to the formation of the New Labour government in 1997 (Houlihan and White 2002), it was this administration that significantly altered the relationship between sport and the British state (see Chapters 5 and 13). Here, both elite and grassroots sport were given significant public funding – through the exchequer and the National Lottery – in return for assistance in delivering a range of government policies in areas such as health, crime prevention, education, community cohesion and social inclusion (Coalter 2007). Such public funding has helped governing bodies significantly increase the development of their sports at the grassroots level, enabling them to employ full-time staff and professionalize their activities. Funding has come with a number of conditions, including some around social equality. Following this new public investment, Sport England, the body responsible for allocating public funding to English sport, was to insist that organizations in receipt of public money must comply with a range of commitments to equality, including race equality:

> The Government has clearly indicated its intention to ensure that all organisations in receipt of public funds make a genuine commitment to provide for all sectors of the public ... Included in the Funding Agreement is a commitment to ensure that 'the modernising' of sports governing bodies takes place. Proposals should include how these bodies intend to address issues relating to equal opportunities and a greater representation of minority groups in formal positions within the organisation.
>
> (Sport England 2000: 5)

This public investment in sport has forced sports organizations to consider a range of new responsibilities and areas of concern, including race equality. By meeting the funding conditions through having things like race equality policies and provisions, organizations have been able to unlock significant funding. In short, race equality has become a more pressing political concern in the UK: through the increase in government funding of sport – and the conditions attached to it – organizations have had to be seen to be meeting such conditions through the implementation of strategies and policies, including race equality. Those organizations that are not seen to adopt such principles are at risk of losing funding, which has become often the major source of income for many UK sports organizations in recent years.

Similarly, prior to 2000 UK antidiscrimination law (notably the Sex Discrimination Act 1975, Race Relations Act 1976 and Disability Discrimination Act 1995) was generally aimed at the delivery of public services and employment procedures, neither of which particularly applied to the predominantly voluntary-sector sport organizations; these were generally seen by the courts as private members' associations and thus exempt from many of the clauses of such laws (Gardiner 2004). As such, many sport organizations – particularly small, localized and voluntary organizations – had little need to concern themselves with antidiscrimination law. More recently, however, successful claims of discrimination have been made against sports organizations, reflecting the strengthening and widening of scope of legislation, in part as a result of the influential MacPherson report that challenged previous understandings of racial discrimination in 1999 (Gardiner and Welch 2011). Vanessa Hardwick, a female football coach, successfully won her sex discrimination case against the FA in 1999 after failing an advanced football coaching licence in 1996, while in 2001 football referee Gurnam Singh won his case for racial discrimination against the Football League after being passed up for promotion. Failing to comply with antidiscrimination legislation places sport organizations at the risk of not only costly legal battles but also obvious damage to the reputation and public image of the bodies involved. Thus, sport managers may find that race equality can be sold to an organization on the basis that it can provide some protection against potentially costly litigation and the loss of future funding.

It is probably fair to say that the political/legal case has been the most influential in prompting the development of policies and activities associated with race equality in UK sport. A casual comparison of the timings of the emergence of equality policies in sport, the changes in political funding and utilization of sport, and the changes in antidiscrimination law indicates the interconnectedness of politics, the law and sport in this context. The general lack of any obvious race equality work prior to the significant rise in public funding for sport and the strengthening of antidiscrimination law at the turn of the new millennium, combined with the rapid emergence of race equality policies among national sporting bodies soon after this time, points to the core mechanism that has prompted such policy development. In their assessment of the uptake of race equality in cricket, Carrington and McDonald (2008) point to both the pressure to respond to the MacPherson report and the vigour of Sport England's promotion of equity as two of the core reasons why the English Cricket Board began to address race equality formally. In my own research, changes to both the funding requirements and legal context were seen to influence the FA's move towards creating its own equity strategy (Lusted 2009), mechanisms that were also identified by local County Football Association respondents (Lusted 2011). And while we might say that this case has been successful in placing race equality firmly on the agenda, there are some important implications and controversies associated with this approach that a sport manager should have some awareness of.

Perhaps unlike the moral case, which can encourage *some* local ownership and commitment to race equality, the political/legal approach is very much *externally* driven, with sports organizations generally *compelled* to change, usually to avoid the risk of some kind of financial penalty. This externally driven approach to equality is a key source of controversy that can be seen to hinder the implementation of race equality policies in local sports organizations significantly (Lusted and O'Gorman 2010). Firstly, this imposition of race equality can connect to broader power struggles in the control of local sports. In English football, County Football Associations have historically enjoyed virtual autonomy in the governance of their local football. Nationally led policies such as the FA's Ethics and Sports Equity Strategy have been interpreted by some as a threat to this local autonomy of decision-making; thanks largely to the increase in external funding at national level, local members feel that the priorities and policies for grassroots football are increasingly being imposed from above, with little consultation with local representatives (Lusted and O'Gorman 2010). Relatedly, where race equality is seen as an explicit political project – originating in government but also taken up by the national FA – it is often interpreted as both a crude form of political interference in an otherwise strongly apolitical setting (drawn from early amateurist ideas of sport for sport's sake) and, in the specific case of race equality, an example of both overt social engineering and excessive political correctness (Lusted 2011). In my own research, for many working in grassroots football, race equality policies represented the wider attempt by national bodies to centralize the governance of their sport and reduce local decision-making and prioritizing of activities, while also overtly politicizing what local stakeholders perceived to be an otherwise 'neutral' social setting (Lusted 2011).

Alongside the potential for the political/legal case for race equality to generate discomfort and scepticism from representatives from local sports organizations, this approach can often engender a minimalist approach to race equality. In her assessment of the UK Equality Standard – a set of guidelines established in 2004 to help sports organizations adopt equality principles in their sports – Shaw (2007) suggests that, like many policies drawn from government and other regulatory bodies, many of these race equality policies in sport are informed by a wider 'audit culture'. This audit culture assesses policy achievements mainly through evidence-based outcomes, such as counting the numbers of ethnic minority participation in certain activities. As such, race equality activities are often limited to meeting these prescribed outcomes or targets related to funding requirements (such as those conditions set by Sport England) rather than addressing both the broader structural and organizational sources of racialized inequalities in sports (see Chapter 11 for a similar discussion around tackling gender inequalities). Quite often, these funding conditions can be very basic: the foundation level of the UK Equality Standard, for example, requires a public commitment to equality, the formation of a policy document and a basic demographic audit of an organization (UK Sport 2004). In complying with funding requirements and legislation, there is little obvious benefit to sports organizations in doing more than the minimum requirements (Spracklen et al. 2006; Shaw 2007). This can be seen as an example of what Carrington and MacDonald (2008) call 'bureaucratic managerialism' – where the formation of policy documents and a rhetorical commitment to the basic principles of race equality and antiracism are often all that organizations feel is needed to be done. In particular, this paper-based commitment to promoting race equality fits relatively well with the type of ideological attachment to amateurist ideas of fairness that I outlined previously; there is little controversy associated with sports organizations making public statements saying, in effect, that they believe racism is wrong and should be challenged. Much harder to 'sell' is a policy commitment to proactively tackling racism, particularly when the implication is that organizations themselves are culpable, compliant or even the source of racialized inequalities in their sport (Carrington and MacDonald 2008).

With regard to the role of legislation, there is evidence to suggest that there are limits to the ability of the law itself to produce social change, particularly in relation to sport and tackling discrimination (Gardiner and Welch 2001, 2011; Gardiner 2004). Gardiner and Welch (2011) remind us that challenging racism through the law is necessarily limited because it is usually applied on an individualized case-by-case basis, can only retrospectively punish racist acts and is much less able proactively to prevent racism occurring in the first place. In addition, while the newly formed UK Equality Act (2006, 2010) was initially seen to strengthen and broaden antidiscrimination law, recent political changes have seen a watering down of some of the more aggressive (and controversial) elements of the law.

Given the above, one might argue that the political/legal case for race equality is necessarily a negative, punitive case for implementing policy; one that is likely to characterize a race equality policy as a 'shield' to a number of external threats – largely financial in nature. Equally, there is evidence to suggest that the race equalities that do emerge from these pressures tend to have little local ownership and are often characterized by a 'bureaucratic managerialist' approach that can promote a tickbox, minimalist approach to tackling racialized inequalities. The sport manager who finds that race equality has been adopted in his or her organization for political/legal reasons is likely to face a challenge in convincing key players of the need for any interventions that go above and beyond the minimum requirements for legal compliance and future funding requirements.

The business case for race equality

The most recent way that race equality has been sold to sports organizations is through the claim that it makes good business sense, particularly in relation to increasing the diversity of their workforce – but also their potential customer base. Bleijenbergh *et al.* (2010) suggest that it is increasingly recognized that promoting ethnic diversity has the potential to facilitate competitive advantage, through improving the corporate image of an organization, improving group and organizational performance and attracting and retaining the best possible staff. Promoting ethnic diversity can also be seen as a useful complement to wider business goals associated with increased productivity and efficiency, the quality of service delivery and a source of new markets and consumer bases (Noon 2007). In short, race equality can be seen to make simple business sense.

The business case for race equality might be seen more readily in professional sport, particularly those organizations such as professional clubs that have a relatively long history of being run as businesses. Professional football clubs have increasingly recognized the need to widen their customer base – predominantly fans – and have looked to exploit consumer markets that have previously been untapped; this includes female fans (Pope and Williams 2011) and also those drawn from ethnic minorities, who have historically been absent from football stadia in the UK (Sportswise 2008). Additionally, professional clubs have an obvious need to recruit the best players – particularly at youth level through their academies – and have an interest in identifying potentially untapped markets of player talent. Kick It Out's equality standard for professional football clubs highlights this approach in matching the business needs of clubs to issues of equality:

> If professional clubs … are to meet the challenges posed by … the need to attract new live audiences, and to maximise the talent available to them, they will ensure all areas of their operation draw on the principles of equality and fairness as part of their commercial model.
>
> (Kick It Out 2009: 4)

At grassroots level, this business approach to race equality is still in its infancy, primarily because most local sports organizations (in the UK at least) have effectively been run as voluntary associations for the majority of their histories. In recent years, however, local sports associations have increasingly been encouraged to professionalize their activities and procedures (Garrett 2004), in part as a result of the increased government investment in sport outlined earlier in this chapter but also due to the rising financial pressures facing such organizations, many of which have seen a significant reduction in participation and associated revenue from membership fees. In the case of English grassroots football, many local County Football Associations have recently been encouraged to become limited companies, effectively changing status from voluntary associations to private businesses (Lusted 2008). This has led to the recruitment of paid staff to undertake administrative duties, and an increasing use of business principles to help grow local participation and generate new streams of revenue. These are very new developments in local sport, but there are already signs of an increasing appetite to adopt business principles in local sport and explore ways of reducing local costs and increasing revenue streams and participation bases (see Chapter 13).

Selling race equality in this way can potentially avoid some of the controversies associated with both the moral and the political/legal cases we have discussed so far. The emphasis on recognizing and managing diversity that this approach favours avoids some of the tensions associated with the different interpretations of the language of equality and fairness outlined earlier; couched in terms of increasing ethnic diversity, it more clearly describes the benefits of race equality to sport and its organizations, rather than contributing to any wider ideological or political project that can be interpreted as social engineering through sport or imposed conformity with perceived political correctness (Bleijenburgh *et al.* 2010). This is primarily because such activities are developed *internally* by power-holders themselves in local sports organizations rather than externally imposed. This can encourage greater local ownership and commitment to race equality policies and activities, as they are often designed to complement existing strategies and plans that sports organizations are guided by. For example, a central concern of the vast majority of local sports organizations is to retain and grow their participation base; race equality activities can be seen as a kind of targeted recruitment drive, aimed at local ethnic minority communities that are often underrepresented in the formal structures of local sport. Certainly, a sport manager following this line of argument for race equality has the potential to garner early support from key power-holders regarding the benefits of such activities. This interest convergence is recognized by governing bodies such as the FA, as seen in this quote from an FA Council Chairman in 2010:

> Under-represented groups are some of the untapped markets of football. Doing what we can to affiliate new teams and retain existing ones, engage fans from new and different communities and bringing in new volunteers (the life blood of our game) and widening representation within the infrastructure of football, is key to our strategy to grow and develop the Nation's favourite game.
>
> (The Football Association 2010)

Additionally, the business case for race equality can promote a form of self-regulation among sport organizations and avoid the controversies associated with externally imposed regulation, through government funding or legislation. This case encourages organizations to consider race equality as part of their broader corporate social responsibilities; if they can be seen to be adopting their own race equality policies, calls to impose external pressure to enforce change are likely to be reduced. Related, a case can be made that the public image of a sport organization, particularly one with governance responsibilities, can be enhanced with a socially responsible policy such as one that promotes race equality (Bleijenbergh *et al.* 2010). Confidence in its ability to run the game among local participants and wider population is likely to be enhanced if it is seen to be accessible to all, transparent in its activities and fair in its treatment of clubs and players.

The business approach to race equality is not without its critics; sport managers should be aware that following this path to promote the uptake of race equality can, in the long run, lead to a mixed reception of local initiatives. Kirten and Greene (2009) suggest that this approach has shifted the emphasis away from social equality and equal opportunities on to a narrower and more instrumental concern with 'diversity management', with much less of an emphasis on challenging institutional discrimination. Many have argued that the increasingly popular 'business' approach to diversity has detached such activities from the broader concerns of equality and social justice (Dickens 1999; Hutchings and Thomas 2005; Noon 2007; Wrench 2005). One of the consequences of this is that 'support for equal opportunities becomes associated with a set of values unrelated to equality, difference, diversity' (Forbes 1996, cited in Dickens 1999: 10) and can even be used to deflect any accusation of inequality or discriminatory practice within the organization itself (Wrench 2005). Wrench (2005) also suggests that the diversity management approach can be *damaging* to race equality principles, by diluting the specificity of such policies to multiple areas of difference (e.g. gender, disability, age) while also reifying simplistic generalizations and assumptions about cultural differences. This diversity management approach also reflects a longer trend towards the 'privatization' or self-regulation of equality action through reduced government intervention, allowing the private sector to shape and dictate the nature and level of commitment to race equality as part of its broader corporate social responsibilities (see Chapter 16).

Dickens (1999: 9) suggests that 'leaving EO [equal opportunities] to individual organisations taking voluntary business case-driven initiatives is an insecure foundation for general overall improvement in the position of ... ethnic minorities'. This insecure foundation can be seen in a number of ways. Firstly, the business case allows existing power-holders to set the agenda and priorities for local race equality activities. This could be an advantage, in that local representatives might be seen as best placed to understand the needs of their sport with regard to race equality, as well as increasing local ownership of policies, as previously mentioned. The downside to this is the assumption that current power-holders in sport are indeed best placed to judge the needs of ethnic minority communities and identify the sources of racialized exclusion in their sports; there is evidence to suggest the contrary, with large parts of local sport still fail even to see the need for any form of race equality work at all (Long 2000; Spracklen *et al.* 2006). This can also engender little appetite for reforms to internal organizational structures or ideologies and even existing power relations that may actually be an important source of racialized exclusion (Lusted 2009). Sport managers may soon find that some of their objectives with regard to race equality – or the elements that they are required to implement – are either amended to a point where they bear little resemblance to their initial aims, or simply dropped if they do not readily meet the perceived business goals of the organization. For example, wider structural changes that are often proposed in race equality policies, such as changes to decision-making structures and personnel, perhaps advocating the co-option of ethnic minority representatives on to boards, councils and other positions of power, are regularly sidelined or dropped, highlighting the ways that current power-holders can deflect any attempt at wider reform through race equality policies (Lusted 2011). Second, the business case necessarily encourages a selective approach to race equality. Because it is sold as being complementary to existing strategies and organizational goals, those activities that do not readily show signs of obviously 'helping' the organization are unlikely to be pursued, regardless of whether such activities might contribute to increasing race equality in the sport. Policies and activities are cherry-picked by organizations to ensure the greatest success with the minimum resource. This cost–benefit approach to race equality (Noon 2007) can encourage a short-term approach and prioritize activities that can be easily measured and are likely to be most easily achieved. So, while running a coaching session targeted at a specific community might produce an obvious rise in ethnic minority participation figures, other activities such as tackling racist abuse among spectators or players might involve addressing a range of complex factors that do not lend themselves well to short-term projects and are unable to produce easily measurable outcomes (Shaw 2007). The sport manager is likely to face a much tougher task 'selling' a project associated with race equality that has little obvious signs of early success, regardless of the fact that it may have much longer-term benefits and rewards.

CONCLUSION

There continues to be a disparity between the rhetorical commitment to race equality in contemporary sport policies and the current picture of sport in the UK in relation to the involvement of ethnic minorities. While we might expect sport to embrace race equality initiatives warmly, given its legacy of fairness and more recent antiracist consensus, research evidence indicates a fair degree of scepticism toward these types of interventions in sport. Implementing race equality activities at the local level appears to be much more complex and fraught with a number of controversies that can hinder the implementation process. This chapter has attempted to make some sense of why policies of this kind have so far been of limited success; I have suggested that a better understanding of the underlying reasons behind a sport organization deciding to adopt a race equality policy may shed some light on the slow progress in this area. I have offered a model outlining three key ways in which race equality has been 'sold' to organizations. This model helps us to identify some of the main reasons why race equality policies have emerged within UK sport organizations in recent years. A number of specific controversies and limitations can be seen to emerge from adopting race equality for moral, political/legal or business purposes. Sport and leisure managers may find that if they are able to identify the underlying reasons for the adoption of race equality policies and initiatives within their organizations, they may in turn be better placed to anticipate some of the controversies that are likely to emerge when doing such work, particularly at a localized level. The

103

underlying message here is that sport organizations appear to need some convincing of the *need* for such policies in the first place. Part of this can be explained by the hegemonic position of the ideology of fairness in sporting cultures, one that makes a number of claims about the existing status of sport which does not lend itself well to either an acceptance of inequalities and discrimination in sport (particularly among governance organizations) or a proactive attitude toward implementing sometimes radical organizational changes. More often than not, race equality activities in sport have emerged as a result of some form of 'prodding' from an external source rather than any internal lobbying, be it government policy and/or funding, changes in legislation or a national sport organization attempting to reform its regional branches. In whatever case, the sport manager should be aware that, far from race equality being an easy 'sell' to an organization, the antiracist consensus in sport is much more complex and contested than we might otherwise imagine.

NOTE

1 The term 'race' is placed in inverted commas in this chapter to reflect a convention in the social sciences that indicates the contested and socially constructed nature of the concept (Miles 1993).

REVIEW QUESTIONS

1 Discuss which of the cases for equality – moral, political/legal or business – is most likely to ensure more representation of ethnic minorities in positions of power in sport.
2 Which of the cases would you say is least likely to facilitate radical organizational changes? Why?
3 What might be the pros and cons of making the implementation of a race equality policy a requirement for an organization to receive future government funding?

FURTHER READING

Carrington, B. and McDonald, I. (2008). "The Politics of 'Race' and Sport Policy in the UK," in Houlihan, B. (ed.) *Sport and Society: A student introduction,* 2nd edn. London: Sage.
Dickens, L. (1999). "Beyond the Business Case: A Three-pronged Approach to Equality Action." *Human Resource Management Journal* 9(1): 9–19.
Spracklen, K., Hylton, K. and Long, J. (2006). "Managing and Monitoring Equality and Diversity in UK Sport: An Evaluation of the Sporting Equals Racial Equality Standard and its Impact on Organizational Change." *Journal of Sport and Social Issues* 30(3): 289–305.

WEBSITES

Kick It Out:
www.kickitout.org

Sporting Equals:
    www.sportingequals.org.uk
The English Football Association – EqualityFootball for All:
    www.thefa.com/TheFA/WhatWeDo/Equality.aspx
UK Equality Standardin Sport: Sports Council Equality Group:
    www.equalitystandard.org
UK Sport Race Equality Scheme:
    www.uksport.gov.uk/publications/uk-sport-race-equality-scheme

REFERENCES

Back, L., Crabbe, T. and Solomos, J. (2001). *The Changing Face of Football.* Oxford: Berg.

Bagilhole, B. (2009). *Understanding Equal Opportunities and Diversity: The social differentiations and intersections of inequality.* Bristol: Policy Press.

Baker, J., Lynch, K., Cantillon, S. and Walsh, J. (2009). *Equality: From theory to action,* 2nd edn. Basingstoke: Palgrave Macmillan.

Bleijenbergh, I., Peters, P. and Poutsma, E. (2010). "Diversity Management Beyond the Business Case." *Equality, Diversity and Inclusion: An International Journal* 29(5): 413–421.

Brailsford, D. (1991). *Sport, Time and Society. The British at play.* London: Routledge.

Burdsey, D. (2007). *British Asians and Football.* London: Routledge.

Carrington, B. and McDonald, I. (2008). "The Politics of 'Race' and Sport Policy in the UK," in Houlihan, B. (ed.) *Sport and Society: A student introduction,* 2nd edn. London: Sage.

Coalter, F. (2007). *A Wider Social Role for Sport: Who's keeping the score?* London: Routledge.

Coleman, R. (2002). "Characteristics of Volunteering in UK Sport: Lessons from Cricket." *Managing Leisure* 7(4): 220–238.

Dickens, L. (1999). "Beyond the Business Case: A Three-pronged Approach to Equality Action." *Human Resource Management Journal* 9(1): 9–19.

Dunning, E. (1999). *Sport Matters: Sociological studies of sport, violence and civilisation.* London: Routledge.

Dunning, E. and Sheard, K. (2005). *Gentlemen, Barbarians and Players: A sociological study of the development of rugby football.* London: Routledge.

Equality Act 2006. Available from: http://www.legislation.gov.uk/ukpga/2006/3/contents (accessed 10 January, 2012).

Equality Act 2010. Available from: http://www.legislation.gov.uk/ukpga/2010/15/contents (accessed 10 January, 2012).

Forbes, I. (1996). "The Privatisation of Sex Equality Policy," in Lovenduski, J. and Norris, P. (eds.) *Women in Politics.* Oxford: Oxford University Press.

Gardiner, S. (ed.) (2004). *Sports Law,* 3rd edn. London: Cavendish.

Gardiner, S. and Welch, R. (2001). "Sport, Racism and the Limits of 'Colour Blind' Law," in Carrington, B. and McDonald, I. (eds) *Race, Sport and British Society.* London: Routledge.

Gardiner, S. and Welch, M. (2011). "Football, Racism and the Limits of 'Colour Blind' Law: Revisited," in Burdsey, D. (ed.) *Race, Ethnicity and Football: Persisting debates and emerging issues.* London: Routledge.

Garland, J. and Rowe, M. (2001). *Racism and Anti-Racism in Football.* Basingstoke: MacMillan.

Garrett, R. (2004). "The Response of Voluntary Sports Clubs to Sport England's Lottery Funding: Cases of Compliance, Change and Resistance." *Managing Leisure* 9(1): 13–29.

Holt, R. (1989). *Sport and the British.* Oxford: Oxford University Press.

105

Horne, J. (1995). "Local Authority Leisure Policies for Black and Ethnic Minority Provision in Scotland," in Fleming, S., Talbot, M. and Tomlinson, A. (eds) *Policy and Politics in Sport, Physical Education and Leisure.* LSA Publication no. 55. Eastbourne: LSA, pp. 159–176.

Houlihan, B. and Green, M. (2009). "Modernization and Sport: The Reform of Sport England and UK Sport." *Public Administration* 87(3): 678–698.

Houlihan, B. and White, A. (2002). *The Politics of Sports Development.* London: Routledge.

Hutchings, E. and Thomas, H. (2005). "The Business Case for Equality and Diversity: A UK Case Study of Private Consultancy and Race Equality." *Planning Practice and Research* 20(3): 263–328.

Jarvie, G. and Reid, I. (1997). "Race Relations, Sociology of Sport and the New Politics of Race and Racism." *Leisure Studies* 16(4): 211–219.

Kick It Out. (2009). *Equality Standard for Professional Clubs.* London: Kick It Out.

Kirten, G. and Greene, A. (2009). "The Costs and Opportunities of Doing Diversity Work in Mainstream Organisations." *Human Resource Management Journal* 19(2): 159–175.

Long, J. (2000). "No Racism Here? A Preliminary Examination of Sporting Innocence." *Managing Leisure* 5(3): 121–133.

Long, J., Robinson, P. and Spracklen, K. (2005). "Promoting Racial Equality Within Sports Organisations." *Journal of Sport and Social Issues* 29(1): 41–59.

Long, J., Hylton, K., Spracklen, K., Ratna, A. and Bailey, S. (2009). *A Systematic Review of the Literature on Black and Minority Ethnic Communities in Sport and Physical Recreation.* Birmingham: Sporting Equals.

Lusted, J. (2008). Sports Equity Strategies and Local Football in England. Unpublished PhD thesis, University of Leicester, UK.

Lusted, J. (2009). "Playing Games with 'Race': Understanding Resistance to 'Race' Equality Initiatives in English Local Football Governance." *Soccer and Society* 10(6): 722–739.

Lusted, J. (2011). "Negative Equity? Amateurist Responses to Race Equality Initiatives in English Grass-roots Football," in Burdsey, D. (ed.) *Race, Ethnicity and Football: Persisting debates and emergent issues.* London: Routledge. pp. 207–222.

Lusted, J. and O'Gorman, J. (2010). "The Impact of New Labour's Modernisation Agenda on the English Grass-roots Football Workforce." *Managing Leisure* 15(1): 140–154.

McFee, G. (2004). *Sport, Rules and Values: Philosophical investigations into the nature of sport.* London: Routledge.

Miles, R. (1993). *Racism after Race Relations.* London: Routledge.

Noon, M. (2007). "The Fatal Flaws of Diversity and the Business Case for Ethnic Minorities." *Work, Employment and Society* 21(4): 773–784.

Pope, S. and Williams, J. (2011). "Beyond Irrationality and the Ultras: Some Notes on Female English Rugby Union Fans and the 'Feminised' Sports Crowd." *Leisure Studies* 30(3): 293–318.

Robinson, L. and Palmer, R. (eds) (2011). *Managing Voluntary Sports Organisations.* London: Routledge.

Shaw, S. (2007). "Touching the Intangible? An Analysis of the 'Equality Standard: A Framework for Sport'." *Equal Opportunities International* 26(5): 420–434.

Sport England. (2000). *Making English Sport Inclusive: Equity guidelines for governing bodies.* London: Sport England.

Sporting Equals. (2001). *Achieving Racial Equality: A standard for sport.* Birmingham: Sporting Equals.

Sport England. (2002). *No Limits: Sport England's Equity Policy.* London: Sport England.

Sportswise. (2008). *National Fan Survey Summary Report.* London: Premier League.

Spracklen, K., Hylton, K. and Long, J. (2006). "Managing and Monitoring Equality and Diversity in UK Sport: An Evaluation of the Sporting Equals Racial Equality Standard and its Impact on Organizational Change." *Journal of Sport and Social Issues* 30(3): 289–305.

St Louis, B. (2004). "Sport and Common-sense Racial Science." *Leisure Studies* 23(1): 31–46.

Swinney, A. and Horne, J. (2005). "Race Equality and Leisure Policy Discourses in Scottish Local Authorities." *Leisure Studies* 24(3): 271–289.

The Football Association. (2004a). *Ethics and Sports Equity Strategy*. London: The Football Association.

The Football Association. (2004b). *Football For All*. London: The Football Association.

The Football Association (2010). "Equality Standard: CFAs Recognised for their Work in Equality." [Available from: http://www.thefa.com/TheFA/WhatWeDo/Equality/NewsAndFeatures/2010/framework-231110 (accessed 10 January, 2012).

The Guardian. (2011a). "*Hugh Robertson: 'Football is Worst Governed Sport in UK'*." Available at: http://www.guardian.co.uk/football/2011/jan/20/hugh-robertson-football-worst-governed?intcmp=239 (accessed 9 January, 2012).

The Guardian. (2011b). "Racism in Football: Keep on Kicking it Out." Available at: http://www.guardian.co.uk/commentisfree/2011/dec/21/john-terry-race (accessed 9 January, 2012).

The Mail Online. (2011). "*Sports Minister Robertson Slams English Football as Worst Run Sport in the Country.*" Available at: http://www.dailymail.co.uk/sport/football/article-1380809/Hugh-Robertson-slams-English-football.html (accessed 9 January 2012).

UK Sport. (2004). *The Equality Standard: A Framework for Sport*. London: Sport England.

Wrench, J. (2005). "Diversity Management can be Bad for You." *Race and Class* 46(3): 73–111.

Chapter 7

Sport and disability

The Special Olympics Youth Unified Sports programme

Sandra Dowling, Sabine Menke,
Roy McConkey and David Hassan

TOPICS

Inclusive sports – Special Olympics Unified Sports programme • The organization of inclusive sports • The role of leaders and coaches in delivering inclusive sports • The broad value of such sports in the lives of people with multiple, if primarily intellectual, disabilities.

OBJECTIVES

By the end of this chapter, you will be able to:

- Understand the challenges of discrimination faced by people with intellectual disabilities and describe the Special Olympics Unified Sports programme;
- Discuss the value of sport in promoting social inclusion for those with disabilities;
- Discuss the value of participation in inclusive sports to non-disabled players;
- Understand the role of the Special Olympics, as the sponsoring body in delivering Unified Sports, as an agent for social change;
- Understand the role of leaders and coaches in delivering the Unified Sports programme and developing attitudinal change among participants and within the community in which such programmes operate.

KEY TERMS

Intellectual disability – a significantly reduced ability to understand new or complex information and to learn and apply new skills (impaired intelligence). This results in a reduced ability to cope independently (impaired social functioning), and begins before adulthood, with a lasting effect on development. Disability depends not only on a child's health conditions or impairments but also, and crucially, on the extent to which environmental factors support the child's full participation and inclusion in society. The use of the term 'intellectual disability' includes people with autism who have intellectual impairments. It also encompasses children who have been placed in institutions because of perceived disabilities or family rejection and who consequently acquire developmental delays and psychological problems (World Health Organization).

Special Olympics – an international sporting organization delivering sports training and opportunities for competition to people with intellectual disabilities, as well as presenting a challenge to the negative stereotypes often held about people with intellectual disabilities.

Stakeholder – a person, group or organization that has a direct or indirect stake in an organization because it can affect or be affected by the organization's actions, objectives and policies.

Unified Sports – a programme delivered by Special Olympics which brings young people with and without intellectual disabilities together to train and compete in team sports.

OVERVIEW

The value of sport extends beyond its physical challenges, health benefits or competitive expression: it is known to hold an integral social value with the potential to bring together disparate groups, dispel stigmatizing myths and promote community cohesion. In 2007 the European Commission highlighted the importance of sport as a vehicle for generating a shared sense of belonging and participation and as a valuable tool in the development of social inclusion, particularly among marginalized groups. People with disabilities represent one such marginalized group. The Commission recommends that sports organizations should adapt their infrastructure to take account of the needs of people with disabilities. Primarily this is in terms of ensuring the accessibility of buildings, and providing training to volunteers and staff in sports clubs so that they are able to welcome people with disabilities (ec.europa.eu/sport/white-paper/index_en.htm?cs_mid=116).

This chapter will discuss a programme hosted by Special Olympics that aims to promote the inclusion of people with intellectual disabilities through sport, namely the Unified Sports programme. During 2009–2010, an evaluation of this programme, as a model for social inclusion, was carried out by the University of Ulster in Northern Ireland, in association with Special Olympics Europe-Eurasia. This chapter will draw on data (using quotations from participants) from this evaluation as it examines the organization of the Unified Sports programme, at both a structural and practical level. The chapter will also discuss the critical role of programme leaders in delivering the Unified concept. First, following a brief summary of the evaluation methods, and by way of context, this discussion will highlight the common forms of marginalization experienced by people with intellectual disabilities, and the known benefits to this group of participation in sport whilst it will also provide some background on the Special Olympics movement in a broader sense.

CASE STUDY: SPECIAL OLYMPICS UNIFIED SPORTS PROGRAMME

Two extracts follow. They are both statements made by young people who take part in the Special Olympics Unified Sports programme. The first is from a young person with intellectual disabilities (special needs) who plays a sport with team mates who do not have an intellectual disability – as the Unified Sports programme provides. The second is from a young man without intellectual disabilities who is also a member of such a team. These testimonies give insight into some of the personal growth, understanding and friendship gained through taking part in this programme, which is the subject of this chapter.

Statement 1

I am 18 years old and I go to special school in our city. I am educated to work with wood after I leave school. I am also a member of our SO [Special Olympics] club for 4 years now. I like to play football and basketball and I also like to ski. I have been working with our Unified football team. I learned through my friends, who were involved in SO athletics teams, of what a good thing it is to be a member of such a team. And when my coach came to our club to ask who wants to join their new Unified sports team, I said I wanted to go to try out. I wasn't that good at playing football at first but now I think I am better and I am very glad that I decided to join in.

I have improved my football skills very much, now I can run faster and I can control the ball much better and easier. I have also met lots of new and nice people and I have travelled a lot where I met people from other towns. And of course we have won lots of awards and lots of medals.

I think I have learned some new things in Unified Sports that help me in my life. I make friends more easily, I have met lots of people and I have learnt a few things from them. I go with my friends after training to town and I walk around with them. They show me some new comic books that I have not read before and they have given me some new music to share with me and through that I have learnt some new stuff. I started listening to rap music because one of my friends on the team introduced me to it and sent me a rap melody to my phone. Then I realized I like rap music and he sent me a few more things, so I learnt some new things that I was not aware of before, something that I would not have known that I would like.

When we meet after training, we go to town, sometimes we go for a drink or we go to eat something, some kind of hamburger or for an ice-cream or we just sit around the city square. There is a place in our city square where all the young people go to sit, so we go there. It is very interesting if you go there after training and we all have the same t-shirt, so people ask us if we are all a member of the same team, what do we do ... and we start to talk to them. A few times they have told me that they recognize me from the newspaper or from the TV and that is really cool for me.

Statement 2

I am glad that I am a part of this programme because it helps me to understand that people with intellectual disabilities are just like other people, but they only need help sometimes. I think that it is very important for people with disability to take part in sports, of course it is good for health, but it is good for them because they can connect with other people, communication is better, it helps them to get into society. Communication is very important, the most important. Many people in my country do not know of these activities and even if they know they do not understand … people just close eyes on this problem and don't want to talk about it. Before I became involved I knew that but I did not what to talk about it. I changed my mind when I came first and I saw how these people can gather and talk and they are able to take an active part in the life of society and community, and I understood it and I changed my mind. I think that people need to know more about these people and then maybe something will change. They would understand that people with problems are just like us, it's simple – they are just like me.

SUMMARY OF THE RESEARCH APPROACH USED IN THIS EVALUATION

The research project (into the impact of the Unified concept) ran for 15 months and was a qualitative study gathering data principally through interview and life – story work with a range of stakeholders – young Special Olympics athletes and non-disabled partners aged 12–25 years, coaches, parents and representatives of the local communities in which the clubs were located.

Following pilot work in the UK, the research team worked across five countries within the Special Olympics Europe-Eurasia region, namely Serbia, Poland, Ukraine, Germany and Hungary, with fieldwork taking place with the various stakeholders in each of these countries. Participants numbered over 220 individuals in total. The work was supported by partnerships developed with local university personnel and with Special Olympics programme staff in each of the participating countries. Training and/or competition events were organized in each country as a backdrop to data collection, with representatives of each of the stakeholder groups attending the events. Data were collected in local languages and later translated, transcribed and analysed. Reports on the project findings and the methods used can be found on the website, www.science.ulster.ac.uk/unifiedsports, where much more information on Special Olympics activities within the Europe-Eurasia region can be found.

CHALLENGES FROM THE MARGINS

Lives lived through the lens of social discrimination, exclusion and marginalization continue to be a common experience of many people with intellectual disabilities. Whilst our postmodern world is familiar with marginalized groups taking direct action to unseat discrimination and provoke changes in attitudes and practices, challenges from or on behalf of people with intellectual disabilities lag far behind those of other excluded groups. It follows that the routine inclusion of people with intellectual disabilities in their local communities and within wider society remains some way off in many countries.

A vision of social inclusion is contained in various Rights Statements that the United Nations has promoted for people with disabilities, such as the recent Convention (2006), which has the aim of ensuring: 'the full and equal enjoyment of all human rights and fundamental freedoms by all persons with disabilities, and to promote respect for their inherent dignity'.

However, for people with an intellectual disability the rhetoric of rights often fails to reflect their lived experiences. The reasons underlying their marginalization are multifaceted (Emerson *et al.* 2008). Many people with intellectual disabilities are born into poverty and because of their disabilities they are perceived to have limited productive capacity. Commonly they and their families have little economic power and are unlikely to be active decision-makers within communities so they have little political power. Moreover the stigma associated with their disability has often resulted in their active exclusion from society (O'Toole and McConkey 1995; Akrami *et al.* 2006).

Yazbeck *et al.* (2004) report how social policy internationally is broadly intended to support the integration, inclusion and acceptance of people with intellectual disabilities into mainstream society (United Nations 1975, 1993; International Association for the Scientific Study of Intellectual Disabilities 2001), engendering a community where people with intellectual disabilities are 'able and allowed to be themselves among others' (Nirje 1985: 67). A rights-based agenda arguing that people should be defined by way of their common humanity rather than their disparate abilities informs a growing movement of advocates and self-advocates for the inclusion of people with intellectual disabilities (Wolfensberger 2000; Parmenter 2001). Nevertheless, attitudes towards this diverse group, which have been the subject of much academic scrutiny internationally, continue, to a significant degree, in a negative vein (Novak 1993; Gething 1994; Yazbeck *et al.* 2004;). Siperstein *et al.* (2003) conducted an international study across nine countries, drawn from five continental regions, of the general public's attitudes towards people with intellectual disabilities. The overall findings suggested an underappreciation of the potential abilities of people with intellectual disabilities with consequent low expectations of achievement, although they do need to be understood within their prevailing social and cultural contexts. A prevailing attitude towards the segregation of people with intellectual disabilities in community, housing and educational settings was also found. The family was thought to be the most appropriate place for people with intellectual disabilities to live and a lack of resources and services was seen as an obstacle to inclusion. Moreover the attitude of others was also regarded as a barrier to inclusion.

SPORT AND INTELLECTUAL DISABILITY

There are a range of organizations which focus on athletes with disabilities. Notably, on the international stage, the Paralympics organization provides high-level competition for elite athletes with, in the main, physical disabilities. Additionally, on a national and local level, inclusive sporting activities for people with physical disabilities are to be found, and whilst these do not provide a vital function, neither they nor mainstream sports clubs typically include people with intellectual disabilities. Nonetheless, whilst the research base is limited and sample size is often small, it is reported that, just as in the wider population, people with intellectual disabilities gain a range of benefits through participating in sport and recreational activities in terms of increased community integration, improved quality of life, greater sense of satisfaction and well-being, the development of friendships as well as enhanced social skills (Valdee 2002; Cummins and Lau 2003; King *et al.* 2003; Duvdevany and Arar 2004; Orsmond *et al.* 2004;). However, the benefits are offset by the limited opportunity for many persons to take part in sporting activities (Abells *et al.* 2008). Where there are examples of the participation of young people with intellectual disabilities in sport, the reported personal outcomes are largely positive, for example relieving tensions, and building and maintaining relationships with family and friends as well as increasing self-esteem and enhanced physical health and fitness, opportunities for learning, skill development, risk-taking, reducing the risk of illness, and helping to build and maintain social relationships and networks (Dattilo *et al.* 1996; Dattilo, 2002; Aitchison 2003; Pegg and Compton 2004; Stumbo and Pegg 2004).

Special Olympics

The Special Olympics movement was founded in 1968, with the First International Special Olympics Games held at Soldier Field in Chicago. It has grown from its origins as a backyard summer camp for around 50 young people with intellectual disabilities and a similar number of volunteers to a worldwide federation now providing sporting opportunities to over three million children and adults with intellectual disabilities in over 180 countries. The mission of Special Olympics is to provide year-round sports training and opportunities for competition for people with intellectual disabilities with the goal of providing opportunities to 'develop physical fitness, demonstrate courage, experience joy and participate in sharing gifts, skills and friendship with their families and other athletes' (www.specialolympics.org/mission. aspx). This is achieved through the provision of a wide range of Olympic sports, as well as adapted sports activities, delivered through local clubs within national programmes in participating countries. Special Olympics clubs are highly dependent on volunteer support, which comes in the form of coaching as well as administrative and organizational roles, and on local fundraising, to sustain the delivery of their programme. Competitions are organized on a local, national, regional and world level, with World Games (alternating between summer and winter games) held every two years.

Whilst Special Olympics is about sport, it is also about much more besides – that is, through sport Special Olympics aims to empower athletes, encourage healthy lifestyles, challenge stigma, promote inclusion and build communities. Therefore, this sporting organization also intends to be a movement for social change and one of the Special Olympics programmes which articulates this agenda clearly is Unified Sports.

The Special Olympics Youth Unified Sports programme

The Unified Sports programme brings together young people with and without intellectual disabilities to play on the same sports teams. This is an ever-expanding programme: recent figures gathered in 2010 account for 44,400 Unified players in the 57 countries of the Special Olympics Europe-Eurasia region alone, with 26,000 of them in the youth programme and aged between 12 and 25 years.

113

The Unified Sports programme's aims are broad. Whilst the development of sporting skills is a central goal, there are wider social aims which include encouraging friendship between players and so enabling participants with an intellectual disability to participate in their local community and to experience social inclusion. Unified teams train regularly together and engage in competition with other Unified teams at a local, national and international level within Special Olympics. Although available in other sports, Unified Sports is typically offered in team sports, commonly association football and basketball. The programme is not time-limited but ongoing, giving participants the opportunity to develop as players, as a team and potentially as friends.

One coach who participated in the evaluation articulated the meaning of the Unified concept:

> Look, the thing is in Unified Sports we love the sport but we also care about the people who are taking part. We think these sports activities, I mean being involved, can change things for people. We approach our training in a way that will encourage the young people to share in the experience with each other, to be a team, sure a team that can win but first to all be part of something that they care about. This of course influences how we go about things, how we talk to them and show them the game – the big game.
>
> (coach, Germany)

The role of the parent organization in supporting the Unified programme and promoting social inclusion

The Unified Sports programme, as described above, is one of many programmes hosted by Special Olympics. The role of the organization in the development and support of the programme is central to its implementation.

Culture of inclusion

The Special Olympics movement supports an ethos of the positive integration of people with intellectual disabilities into their wider communities. The organization expressly challenges discrimination and promotes empowerment, competence and acceptance through sport. The culture of the organization can be understood to provide a critical platform on which the concept of Unified Sports is based. For instance, coaches interviewed in the course of the evaluation link the culture of the organization and its practical articulation through Unified Sports:

> Special Olympics is the basis of where we can get good ideas and inspiration about inclusion and change. Through Unified Sports we can try to overcome some of the challenges that we have and integration can be much better through what we do in this project.
>
> (community representative, Serbia)

The longevity, reach and success of Special Olympics are shown to inspire confidence in the potential for individuals to make the Unified programme a reality:

At first I was nervous of this idea – whether it could work or not, and then my colleague told me that it was part of Special Olympics and I say that yes this can work so I would really give it a go in my school.

(coach, Poland)

Crucially the culture of inclusion can be seen to influence the approaches taken by programme leaders. In each country a national coordinator provides overall leadership for Special Olympics national programmes and locally, in Special Olympics clubs, there is reliance upon coaches who, typically voluntarily, work in a coaching and sports development role. Clubs are assisted by additional volunteers who variously work in administrative and other practical support roles. The positive approaches taken by these leaders translate into the active encouragement of inclusion and an attitude of equal treatment of all players whilst valuing each individual for his or her contribution to the team. As one coach stated:

The very interesting thing about this is that this project promotes everyone. As a coach this is what you work for. Everyone is a member of the team and you do not have to look on the team and see who is with and who is without intellectual disability, it is the team, the whole that counts.

(coach, Serbia)

Established position within the community

Unified Sports programmes are typically sited within existing and established Special Olympics clubs either in schools or as independent local community organizations. The programmes benefit from the profile that the clubs have already established in their local communities and regions. The benefits can have a tangible impact in terms of integration and inclusion as the leaders and coaches are able to tap into sources of support and networks that enable the development of the project within their area. The passage of time influences attitudes towards participation and the support the club receives from parents is well described by this participating coach:

In the beginning it was more difficult to convince people that this [Unified Sports] was a good idea. In general – you have to explain to parents about what you are asking of their children, both athletes and partners, because both of them are scared … parents of athletes worry that their child would not be able to achieve as good as the partners are, and parents of partners, they don't want their kids to be on a team that might not be able to offer their child to develop to their full potential as a sports person. Today it is different. It is all in the spirit of Special Olympics. Now parents come, they come with their friends, they come to cheer and they often ask if they can volunteer at events. It is getting better all the time.

(coach, Serbia).

A further example can be found in the links with mainstream schools, which often predate the establishment of the Unified Sports programme. For instance, they may support the

115

programme through the use of school sports pitches for training and competitions, a consequence of which is the increased visibility of athletes in their local community through their regular visits to train at mainstream school premises. Further, partnerships with schools may encourage mainstream sports teachers to become Unified Sports coaches.

Another example is that of a headteacher in a special school who has made a commitment to keep his school building open every day of the year for young people to use as a recreation facility, as he had witnessed the value of sport in the lives of the young people at his school. Moreover, contacts with the local community can lead to the establishment of links with a regional mainstream sporting organization:

> Unified Sports is a very good, important and noble project because it helps people with intellectual disabilities become more socially included and to become involved in different spheres of society through sports. Because of this when the Special Olympics programme asked me to contribute of course I agreed. We started the collaboration with this organization and we tried to help them out as much as possible. We provided them with equipment, sports facilities. There is no doubt that we want to continue to collaborate with this organization.
>
> (community representative,[1] Ukraine)

Unified Sports programmes were therefore found to benefit through being part of an established network of support and with an existing profile within the community.

Enduring programme

Many of the Unified Sports programmes that took part in the evaluation had been operating for several years and many participants, particularly athletes, had played on the team since its inception. Unified programmes are not time-limited, that is, they are not, for example, a 6-week or 6-month programme, but they are ongoing with no specified end date. This enables participants to get to know one another and gradually break down the preconceptions about each other which may have previously divided them. In the evaluation study it was found that, although partners tend to stay in the team for a shorter period than athletes, they do frequently remain for over 2 years and their departure from the team is commonly linked to changes in their lives such as leaving school or going to university. Many partners maintain contact with the club after their departure. Coaches also tend to remain within the club and continue coaching their teams over extended periods of time.

Many coaches with whom the research team spoke had been responsible for bringing the Unified teams together and had then continued as their coaches. There was a strong commitment to the programme and to the players.

> These activities bring about changes for these kids. I have seen very big changes in them in their game, their physique and how they act with others. This is something that I want to continue, I have a strong commitment to these kids.
>
> (coach, Hungary)

The enduring nature of the programme is important in creating social inclusion. It provides for the ongoing building of relationships based on mutual trust and shared values. Because of the enduring nature of this programme strong ties were developed between team members. From these, participation in networks within the community were also built.

Coaches and players – constructing a Unified team

Once a national Special Olympics programme has opted to initiate Unified Sports as part of its repertoire of sporting activities, it is often coaches, attached to local clubs, who are called upon to bring teams together. Recruiting players to join teams is an initial activity. In contrast, players with intellectual disabilities, who are known as 'athletes', are usually already members of the local Special Olympics club. Those with milder intellectual disabilities and a relatively high level of sporting ability are very often the ones who are asked whether they might like to take part in Unified teams. Team mates without intellectual disabilities, known as 'partners', are often recruited from local high schools. Typically the links are established with mainstream schools, or existing links are expanded, and sports educators from mainstream and special schools work together to attract non-disabled players to Unified teams. This activity is considered critical to the success of teams. It is important that partners are open to playing with people with intellectual disabilities, that they are able to behave without prejudice, are willing to adapt to new experiences but are also not intent on helping their team mates with disabilities, and are willing to share the game and to play together. Some coaches described the ideal attributes of partners:

> Partners should be a particular personality, not a champion who has to be first but someone who will cooperate and who will put another before themselves.
>
> (coach, Hungary)

Because as another coach described it:

> If the partner is too ambitious it will be hard for them to play on a Unified team.
>
> (coach, Germany)

For many of the partner players, taking part in Unified Sports is their chance to train and compete in a team sport. They may not have been picked to play on their school team and they may not be a star player, so becoming a member of a Unified team is not a charitable act, but a valued opportunity for them to enjoy and develop their sport.

Once recruited, coaches aim to match players with and without intellectual disabilities in terms of their skill level to form a cohesive team. This skill-matching across the two sets of players is critical to the Unified concept. It promotes the idea of a level playing field, so that athletes and partners can train and improve together without a bold distinction in terms of ability between players, thus encouraging team unity and cohesion.

117

TEAM ACTIVITIES

Training

Teams meet regularly, often on a weekly basis, for training. Training of course focuses on the technique, rules and practice of the particular sport, as well as on individual fitness of players; however, it also has a strong emphasis on team building. This is more complex and delicate than it might be in typical team sport coaching, as there is an initial need to assist players to break down the myths each group has constructed of the other. Often those with an intellectual disability will have absorbed the negative attitudes directed towards them and will therefore feel at a disadvantage to the young partners who may be considered to be previously unattainable as friends. Likewise, those without an intellectual disability will be taking the first steps in challenging the negative attitudes, which commonly prevail, to varying degrees, in their communities. The bridge to bringing together these two groups is sport. A shared interest in their chosen sport and a desire to play and compete together becomes the vehicle through which mutual understanding and respect take their first tentative steps.

Competition

Beyond the weekly meetings teams are usually involved in competition on a regular basis. These might be at a local level between Special Olympics Unified teams in neighbouring areas, or at a regional level within their country. National Special Olympics programmes typically hold annual games, and Unified teams are increasingly represented at such events. Additionally there are international Special Olympics competitions, held within Special Olympics regions, or every four years World Summer Games bring together national teams from around the world and Unified squads represent their countries at these events.

These comparatively unusual opportunities to travel and compete provide an additional draw, which encourages participants to get involved. This is particularly the case with partners and the chance to travel within their country, or even internationally, raises the profile for Unified Sports amongst the partners and critically amongst their peers. These young people are not simply playing on a team with the 'disabled guys from the Special School', they are involved in a team sport where they have regular training and the chance to compete, to travel and possibly to represent their country at international competitions. This is something that all participants are proud to be a part of and they closely guard their place on the team so as to maintain their involvement through regular attendance and close attention to what is expected of them. That these opportunities are available through becoming involved with an organization that provides sports programmes primarily for people with intellectual disabilities challenges the very perception of intellectual disability. In this way Unified Sports adds value to the notion of intellectual disability and subverts some of the stigma which is typically found.

Non-sporting activities

Many of the young people and coaches who took part in the evaluation of Unified Sports described the informal activities that young people engage in outside of their sporting engagement. These are based on the regular association of players and the emerging friendships between players, which span the initial separateness of those with and without intellectual disabilities. Young people begin to spend time together doing activities they enjoy. This is a natural consequence of their getting to know one another and their shared interest in sport. Unified Sports offers a comparatively neutral space for young people to come together. Their focus is less on what distinguishes them from each other and more on the fun and enjoyment they derive from the games, the training associated with being a member of a team and the sense of camaraderie and friendship they get from being with likeminded people. This is a very important outcome of the Unified Sports programme in terms of promoting social inclusion. Further discussion of it is beyond the scope of this chapter; however it is discussed extensively in the project report available on the project website (www.science. ulster.ac.uk/unifiedsports).

The role of Unified coaches and their contribution to building inclusivity

The core drivers of Unified Sports in each country are the programme national coordinators assisted by the sports directors. However, at the frontline, the role of coaches both provides the impetus to teams and steers the course of their development. Coaches' roles were found to be complex and multifaceted, as one coach confirmed:

> In a Unified team the coach is the main person who has to connect all the blocks of the team.
>
> (coach, Serbia)

As one would expect, the coaches' role included the usual work involved in training and coaching players in the sport. Additionally they are responsible for the selection of players and matching athlete and partner skills to create a team based on the Unified model. However, there were additional tasks which result from the aims and nature of the Unified project and which are expanded on here, as these are probably crucial to producing teams that are truly unified.

The coaches have to make clear the concept of Unified Sports and encourage the development of a team of players who are not divided by labels or supposed differences, but are united in purpose and equal as team members:

> The idea is that we are all the same, that there are no differences between us and it is the motto under which we work.
>
> (coach, Serbia)

Another coach explained this:

> The coach has several main tasks, to teach and then to create the conditions in which a person with intellectual disabilities can feel equal rights to other people without problems.
>
> (coach, Ukraine)

Support beyond sport: mentoring

Coaches also commonly emphasized that they needed to know all players on the team and to assess their strengths and needs and be able to offer support that may be beyond what is commonly expected from a sports coach:

> It is important to really know your team, all of them as individuals, because they often need some help with something that is not a sports problem but maybe something at school or at home. We include them and they have belief in us – it is part of what we do as Unified coaches.
>
> (coach, Hungary)

Another stated:

> Also you realize that the role of the coach, as well as a sports person, should be someone that athletes and partners can come to talk to if they have a problem and that the coach has to know each one of them.
>
> (coach, Serbia)

Role model

A further aspect of the role described by coaches was that of a role model to young people in the team. This was in relation to the development of positive relations within the team. Coaches were aware of the initial uncertainty felt by many players on first meeting one another, given that these were young people from two groups in society who previously had little or no contact with one another, but who had been exposed to the social myths pertaining to people with intellectual disabilities.

> I treat everybody equally right from the start, it is important for players and athletes to see that they are the same in the team. I am also careful to talk to them in a pleasant way, and to joke with them. I do not give athletes special treatment and I do not give partners special treatment and they all see this and it affects how they treat each other, they too are willing to behave as an group of equals. In a Unified team we are all the same.
>
> (coach, Ukraine)

Encouraging relationships within the team

Some coaches also highlighted a further aspect of their work with young people on the Unified teams, which was to 'initiate bonds between partners and athletes' (coach, Germany).

120

Another coach described this part of the work in more detail:

> We in the club push people together to do different sports activities, and we want them to hang around together after school [...] we organize for different sports activities, rafting, rowing, swimming, and we have lots of non-sports activities to connect people and everyone is invited and welcome.
>
> (coach, Serbia)

This aspect of the work was not mentioned by all coaches as a part of the role; however, when it was mentioned it was supported by evidence of a greater degree of interaction between athletes and partners outside the playing field, as reported in the interviews conducted with them. It would seem that the approach of coaches in relation to motivating partners and athletes to form friendships, which extended beyond their training and competition, was one factor influencing the development of these relationships. As one coach stated:

> I know that friendships exist off the field between athletes and partners and I have to tell you that we in the club push people together to do different activities, not sports activities, and we want them to hang around together after school, go to dances, go to discos, go to towns, and we also organize for nature walks, and we invite everyone to participate in this. So we have lots of different non-sports activities that connect people and this helps them to spend more time together.
>
> (coach, Serbia)

Coaches themselves also often described another aspect of their relationship with players on their Unified team as one of friendship. Coaches recognized that they needed to be able to adapt their role in response to varying situations and contexts in their work with players:

> Sometimes you are their trainer, but sometimes you are also responsible for them. It is the same when we travel, then we form a special bond together, which is something quite unique. So they see you as a coach and while we play they listen to your instructions, but after training or competition is over you somehow become a different person to them, you take a different role, you have to know what is going on with your team and your team members, if someone has a problem or if there are any questions or is there something they need to do, so I think through being a coach you become a friend.
>
> (coach, Serbia)

The evaluation gave a clear picture of the multifaceted role of coaches working with Unified Sports teams. Further it suggests that this complex role is of crucial importance in promoting the concept and reality of social inclusion for players with intellectual disabilities in sports. This is seen through their pedagogic approach to training, the function as a role model and mentor for athletes and partners and in consciously promoting the development of inclusion for athletes through both changes in attitude and encouraging the active involvement of athletes and partners outside the playing field. The coaches in large part therefore were found to provide the conditions upon which both the sporting involvement and the wider social outcomes of developing inclusion through participation in Unified Sports are founded.

KEY THEMES

The challenge

It is worth emphasizing that the idea of young people with and without intellectual disabilities coming together in a sports team (or indeed other setting) is, in many instances, in many parts of the world, a new and challenging one. Young people with intellectual disabilities often live separate lives to their non-disabled peers in the mainstream of society. Many attend special schools whilst some live in institutions distinct from community life. Stigma continues around the idea of intellectual disability and this is perpetuated by a lack of direct knowledge of or association with people who have an intellectual disability. Negative attitudes and fear born of imagined stereotypes often form barriers to young people from mainstream society when meeting their peers who have an intellectual disability. This is the challenge met by Unified Sports. It is one that requires a willingness to take a chance and be open to the possibilities that may be enabled through the shared experience of team sport.

The response

In response to the significant challenges posed by negative attitudes and historical practices, Unified Sports is in essence a fairly simple idea, providing, as it does, a forum for young people with intellectual disabilities to connect with their wider community and meet with other young people around a shared interest in sports. However, in its operation the programme works through a complex dynamic of connections at three levels – that of the people participating in the programme, the organization underlying it and the interaction with local community. These three are interactive and mutually transforming concepts.

This chapter has focused on the organization of Unified Sports both at a structural and at a personnel level. The wider movement of Special Olympics provides a substantial platform, both philosophically and practically, from which to launch this programme and the movement's established position in many communities provides credibility to the idea, which in turn encourages individuals to try something new. Likewise the longevity of the Special Olympics movement means that the programme can also enjoy an enduring scope and not be limited by time.

Coaches play a complex and critical role and are central to the delivery of the programme. The vast majority of Special Olympics and Unified coaches work on a voluntary basis; additionally, many are highly qualified in the field of sports coaching. The commitment then to the task of not only providing coaching, but also generating belief in change through sport is both considerable and laudable. The importance of the leadership provided by coaches cannot be underestimated.

The evaluation, which has formed the basis of this chapter, concluded that in many ways Unified Sports poses a challenge to the social exclusion of people with intellectual disabilities from their communities. Young athletes who participated tend to be more visible in their locality, they come to be valued for their achievements within the team and crucially they make friends with other young people who themselves tend to enjoy the freedoms of inclusion. The shared experiences on the sport field appear for many to extend into the social world beyond sports and to enable young people to have access to more typical life experiences.

Limitations of the programme

There are some internal challenges and limitations to the Unified programme. Firstly, at present it is mainly those with mild/moderate intellectual disabilities who are able to take part in the activities. This is due to the skill matching, which is a central component of the programme and enables a relatively level playing field for participants. How this could be achieved for people with more complex disabilities is a challenge to the Unified idea.

There are also a limited number of sports at present which provide Unified opportunities for young people with intellectual disabilities, particularly females. However, it is anticipated that in time there may be an augmented list of sports available, thus providing greater choice and enabling more people to take part.

An ongoing challenge to Unified programmes (and indeed Special Olympics clubs) is the recruitment and training of qualified and committed coaches. Many coaches come from special educational or sporting backgrounds; however with an expanding programme the need for additional coaches is an ever-present reality. Ongoing initiatives to recruit, train and ultimately retain Unified coaches must be a central focus in order to continue to deliver this programme in the time ahead.

On a practical level, financial challenges are a potential constraint. Coaches commonly act in a voluntary capacity and encouraging people to take on this work without financial remuneration may provide an additional obstacle in the time to come. Moreover, the costs of running the programme, of travel to competition and the purchase of equipment present a need for ongoing fundraising by Special Olympics clubs.

In terms of continuity within clubs, it is apparent that Unified partners are more likely than athletes to leave the Unified team after 1 or 2 years as their circumstances change, whereas athletes remain for much longer. The opportunities for partners to go to university, travel and embark on intimate relationships are not readily available to athletes. This is difficult as it re-emphasizes the different opportunities available to athletes, despite the work within Unified Sports to erase them. It means too that athletes do not easily progress, but may remain caught in an activity, which, although rewarding, has no progression. One approach is the development of adult Unified teams and there are some growing opportunities for athletes to progress on to coaching roles, although these remain limited in reality.

SUMMARY

Ignorance of, or the casual acceptance of, stigma or social discrimination is subject to increasing challenge by those who experience such marginalization, as well as by their advocates and supporters. Challenges are multifaceted and are to be found at governmental, policy as well as at grassroots levels. Sport is one vehicle through which changed attitudes and practices are promoted and a strong example of this is found in the Special Olympics Unified Sports programme.

Regular and structured contact between people with and without intellectual disabilities, enabled through training and competing in team sports within the Unified programme, has been found to promote understanding, dispel stigmatizing myths and develop a range of social and sporting skills. Through this programme people with intellectual disabilities become valued because of their abilities rather than their supposed inabilities. They experience this through being respected team members and the resultant growth of self-esteem and confidence impacts on improved communication and social skills. Personal fitness and well-being as well as, critically, the development of friendships provide further important benefits. The personal growth, confidence and ease in contact with others are tools that empower young people with intellectual disabilities to be active participants in the transactional relationship involved in meaningful inclusion. That is, young people may actively experience, contribute to and generate their own inclusion as well as take up opportunities developed through the efforts of others on their behalf.

This valuable programme is dependent on the leadership provided by coaches, who largely work on a voluntary basis. Their role as sports instructors as well as mentors and role models is critical to the success of the programme. The programme requires a strong philosophical basis, which promotes inclusion and equality, and able coaches' work to translate these ideas into their practical application within Unified teams.

To further the advantages found within the Unified Sports model there is the potential that mainstream clubs could adopt a similar approach so as to encourage the greater inclusion of people with intellectual disabilities in their activities. On a practical level this could involve forging links with special schools or encouraging shared learning between sports coaches and physical educators in special schools. Another strategy could be through establishing links between Special Olympics clubs and mainstream sports clubs, even to the extent of shared facilities and coaching expertise. A disability champion within mainstream clubs would provide advice and likely encourage activities such as additional training around disability for coaches, or the institution of a proactive recruitment strategy within marginalized populations, such as people with intellectual disabilities, amongst others.

Whilst the benefits of this programme are clear, it is vital to note that inclusion in sport alone is insufficient to promote the kind of social change sought by people with intellectual disabilities and their advocates. Further initiatives to promote inclusion and opportunities for people to experience inclusion are needed through the range of social and community places, for example, schools, places of employment and housing options are all sites wherein inclusion and the growth of equality can be located. Unified Sports cannot alone solve the challenges faced daily by this marginalized population; it is however a step in the right direction or, in the words of one young participant: 'Unified gives us a chance'.

NOTE

1   In each participating country, in addition to players – athletes (with disabilities) and partners (without dis-
    abilities), coaches and parents, we included in our sample 'community representatives'. These were members
    of the local community who in their role as, for example, local government representatives, social workers,
    teachers or members of sporting organizations, could comment on the impact of Unified Sports in relation to
    encouraging the social inclusion of people with intellectual disabilities more widely within the community.

REVIEW QUESTIONS

1   What are the processes within inclusive sports programmes that can challenge stigma and
    social marginalization of minority groups?
2   What are coaches' roles in providing a platform for the growth of social inclusion through
    the Unified programme?
3   How is Unified Sports supported by the parent organization Special Olympics?

FURTHER READING

Burnett, C. (2006). "Building Social Capital Through an Active Community Club." *International
    Review for the Sociology of Sport* 41: 283–294.
Coleman, J. (1998). "Social Capital in the Creation of Human Capital." *American Journal of
    Sociology* 94: 95–120.
Grant, G., Ramcharan, P., Flynn, M. and Richardson, M. (eds) (2010). *Learning Disability: A life
    cycle approach,* 2nd edn. Maidenhead: Open University Press.
McConkey, R., Dunne, J. and Blitz, N. (2009). *Shared Lives: Building relationships and community
    with people who have intellectual disabilities.* Amsterdam: Sense Publishers.
Norins, J., Harada, C. and Brecklinghaus, S. (2007). *Inclusion of Young People with Intellec-
    tual Disabilities in Europe Through Special Olympics Unified Sports.* Washington, DC: Special
    Olympics Internaitonal.

WEBSITES

Special Olympics:
    www.specialolympics.org
University of Ulster Special Olympics – Unified Sports evaluation:
    www.science.ulster.ac.uk/unifiedsports

REFERENCES

Abells, D., Burbidge, J. and Minnes, P. (2008). "Involvement of Adolescents With Intellectual Dis-
    abilities in Social and Recreational Activities." *Journal of Developmental Disabilities* 14(2):
    88–94.

125

Aitchison, C. (2003). "From Leisure and Disability to Disability Leisure: Developing Data, Definitions and Discourses." *Disability and Society* 18: 955–969.

Akrami, N., Ekehammar, B., Claesson, M. and Sonnander, K. (2006). "Classical and Modern Prejudice: Attitudes Towards People with Intellectual Disabilities." *Research in Developmental Disabilities* 27: 605–617.

Cummins, R.A. and Lau, L.D. (2003). "Community Integration or Community Exposure? A Review and Discussion in Relation to People with Intellectual Disability." *Journal of Applied Research in Intellectual Disabilities* 16: 145–157.

Dattilo, J. (2002) *Inclusive Leisure Services,* 2nd edn. State College, PA: Venture.

Dattilo, J., Hoge, G. and Malley, S.M. (1996). "Interviewing People with Mental Retardation: Validity and Reliability Strategies." *Therapeutic Recreation Journal* 30: 163–178.

Duvdevany, I. and Arar, E. (2004). "Leisure Activities, Friendships, and Quality of Life of Persons with Intellectual Disability: Foster Homes vs. Community Residential Settings." *International Journal of Rehabilitation Research* 27(4): 289–296.

Emerson, E., McConkey, R., Walsh, P.N. and Felce, D. (2008). "Editorial: Intellectual Disability in a Global Context." *Journal of Policy and Practice in Intellectual Disability* 5(2): 79–80.

European Commission (2007). *White Paper on Sport: the Societal Role of Sport.* Brussels: European Commission.

Gething, L. (1994). "The Interaction with Disabled Persons Scale." *Journal of Social Behaviour and Personality* 9: 23–42.

International Association for the Scientific Study of Intellectual Disabilities. (2001). *The Edinburgh Principles.* Clifton Park, NY: International Association for the Scientific Study of Intellectual Disabilities.

King, G., Law, M., King, S., Rosenbaum, P., Kertoy, M.K. and Young, N.L. (2003). "A Conceptual Model of the Factors Affecting the Recreation and Leisure Participation of Children with Disabilities." *Physical and Occupational Therapy in Pediatrics* 23(1): 63–90.

Nirje, B. (1985). "The Basis and Logic of the Normalization Principle." *Australian and New Zealand Journal of Developmental Disabilities* 11: 65–68.

Novak, A. (1993). *Friendships and Community Connections Between People with and Without Developmental Disabilities.* Baltimore: Brookes.

O'Toole, B. and McConkey, R. (1995). *Innovations in Developing Countries for People with Intellectual Disabilities.* Chorley, Lancs: Lisieux Hall Publications.

Orsmond, G.I., Krauss, M.W. and Seltzer, M.M. (2004). "Peer Relationships and Social and Recreational Activities among Adolescents and Adults with Autism." *Journal of Autism and Developmental Disabilities* 343: 245–256.

Parmenter, T. (2001). "Intellectual Disabilities – Quo Vadis," in: Albrecht, G., Seelman, K. and Bury, M. (eds) *Handbook of Disability.* London: Sage, pp. 267–296.

Pegg, S. and Compton, D. (2004). "Creating Opportunities and Insuring Access to Leisure and Recreation Services Through Inclusion in the Global Community." *Leisure/Losir* 1–2: 5–26.

Siperstein, G.N., Norins, J., Corbin, S. and Shriver, T. (2003). *Multinational Study of Attitudes towards Individuals with Intellectual Disabilities, General Findings and Calls to Action.* Washington, DC: Special Olympics International.

Stumbo, N. and Pegg, S. (2004). "Choices and Challenges: Physical Activity and People with Disabilities." *Annals of Leisure Research* 7(2): 104–128.

United Nations. (1975). *Declaration on the Rights of People with Disability.* New York: United Nations.

United Nations. (1993). *The Standard Rules on the Equalization of Opportunities for Persons with Disabilities.* New York: United Nations.

United Nations. (2006). *Convention on the Rights of Peoples with Disabilities.* New York: United Nations.

Wolfensberger, W. (2000). "A Brief Overview of the Principles of Social Role Valorization." *Mental Retardation* 38: 105–124.

World Health Organization (WHO) Definition: intellectual disability. http://www.euro.who.int/en/what-we-do/health-topics/noncommunicable-diseases/mental-health/news2/news/2010/15/childrens-right-to-family-life/definition-intellectual-disability (accessed May 2011).

Yazbeck, M., McVilly, K. and Parmenter, T.R. (2004). "Attitudes Toward People with Intellectual Disabilities." *Journal of Disability Policy Studies* 15(2): 97–111.

Chapter 8

Pain and Injury in Sporting Cultures of Risk

Lara Killick, Todd Davenport and Jodi Baker

TOPICS

Sports pain and injury • Sporting cultures of risk • Corporate responsibility and health versus performance tensions

OBJECTIVES

By the end of this chapter you will be able to:

- Evaluate the case for sporting pain and injury as a management concern;
- Describe the characteristics of sporting cultures of risk;
- Appraise the role of sports managers in the production of sporting cultures of risk;
- Identify and evaluate the core ethical issues associated with the organizational management of sporting pain and injury.

KEY TERMS

Corporate responsibility – the degree to which corporations are responsible for the intended and unintended consequences of their operational practices.

Cultures of risk – a sociohistorical and cultural milieu in which the glorification of risk, normalization of pain and rationalization of playing hurt are reinforced through embodied practices, mediated messages and the network of people and activity spaces involved in the production of sport.

Health versus performance outcomes – the tension between clinical practices that promote the optimal health of the athletes and those that promote favourable performance outcomes (e.g. a winning result).

> **Sports injury** – a process which prevents the body from carrying out the functions necessary to maintain an athletic, embodied identity. The process of becoming, being and recovering from injury contains physical, emotional, social, biological, cultural, historical and existential dimensions.

OVERVIEW

Whilst the medical management of sporting pain and injury has received academic attention (Safai 2004; Walk 2004; Malcolm 2006; Waddington 2006), organizational involvement in this dimension of sporting performances has received far less consideration. However, as this chapter will explore, the organizational structure and personnel of sports worlds have an important role to play in the management of the physical consequences of sporting performance. Blending sociological theory and the insights of sports medicine practitioners, this chapter will examine some of the key issues that arise when we think socioculturally about sporting pain and injury. Drawing attention to the distinct tensions facing sports management personnel in elite achievement sport, this chapter further offers two case studies and associated application questions to help the reader better explore the issues at hand. Whilst the emphasis of this chapter is on elite achievement sport, research suggests that the issues raised here exist, to varying degrees, across all aspects of the participation spectrum (Pike 2000; Charlesworth and Young 2004; Howe 2004; Killick 2009). Thus, the discussion points raised by this chapter are of interest to sports management personnel engaged in all forms of sports participation, from recreational youth sport right up to international competition.

This chapter will first present the case for sporting pain and injury as a management concern before mapping out what it means to think socioculturally about this dimension of sports performance. In so doing, it will explore what researchers have termed a sporting 'culture of risk' and examine some of the implications of this distinct cultural space for sports management personnel (Nixon 1994: 79). Particular attention will be paid to the tension between health and performance outcomes in elite sport and the corporate responsibility of franchises and sports teams when injuries occur to professional athletes. But first, why should sports managers be concerned with issues of pain and injury in sport?

CASE STUDY: THE $100 MILLION ATHLETE: EXAMINING THE COST OF TIGER WOODS' INJURIES

Tiger Woods originally damaged the anterior cruciate ligament (ACL) in his left knee during the 2007 season, ironically whilst jogging near his home following a tournament. Woods elected against surgical repair of the ligament at that time. Instead, he continued to train and compete, winning five of the six events he subsequently entered. Two days after the US Masters' tournament held in April 2008, Woods underwent arthroscopic meniscectomy to address potential cartilage damage in his knee. Two months later, he competed in the 108th US Open golf tournament. Playing in visible pain and often using a golf club as a makeshift walking stick, Woods won the tournament in what is widely considered to have been amongst the most exciting golf tournaments in the history of the game. After the competition, Woods was revealed to have sustained an ACL tear, as well as tibial plateau stress fractures associated with the intensive training necessary to compete at elite-level golf. Woods provided a press release that described his injury and the rationale for its handling:

> I know much was made of my knee throughout the last week, and it was important to me that I disclose my condition publicly at an appropriate time. I wanted to be very respectful of the US GA [US Golf Association] and their incredibly hard work and make sure the focus was on the US Open. Now, it is clear that the right thing to do is listen to my doctors, follow through with this surgery and focus my attention on rehabilitating my knee.

One possible explanation for Woods' decision to delay necessary treatment may have included the fact that typical accelerated rehabilitation programmes after uncomplicated ACL reconstruction require between 6 and 8 months out of competitive sport. This is a prolonged period for both athletes and sporting organizations to sustain the economic impact of a star athlete's absence.

One risk of Woods' absence might be a potential reversal of interest in golf, particularly amongst youth and minority golfers, who are important to the ongoing growth of the sport (Branch 2000). In addition, Woods' participation in tournaments is associated with increased television viewership and, more desirable still, and therefore more expensive, opportunities for advertising. Beginning in 1997, higher viewing figures were recorded for major tournaments won by Woods (Anonymous 2005). Conversely, television viewership declined by 46% during Woods' injury-induced absence (Nielsen Company 2009). This data suggests an economic motivation for delaying necessary treatment. However, in the long term, delayed treatment may lead to a worsening injury that can jeopardize the athlete's prognosis. In turn, this delayed prognosis can result in longer-term economic harm to sports organizations.

SPORTING PAIN AND INJURY AS A MANAGEMENT CONCERN

Often bypassed as a distinctly medical issue, incidences of sporting pain and injury should be considered and understood by management personnel as an integral part of their occupational responsibilities. With a growth in domestic and international competition, developments in technology and training practices and the increased demands placed on athletes to produce high-quality performances, the injury rates associated with elite sport have experienced a concurrent increase (White 2004). Injury-induced absences from games are commonplace and a quick search of teams' webpages reveals several 'injury lists' containing the names, details and projected return date of injured players in a range of sports. This growing prevalence of sports injuries should be a concern to sports management personnel for several reasons, including, but not limited to, the potential detrimental effect these injuries may carry for the performance of the team, the psychological health of the players and the financial health of the organization as a whole.

Tolpin and Bentkover (1986) identify both direct and indirect costs associated with sports injuries. The indirect costs of sports injuries, whilst often traumatic and long-lasting, are notoriously difficult to measure quantitatively. Similarly, there is a dearth of longitu-dinal data on the direct costs of sports injuries, in part due to the powerful rhetoric sur-rounding the perceived health benefits of sports participation. Indeed, White (2004: 310) acknowledges that 'epidemiological information on the costs of sport ... is inconsistent, far from complete and merits further attention'. However, in mapping out the 'injury toll' of recreational and elite sport across the globe, he presents some alarming data on the size and scope of the economic dimension of sports injury (White 2004: 312). Data collected in Canada in 1998/1999 estimated the costs of sports injuries at C$428 million, of which C$155 million was borne by the taxpayer in direct medical costs (White 2004). Similarly, it has been reported that sports injuries cost the USA an estimated $217 billon a year and result in 147 million lost workdays per annum (White 2004). The UK sports market exhibits corresponding trends, with the National Sports Medicine Institute estimating the annual cost of sports injuries exceeding £500 million (Cole 1995). In 1994, eight million working days were reportedly lost due to sports injuries, at a cost of £405 million to the British economy (Goodbody 1995).

Definition

Direct costs: those expenditures paid for by the injured party, his or her family and/or third-part reimbursement agencies. For example, cost of treatment, physicians, drugs, medical supplies, physical therapy and follow-up care.

Indirect costs: costs that are not directly related to the care of the injury but are incurred as a result of the injury. For example, loss of earnings, increased presence of illness or dis-ease, disruption to identities, decreased quality of life and increased mortality.

Furthermore, the network of people required to manage incidences of sporting pain and injury is growing in size and, subsequently, attracting a larger wage bill. It is now commonplace for professional teams to employ a full-time club doctor, strength and con-ditioning coaches and a team of physiotherapists[1]. However, the impact of injuries on sports teams extends beyond the economic burden felt by athletes, their families and the organization. Sociocultural research describes injuries as a 'fatal flaw' to athletes' sense of self (Sparkes 1996: 463) and testimonies of former athletes frequently point to the disruptive effect injuries have on the psychological strength and unity of teams. Indeed, the recent suicide of Denver Broncos' wide receiver Kenny McKinley has been linked with his inability to cope with his knee injury and subsequent surgery (Anonymous 2010). It is with a sociocultural approach that this chapter is concerned. So what does it mean to think socioculturally about sports injuries? And why should sports management personnel adopt this approach?

THINKING SOCIOCULTURALLY ABOUT SPORTING PAIN AND INJURY

Moving towards a more sociocultural understanding of sporting pain and its management requires a reorientation of thinking about what it means to be 'in pain' or 'injured'. This proc-ess necessitates a shift away from physiology and perception of pain by individuals towards a broader understanding of how perspectives of pain experiences among members of a sport organization result in the formation of pain networks. In turn, enhanced understanding of pain networks within a sport organization can inform effective sport management practices that balance the needs of both the sport organization and its athletes. This perspective requires a paradigmatic repositioning, which involves a consideration of the ontological and epistemological foundations of pain and injury and carries significant implications for those performing, rehabilitating and managing others within sports worlds.

Definitions

Cartesian dichotomy – the separation of mind and body as two distinct entities. Grounded in the ideas of Descartes, this dichotomy presents the body (*res extensa*) as a physical object that follows the deterministic laws of nature and is incapable of free thought and action. It is considered to exist separately from 'thinking' substances (*res cogitans*), for example, consciousness, rationality, freedom and the human mind.

Epistemology/epistemological – the branch of philosophy that deals with how knowledge is acquired. It addresses questions such as: how do we know what we believe to be real and/or true? Through what mechanisms do we acquire knowledge about phenomena?

Ontology/ontological – the branch of philosophy concerned with the existence and nature of phenomena. It addresses questions such as: what is reality? What is truth?

To date, theories of pain and understanding of injury have been largely dominated by the classical biomedical model and its emphasis on neurophysiology and pain pathways (Ekstrand *et al.* 1983; Van Mechelen *et al.* 1992). Underpinned by a Cartesian mind–body dichotomy, this paradigm predominantly understands pain and injury in functional and physiological terms. Pain is perceived as a biological process that 'informs the higher centres of the organism of threats and dangers which have physical causes' (Loland 2006: 51). Thus, it is viewed as 'an unpleasant sensory and emotional' sensation governed by the deterministic laws of the physical world (International Association for the Study of Pain 1979: 240). Similarly, injury is approached as a static concept concerned with physical 'damage to the body caused by mechanical stress', for example, a fractured femur or torn Achilles tendon (Howe 2004: 91). Evident in the fields of anatomy, physiology, biomechanics and traditional sports medicine, this approach argues that pain, as indeed any bodily function, can be described accurately, explained causally and predicted or treated systematically. Whilst biomedical models have undeniably generated valuable practical knowledge about sporting pain and injury, we must question whether they capture the whole picture necessary for sports management practitioners to manage these episodes effectively and ethically.

The degree to which biomedical frameworks reflect the multifaceted realities of lived sporting pain and injury experiences can be questionable. Maintaining pain's position solely within a physiological realm reduces a decidedly complex phenomenon that sits at the intersection of biology, culture, history and religion to matters of nerves and neurotransmitters. Biomedical frameworks downplay the social and cultural significance of pain. As this chapter will demonstrate, pain is 'always saturated with the visible and invisible imprint of specific human cultures' (Morris 1991: 14). For example, in sports worlds the ability to play whilst injured and in pain is viewed as a badge of honour, an embodied representation of strength, courage and bravery. Conversely, obtaining the label of 'injured' leaves athletes vulnerable to being dropped from the roster, isolated from their team mates and subjected to ridicule by the media (Roderick *et al.* 2000). In addition, the narrow perspective of biomedical models neglects the broader networks of people, ideologies and practices in which injured athletes are enmeshed. It is through these pain networks that our frameworks for defining, understanding and responding to sporting pain and injury emerge and are subsequently developed, reproduced and reinforced.

In light of these observations, this chapter joins the call for the employment of a:

> more sophisticated model of pain … one which locates individuals within their social and cultural contexts and which allows for the inclusion of feelings and emotions (Bendelow and Williams 1995: 146).

Adopting a sociocultural perspective when examining sporting pain and injury offers one such model. This approach considers pain to be 'inscribed with meaning (or meaningless) based on the sociocultural context in which it is situated' (Loland 2006: 54). It moves away from understanding pain and injury as purely physiological towards a position that recognizes the multifaceted and embodied characteristics of these experiences. From a sociocultural perspective, pain is approached as simultaneously 'physical *and* emotional, biological *and* cultural, even spiritual *and* existential' (Bendelow and Williams 1995: 160: emphasis added). The physiology of pain, given such primacy within the classical biomedical model, becomes only one aspect of a broader, interconnected phenomenon.

Attention is drawn to aspects of pain shrouded or neglected by biomedical approaches, namely social, psychological, historical and cultural dimensions of pain experiences. In the first instance, how and what we come to understand to be 'painful' is shaped by our historical context. Elias (1986) mapped out the mimetic distance between 'games contests' and 'battle contests' from Ancient Greece to modern-day sport. In so doing he demonstrated that death and debilitating injuries were a common feature of early sport forms and the 'internalized inhibitions against physical violence were lower' than the present day (Mennell 1992: 145). As such, it is unlikely that Roman gladiators, medieval knights or public schoolboys from the nineteenth century would have labelled the 'serious' injuries associated with contemporary modern sport in the same way. Similarly, our cultural context influences and infuses our frameworks for understanding what it means to be 'in pain'. Research has demonstrated that different cultural groups conceptualize, interpret, manage and assign meaning to pain in different ways (Kotarba 1983; Howe 2001, 2004; Killick 2009). For example, athletes have been shown to play through severe pain, glorify pain experiences and rationalize their decision to place their short- and long-term health in jeopardy through their continued participation (Young 2004).

These pain and injury experiences become part of the ways in which we develop an understanding of who we are and where we are located in our social worlds. Shilling (2003: 4) asserts that in the modern, affluent West there is a tendency for the body to be viewed as a '*project*, which should be worked at and accomplished as part of an *individual's*

133

self-identity'. Within sports worlds, pain and injury experiences can be perceived as a means to both develop and disrupt these body projects. On the one hand, acute sports injuries and pain episodes may act as 'disruptions' to ongoing 'body projects' since they potentially 'prevent the body from carrying out the functions which are necessary in order to maintain an embodied identity as an athlete' (Pike and Maguire 2003: 233). Likewise, chronic pain or injury episodes can be perceived as 'fatal flaws' that must be contained, managed and ultimately dismissed given their far more long-term impact on self-identities (Sparkes 1996: 463). On the other hand, these experiences may be mobilized by afflicted individuals to probe their bodily limits, develop corporeal knowledge about themselves and exercise a degree of relative autonomy over their bodies (Killick 2009). In this way, pain and injury experiences may also be spaces in which people engage in a 'quest for exciting significance' and develop rather than disrupt aspects of their embodied sense of self (Maguire 1991: 29). Sociocultural approaches therefore posit that pain and injuries are not merely physiological conditions. Rather these experiences are shaped by our historical, social and cultural contexts and are significant for both our physical existence and individual and collective senses of identity(s) (Table 8.1).

Table 8.1 *Two approaches to the study of sporting pain*

Classical biomedical approach	Sociocultural approaches
Pain as physiological phenomenon	Pain as multidimensional (physiological, emotional, social, psychological, cultural, historical)
Pain pathways	Pain networks
Pain as sensation	Pain as embodied experience
Pain as warning system	Pleasure–pain continuum
Injury as mechanical distress to body	Injury as rupture to embodied identities
Grounded in Cartesian ideology	Challenges Cartesian ideology

CASE STUDY: EXPLORING INJURED SPORTING BODIES: COMPARING AND CONTRASTING BIOMEDICAL AND SOCIOCULTURAL APPROACHES

It's 2007, fourth round at Wimbledon and one of the most dominant forces of women's tennis in the twenty-first century, Serena Williams, walks on to court amidst wild cheering and chanting. She begins her warm-up, striking the ball masterfully. Her opponent, Daniela Hantuchova, awaits. Williams takes the first set 6–2, dominating with blistering groundstrokes. Second set, five games all, 30–15 with Hantuchova serving. Hantuchova throws the ball up, it seemingly hangs there, suspended in mid-air, the whoosh of her racket, thud, sweet strike, Serena returns the ball and then with a guttural cry, grabs her left calf and falls to the turf. The crowd inhales deeply; the TV coverage cuts to her sister Venus in the crowd, who is covering her mouth in worry. Disturbed murmurs echo around the court; the crowd's unsure what's wrong. A man sitting close to you mutters under his breath 'jeez, it's only cramp, get up, my boy plays through worse every Saturday in his U11 rugby game'. Serena lies prostrate on the turf. A physiotherapist runs to her side.

A medical time-out is called, allowing 3 minutes to treat the injury before Serena must either play on or retire from the game. The physiotherapist asks Williams several questions and sets to work on her calf. Serena wipes away tears as the clinician treats her. She returns to the game with her leg heavily strapped. The crowd applauds enthusiastically as she gets to her feet and walks gingerly to the baseline. She continues to play, each shot accompanied by a cry of agony and grimace. As the game progresses the commentators continually reference her injured calf and reflect on her 'tenacity' and 'determination' (ESPN 2007).

It begins to rain, and the players leave the court for 1 hour and 50 minutes. During the rain delay, Williams is told by doctors to retire from the game due to the severity of her injury. However, she returns to continue the game after the rain delay to rapturous applause from the crowd. She plays through the pain and in obvious discomfort, her left leg heavily strapped. Williams wins in the third set and proceeds to the quarter-final. The following day, the back pages are filled with articles praising Williams' 'courage', 'tenacity' and 'bravery'. Fans rave about Serena's 'fighting spirit' and 'warrior girl' status on their blogs. YouTube is flooded with videos dedicated to Serena's 'toughness' and her 'win against all odds' attitude. However, Williams loses the subsequent quarter-final against Justine Henin. She receives widespread criticism in the media for her claims that she would have won the game if she had not been suffering from multiple injuries.

MANAGING NETWORKS OF SPORTING PAIN AND INJURY

What does the adoption of a sociocultural approach to pain and injury mean for future or current practitioners within the field of sports management? Firstly, it highlights the significance of sporting pain and injury for sports managers and emphasizes the need for the ethical and socially responsible management of these experiences. Through the recognition of social, cultural and historical dimensions of pain experiences, athletes are no longer perceived as 'individuals in pain' but rather, part of a broader web of people who construct ever-changing systems of meaning about what pain is, what injuries represent and how suffering should be 'managed'. A sociocultural approach emphasizes the role of sports managers in the production of this knowledge connected to sports injury and the development of potentially damaging ideologies and practices related to sporting pain management.

Practitioners in the field of sports management are an integral part of these webs of people. These pain networks produce knowledge about the ways in which athletes should respond to injuries, what treatment they should undertake and how they should conduct their return to activity. Drawing on the central principles of a sociocultural approach reminds us that people define, interpret and respond to these experiences in different ways, depending on the social, historical and cultural context in which they are located. This raises important questions about the unique ways in which members of sporting pain networks define and respond to pain and injury. What do pain and injury episodes mean to athletes, clinicians, fans and managers? And

135

how do athletes or their fans respond when they are becoming or being injured or recovering from injuries? Whilst the assumption may be that members of these networks seek to protect the short- and long-term health of athletes, research suggests that sports participation is occurring in a 'public culture of risk, pain and injury' that places the health of athletes in jeopardy (Nixon 1994: 79).

SPORTING CULTURES OF RISKS

In contrast to the dominant rhetoric that stresses a positive relationship between sport and good health, sociological research contends that sports participation occurs in an embodied 'cultural context that glorifies risk and normalises pain, injuries and playing hurt' (Nixon 1994: 79). Research has identified several broad characteristics of this embodied cultural space. Central to these are:

- athletes' uncritical acceptance and normalization of sporting pain and injury (Curry 1993);
- the practice of 'playing hurt' (Roderick *et al.* 2000: 165);
- forms of athletic 'injury talk' that serve to discredit, dismiss and depersonalize sporting pain (Young *et al.* 1994: 182);
- devastating emotional repercussions akin to grieving processes (Pike 2000; Sparkes and Smith 2002; Smith and Sparkes 2004, 2005).

A substantial body of research across a number of sports[2] provides empirical evidence demonstrating:

> a willingness of athletes ... to repeatedly place their bodies at risk by training while they are in pain, competing while they are injured or by returning to sport before they are fully recovered.
>
> (Charlesworth and Young 2004: 163)

Described in the literature as 'playing hurt', the athletic practice of playing through pain and with injuries appears to be one of the foremost characteristics of a sporting culture of risk (Roderick *et al.* 2000: 165). This practice appears to be highly valued and respected by many athletes, coaches, fans, managers, support staff and media representatives (Nixon 1993, 1994). Demonstrations of a stoic response in the face of pain and a desire to push through injuries receive high accolades from others. Conversely, failure to maintain a 'game face' (Zurcher 1982) and conform to the 'pain principle' often results in the stigmatization of athletes, a questioning of their status on the team and a subsequent devaluation of their self-worth (Messner 1992: 72).

Sociologists have explored this phenomenon in a variety of settings, including professional (Nixon 1993; Howe 2001; Frey *et al.* 2004; Roderick 2004, 2006), university (Charlesworth 2002; Liston *et al.* 2006), recreational (Pike 2000) and youth (Killick 2007, 2009) sport.

Their research demonstrates how ideologies and practices associated with sporting cultures of risk can be identified along the full spectrum of sports participation, from the supposedly health-affirming environment of school physical education to elite, achievement sports cultures. How might we explain the development and widespread occurrence of such practices? And what role do sports managers play in this process?

MANAGING SPORTING NETWORKS OF PAIN AND INJURY WITHIN CULTURES OF RISKS

Several conceptual frameworks have been employed in the literature to make sense of athletes' adherence to this culture of risk. These have included matters of victimization (Young 1991), the influence of athletic social networks (Nixon 1992), issues of 'edgework' (Lyng 2005) and over-conformity to the sports ethic (Hughes and Coakley 1991). It has also been suggested that sporting experiences of pain and injury play a central role in the creation, performance and maintenance of a host of embodied identities, including athletic (Pike 2000), gendered (Sabo 1986; Messner 1990, 1992; Messner and Sabo 1990; Young et al. 1994) and age-related (Killick 2009). Robert Hughes and Jay Coakley (1991) argue that athletes play hurt and accept the physical risks associated with sports participation in order to be defined as a 'real' athlete. They consider practices connected to sporting cultures of risk to be core components of the 'sports ethic', a relatively universal set of ideas about what it means to be an athlete (Hughes and Coakley 1991: 307). Thus, within sports worlds, playing hurt is seen as a necessary bodily sacrifice to achieve excellence and the onset of pain is interpreted as 'limit', which athletes must overcome in their pursuit of success.

Other authors extend the analysis of a sporting culture of risk beyond individuals' quest for athletic identity and begin to incorporate the broader social interactions in which the athlete is located (Walk 1997; Roderick et al. 2000; Safai 2003; Nixon 2004). Their research draws important attention to the structural environment in which sporting pain and injury take place and the ways in which interconnected structural constraints, inducements and processes of institutional rationalization mediate messages around playing hurt. Central to their observations is the claim that contemporary body cultures are 'locked in the iron cage of modern achievement sport' in which the pursuit of performance efficiency is paramount (Maguire 2004: 299). In this increasingly commercialized environment, the pressure to win and maintain a commercial image of the 'healthy' competitor is notable. Thus sporting practices that result in the increased alienation of athletic bodies are promoted and far more currency is placed on the outcome of sporting encounters than the enjoyment gained from bodily expression.

Thus, Nixon draws heavily on a social network approach to aid understanding of elite athletes' rationale for enduring 'the sheer physical and mental anguish of pushing [themselves] through the pain barrier time and time again' (Stratford 1988: 67). He maps out the 'relations among persons, positions, roles or social units' and to display the ways in which these interactions reinforce 'cultural and interpersonal messages exhorting and encouraging [athletes] to play with pain or injuries' (Nixon 1992: 127–128). Nixon (1992: 133) conceptualizes these networks of interaction as 'sportsnets' and presents them as isolated, closed networks 'structured to limit, block, deflect or discredit contact with people who might challenge the nature of risk in sport'. He describes a conspiratorial alliance of coaches, athletic administrators, sports medicine personnel and others who produce 'implicit and explicit messages about risk, pain and injury that provide biased support' for athletes (Nixon 1992: 130). Integral to this 'conspiratorial alliance' are sports management personnel, since they are directly responsible for fundamental operational decisions that shape the work ethic and ethos of the organization (e.g. the employment of coaches). Indeed, Nixon argues that the organizational cultures led by these managers continually reinforce and rarely challenge the acceptance of risk, pain and injury, fostering the belief that playing hurt is the only viable option open to the athletes. He conceptualized athletes as passive 'receivers' of cultural messages to play hurt and, in so doing, implies that sports managers are one source of such messages (Nixon 1992: 130).

Several researchers have used Nixon's work as a point of departure and suggest that the ways in which athletes engage with sporting risk, pain and injury are perhaps more complex than initially suggested (Walk 1997; Roderick 1998; Pike and Maguire 2003; Safai 2003; Charlesworth and Young 2004; Singer 2004; Theberge 2006). For example, through her study of sport medicine clinicians and injured athletes in Canadian intercollegiate sport, Safai (2003: 127) indicated a level of negotiation between the clinicians and athletes over the athlete's injury experiences and concluded that:

> a 'culture of risk' was reinforced under certain circumstances during negotiation, but was also tempered by the existence of a 'culture of precaution' that worked to resist those influences.

Her evidence suggested that, as well as reinforcing core elements of a culture of risk, the environment of Canadian intercollegiate sport is also a site in which concern and caution for the health and welfare of student athletes are voiced. Similar conclusions were drawn in studies of American student athletic trainers (Walk 1997), English physical education environments (Killick 2009) and the British Olympic Committee's sports medicine community (Scott 2010). This body of research suggests that members of sports worlds actively negotiate many different aspects of the injury process and, whilst a culture of risk remains the dominant set of ideologies shaping pain and injury experiences, it is 'not as homogeneous and all encompassing' as the early research implied (Safai 2003: 131).

Sports management practitioners sit at a pivotal point in these interpersonal negotiations. They have the potential either to reinforce or provide counter-messages to the dominant culture of risk. However, managers, like the athletes, will themselves be subjected to interconnected structural constraints, inducements and processes of institutional rationalization that will shape their own management practices. The final section of this chapter explores two core issues you may face in efforts to manage sporting pain ethically and responsibly.

BALANCING HEALTH AND PERFORMANCE OUTCOMES

The financial health of sports organizations, by nature, is driven by the successful performance of its athletes. In turn, athletic performance and its related chances of success are optimal when athletes' health is maximal. Thus, the balance between health and performance is a critical issue in sports organizations. Often, sports organizations maintain a clinical apparatus that is geared toward performance enhancement rather than health maintenance (Waddington 1996). In so doing, decisions are often made that favour performance outcomes at the expense of the optimal health of the athletes (Safai 2003; Johnson 2004; Mathias 2004). Within these decisions, the consequences to the long-term health of the athlete are often minimized or even discounted in the pursuit of success, personal achievement and the establishment of a winning record.

A major component of the everyday practices of healthcare providers within sports organizations involves balancing the often-competing agenda of their primary responsibility to advocate for the optimal well-being of athletes under their care with the agenda of an organizational framework that subsists on athletic performance (Safai 2003; Theberge 2007, 2009). From a practitioner's point of view this is one of the most difficult aspects of working within a sports organization. There exists a constant tension between what is physiologically best for the athlete from a healthcare standpoint and the desires of that athlete, and associated members of sports networks, for performance. Although it is easy to become involved in the desires of the athlete, coach and even management of the sports organization, it is often necessary that the sports medicine practitioner be the 'voice of reason' in an injury situation.

Though it is the responsibility of the healthcare professional to be the advocate for athletes' health and well-being, there are many factors that are involved in the decision-making process following an injury. Some of these include the time and importance of the competition, the playing status of the athlete, the health and mental well-being of that athlete and the potential for further damage to the athlete. It is important that sport management personnel understand this tension so they are able to provide support to the sports medicine personnel employed within their organization and advocate for the long-term best interests of both the injured athlete and the health of the organization. The steps taken by sports organizations to facilitate effective advocacy on behalf of their athletes from their healthcare providers appears to be an important investment in the long-term quality and longevity of individual athletes' careers. This investment by sports organizations to extending the viability of athletes' careers ensures the financial viability of the sports organization itself.

PAIN, INJURY AND CORPORATE RESPONSIBILITY

Exploring sport, and the injuries and risk inherent in many of these activities, from a sociocultural perspective raises questions about the ethical and legal responsibilities of sports organizations and sports management personnel. One of the many responsibilities of sports management personnel is to ensure that the business activities of the organization adhere to national and international regulations and laws. Many professional sports organizations employ a large legal department or, at a minimum, consult legal counsel to ensure their management practices and operations meet these legislative standards. In addition, awareness of potential legal ramifications leads sports management personnel to purchase liability insurance, become educated in the legalities of sport and apply certain rules and standards within the organization (Ray 2005).

139

In the interest of protecting sporting organizations and the athletes who play for them, it is critical to consider the legal dimension of sporting pain networks. In most cases, the legal implications of acute pain and injury are often recognized through concepts such as negligence, duty of care and assumption of risk.

Definitions

Negligence: a legal wrong in which an individual fails to act as a reasonably prudent person would act under the circumstances (Ray 2005)

Duty of care: the existence of a responsibility for an individual to provide a standard of care when caring for others (Osborne 2001)

Assumption of risk: the act or agreement to take on a risk of damage, injury or loss, to the participant upon the occurrence of a certain event

---

Evident in the 1995 court case between the University of Tennessee and University of Tennessee footballer Michael Pinson, the legal concept of negligence is prominent in many cases that make it to the courts. In *Pinson* v. *State of Tennessee*, the athletic trainer and the university were sued for negligence in the care of Pinson's injury. Pinson was struck in the head during a football practice and was unconscious for 10 minutes. Upon examination, the athletic trainer found substantial neurological symptoms; however he did not call for emergency personnel and instead sent the athlete to the emergency room with an athletic training student. The student was misinformed of Pinson's condition and, as a result, physicians did not perform the appropriate diagnostic tests. Although Pinson continued to be symptomatic, he was allowed to return to participation approximately 1 week after the incident and it was eventually discovered that he had suffered a significant brain injury 3 weeks prior to the practice session (Richardson and Lorek 2003). He now suffers from permanent brain damage and is unable to perform normal functions, including maintaining regular employment. The court found the defendant guilty of negligence and awarded Pinson $1.5 million in compensation.

Often connected to negligence, the concept of duty of care is also prevalent in legal cases involving sports injuries. West and Ciccolella (2004) contend that individuals who have been recruited or are employed by a sporting organization are entitled to a specific duty of care regarding medical injuries and conditions. This duty requires that the organization provide appropriate and prudent medical care for its athletes and is evident in *Kleinknecht* v. *Gettysburg College*. Kleinknecht, a varsity lacrosse player at Gettysburg College, died of cardiac arrest during a practice in which no trained medical personnel were present. The US Court of Appeals for the Third Circuit sided with the plaintiff, ruling that Gettysburg College owed a specific duty of care to the athlete during college-sponsored athletic activities. The Court attested that Kleinknecht should have had access to life-saving emergency techniques during scheduled training sessions.

Although the responsibility of care and issues of negligence are often attributed to the medical personnel who provide direct medical care for the athletes (for example, sports physiotherapists, club doctors or certified athletic trainers), it is important that sports management personnel are aware of these legal aspects of sport. In most cases, sport managers oversee the hiring process of the medical support staff and, in the majority of these cases, the entire organization is included in the lawsuit, even if the negligent act was the responsibility of the medical staff. Moreover, management personnel must be in a position to implement policies and procedures effectively that will successfully protect the organization and participants in case of injury.

There is a pressing need for sports management personnel to understand better the legal dimension of sporting pain networks. In recent years there has been a growth in concern around issues of negligence, duty of care and assumption of risk. This increased concern has given rise to the creation of distinct rules, regulations and legal strictures controlling sport practices. Many of them are designed to protect both the participants from harm and the organizations from associated lawsuits. For example, in 2010 the California Interscholastic Federation (CIF), the organization responsible for high-school athletics in California, implemented a rule governing the management of head injuries in the 2010–2011 season (California Athletic Trainers' Association 2010). The rule states that an individual who suffers a head injury in either practice or competition will be removed from participation for the remainder of the day. The individual must also be given written clearance by a licensed healthcare professional prior to return to activity (CIF 2010). It will be critical, as further rules and laws come into effect, that sport managers stay abreast of these changes and be able to understand and implement them immediately to avoid any potential penalties to the organization. However, although many of these regulations address substantial and acute injuries, what happens in the case of long-term cumulative effects of sporting participation? Does the organization have a responsibility to the long-term health and well-being of the athletes who play for them or is it the responsibility of athletes to assume all risk associated with their participation and waive their protection of long-term health?

SUMMARY

Whilst it is frequently assumed, often uncritically and without empirical evidence, that 'sport is good in itself' and participation in sporting activities leads to wholesale health benefits, research suggests that many athletes are developing lengthening and often debilitating sport injury histories, continuing to play sport whilst in pain or suffering from known injuries and rejecting medical advice to cease activity and undergo periods of rehabilitation (Young 2004). These damaging practices are not restricted to injuries with limited, minimal, short-term effects. Several athletes' narratives reveal their propensity to play hurt with injuries that carry significant health warnings (e.g. concussions), the ramifications of which can be felt on a physical, psychological, emotional, social and moral level.

Thinking socioculturally about these observations draws attention to the role of sports management practitioners in the (re)production of potential harmful cultural messages and practices concerned with sporting pain and injuries. This chapter has explored some of the ethical and legal issues that arise when engaging with sporting pain and injury from a management perspective grounded in a sociocultural approach. It calls for future and current sports management personnel to think critically about their role within sporting pain networks and attempt to develop management practices that strike a balance between the demands of high performance and the ethics of health protection and promotion. In so doing, it is hoped they will contribute to the emergence of more ethical and responsible achievement sports worlds.

NOTES

1   For our North American readers, the term 'physiotherapist' refers to athletic trainer.
2   Including, but not limited to, rugby union (Howe 2001), rugby league (Liston et al. 2006), association football (Roderick et al. 2000), rowing (Pike 2000), cycling (Albert 1999), softball (Malcolm 2006), ballet (Turner and Wainwright 2003), triathlon (Atkinson 2008), skateboarding (Young and Dallaire 2008) and the multi-sport context of physical education (Killick 2007, 2009).

REVIEW QUESTIONS

1   What is the relationship between an athlete's health and the financial health of a sport? Use the first case study to help you.
2   What are the potential consequences of this relationship for: (a) the athlete and (b) the organization?
3   Identify the major differences between a biomedical and sociocultural approach to Serena Williams' experience in the fourth round at Wimbledon (see second case study).
4   What messages about sporting pain and injury were conveyed in this case study?
5   What conflicts of interest may occur between athletes' health and performance both within and between members of pain networks within a sports organization?

FURTHER READING

- Liston, K., Reacher, D., Smith, A. and Waddington, I. (2006). "Managing Pain and Injury in Non-elite Rugby Union and Rugby League: A Case Study of Players at a British University." *Sport in Society* 9(3): 388–402.
- Maguire, J. (2004) "Challenging the Sports–Industrial Complex: Human Sciences, Advocacy and Service." *European Physical Education Review* 10(3): 299–322.
- Roderick, M. (2004). "English Professional Soccer Players and the Uncertainties of Injury," in: Young, K (ed.) *Sporting Bodies, Damaged Selves: Sociological studies of sports-related injury.* Oxford: Elsevier Science Press, pp. 137–150.

WEBSITES

BBC:
    news.bbc.co.uk/sport1/hi/academy/4244782.stm
Brain Injury in Sport:
    www.headinjury.com/sports.htm

142

REFERENCES:

Albert, E. (1999). "Dealing with Danger: The Normalization of Risk in Cycling." *International Review for the Sociology of Sport* 34(3): 157–171.

Anonymous. (2005). Tiger Woods boosts TV, playing or not. *Golf Today.* http://www.golftoday. co.uk/news/yeartodate/news00/woods13.html (accessed 10 September 2010).

Anonymous. (2010). Broncos address Kenny McKinley death. *ESPN: NFL.* http://sports.espn. go.com/nfl/news/story?id=5600395 (accessed 5 December 2010).

Atkinson, M. (2008). "Triathlon, Suffering and Exciting Significance." *Leisure Studies* 27(2): 165–180.

Bendelow, G.A. and Williams, S.J. (1995). "Transcending the Dualisms: Towards a Sociology of Pain." *Sociology of Health and Illness* 17(2): 139–165.

Branch, J. (2000). Woods part of the crusade: minority golf numbers growing. *TigerTales.com.* http://www.texnews.com/tiger/part0607.html (accessed 10 September 2010).

California Athletic Trainers' Association. (2010). CIF concussion ruling and the CATA position. http://ca-at.org/2010/05/the-cif-concussion-ruling-and-the-cata's-position (accessed 16 June 2012).

California Interscholastic Federation. (2010). Concussion management guidelines. http://205.214. 168.16/health_safety/concussion/index.html (accessed 16 June 2012).

Charlesworth, H. (2002). Sports-related injury, risk and pain: the experience of English female university athletes. Unpublished doctoral dissertation, Loughborough University, UK.

Charlesworth, H. and Young, K. (2004). "Why English Female University Athletes Play with Pain," in Young, K. (ed.). *Sporting Bodies, Damaged Selves: Sociological studies of sports-related injury.* Oxford: Elsevier Science Press, pp. 163–180.

Cole, J. (1995). "Wimbledon Foul Underlines Need to Know Insurance Score." *The Guardian* 1 July.

Curry, T. (1993). "A Little Pain Never Hurt Anyone: Athletic Career Socialization and the Normalization of Sports Injury." *Symbolic Interaction.* 16(3): 273–290.

Ekstrand, J., Gillquist, J., Moller, M., Oberg, B. and Liljedahl, S.O. (1983). "Incidence of Soccer Injuries and their Relation to Training and Team Success." *American Journal of Sports Medicine* 11(2): 63–67.

Elias, N. (1986). "An Essay on Sport and Violence," in Elias, N. and Dunning, E. (eds) *Quest for Excitement: Sport and Leisure in the Civilising Process.* Oxford: Blackwell Publishing, pp. 150–176.

ESPN. (2007). Serena Williams 4th Round Wimbledon. http://www.youtube.com/watch?v= MxpQSWLDekU (accessed 10 September 2010).

Frey, J.H., Preston, F. and Bernhard, B. (2004). "Risk and Injury: A comparison of Football and Rodeo Subcultures," in Young, K. (ed.) *Sporting Bodies, Damaged Selves: Sociological studies of sports-related injury.* Oxford: Elsevier Science, pp. 211–222.

Goodbody, J. (1995). "Injury Time Costs Economy 405 Million Pounds." *The Guardian* 7 June.

Howe, P.D. (2001). "An Ethnography of Pain and Injury in Professional Rugby Union: The Case of Pontypridd RFC." *International Review for the Sociology of Sport* 36: 289–303.

Howe, P.D. (2004). *Sport, Professionalism and Pain: Ethnographies of injury and risk.* London: Routledge.

Hughes, R. and Coakley, J. (1991). "Positive Deviance among Athletes: The Implications of Overconformity to the Sports Ethic." *Sociology of Sport Journal* 8: 307–325.

International Association for the Study of Pain. (1979). "Pain Terms: A List with Definitions and Notes on Usage." *Pain* 6: 240.

Johnson, R. (2004). "The Unique Ethics of Sports Medicine." *Clinics in Sports Medicine* 23(2): 175–182.

Killick, L. (2007). "PE Kits, Playgrounds and Pain: An Exploration of Children's Experiences of Risk, Pain and Injury in Sport," in Scott-Jones, J. and Raisborough, J. (eds) *Risks, Identities and the Everyday.* Hampshire, Ashgate: pp. 51–66.

Killick, L. (2009). "Walking the fine line?" Young people, sporting risk, health and embodied identities. Unpublished doctoral dissertation, Loughborough University, UK.

Kleinknecht v. *Gettysburg College.* 989 F2D 1360 (1992).

Kotarba, J. (1983). *Chronic Pain: Its Social Dimensions.* Newbury Park, CA: Sage Publications.

Liston, K., Reacher, D., Smith, A. and Waddington, I. (2006). "Managing Pain and Injury in Non-elite Rugby Union and Rugby League: A Case Study of Players at a British University." *Sport in Society* 9(3): 388–402.

Loland, S. (2006). "Three Approaches to the Study of Pain in Sport," in Loland, S., Skirstad, B. and Waddington, I. (eds) *Pain and Injury in Sport: Social and ethical analysis.* Abingdon: Routledge, pp. 49–62.

Lyng, S.L. (2005). *Edgework: The Sociology of Risk-Taking.* London: Routledge.

Maguire, J. (1991). "Towards a Sociological Theory of Sport and the Emotions: A Figurational Perspective." *International Review for the Sociology of Sport* 26(1): 25–33.

Maguire, J. (2004). "Challenging the Sports–Industrial Complex: Human Sciences, Advocacy and Service." *European Physical Education Review* 10(3): 299–322.

Malcolm, N.L. (2006). "'Shaking it Off' and 'Toughing it Out': Socialisation to Pain and Injury in Girls' Softball." *Journal of Contemporary Ethnography* 35(5): 495–525.

Mathias, M.B. (2004). "The Competing Demands of Sport and Health: An Essay on the History of Ethics in Sports Medicine." *Clinics in Sports Medicine* 23(2): 195–214.

Mennell, S. (1992). *Norbert Elias: An Introduction.* Dublin: University College Dublin Press.

Messner, M. (1990). "When Bodies are Weapons: Masculinity and Violence in Sport." *International Review for the Sociology of Sport* 25: 203–219.

Messner, M. (1992). *Power at Play: Sports and the problem of masculinity.* Boston: Beacon Press.

Messner, M. and Sabo, D. (1990). *Sport, Men and the Gender Order: Critical feminist perspectives.* Champiagn, IL: Human Kinetics.

Morris, D. (1991). *The Culture of Pain.* Berkeley, CA: University of California Press.

Nielsen Company. (2009). Tiger's return expected to make PGA ratings roar. *Nielsen Wire.* http://blog.nielsen.com/nielsenwire/online_mobile/tigers-return-expected-to-make-pga-ratings-roar/ (accessed 10 September 2010).

Nixon, H.L. (1992). "A Social Network Analysis of Influence on Athletes to Play with Pain and Injuries." *Journal of Sport and Social Issues* 19: 127–135.

Nixon, H.L. (1993). "Accepting the Risks of Pain and Injury in Sport: Mediated Cultural Influences on Playing Hurt." *Sociology of Sport Journal* 10: 183–196.

Nixon, H.L. (1994). "Coaches' Views of Risk, Pain and Injury in Sport: With Special Reference to Gender Differences." *Sociology of Sport Journal* 11: 79–87.

Nixon, H.L. (2004). "Cultural, Structural and Status Dimensions of Pain and Injury Experiences in Sport," In: Young, K. (ed.). *Sporting Bodies, Damaged Selves: Sociological studies of sports-related injury.* Oxford: Elsevier Science Press, pp. 81–98.

Osborne, B. (2001). "Principles of Liability for Athletic Trainers: Managing Sport-Related Concussion." *Journal of Athletic Training* 36(3): 316–321.

Pike, E. (2000). Illness, injury and sporting identity: a case study of women's rowing. Unpublished doctoral thesis, Loughborough University, UK.

Pike, E. and Maguire, J. (2003). "Injury in Women's Sport: Classifying Key Elements of 'Risk Encounters'." *Sociology of Sport Journal* 20: 232–251.

Pinson v. *State of Tennessse.* C.A. no. 02A01-9409-BC-00210 (Tenn. App. 1995).

Ray, R. (2005). *Management Strategies in Athletic Training,* 3rd edn. Champaign, IL: Human Kinetics.

Richardson, J.J. and Lorek, J.J. (2003). Memorandum: athletic trainers' legal duties. http://www.collegeathletictrainer.org/symposiums/symposium2003/00463593.pdf (accessed 25 November 2010).

Roderick, M. (1998). "The Sociology of Risk, Pain and Injury: A comment of the Work of Howard L. Nixon II." *Sociology of Sport Journal* 15: 64–79.

Roderick, M. (2004). "English Professional Soccer Players and the Uncertainties of Injury," in Young, K. (ed.) *Sporting Bodies, Damaged Selves: Sociological studies of sports-related injury.* Oxford: Elsevier Science Press, pp. 137–150.

Roderick, M. (2006). "Adding Insult to Injury: Workplace Injury in English Professional Football." *Sociology of Health and Illness* 28(1): 76–97.

Roderick, M., Waddington, I. and Parker, G. (2000). "Playing Hurt: Managing Injuries in English professional football." *International Review for the Sociology of Sport* 35(2): 165–180.

Sabo, D. (1986). "Pigskin, Patriarchy and Pain." *Changing Men: Issues in Gender, Sex and Politics* 16: 24–25.

Safai, P. (2003). "Healing the Body in the 'Culture of Risk': Examining the Negotiation of Treatment Between Sport Medicine Clinicians and Injured Athletes in Canadian Intercollegiate Sport." *Sociology of Sport Journal* 20: 127–146.

Safai, P. (2004). "Negiotating with Risk: Exploring the Role of the Sports Medicine Clincian," in Young, K. (ed.). *Sporting Bodies, Damaged Selves: Sociological studies of sports-related injury.* Oxford: Elsevier Science Press, pp. 269–286.

Schwarz, A. (2009a). Dementia risk seen in players in NFL study. *New York*

Scott, A. (2010). The occupational practices of sports medicine clinicians working with British Olympic athletes. Unpublished doctoral thesis, Loughborough University, UK.

Shilling, C. (2003). *The Body and Social Theory,* 2nd edn. London: Sage Publications.

Singer, R.L. (2004). "Pain and Injury in a Youth Basketball League," in Young, K. (ed.) *Sporting Bodies, Damaged Selves: Sociological studies of sports-related injury.* Oxford: Elsevier Science Press, pp. 223–235.

Smith, B. and Sparkes, A. (2004). "Men, Sport and Spinal Cord Injuries: An Analysis of Metaphors and Narrative Types." *Disability and Society* 19(6): 613–626.

Smith, B. and Sparkes, A. (2005). "Men, Sport, Spinal Cord Injury and Narratives of Hope." *Social Science and Medicine* 61: 1095–1105.

Sparkes, A. (1996). "The Fatal Flaw: A Narrative of the Fragile Body-Self." *Qualitative Enquiry* 2: 463–494.

Sparkes, A. and Smith, B. (2002). "Sport, Spinal Cord Injuries, Embodied Masculinities and Narrative Identity Dilemmas." *Men and Masculinities* 4(3): 258–285.

Stratford, T. (1988). *Guts, Tears and Glory.* Auckland: New Women's Press

Theberge, N. (2006). "The Gendering of Sports Injury: A Look at 'Progress' in Women's Sport Through a Case Study of the Biomedical Discourse on the Injured Athletic Body." *Sport in Society* 9(4): 634–648.

Theberge, N. (2007). "It's Not About Health, It's About Performance," in Hargreaves, J. and Vertinsky, P. (eds) *Physical Culture, Power and the Body.* London: Routledge.

Theberge, N. (2009). "Professional Identities and the Practice of Sport Medicine in Canada. A Comparative Analysis of Two Sporting Contexts," in: Harris, J. and Parker, A. (eds) *Sport and Social Identities.* Basingstoke: Palgrave McMillan.

Tolpin, H. and Bentkover, J. (1986). "The Economic Costs of Sports Injuries," in: Vinger, P. and Hoerner, E. (eds) *Sports Injuries: The unthwarted epidemic.* Littleton, MA: PSG Publishing.

Turner, B.S. and Wainwright, S.P. (2003). "Corps de Ballet: The Case of the Injured Ballet Dancer." *Sociology of Health and Illness* 25(4): 269–288.

Van Mechelen, W., Hlobil, H. and Kemper, H.C.G. (1992). "Incidence, Severity, Aetiology and Prevention of Sports Injuries: A Review of Concepts." *Sports Medicine* 14: 82–99.

145

Waddington, I. (1996). "The Development of Sports Medicine." *Sociology of Sport Journal* 13(2): 176–196.

Waddington, I. (2006). "Ethical Problems in the Medical Management of Sports Injuries: A Case Study of English Professional Football," in: Loland, S., Skirstad, B. and Waddington, I. (eds) *Pain and Injury in Sport: Social and ethical analysis.* Abingdon: Routledge, pp. 182–199.

Walk, S. (1997). "Peers in Pain: The Experiences of Student Athlete Trainers." *Sociology of Sport Journal* 14: 22–56.

Walk, S. (2004). "Athletic Trainers: Between Care and Social Control," in: Young, K. (ed.) *Sporting Bodies, Damaged Selves: Sociological studies of sports-related injury.* Oxford: Elsevier Science Press, pp. 251–268.

West, S.A. and Ciccolella, M.E. (2004). "Issues in the Standard of Care for Certified Athletic Trainers." *Journal of Legal Aspects of Sport* 14(1): 63–74.

White, P. (2004). "The Costs of Injuries from Sport, Exercise and Physical Activity: A Review of Evidence," in: Young, K. (ed.). *Sporting Bodies, Damaged Selves: Sociological studies of sports-related injury.* Oxford: Elsevier Science Press, pp. 309–323.

Young, K. (1991). "Violence in the Workplace of Professional Sport from Victimological and Cultural Studies Perspective." *International Review for the Sociology of Sport* 26: 3–13.

Young, K. (ed.) (2004). *Sporting Bodies, Damaged Selves: Sociological studies of sports-related injury.* Oxford: Elsevier Science Press

Young, A. and Dallaire, C. (2008). "Beware *@! SK8 at Your Own Risk: The Discourses of Young Female Skateboarders," in: Atkinson, M. and Young, K. (eds) *Tribal Play: Subcultural journies through sport.* Bingley: JAI Press, pp. 235–254.

Young, K., White, P. and McTeer, W. (1994). "Body Talk: Male Athletes Reflect on Sport, Injury and Pain." *Sociology of Sport Journal* 11: 175–194.

Zurcher, L. (1982). "The Staging of Emotion: A Dramaturgical Analysis". *Symbolic Interaction* 5: 1–22.

146

Chapter 9

Sport labour migration

Managing a twenty-first-century global workforce

Pete Schroeder and Chris Janssen

TOPICS

Factors facilitating sport labour migration • Trends in sport labour migration • Managing sport labour migration

---

OBJECTIVES

By the end of this chapter you will be able to:

- Define sport labour migration;
- Understand the significance of sport labour migration to sport managers;
- Explain the economic, political, geographical/cultural, competitive and technological factors facilitating sport labour migration;
- Identify common patterns of sport migration in professional team sports, individual professional/Olympic sports and American intercollegiate athletics;
- Understand how the concerns and issues of sport labour migration apply to sport managers;
- Develop practical solutions to facilitate migration processes for athletes.

KEY TERMS

Deskilling – the process whereby a nation produces and develops, in this case, talented athletes, but loses those athletes to other nations due to a variety of factors.

Donor nation – a nation that produces large numbers of emigrating sport labour migrants.

Host nation – a nation to which large numbers of sport labour migrants immigrate.

Sport labour migration – the fluid movement of athletes across international and cultural barriers.

Sport opportunity structure – national imbalances between the number of athletes and the amount of competitive opportunities, creating a flow of sport labour migrants from nations of fewer opportunities to nations with greater opportunities.

OVERVIEW

Globalization is the defining attribute of twenty-first-century life (Friedman 1999; Giddens 2000; Flanagan 2001). Researchers have suggested that sport is an excellent microcosm of the economic, political, cultural and technological trends creating globalization (Bale 2003; Sage 2010). Some of these trends have made sports stars like David Beckham, Michael Jordan and Roger Federer global icons, and these athletes have also contributed significantly to sport's global popularity (Maguire 2005). These outcomes result from the process of sport labour migration. Sport labour migration refers to the fluid movement of athletes across international and cultural barriers (Maguire *et al.* 2002). This movement applies primarily to athletes, but can also include coaches, officials, administrators and sport scientists.

Researchers have identified three forms of sport labour migration (Maguire *et al.* 2002; Sage 2010): within-nation, intracontinental, and intercontinental. The recruitment of a high-school basketball player from New York to play for the University of California in Los Angeles exemplifies within-nation migration. When Canadian ice hockey players are drafted by National Hockey League (NHL) franchises in the USA, intracontinental migration has occurred. Intercontinental migration occurs frequently in the English Premier League when clubs sign players from across the world, including Africa or South America.

Such forms of migration stem from an interaction of political, economic, cultural and technological factors. The management of sport requires an understanding of these factors and their interactions for several reasons. First, most sport managers will work in organizations that employ sport migrants. Professional individual sports, like tennis and golf, feature athletes from across the globe, and the rosters of many professional football, rugby, cricket, basketball or baseball teams are equally cosmopolitan. Second, sport managers are often responsible for the processes involved in finding and signing sport migrants. International scouting, contract development and representation all demand variable skill sets based on the sports and nations in which sport managers work. Third, once migrants are hired, sport managers are responsible for creating environments in which migrant labor can best contribute to the sport organization's success.

Therefore, this chapter will examine the causes, patterns and motivations of sport labour migration and provide particular emphasis on the range of potential consequences for sport managers. It will begin with a contextualization and exploration of the factors facilitating modern sport migration. Next, resulting migration patterns common in professional, individual/Olympic and intercollegiate sports will be presented along with the motivations associated with these patterns. The chapter concludes with practical recommendations for sport managers who must come to terms with some of the issues associated with labour migration.

CASE STUDY: MIGRATION CONCERNS IN AMERICAN INTERCOLLEGIATE ATHLETICS

In the autumn of 2009, Elsa, a 6'1" (1.85-metre) volleyball player from the Czech Republic, arrived at Los Angeles International Airport in preparation for her first year at Western University. Western had a top volleyball programme and had used a recruiting service operated by a former German volleyball player to recruit Elsa to the USA. Elsa had hired the recruiting service because she wanted to attend an American university, but she had never travelled outside Europe. The coaching staff at Western had never met Elsa, but had seen a video of her playing for the junior national team. They offered Elsa a full scholarship with the expectation that she would immediately become a top player.

Upon arrival, Elsa began practising with Western's team, but was told to stop practising after 2 days because she was not academically eligible. Elsa was confused because she had graduated from high school with honours and was admitted by Western University. However, Western's coaching staff explained to her that the National Collegiate Athletics Association (NCAA) did not accept all of her coursework because she attended a technical high school. In a separate meeting, an NCAA representative explained to Elsa that all prospective student athletes must take a core set of high-school courses before being allowed to play NCAA athletics. They further indicated that Western's staff did not clear her high-school coursework before they offered her a scholarship. Lacking familiarity with the American university sport culture, she could not understand why the university could accept her but the NCAA would not allow her to play, or even practise, with the volleyball team.

Elsa was left with three options. First, Western officials said they would honour her scholarship for 1 year, but she could not play volleyball. Second, the school offered to pay her travel expenses home. Third, Western's coach said he would help Elsa obtain admission to a college preparatory school that would allow her to play volleyball at a less competitive level while becoming academically eligible for NCAA. However, he could not guarantee her a scholarship the following year. Elsa did not want to miss out on a year of volleyball because she was hoping to make the Czech national team. She did not want to go home because she felt like a failure. Elsa did not think the preparatory school option would help her athletically and she was unsure what would happen after the school year.

FACTORS FACILITATING SPORT LABOUR MIGRATION

Although the patterns of migration can be relatively easy to understand, the factors facilitating sport labour migration result from broader global processes. While the term 'globalization' is very much contested, there are commonalities in the way theorists characterize it (Giddens 2000; Held and McGrew 2002; Maguire 2005). First, globalization arises from political, economic, cultural and technological factors (Giddens 2000). While these factors have singular influences, it is the interconnectedness of them that is the hallmark of globalization (Maguire 2005). Second, globalization has intensified in the last 25 years (Giddens 2000; Jarvie and Maguire 2000). While globalization is not new, the factors facilitating it, particularly communication technology, have evolved so rapidly that the momentum of globalization is 'revolutionary' (Giddens 2000: 28). A third characteristic of globalization is the shrinkage of time and space (Giddens 2000; Jarvie and Maguire 2000; Flanagan 2001; Held and McGrew 2002; Maguire 2005). People, ideas and capital can move freely and easily across the globe, creating 'an increased awareness of a sense of the world as a whole' (Jarvie and Maguire 2000: 231). With time and space compressed, the resulting conflict between local and global cultures is the fourth characterization of globalization. Political, technological, economic and cultural forces can lead to the development of a singular transnational culture (often dominated by Western capitalism), but they can also strengthen and revive local identities or fuel reactionary politics (Giddens 2000; Held and McGrew 2002; Maguire 2005). The fifth attribute is that globalization is complex, unpredictable and in some cases contradictory (Giddens 2000; Jarvie and Maguire 2000). The outcomes that arise from the interactions of globalization factors do not maintain consistent patterns, which may actually result in a more 'archaic, haphazard' (Giddens 2000: 37) global order.

These dimensions and complexities are clearly evident in sport labour migration. Economic, political, cultural and technological factors all play roles in sport migration, but no single factor best explains the process. Furthermore, the competitive nature of sport further accelerates the speed at which athletes migrate. Thus, it is the interaction, or 'interconnectedness' (Elliot and Maguire 2008b: 485), of these factors that shapes sport migration (Sage 2010). Five common facilitators will be presented below for simplicity of analysis, although it is once again acknowledged that the processes are invariably more complex and multifaceted than presented on first inspection.

Economic factors

Economic factors are often seen as the primary motivation for sport labour migration. Athletic skill is a commodity with a short lifespan. Thus, athletes are willing to move quickly and widely in order to maximize their value during such narrow windows of opportunity. David Beckham's lucrative journey (from Manchester United to Real Madrid to the Los Angeles Galaxy, loan to Inter Milan, and back to the Galaxy, a second loan to Inter Milan and once again back to Los Angeles) exemplifies this. However, Sage (2010: 90) adds that the sport opportunity structure 'accounts for a great deal of sports migration'. This refers to the notion that some countries have many professional opportunities but a scarcity of athletic talent. Conversely, some countries produce a talent in excess of their available positions. Thus, athletic talent regularly flows to the locations with economic opportunity in sport (Klein 2006; Alegi 2010; Sage 2010).

Athlete movement stemming from the sport opportunity structure has been facilitated by the increase in economic freedom and international trade that emerged in the wake of the Cold War. The Cold War between the USA and former Soviet Union (USSR) dominated much of the world's economic (and political) climate following World War II (Giddens

2000; Flanagan 2001). During this period, rigid economic and political boundaries existed between predominantly communist and predominantly capitalistic nations. The formation of economic trading blocs, like the North American Free Trade Agreement and, particularly, the European Union (EU), has had a notable effect on sport migration. One core objective of the EU was to create a single market that would facilitate four freedoms: movement of people, goods, services and capital (European Commission 2010). Despite this, athletes were still subject to restrictive transfer rules and Union of European Football Associations (UEFA) quotas. However Jean Luc Bosman sued for the right to change clubs, and in 1995, the European Court of Justice ruled that players were free to transfer at the conclusion of their contracts. As a result of what became known as the Bosman ruling, 'clubs could sign any number of players from European Union countries' (Fordyce 2005; news.bbc.co.uk/sport2/hi/football/4528732.stm).

Such signings often result from interrelated recruiting and marketing efforts that are underscored by economic motivations. American college coaches will personally scout and recruit athletes as well as rely on professional contacts in talent-rich countries to find and steer talent to their institutions (Bale 1991; Berkowitz 2006; Pierce *et al.* 2010). Major League Baseball (MLB) teams have established academies in countries like the Dominican Republic to train systematically young baseball players, the best of whom are given work permits to play in the USA (Klein 2006; Sage 2010). Similar academies exist in African youth football too. Many are funded in part by European clubs or western corporations and export top players north to Europe (Alegi 2010). Finally agents, buscones[1] and other *ad hoc* coaches facilitate migration by serving as intermediaries. Such individuals find remote pools of talent, board and train their athletes, then market them to professional teams in return for a percentage of the athlete's signing bonus (Wertheim 2004a; Klein 2006, 2008; Alegi 2010).

Political factors

A nation's political system often contributes to its level of sport opportunity structure. Without fair pay, freedom or diverse occupational opportunities, athletes will use sport as a means to emigrate. In some cases, political corruption creates a sport structure in which players are unable to attain fair market value for their services. Foer (2004) described how the culture of political bribery in Brazil led to the mass exodus of its top players. He estimated that over 5,000 players emigrated primarily in search of more equitable offers.

Changing political systems and the associated redrawing of political boundaries have also contributed to an increase in sport labour migration. The change in political boundaries resulting from the end of the Cold War opened up competitive opportunities for athletes in countries that had been previously off limits. The exodus of Russian hockey players to the NHL was a prime example of this movement. From 1956 to 1988, the USSR dominated international ice hockey, winning seven Olympic gold medals, yet their players were unable to play professionally in North America. Following the fall of Communism, Russian players became a common and transformational presence in the NHL (Glennon 2008; Allen 2009). More recently, China has begun to allow its most talented athletes to migrate to professional leagues outside its borders (Beech 2003). Yao Ming and Yi Jianlian were top draft picks

151

in the National Basketball Association (NBA), Li Na became the first Chinese Grand Slam champion (French Open) and Liu Xiang has been a world-class hurdler on the International Association of Athletics Federation (IAAF) World Athletic Series (Yilei 2010). In other cases, sport migration is driven by the desire of athletes to free themselves from restrictive political systems. While political asylum was more commonly sought through sport during the Cold War, athletes from countries like Cuba and Eritrea still use sport, or the status it provides, as a means of defecting overseas (Woolf *et al.* 2000; Pfeil 2009; Montague 2011).

Political factors contributing to migration are often linked to the aforementioned economic factors. In some African and Latin American countries with weak political structures, especially those with poor educational systems, sport emerges as a visible and legitimate occupation for individuals wishing to improve their economic standing (Klein 1991, 2006; Aranguré and Cyphers 2009a; Alegi 2010). The Dominican Republic provides an excellent case study. Suffering from the colonial legacy of Spain and the USA, the Dominican Republic's political history has been 'filled with internal struggle, corrupt, power-hungry leaders' (Klein 1991: 14). Economically, these struggles have resulted in a 'historic overdependence on sugar' production (Klein 1991: 14). Beside the sugar industry, the only legitimate option for many Dominican boys is baseball, and, as Klein notes, 'there are not national heroes with machetes in their hands' (Klein 1991: 58). According to Klein (2006: 125), the concept of 'grow[ing] players for export' is encouraged by Dominican politicians through the subsidization of academies, provision of youth coaching, and use of elite Dominican players in government propaganda. Alegi (2010) presents a similar picture in African countries like Senegal and Nigeria, whose politicians facilitate the exporting of young football talent.

Geographical and cultural factors

The locations of sport opportunities and the cultures in those locations comprise a third factor influencing the movement of athletes (Maguire *et al.* 2002). Close or common boundaries and short travel distances between athletes' homes and host countries certainly increase the likelihood of migration. This can be seen in the movement of Eastern European footballers to the Spanish and Italian leagues as well as the influx of Latin American baseball players to the USA (Klein 1991; Maguire *et al.* 2002). However it does not account for common migration patterns over significant distances.

In these cases, shared cultural elements like history, language, religion and ethnicity are important considerations (Maguire *et al.* 2002). The transition between sport worlds becomes much easier when athletes share cultures with their hosts. Stead and Maguire (2000) noted that the transition for Scandinavian football players into English leagues was fairly seamless because most athletes knew how to speak English, maintained a similar work ethic and were familiar with the culture. Likewise, Maguire (1996) found that the migration of French-Canadian ice hockey players to French-speaking countries was primarily due to cultural parallels. Sport culture may also play a role in migration patterns. Researchers have argued that South American football players migrate most frequently to Spain and Italy not only due to shared cultural elements, but also because of the similarity in playing style (Maguire *et al.* 2002; de Vasconcellos Ribeiro and Dimeo 2009).

152

Competitive factors

Although fairly simplistic, a common motivation for sport migration is the desire of athletes to seek out the best competitive opportunities available to them. Sport migration is replete with examples of athletes moving to challenge their skills against the best athletes in their sports. After Ichiro Suzuki dominated the Japanese league of baseball, 'he simply wanted to play the game at the highest level possible, and Ichiro felt that place was the United States' (Leigh 2004: 63). His success has led to a shift in Japan where 'schoolboy players yearn to play in the American Major Leagues' instead of Japanese professional baseball (Gordon 2006: 18). Research has also demonstrated that football players in less prominent leagues migrate to the top leagues in Western Europe because the competition level there is higher (Stead and Maguire 2000; Molnar 2006).

Competitive motivations for migration also include the desire to learn from elite coaches who can maximize an athlete's potential. Such migrations have been common in youth gymnastics and tennis. However, IMG, the global sports marketing agency, has created an academy in Florida that extends its reach to a variety of sports. Athletes migrate internationally and within the USA to obtain comprehensive athletic coaching in typical individual sports like golf and tennis as well as team sports like lacrosse, baseball, American football and basketball. Coaching at such academies is not only sport-specific, but also includes instruction in nutrition, strength and conditioning and sport psychology (King 2002; Sokolove 2004).

Technological factors

The rapid development in communication and transportation technologies comprises the final factor facilitating sport labour migration. The dramatic growth of communication technologies in the late twentieth century has made sport migration more plausible. A first benefit of communication technology is that developing athletes are able to see international competition with regularity. Whether through live television, internet broadcasts or websites like YouTube, fans can watch the world's best athletes perform in virtually any sport. Although there is little formal research on the impact of internet communication technology on sport labour migration, it has obvious significance for developing athletes. Not only do young athletes learn how a particular sport is played at the highest level, they also learn to see a particular league or country as the pre-eminent playing destination. For example, German Dirk Nowitzki watched telecasts of Larry Bird playing in the NBA, and ultimately became the most valuable player of the NBA. NBA officials reportedly believe that German broadcasts of Nowitzki playing in the NBA have the potential to perpetuate further sport migration (Wertheim 2004b).

Improved scouting is a second benefit of communication technology. Use of the internet and social media to recruit international athletes is increasingly commonplace (Pierce et al. 2010). Athletes in sports ranging from basketball, water polo, volleyball, tennis, golf to athletics depend heavily on the internet to email coaches and/or post video highlights on websites like YouTube. Conversely, many coaches in these sports request video or use statistical databases on the internet to find prospective athletes (NCAA 2010; Popp et al. 2010;

153

Schroeder and VanHollebeke 2010). Furthermore, recruiting-specific websites like aussie-sportsamerica.com, avsrglobal.com or netscoutsbasketball.com connect coaches and athletes through platforms designed specifically to facilitate the recruiting process.

A third way communication technology enhances sport migration is by enabling migrant athletes to stay in contact with their friends and family. Communication websites (e.g. Skype or Facebook) can help alleviate the loneliness that is a common consequence of sport migration (Schroeder and VanHollebeke 2010). Such communication has been shown to lead to another outcome of labour migration: talent pipelines. A talent pipeline is a relationship that is built between a sport organization and a country's athletes based on previous dealings and exchanges of players and coaches (Maguire *et al.* 2002). With established connections, players are more likely and willing to join an organization about which they have heard positive feedback. Similarly, organizations or coaches are more willing to recruit players from countries that have a history of good talent. Talent pipelines have existed for many years. For example, Klein (2006) notes that MLB teams began sending baseball scouts to the Dominican Republic in 1955. The number of Dominican players in the MLB rose steadily through the twentieth century and, by 2009, almost 10 per cent of MLB players were Dominican. However, communication technology can accelerate and solidify such pipelines for coaches. In 2001, St Mary's College in California recruited one Australian basketball player and by 2009, 33 per cent of the basketball team was comprised of Australians (Dienhart 2010). In a study on migrant college athletes in the USA, an American tennis coach commented on the frequency and role of communication technology:

> Also you'll see a lot in college tennis, and you will see it here, is you'll get sort of a pipeline going where I think we, for a while, had quite a few Germans. You get one German and then he Skypes his friends, 'Hey I love it over here. Why don't you come join me?' And then it kind of goes in that cyclical formula, and that's what happened with the Brazilians. We had Chris who was here, and then I started recruiting the guy who came in the fall. Then he knew the guy who just came in January. So now we have three Brazilians ... I give him a lot of the credit for pushing him and pushing him to go here because he had quite a few offers from bigger schools than here.
>
> (Schroeder and VanHollebeke 2010)

Innovations in transportation technology over the past two decades have increased the number of destinations served by air travel and decreased the costs and flight times to those destinations. This has facilitated sport migration in several ways. First, scouts and agents have been able to broaden their recruiting bases. In professional football, baseball and hockey, scouts and agents fly all over the world to find new prospects (Wertheim 2004a; Gleason 2008). At intercollegiate level, coaches also travel internationally to recruit players, but the ease of international travel also allows coaches to bring these recruits to American campuses on 'official visits' (Berkowitz 2006; Weston 2006). These visits enable international athletes to assess the university, its sports facilities and campus life to determine if it will meet their needs. Finally, professional teams and leagues have been able to play internationally due to the increasing ease of travel. For example, MLB, the NBA, NHL, and National Football League

(NFL) all play regular season games abroad. Major football clubs commonly conduct preseason tours in other continents and countries (e.g. Chelsea in Asia in 2011; Inter Milan in the USA in 2010). These international competitions not only increase revenue and visibility, they also maintain the leagues' and teams' status as premier destinations for migrants.

TRENDS IN SPORT LABOUR MIGRATION

Due to a combination of the above factors, athlete migration is present in most professional team sports throughout the world, individual professional/Olympic sports, and common in many American universities. While a detailed analysis of all sport labour migration patterns is beyond the scope of this chapter, this section will provide an overview of the major trends at each level of competition.

Professional sport

Perhaps with the exception of the NFL[2] in the USA, most major professional leagues rely to some degree on imported labour. As the world's most popular sport, association football has the largest talent pool, and top professional teams spend significant amounts of money scouting and signing the best international players (Sage 2010). In 2009–2010, migrants represented 42.6 per cent of the total number of footballers in the leagues of England, France, Spain, Italy and Germany (see Table 9.1 for a breakdown by country). In the top five leagues, this percentage rose above 60 per cent. Furthermore, migrants claimed a greater proportion of playing time than these percentages would warrant. Thus, the higher the level of football, the more migrants on the roster and the more playing time they received (Poli *et al.* 2010).

Table 9.1 *The percentages of foreign players in the top five European football leagues or countries*

Country	Foreign players (%)
England	59.8
Germany	47.4
Italy	42.1
Spain	32.8
France	31.8

Professional baseball in the USA is also increasingly cosmopolitan. While MLB has had a stream of players from Latin America since the 1930s, that stream has increased and broadened in the past 25 years. More recently, the number of players hailing from Pacific Rim nations has risen. Migrant baseball players made up 28 per cent of 2009 opening-day rosters and these 229 players migrated from 15 countries (Table 9.2). In addition, nearly half (47.8 per cent) of all Minor League Baseball players came from 41 countries outside the USA (MLB. com 2009).

155

Table 9.2 *Number of foreign-born Major League Baseball players by country in 2009*

Country	Number of professionals
Dominican Republic	84
Venezuela	52
Puerto Rico	28
Mexico	14
Canada	13
Japan	13
Cuba	7
Curaçao	4
Panama	4
Australia	3
South Korea	3
Colombia	2
Nicaragua	2
Taiwan	2
Netherlands	1

Source: MLB.com (2009).

Basketball is notable for having two distinct labour flows across the globe. First, the world's best players migrate to the NBA and Women's National Basketball Association (WNBA) with regularity. At the beginning of the 2009–2010 season, 83 players representing 36 countries were on NBA rosters, and in the WNBA, 22 per cent of the players were from outside the USA (NBA.com 2009). Second, the USA is a large exporter of basketball talent. Many American players who are not signed by American professional teams seek opportunities in European leagues. In fact, more than half of WNBA players also compete in non-American leagues during the WNBA's off-season (Wolff 2008; Poms 2009).

Ice hockey was the first international league, with five franchises in Canada and one in the USA. While hockey has always moved players across the American–Canadian border, the aftermath of the Cold War marked an enormous European influx to the NHL. In 1990, only 12 per cent of NHL players were born outside the USA, but by 2001, over 30 per cent of NHL hockey players were from Europe (Glennon 2008; Podnieks 2008). However, as European leagues have become more financially viable and legal barriers have increased, the migration patterns have shifted (Gleason 2008; Podnieks 2008). Fewer Europeans are migrating to North America, and many North American players are pursuing opportunities across the Atlantic (Elliot and Maguire 2008a).

Individual/Olympic sports

The structure of individual sports like tennis, golf, athletics and Formula One racing creates a nomadic existence for its athletes. In such sports, many governing bodies have international divisions or offices and host competitions throughout the world for athletes from a wide variety of nations. Tennis is a prime example of the increasing globalization of sport. The Association of Tennis Professionals (ATP) has offices in London, Sydney, Monte Carlo and Florida and hosts events in 32 countries (ATP 2010a). Its top 100 singles players hail from 36 different countries, and between 2000 and 2010, every inhabited continent had a player ranked in the ATP's top ten (Wertheim 2009; ATP 2010b). Thus, in sports like tennis, globalization sports has moved athletics beyond migration and instead created a mobile labour force in which athletes must regularly move around the globe. Maguire and Pearton (2000) refer to such athletes as sport nomads because 'home', as defined as birthplace, is at odds with a 'seemingly constantly shifting workplace and place of residence' (p. 178).

In Olympic sports, transfers of allegiance, or changes in the country for which an athlete competes, have become increasingly common (Bale 2003; IAAF 2012). In some cases, transfers are driven by countries seeking the prestige associated with success in international competitions. Such nations recruit athletes from other countries and provide them with top pay, facilities and coaching in hopes of improving their national medal count. Conversely, some athletes may not be selected by their own national teams so they migrate to nations seeking to import athletic talent. Both of these forms of labour migration were evident during the 2008 Beijing Olympics. Bernard Lagat was a Kenyan runner who participated in intercollegiate athletics in the USA but retained his Kenyan citizenship and was the 1500m silver medalist in the 2004 Olympics. But, in 2005, he was persuaded to become a US citizen and represented the USA in the 2008 Olympics (Moore 2010). On the other hand, American Becky Hammon failed to make the USA women's basketball team and subsequently became a citizen of Russia to pursue her Olympic dreams. She not only led the Russian team to a bronze medal, but was also able to triple her salary for CSKA Moscow because she held a Russian passport (Schwarz 2008; Weeks 2008). On rare occasions, these transfers of allegiance are due to the pressure on host countries to field credible teams in Olympic sports unfamiliar in their nations. In these instances, host nations have recruited players from other countries who excel at the particular sport and usually share some heritage of the host nation. For example, Greece's 2004 Olympic baseball and softball teams were primarily composed of Americans who were only required to be one-quarter Greek, so to speak (Ford 2004; Michaelis 2004).

American intercollegiate athletics[3]

Although intercollegiate sport competition exists in many countries, the American system is quite unique. It features widespread media coverage, highly paid coaches, corporate sponsorship, lavish facilities and financial rewards for successful universities (Eitzen and Sage 2008). Part of this elaborate structure involves athletic scholarships. American coaches recruit top athletes by paying their college tuition and living expenses for up to 5 years. In 1996, 8,851 migrants were playing American intercollegiate athletics (NCAA 1996). A 2008 report by the governing body of American university sport, the NCAA, showed an increase to over 16,000. There are several possible explanations for this increase, related to both migrant athletes and American coaches.

157

From the migrant athlete's perspective, research has indicated that the American 'brand' image appeals to young people throughout the world (Bale 1991; Kaburakis 2007). In addition, the American university system has a strong worldwide reputation, so some international athletes seek out the American system of higher education for its academic strength (Popp *et al.* 2010). The American intercollegiate system can also serve as a gateway to lucrative professional leagues in the USA. In baseball, basketball, golf, hockey and American football, a successful college career enables athletes to attract attention easily from professional scouts and sponsors. Finally, American universities allow athletes to play sport and study at high levels. In other countries, athletes have reported feeling forced to decide between training for a sports career and studying for a traditional occupation (Popp *et al.* 2010; Schroeder and VanHollebeke 2010). By coming to the USA, international student athletes can postpone that decision. For example, a female tennis player indicated to Schroeder and VanHollebeke that:

> a lot of other players from my club in Germany have been to the US and I talked to them and they said, 'Yeah it's really nice. You can do both education and sport.' And if I do it in Germany, I have to decide what I want to do [between] playing tennis and going to a university. And that's the reason why I came here, to do both.
>
> (Schroeder and VanHollebeke, 2010)

American college coaches are also responsible for the rise in sport migration among US universities. At the highest levels of American intercollegiate athletics, coaches are under significant amounts of pressure to produce winning teams (Weston 2006). To that end, coaches need to recruit talented athletes. Recruiting abroad gives American coaches access to larger and deeper talent pools. In football, tennis and ice hockey, more athletes play these sports in other countries and do so at higher levels. The second reason many American coaches recruit abroad is to close the talent gap (Bale and Sang 1996; Weston 2006). The top universities in the USA tend to attract the top American talent. American coaches at smaller universities recruit abroad in an attempt to find undiscovered talent to compete with these 'traditional powers' (Bale and Sang 1996). Several smaller universities have been able to attain national prominence by developing talent pipelines with specific countries (see St Mary's College basketball example, above) (Bale and Sang 1996; Pierce *et al.* 2010).

MANAGEMENT ISSUES ARISING FROM SPORT LABOUR MIGRATION

As the frequency of sport migration has increased, so have the number of concerns and issues raised by the global flow of labour. The consequences primarily arise for three types of stakeholders: donor nations, host nations and athletes (Sage 2010). Donor nations, those from which large pools of athletes migrate, suffer from deskilling and underdevelopment (Maguire *et al.* 2002; Klein 2006; Alegi 2010). Host nations, those which frequently import athletes, must deal with legal issues and xenophobia (Maguire *et al.* 2002). For athletes, particularly those from poor and undeveloped nations, exploitation in the form of low pay is a major concern. Athletes may also experience difficulty adjusting to new cultures, especially when new cultures significantly differ from their own (Bale and Sang 1996; Bretón 2000).

Concerns for donor nations

From the standpoint of sport labour migration, donor nations are primarily poorer countries that produce large pools of athletic talent but fail to provide lucrative and/or competitive professional prospects. Therefore their athletic talent often emigrates to nations with more lucrative playing opportunities. Donor nations highlighted in the literature include Nigeria and Cameroon in football and the Dominican Republic and Venezuela in baseball (Klein 1991; Alegi 2010). In these and other cases, deskilling often emerges. Deskilling refers to the process whereby nations expend resources to produce athletic talent and, when that talent matures, teams from other nations lure it away (Maguire *et al.* 2002). As exemplified in African football and Latin American baseball, deskilling frequently occurs to less developed nations and primarily benefits more economically advanced countries. Alegi (2010) writes that nearly 800 Africans were playing in UEFA leagues and as a result 'in the 2006 World Cup, only about one in five African players came from African clubs' (p. 102). Not surprisingly, this has devastated African leagues where the lack of talent has diminished public interest. Although much less common, there are cases where developed nations are also deskilled. Concerns have been expressed about top American footballers moving to European leagues and Japanese baseball players migrating to the USA (Fackler 2004; Farley 2010).

Donor nations may also suffer from the symbiotic processes of underdevelopment and dependent development. According to Klein (1991), underdevelopment refers to the lack of diversity in a nation's economy, often stemming from an overreliance on one or two basic industries. Sport can contribute to underdevelopment when government resources that are spent on football or baseball siphon off funding for education or economic development. Furthermore, when children view sport as one of the only legitimate job options, they are liable to spend less time in school or on occupational training (Alegi 2010; Klein 2006). These issues are endemic to countries like the Dominican Republic where the educational funding is the fourth worst in the world, and 'the amount of energy people expend in pursuit of a career in baseball appears grotesquely out of proportion to the number of opportunities actually available' (Klein 1991: 59; Aranguré and Cyphers 2009a).

The underdevelopment of such nations is further reinforced by the dependent development of countries benefiting from sport migration (Klein 1991; Maguire *et al.* 2002; Alegi 2010). In dependent development, teams, leagues and, in some cases, corporations from wealthy nations infuse millions of dollars into the economies of poor nations for the sole purpose of training, and ultimately importing, young athletes. This narrow form of development creates a 'pauperization' (Alegi 2010: 103) in donor nations and perpetuates the myth of a professional sports career among its young athletes (Klein 2006; Alegi 2010). Alegi (2010) illustrates these problems in the football academy systems across Africa. A prototype is the Pepsi Football Academy in Nigeria, which has 'a national network of fourteen centers with fifty-four coaches training three thousand boys from the ages of six to eighteen' (p. 119). While it has placed graduates in over 12 European countries, 'for the thousands of boys not good enough for admission to the academies or unable to reach the professional ranks, the future looks bleak' (Alegi 2010: 119–120).

159

Issues in host nations

Host nations tend to be wealthy countries that lure migrant athletes with better pay, competition, coaching or training facilities than the athletes' home nations. While host nations largely benefit from sport migrants, this importation does create concerns. In some places xenophobia, a fear or opposition to immigration and a preference for local players over immigrants, has arisen (Sage 2010). Legal barriers such as league quotas, immigration issues, questions of amateurism and league transfer agreements comprise a second concern in host nations (Weston 2006; Gleason 2008; Sage 2010). For sport managers, these concerns can limit an organization's ability to attract top athlete migrants, influence marketing and create onerous recruiting and hiring processes.

Cases of xenophobia tend to arise as leagues or teams rely overwhelmingly on imported labour. Maguire *et al.* (2002) indicate that these concerns typically centre on the perceived threat to national team performance and the underdevelopment of national talent. England's Professional Footballers Association (2007) contends that the country's poor showings during the FIFA World Cup are due to the high percentage of sport migrants in the English Premier League, especially employed by the League's top teams. As a result, English players are relegated to lower levels of domestic competition that do not adequately prepare them for international play. Similarly, some American players, coaches, administrators and parents pin the demise of American tennis on the vast recruiting of tennis migrants in NCAA tennis (Weston 2006). Another concern stemming from xenophobia is job loss. Immigrant labour is often hired at a lower wage and thus robs native citizens of well-paying jobs (Friedman 1999; Weston 2006). The waning participation of African-Americans in baseball is a prime sports example of this concern. Although the decline in participation stems from many factors, some critics argue that it is due to the MLB's preference for the cheaper and more 'controllable' labour of Latin Americans (Howard 2010). Although research (Weston 2006; Elliot and Weedon 2010) is sceptical of these migration effects, sport managers must account for them when communicating and marketing to fans.

An outgrowth of these xenophobic tendencies is the establishment or strengthening of policies that can serve as migration barriers. Although EU members can migrate freely, some European sports leagues still commonly maintain quotas for EU players and place limits on the number of non-EU athletes (Maguire *et al.* 2002). This protectionism is evident in Japanese and Australian leagues as well (Kelly 2006). Concerns about illegal immigration and underage signings have emerged in response to high numbers of teenage talent migrating from underdeveloped nations. In 2001, FIFA passed an age restriction rule for international transfers and the signings of 14- and 15-year-old baseball players has led to an increase in documentation and regulations in the US visa process (Klein 2006). Although both sets of regulations temporarily curtailed youth recruitment, sports organizations have found means of circumventing these rules (Aranguré and Cyphers 2009b; Alegi 2010). Thus, sport managers will still be forced to find ways to change the xenophobic fan cultures that dot the sport landscape.

International athlete transfer agreements also affect sport labour migration. Transfer agreements are contracts between sport governing bodies in different countries that govern the manner and price by which players are allowed to move from one league to another. Disputes between teams and leagues in multiple sports have created numerous headaches for

160

sport managers (Gleason 2008; Lefton 2011). For example, MLB teams wishing to sign players from the Japanese professional league must pay a huge sum to the Japanese team, referred to as a posting fee (i.e. $20 million) just for the right to negotiate with a player. If that player does not sign with an MLB team in 30 days, the posting fee and player are lost. This gives Japanese players excellent leverage in the negotiation process, so MLB teams must have deep pockets to sign these players (Lefton 2011). The absence of an international transfer policy can be even more problematic (Gleason 2008). The NHL has transfer agreements with all major donor nations except Russia because Russian clubs were unhappy with the transfer fees offered by the NHL. The lack of a transfer policy has left NHL and Russian teams unsure about where individual athletes will play (Gleason 2008; Glennon 2008). Athletes unhappy with contracts or playing conditions have simply changed allegiances in the midst of their contracts. But without a transfer agreement, there is little either NHL or Russian clubs can do to retain their players (Gleason 2008). For sport managers, at least in the NHL, this makes drafting migrant athletes very risky due to 'the expense and difficulty teams encounter when attempting to pull their draft picks away from international teams and into the NHL' (Gleason 2008: 604). Thus it is imperative for sports executives to research thoroughly migrant prospects' personality, commitment to migration and contract status (Glennon 2008).

In American intercollegiate sport, the NCAA maintains restrictive policies for the recruitment and migration of international student athletes. The NCAA requires amateurism amongst its athletes and strictly defines it as not receiving pay, the promise of pay or having competed on a professional team (NCAA 2010). However, amateurism is not as clearly defined outside the USA, where young athletes may play in clubs that field professional teams or host professional tournaments (Weston 2006; Kaburakis 2007; Pierce et al. 2010). The NCAA used to ban players with such affiliations, but now reduces the number of years they are allowed to compete for American universities (Pierce et al. 2010). Compounding this issue are differences in educational systems. The NCAA requires all prospective student athletes to complete a core of college preparatory classes in order to be eligible for college sport. Yet differences in educational systems 'coupled with language barriers, varied standards and inconsistent record keeping, can lead to uncertain assessments' (Weston 2006: 832) of an international athlete's academic preparation. Thus, athletes can migrate to an American university, but unknowingly end up ineligible for competition upon arrival. While such restrictions would seemingly limit athletes' willingness to migrate to American universities or coaches' desire to recruit migrants, statistics indicate otherwise (NCAA 2008). The number of international athletes in American universities continues to rise. Subsequently, the burden of facilitating this process falls on sport managers (Berkowitz 2006). The tasks of articulating transcripts, coordinating eligibility with the NCAA and integrating migrant athletes into the American university system are all performed by university sport administrators and this process has been described by international advisors as being extremely exhausting (Berkowitz 2006).

Athlete concerns

The most commonly expressed concern about sport migration, and one sport managers should be particularly sensitive to, is the well-being of the migrant athletes. Several authors have discussed the perceived exploitation of young sports migrants, especially those from underdeveloped nations (Klein 1991, 2006; Bale and Sang 1996; Bretón 2000; Maguire *et al.* 2002; Alegi 2010). Cross-cultural adjustments are also common concerns for sport migrants (Bale and Sang 1996; Popp *et al.* 2010). These can occur across a variety of migrant experiences and may lead to poor athlete performances or the return of athletes to their homelands. While these are significant consequences for sport organizations, they are drawbacks which sport managers are well positioned to address.

The first form of sport migrant exploitation has been referred to as the 'boatload mentality' (Bretón 2000: 14). Here clubs and teams, primarily in football and baseball, sign numerous young players from underdeveloped nations at very low prices. The teams then house, feed and train the athletes. The few athletes who develop potential are exported – either sold to football clubs or sent to Minor League Baseball teams. The vast majority of players who do not demonstrate sufficient skill are returned to their home nations with little hope of meaningful employment (Bretón 2000; Klein 2006; Alegi 2010).

A second form of exploitation occurs on the part of agents. Agents serve a variety of functions, depending on the sport or country. While all agents market their clients, others scout, house, feed and train them. In exchange for these services, agents demand a percentage of the athlete's signing bonus. Since these agents are mostly unregulated, their fees can be exorbitant – in extreme cases amounting to 50 per cent of the bonus (Klein 1991; Arangure and Cyphers 2009a).

Ethnic exploitation is a third form. Here, athletes are signed not necessarily for their talent, but instead as vehicles for marketing. One way this occurs is when teams sign a player of unique ethnicity (e.g. Yao Ming) as a means of marketing their team to a new demographic (e.g. China) (Oates and Polumbaum 2004). Another way ethnic exploitation occurs is through the use of stereotypes. Athletic stereotypes exist in all sports and are often based on the perceived styles of play in a specific country (Falcous and Maguire 2005; Alegi 2010). Agents leverage these stereotypes to sell players of marginal quality to clubs at inflated prices. Teams further this exploitation by marketing these migrants to their own fans (Foer 2004; de Vasconcellos Ribeiro and Dimeo 2009). While these forms of exploitation are common, sport managers can help rectify them by using responsible marketing strategies, compensating all stakeholders fairly and only negotiating with reputable agents.

Cross-cultural adjustments are also a common concern for athlete migrants. When athletes encounter a new culture, they commonly report difficulty adjusting to its language, food and customs (Ridinger and Pastore 2000a, b; Berkowitz 2006; de Vasconcellos Ribeiro and Dimeo 2009; Popp *et al.* 2010; Schroeder and VanHollebeke 2010). These adjustments are compounded by the racism to which migrants are often subjected in their new host countries by fans, media and team mates (Bale and Sung 1996; Foer 2004; Alegi 2010) The discrimination in and out of sport often catches migrants off guard as they are not prepared for its presence, intensity or multiple sources. For intercollegiate athletes, the differences in educational style and academic coursework can create additional discomforts (Berkowitz 2006; Popp *et al.* 2010; Schroeder and VanHollebeke 2010).

Sport-specific culture shock adds another layer to the challenge of athlete migration. Migrants commonly struggle to mesh their personal athletic strengths with the style of their host team (Foer 2004; Glennon 2008). Differences in coaching and training can also frustrate sport migrants. The omnipresence of American college coaches can be an affront to migrant athletes while the differences in training intensities have been shown to divide football teams along national lines (Foer 2004; Popp *et al.* 2010; Schroeder and Van Hollebeke 2010). These cultural clashes can be puzzling and discouraging for both parties. Athletes may become depressed about their poor level of play, and managers may regret the significant investments made in the sport migrant (Bretón 2000; Foer 2004; Alegi 2010; Schroeder and Van Hollebeke 2010). Combined, these cultural barriers may not only inhibit the performance of migrants, but, in some cases, compel migrants to return home (Gleason 2008; Glennon 2008).

MANAGING SPORT LABOUR MIGRATION

In the modern, globalized economy, sport labour migration will continue to proliferate (Maguire *et al.* 2002; Sage 2010). As industry leaders, sport managers have a responsibility to frame and shape the labour migration process in an ethical manner. While some of the stakeholders defy management and regulations (e.g. agents), sport managers can take actions that will improve the process for migrants and ultimately their own organization. This can be accomplished through the establishment of support systems for transplanted athletes, development of organizational philosophies about sport labour migration and education about the sport migration process.

The most tangible step sport managers can take to improve this process is to establish legitimate support systems for athletes (Berkowitz 2006). In light of the frequency with which migrants report isolation and loneliness, a variety of steps can help smooth athletes' transitions. Such steps could include the use of cultural mentors and interpreters, formal orientation programmes and cultural education prior to and during migration (Berkowitz 2006). For example, MLB and NBA teams have made widespread use of translators for players from Japan, Taiwan and China (White 2010). Informal networks of mentors often emerge through established talent pipelines, and formalizing these can be even more beneficial. Some American universities have created orientation programmes that connect international athletes on campus, explain the differences in the American educational and athletic systems and provide community support to fight the innate isolation of sport migration (Berkowitz 2006). Such programmes exemplify the type of education needed by sport migrants. To this end, MLB team academies in the Dominican Republic have begun to include cross-cultural and vocational training in their educational programmes (Aranguré and Cyphers 2009b).

The difficulty in establishing support systems is that doing so requires resources. While some sport organizations (i.e. teams) have the resources to assist migrant athletes, others do not see this as a worthy expenditure (Russell and Holowaty 2010). In addition, many of the sport organizations pursing sport migrants are doing so because they are already at an economic disadvantage. Thus, the types of organizations often hiring migrant athletes are those least prepared to support them. For example, Alegi (2010: 100) notes that 'most Africans labor in middle- and lower-tier European leagues' that feature minimal support and ominous working conditions.

163

Subjectively, sport managers can help their organizations develop cultures of inclusion to improve the migration process. Simply ensuring access to native foods, communication devices and ethnic communities is a first way to demonstrate concern for migrant athletes. Second, recognizing and highlighting the strengths that migrants bring to an organization can help create 'a culture ... which enhances the development potential of all players' (Elliot and Weedon 2010: 1). Elliot and Weedon have demonstrated that such an approach has been successful in English Premier League football as migrants improved the work ethic, professionalism and skills in the academy cultures. Third, developing an appropriate philosophical approach to the development and use of sport migrants is critical to successful transitions. According to MLB International, teams that import athletes often feel pressured to develop and play them rapidly. This shortsighted approach leads to cultural frustrations that result in poor athletic performance. Instead, MLB International is working with teams to create an integration model for baseball migrants that slowly introduces regional culture and MLB's baseball culture (Russell and Holowaty 2010).

However, leading such cultural changes within professional and university sport organizations is exceedingly difficult, especially when organizations have been successful (Schein 2004). The public nature of sport adds to these difficulties. Fans and their traditions contribute greatly to the cultures of their favorite teams, yet sport managers have minimal control over their perceptions or actions (Beyer and Hannah 2000). The economic pressures of sport may overwhelm the best development intentions of sport managers. When significant expenses are spent on scouting, transfer fees and salaries, the pressure to play sport migrants may outweigh the desire to provide gradual cultural integration.

Nonetheless, education can help future sport managers grapple better with the sport labour migration process. Being able to identify the key stakeholders and their motivations can help prevent the exploitation common to sport migration and may help ease imbalances between host and donor nations. Sport managers may be able to create competitive advantages for their organizations by knowing where to find talented athletes and developing talent pipelines. In developing such pipelines, knowledge of the migration process can help sport managers navigate the barriers that impede this recruitment. Providing information to athletes about the process, understanding different cultural communication norms and locating strategic partners can make a sport organization more attractive to prospective migrants (Berkowitz 2006). Studying international transfer agreements, national visa processes and regulations of sport organizations (e.g. NCAA) can all improve the legal aspects of migrant athlete employment (Weston 2006). With knowledge of the difficulties facing sport migrants, sport organizations can develop support systems that will facilitate smooth transitions for these athletes.

SUMMARY

The fluid movement of athletes across international and cultural barriers, or sport migration, is a fundamental element of the twenty-first-century sport industry. The process has accelerated since the end of the Cold War, influenced by a range of economic, political, geographical/cultural, technological and competitive factors. During this time, common patterns of migration have developed in professional team sports, individual professional sports and intercollegiate athletics. In professional team sports, athletes often move from less-developed nations to those with more developed economies. Athletes competing individually must travel across the globe simply to remain competitive. For young athletes, universities in the USA have become a common destination. Athletes at these levels migrate intranationally and internationally for a variety of interacting reasons. Economically, many athletes move in search of more lucrative contracts, and conversely, many teams recruit internationally in search of cheaper labour. Other athletes are politically motivated to move to escape repressive regimes or avoid corrupt governments. Migration decisions are also influenced by geographical proximity, cultural similarities and increased competitive opportunities. Sport labour migration can create several concerns. For donor nations, deskilling, underdevelopment and dependent development can result. Host nations must worry about xenophobia and the legal barriers to sport migration. The potential for culture shock and exploitation is a common concern for athletes. Sport managers are well positioned to deal with some of these concerns. By understanding the legal barriers to migration, creating cultures of inclusion and providing support systems, sport organizations can ease the transitions for migrant athletes.

NOTES

1 *Buscones* are found primarily in the Dominican Republic. The term translates literally to 'finders', but *buscones* do more than find baseball talent. According to Klein (2008), 'the *buscón* is someone who finds potential talent, develops it, and, when ready, sells the player to a major league team, reserving a part of the signing bonus as his commission' (p. 126).
2 The National Football League organizes American football. In this chapter, 'football' refers to association football.
3 The chapter uses the American iteration of 'athletics' in which it is synonymous with sport and not specifically track and field.

REVIEW QUESTIONS

1 Why is it important for sport managers to understand the labour migration process?

2 Pick your favorite sport to help discuss the following questions:
   ■ Is your country a donor nation or host nation in that sport? Explain your position.
   ■ Explain which of the factors highlighted in the chapter facilitate migration in this sport.
   ■ Which management issues arising from sport labour migration are of most concern in your favorite sport? Why?
   ■ Explain what management tactics you would use to help minimize these concerns.

3 Make a list of the advantages and disadvantages of sport labour migration for the following parties:
   ■ migrating athletes;

165

- host nation sports;
- donor nation sports.

4 As a sport manager, what actions might you have taken to prevent the problem in the case study?

5 What option would you advise Elsa to take? Why?

FURTHER READING

Alegi, P. (2010). *African Soccerscapes: How a continent changed the world's game.* Athens, OH: Ohio University Press.

Bale, J. (2003). *Sport Geography.* New York, NY: Routledge.

Falcous, M. and Maguire, J. (2005). "Globetrotters or Local Heroes? Labour Migration, Basketball, and Local Identities." *Sociology of Sport Journal* 22: 20–40.

WEBSITES

Moving People Changing Places:

www.movingpeoplechangingplaces.org/identities-cultures/sporting-diasporas.html

The Sport Journal:

www.thesportjournal.org/article/labor-and-immigration-issues-sports

REFERENCES

Alegi, P. (2010). *African Soccerscapes: How a continent changed the world's game.* Athens, OH: Ohio University Press.

Allen, K. (2009). More Russian players saying 'nyet' to NHL. *USA Today* 17 December. http://www.usatoday.com/sports/hockey/nhl/2009-12-16-russian-players_N.htm (accessed 17 November 2011).

Aranguré, J. Jr. and Cyphers, L. (2009a). It's not all sun and games. *ESPN The Magazine.* http://sports.espn.go.com/espnmag/story?id=3974952 (accessed 26 October 2010).

Aranguré, J. Jr. and Cyphers, L. (2009b). Padres' Dominican baseball academy (video). http://espn.go.com/video/clip?id=3967271 (accessed 26 October 2010).

ATP. (2010a). ATP World Tour 2010 event calendar. http://www.atpworldtour.com/Tournaments/Event-Calendar.aspx (accessed 27 October 2010).

ATP. (2010b). 2010 ATP World Tour singles rankings. http://www.atpworldtour.com/Rankings/Singles.aspx (accessed 27 October 2010).

Bale, J. (1991). *The Brawn Drain: Foreign student – athletes in American universities.* Urbana, IL: University of Illinois Press.

Bale, J. (2003). *Sport Geography.* New York, NY: Routledge.

Bale, J. and Sang, J. (1996). *Kenyan Running: Movement culture, geography and global change.* London: Frank Cass.

Beech, H. (2003). Yao Ming: China's incredible hulk of the hardcourt becomes NBA sensation. *TIME Asia 38.*

166

Berkowitz, K. (2006). "From Around the World." *Athletic Management* 18: 39–45.

Beyer, J.M. and Hannah, D.R. (2000). "The Cultural Significance of Athletics in U.S. Higher Education." *Journal of Sport Management* 14: 105–132.

Bretón, M. (2000). Field of broken dreams: Latinos and baseball, *ColorLines*. http://www.colorlines.com/archives/2000/04/fields_of_broken_dreams_latinos_and_baseball.html (accessed 5 October 2010).

de Vasconcellos Ribeiro, C.H. and Dimeo, P. (2009). "The Experience of Migration for Brazilian Football Players." *Sport in Society* 12(6): 725–736 (available through EBSCO database: accessed 15 September 2010).

Dienhart, T. (2010). Saint Mary's built with Aussie talent. *Yahoo! Sports*. http://rivals.yahoo.com/ncaa/basketball/news?slug=td-stmarys031910 (accessed 21 November 2011).

Eitzen, D.S. and Sage, G.H. (2008). *The Sociology of North American Sport,* 8th edn. Boulder, CO: Paradigm Publishers.

Elliot, R. and Maguire, J. (2008a). "'Getting Caught in the Net': Examining the Recruitment of Canadian Players in British Professional Ice Hockey." *Journal of Sport and Social Issues* 32(2): 158–176.

Elliot, R. and Maguire, J. (2008b). "Thinking Outside of the Box: Exploring a Conceptual Synthesis for Research in the Area of Athletic Labour Migration." *Sociology of Sport Journal* 25(4): 482–497.

Elliot, R. and Weedon, G. (2010). "Foreign Players in the English Premier Academy League: 'Feet drain' or 'Feet-exchange'?" *International Review for the Sociology of Sport* 46(1): 61–75.

European Commission. (2010). General policy framework. http://ec.europa.eu/internal_market/top_layer/index_1_en.htm (accessed 27 October 2010).

Fackler, M. (2004). Baseball players are the latest casualty of Japan's slump. *Wall Street Journal* 7 January. http://online.wsj.com/article/0,,SB107343108813904000,00.html (accessed 27 October 2010).

Falcous, M. and Maguire, J. (2005). "Globetrotters or Local Heroes? Labour Migration, Basketball, and Local Identities." *Sociology of Sport Journal* 22: 20–40.

Farley, R. (2010). Major League Soccer players' absence from the 2010 World Cup, *SB Nation Soccer*. http://www.sbnation.com/2010/7/28/1591752/major-league-soccer-players-absence-2010-world-cup (accessed 21 October 2010).

Flanagan, S.J. (2001). "Meeting the Challenges of the Global Century," in: Kulger, R.L. and Frost, E.L. *The Global Century: Globalization and national security.* Washington, DC: National Defense University Press, pp. 7–34.

Foer, F. (2004). *How Soccer Explains the World: An unlikely theory of globalization.* New York, NY: Harper Perennial.

Ford, P. (2004). Greek baseball team, made in the USA. *The Christian Science Monitor.* http://www.csmonitor.com/2004/0818/p02s01-woeu.html (accessed at 27 October 2010).

Fordyce, T. (2005). 10 years since Bosman. *BBC Sport.* http://news.bbc.co.uk/sport2/hi/football/4528732.stm (accessed 23 October 2010).

Friedman, T.L. (1999). *The Lexus and the Olive Tree.* New York: Farrar, Strauss and Giroux.

Giddens, A. (2000). *Runaway World.* New York, NY: Routledge.

Gleason, J.P. (2008). "From Russia with Love: The legal Repercussions of the Recruitment and Contracting of Foreign Players in the National Hockey League." *Buffalo Law Review* 56: 599–654.

Glennon, J. (2008). Move to NHL becomes tough one for Russians. *USA Today.* http://www.usatoday.com/sports/hockey/nhl/2008-08-28-russian-exodus_N.htm?csp=34 (accessed 17 November 2011).

Gordon, D. (2006). "Japan: The Changing of the Guard in High School Baseball," in: Gmelch, G. *Baseball without Borders: The international pastime.* Lincoln, NE: University of Nebraska Press, pp. 3–21.

167

Held, D. and McGrew, A. (2002). *Globalization/Anti-globalization*. Malden, MA: Polity Press.

Howard, J. (2010). Hunter wrong on race, not problems. *ESPN.com*. http://sports.espn.go.com/espn/commentary/news/story?id=4989239 (accessed 19 October 2010).

IAAF. (2012). Transfers of allegiance. http://www.IAAF.org/athletes/transfer/index.html (accessed 20 June 2012).

Jarvie, G. and Maguire, J. (2000). *Sport and Leisure in Social Thought*. New York, NY: Routledge.

Kaburakis, A. (2007). "International Prospective Student-Athletes and NCAA Division I Amateurism." *International Journal of Sport Management and Marketing* 2: 100–118.

Kelly, W.W. (2006). "Japan: The Hanshin Tigers and Japanese Professional Baseball," in: Gmelch, G. (ed.) *Baseball without Borders: The international*. Lincoln, NE: University of Nebraska Press, pp. 22–42.

King, K. (2002). The ultimate jock school. *Sports Illustrated*. http://sportsillustrated.cnn.com/vault/article/magazine/MAG1027520/index.htm (accessed 20 October 2010).

Klein, A.M. (1991). *Sugarball: The American game, the Dominican dream*. New Haven, CT: Yale University Press.

Klein, A.M. (2006). "Dominican Republic: Forging an International Industry," in: Gmelch, G. (ed.) *Baseball without Borders: The international*. Lincoln, NE: University of Nebraska Press, pp. 117–135.

Klein, A.M. (2008). "Progressive Ethnocentrism: Ideology and Understanding in Dominican Baseball." *Journal of Sport and Social Issues* 32: 121–138.

Lefton, B. (2011). Focus on a star and a system. *The New York Times*. http://www.nytimes.com/2011/11/10/sports/baseball/yu-darvish-situation-puts-spotlight-on-japanese-player-posting-system.html?_r=2 (accessed 21 November 2011).

Leigh, D.S. (2004). *Ichiro Suzuki* (e-book). Minneapolis, MN: Lerner Publications.

Maguire, J. (1996). "Blade Runners: Canadian Migrants, Ice Hockey, and the Global Sports Process." *Journal of Sport and Social Issues* 20(3): 335–360.

Maguire, J. (2005). *Power and Global Sport: Zones of prestige, emulation, and resistance*. New York, NY: Routledge.

Maguire, J. and Pearton, R. (2000). "Global Sport and the Migration Patterns of France '98 World Cup Finals Players: Some Preliminary Observations." *Soccer and Society* 1(1): 175–189.

Maguire, J., Jarvie, G., Mansfield, L. and Bradley, J.M. (2002). *Sports World: A sociological perspective*. Champaign, IL: Human Kinetics.

Michaelis, V. (2004). Quest to play softball for Greek Olympic team takes family on odyssey. *USA Today*. March 25: 8C.

MLB.com. (2009). Opening Day rosters feature 229 players born outside the U.S. (press release). http://mlb.mlb.com/news/press_releases/press_release.jsp?ymd=20090406&content_id=4139614&vkey=pr_mlb&fext=.jsp&c_id=mlb (accessed 29 October 2010).

Molnar, G. (2006). "Mapping Migrations: Hungary Related Migrations of Professional Footballers after the Collapse of Communism." *Soccer and Society* 7(4): 463–485.

Montague, J. (2011). Where soccer has been a one-way ticket out. *The New York Times*. http://www.nytimes.com/2011/11/15/sports/soccer/world-cup-qualifying-in-eritrea-soccer-as-ticket-out.html (accessed 21 November 2011).

Moore, K. (2010). Bernard Lagat is not done yet, *Runner's World*. http://www.runnersworld.com/article/0,7120,s6-243-297--13403-F,00.html (accessed 21 November 2011).

NBA.com. (2009). NBA players from around the world: 2009–10 season. http://www.nba.com/players/int_players_0910.html (accessed 21 October 2010).

NCAA. (1996). *1996 NCAA Study of International Student-athletes*. Indianapolis, IN: NCAA.

NCAA. (2008). *2006–07 NCAA Student-athlete Race and Ethnicity Report*. Indianapolis, IN: NCAA.

NCAA. (2010). *Division I Manual*. Indianapolis, IN: NCAA.

Oates, T. and Polumbaum, J. (2004). "Agile Big Man: The flexible Marketing of Yao Ming." *Pacific Affairs* 77(2): 187–210.

Pfeil, G. (2009). The international trade in Cuban boxers. *Spiegel Online International.* http://www.spiegel.de/international/world/0,1518,614370,00.html (accessed 15 October 2010).

Pierce, D., Kaburakis, A. and Fielding, L. (2010). "The New Amateurs: The National Collegiate Athletic Association's Application of Amateurism in a Global Sports Arena." *International Journal of Sport Management* 11: 304–327.

Podnieks, A. (2008). NHL landscape changes. *International Ice Hockey Federation.* http://www.iihf.com/home-of-hockey/news/news-singleview/browse/2/article/nhl-landscape-changes.html?tx_tt news%5BbackPid%5D=187&cHash=5abfb28b5e/ (accessed 25 October 2010).

Poli, R., Ravenel, L. and Besson, R. (2010). *Annual review of the European players' labour market.* http://www.fifa.com/mm/document/affederation/courses/01/09/64/93/professionalfootballplay-ersobservatory-extract2010.pdf (accessed 25 October 2010).

Poms, M. (2009). Foreign affairs spur WNBA to starts its season later. *USA Today.* http://www.usa-today.com/sports/basketball/wnba/2009-06-03-wnba-delays-start_N.htm (accessed 25 October 2010).

Popp, N., Love, A.W., Kim, S. and Hums, M.A. (2010). "Cross-cultural Adjustments and International Collegiate Athletics." *Journal of Intercollegiate Sport* 3(1): 163–181.

Professional Footballers Association. (2007). Meltdown: The nationality of Premier League players and the future of English football. http://edition.pagesuite-professional.co.uk/Launch.aspx?referral=other&pnum=&refresh=J0z715Qso14L&EID=095118a5-4201-40ae-a055-1a7e3cf16837&skip= (accessed 24 October 2010).

Ridinger, L. and Pastore, D. (2000a). "A Proposed Framework to Identify Factors Associated with International Student-athlete Adjustment to College." *International Journal of Sport Management* 1(1): 4–24.

Ridinger, L. and Pastore, D. (2000b). "International Student-athlete Adjustment to College: A Preliminary Analysis." *NACADA Journal* 20(1): 33–41.

Russell, C. and Holowaty, J. (2010). University of the Pacific study abroad meeting. Major League Baseball International (personal communication, 25 May 2010).

Sage, G.H. (2010). *Globalizing Sport: How organizations, corporations, media, and politics are changing sports.* Boulder, CO: Paradigm Publishers.

Schein, E.H. (2004). *Organizational Culture and Leadership,* 3rd edn. San Francisco, CA: Jossey-Bass.

Schroeder, P.J. and VanHollebeke, A. (2010). "The Effect of Sport Participation on Academic Integration of International Student-athletes." Paper presented at the College Sport Research Institute's Annual Scholarly Conference on College Sport, Chapel Hill, NC.

Schwarz, M. (2008). Olympics opportunity too much for Hammon to pass up. *ESPN.* sports.espn.go.com/oly/news/story?id=3427182 (accessed 21 November 2011).

Sokolove, M. (2004). Constructing a teen phenom. *New York Times.* http://www.nytimes.com/2004/11/28/magazine/28ATHLETE.html (accessed 27 October 2010).

Stead, D. and Maguire, J. (2000). "'Rite de Passage' or Passage to Riches." *Journal of Sport and Social Issues* 24(1): 36–60.

Weeks, L. (2008). Changing home teams: Olympians shift allegiances. *NPR.* http://www.npr.org/templates/story/story.php?storyId=93741707 (accessed 27 October 2010).

Wertheim, L.J. (2004a). Hot prospects in cold places. *Sports Illustrated.* http://sportsillustrated.cnn.com/vault/article/magazine/MAG1032317/index.htm (accessed 15 September 2010).

Wertheim, L.J. (2004b). "The Whole World is Watching." *Sports Illustrated* 14 June: 72–86.

Wertheim, L.J. (2009). *Strokes of Genius.* New York, NY: Houghton Mifflin Harcourt.

Weston, M.A. (2006). "Internationalization in College Sports: Issues in Recruiting, Amateurism, and Scope." *Willamette Law Review* 42(4): 830–860.

White, P. (2010). Baseball interpreters bridge gap between players, new culture. *USA Today.*

169

http://www.usatoday.com/sports/baseball/2010-08-03-baseball-interpreters-translators-guillen_N.htm (accessed 29 October 2010).

Wolff, A. (2008). "To Russia with love." *Sports Illustrated* 15 December: 58–67.

Woolf, A., Callegari, R. and Roth, N. (2000). *Greener Grass: Cuba, Baseball and the United States* (video).http://www.pbs.org/itvs/globalvoices/greenergrass.html (accessed 29 October 2010).

Yilei, Y. (2010). G'day II as Li, too, advances. *China Daily*. http://www.chinadaily.com.cn/sports/2010-01/28/content_9388050.htm (accessed 30 October 2010).

Chapter 10

The challenges of managing sport in a divided society
Football in Jordan

Dag Tuastad

'We don't want to see any Palestinians.'
(chant of Faisali supporters in their game against
Wihdat during the 2010–2011 season)

TOPICS

Football in Jordan • The Middle East conflict • Supporter violence • Jordan and the democratization wave in the Arab world • Political management of football and ethnic conflict

OBJECTIVES

By the end of this chapter, you will be able to:

- Acknowledge the political role of football in Jordan;
- Describe the role of UN Relief and Works Agency (UNRWA) in organizing sport for refugees and the importance of sport for marginalized people;
- List the main aspects of the Palestinian refugee problem and the Middle East conflict;
- Understand the challenges of sport management in a politically divided society;
- Explain the main causes for political unrest in Jordan.

KEY TERMS

Ethnic conflict – conflict between social groups retaining different cultural belongings.
National identity – identity is the answer to the question: who are you? National

identity is related to the country you feel you belong to but remains independent of your citizenship.

Social memory – the common memory of members of a social group related to what the members of the group do, such as participating in common rituals.

Symbolic war – war without violence. Football has been referred to as 'war without weapons', as supporters impose other meanings upon the game, that often go beyond the action taking place on the field of play, like a history of war between two countries.

Tribe – a group of people who share a perceived common descent and who inhabit or control a specific, defined territory.

OVERVIEW

The team of the Palestinian refugee camp Wihdat has, over the last number of decades, been the most successful football club in Jordan. Meanwhile the team affiliated with the original Transjordanian inhabitants of Jordan, Faisali, has seen its historical position as the pre-eminent club side in the country diminished and ultimately overcome. Politically there has always been tension in Jordan between Palestinian Jordanians, who are a majority in the country, and the original Transjordanian inhabitants. Because of this tension the authorities have suppressed expressions of national identities other than the Jordanian one. Only during football matches have the suppressed tensions been brought to the surface. Football in Jordan is thus a barometer of the political situation in the country more broadly. Indeed, how the authorities handle supporter violence during football matches has consequently a significant impact upon the political development of the country.

HISTORY OF THE CASE STUDY

Two years after Jordan became an independent state in 1946, its indigenous population, the Transjordanians (referring to Jordanians originating on the east bank of the river Jordan), became a minority within their own country. This took place as Palestinian refugees flooded the country during the Israeli–Arab war, and as King Abdullah of Jordan annexed the Palestinian West Bank. The pan-Arabic and Islamic heritage of the royal family was emphasized in an effort to transcend the different ethnic and national identities of the population. To succeed, the rulers had to ensure that Palestinian national identity was suppressed. This project failed with Black September, the violent confrontation between the Jordanian army and Palestinian resistance fighters in 1970. Since then Palestinian national identity among Palestinians in Jordan has been even more suppressed (Brand 1995).

The lack of opportunity to express national identity has transformed the football arena into a field where ethnic belonging and political messages are communicated. Most strikingly, the success of the Wihdat Club has been tremendous, so that games involving it have often seen this phenomenon in its most fulsome form. The Wihdat Club, from the Palestinian refugee camp with the same name, would long serve as a symbol of national resistance and Palestinian national victory. From 1975 to 1993, Palestinian Jordanians – and in fact all over the world – were filled with pride when Wihdat was playing. But football matches have also served as the social memory of Black September, and supporter violence based on ethnic belonging frequently followed matches between teams affiliated with Palestinian and Transjordanian ethnicity (Tuastad 1997).

Today, the political situation for the Palestinians in Jordan has changed as the establishment of an independent Palestinian state in the West Bank and Gaza appears to be a realistic political scenario. Congruently, the content of political messages communicated during football matches in Jordan has also changed. Now it is Transjordanian nationalists, wanting the Palestinians out of their country, who use the football arena to express Transjordanian, anti-Palestinian nationalism. During the first decade of the new millennium, the more unbeatable the Wihdat club was, the fiercer the political reaction it would meet from Transjordanian nationalists. Football thus represents a barometer of ethnic conflict in Jordan. And for the Jordanian authorities, how unrest at the football matches is managed reflects how the authorities manage ethnic conflict in the state.

CASE STUDY: FOOTBALL IN JORDAN

Faisali–Wihdat 0–0, Zarqa, July 2009

'Jordanian football game halted amidst anti-regime chants, hooliganism towards Palestinians' was the headline of a secret document sent on 28 July 2009 from the American Embassy in Amman (Wikileaks Updates 2010). It referred to a match between the Amman football clubs Faisali and Wihdat. Faisali, it was written, is the proxy champion of the East Bank community in Jordan. The name refers to the Hashemite King Faisal, and the team is the one of the East Bank's prominent tribe Udwan, from their stronghold of Salt. Wihdat, though, is the proxy champion of the Jordanians of Palestinian origin, being named after the large Palestinian refugee camp located south of Amman. During the match between Faisali and Wihdat, played in the industrial town of Zarqa and not in Amman as they used to, in order for the authorities to have better crowd control, slogans and cheers were particularly divisive and controversial, directed against members of the royal family. According to the Wikileaks document,

> Faisali supporters chanted about the Palestinian origins of Queen Rania with the cheer, 'divorce her you father of Hussein, and we'll marry you to two of ours.' The newly appointed Crown Prince did not escape comment either, as he is half Palestinian (and one quarter British) himself.

The incident was notably absent in Jordanian media reporting. When asked to comment on Al-Jazeera, the heads of the fan clubs of Wihdat and Faisali declined to participate, recognizing the sensitivities surrounding criticism of the royal family, it was claimed in the document. The match between Faisali and Wihdat was actually called off before it finished, with the score at 0–0. At the stadium, bottles were thrown at the Wihdat players and their supporters by some of the Faisali fans, sparking a violent reaction. The coaches of the teams ordered their players off the field, fearing for their safety.

The game exposed the growing rift between East Bankers and Palestinians in Jordan, it was said in the document, again released by Wikileaks. The 'ugly side of Jordanian ultra nationalism' had been expressed, a source had told the representative of the American Embassy. The slogans had been evidence that status quo-oriented East Bankers were uncomfortable with increasing pressures from political reforms in the country, which would inevitably lessen their near-monopoly of political and social power in Jordan. The King's silence had been deafening, and had 'effectively empowered the pro-status quo establishment'.

Faisali–Wihdat 0–1, Amman, December 2010

In December 2010, Faisali and Wihdat met in Amman, since locating the game in Zarqa had proven to be of little value in addressing violence during the matches between the two teams. The Al-Wihdat team, stronger than ever before, won the match 1–0. Reportedly, the match went off smoothly, 'fans enjoyed a thrilling match in which sportsmanship prevailed', according to the *Jordan Times* (Omari 2010). After the match the police escorted the Faisali supporters from the stadium. But then someone threw stones at the police and at the remaining Wihdat fans inside the stadium. This created panic, unrest and clashes with the police who tried in vain to control the crowd. Outside the stadium clashes erupted, with stone-throwing, cars set on fire and property damaged. Rumours soon spread that Al Jazeera had reported that several fans had been beaten to death by the police (Montague 2011). Reports indicated that as many as 250 people were in fact injured. The Jordanian Minister of Interior, Saad Hayel Sror, issued a stern warning after the game: 'Those who tried to take advantage of the incident, raising provocative statements should have instead sought to ease the tension and restore calm. Their statements pose a threat to Jordan's rule of law and its integral unity' (Omari 2010). Apparently the Minister had Wihdat leaders in mind when issuing this address. The president of the Wihdat club, Tareq Khouri, was at the stadium, and witnessed the violence. After the match Khouri said that the police had deliberately attacked Wihdat fans, and incited the Palestinians (Omari 2010).

Writing on the event, Mudar Zahran (2010), a former employee of the American Embassy in Jordan, and allegedly one of the sources for the cable sent by the American Embassy diplomat over the match in 2009, supported the claim of the Wihdat president. The Wihdat fans were knowingly locked up inside the stadium and then mercilessly attacked by the police, Zahran claimed. Apparently, Transjordanian nationalists and the police allied against the Jordanian Palestinians. If so, this indeed represented a very serious development. Since the establishment of Jordan as an independent state, the challenge of the royal authorities was always to transcend this alliance, and integrate the Palestinians into the nation state rather than alienate them.

THE ORIGIN OF THE RIFT IN PALESTINIAN JORDANIAN RELATIONS IN JORDAN

Jordan emerged out of British interests in bringing stability to a decentralized tribal region. During their revolt during the First World War, Arabs rose against the Ottoman Empire, allying with British forces, in order to create a unified Arab state from Syria to Yemen. But in the desert of the Syrian province of Transjordan, the Arab tribes sided with the Ottomans (Rogan 2009: 152). The area had been neglected by the Ottomans, leaving the Bedouin tribes of the Transjordanian desert autonomous, and wishing to preserve the status quo. They frequently raided the territories of the region, and were opposed to having international borders established throughout their homelands. The Britons created the 'desert mandate' of Transjordan to control the unruly tribes of the region.

Transjordan was never a political community. It was created as part of the British mandate over Palestine, but as the British foreign secretary Arthur Balfour confirmed during the First World War, Britain had promised Zionist leaders a Jewish state west of the Jordan River. Consequently Transjordan was created as a separate mandate on the east bank of the Jordan River. This would make it easier to control the region of some 300,000 people, who made their home between the steppe and the desert. When Amman was appointed capital of the new mandate of Transjordan in 1921, it had a population of about 2,500 people (Cleveland 2000: 209). During the mandate, which was to last until Jordan (changing its name from Transjordan) was established as an independent state in 1946, the Britons in their effort to control the area built up a reliable armed force. This armed force, the Arab Legion, which the Britons trained and developed as a professional army with modern weapons, armoured cars and airplanes, was recruited from the local population, mainly then the Bedouin tribes. Hence, tribal opposition was eliminated as leading tribes were co-opted, and later became a founding element in the strength of the new kingdom. Moreover, to staff the new administration of the desert mandate, educated people were recruited from towns west of Jordan river, and so Palestinians were introduced into the administration during the 1920s and 1930s. A divide between ethnic Transjordanians and Palestinians was thus created, even before the Palestinian disaster of 1948.

THE PALESTINIAN INFLUX IN 1948

Nowhere was the impact of the Palestinian refugee disaster following the establishment of Israel greater than in Gaza and Jordan. While Egypt occupied Gaza in 1948, Jordan annexed the West Bank. Prior to the 1948 war between Israel and its neighbouring states, Jordan's population was around 340,000 people. With the annexation of the new territory, 900,000 Palestinian refugees – a native West Bank population of 450,000 and 450,000 refugees who had fled or been driven out of Israel – were within the new borders of Jordan. The refugees were generally in a catastrophic situation. The new aid agency established by UN, UNRWA, had a budget of $27 per refugee for food, shelter, clothing and medical services. Degraded habitations of people living in shacks made by flattened petrol cans or tents were to be the new reality, forced upon the refugees by external circumstances beyond their control (Cleveland 2000: 347).

Crucially, though, the Jordanian annexation of the West Bank had an important implication which made the situation better for the Palestinians in Jordan than in other host countries; Jordan granted the Palestinians citizenship. This made many Palestinians able to find employment, and a significant number would enjoy middle-class status as civil servants in the Jordanian state administration, as other Palestinians had done during the British mandate. They became 'the core of a post-1948 Palestinian exile bourgeoisie, emotionally committed to the ideal of the return to Palestine but practically devoted to the niceties of middle-class existence', according to Cleveland (2000: 349). These were the urban Palestinians, who had arrived into Jordan from the towns. It meant that – unlike in Gaza where there was no economic differentiation between the refugees – the divide which had always existed in Palestine between local peasants, distrustful of the urban elites, was maintained in terms of social and economic considerations, and that divide was aggravated still further in exile. Initially a third of the Palestinian refugees in Jordan settled in refugee camps, but this proportion gradually increased as many of the refugees from the villages could not sustain their lives in Jordan outside these camps. For Palestinians of peasant origin the new circumstances were devastating, and their initial time in Jordan was later referred to as 'the years of famine.'

As the camps were organized by UNRWA, the political identity of Palestinian camp residents, although granted Jordanian citizenship, was strengthened. UNRWA would grant the refugees a form of permanent emergency aid, and it would also provide education and health services, and, for some, employment. The UNRWA-administered camps were like autonomous islands within the state. Although the camp refugees constituted more than 25 per cent of the Jordanian population, not one camp resident was elected to the Jordanian parliament between 1948 and 1965 (Kimmerling and Migdal 2003: 223). The political isolation of the camps made them a fertile ground for an emerging political consciousness and organization among the refugees. Thus, when Israel crushed the neighbouring states in 1967, occupying Gaza which had been occupied by Egypt, and the West Bank which had been annexed by Jordan, this was paradoxically a moment of liberation for many Palestinians in the sense that they would start to participate in an armed struggle (Rogan 2009: 345). With this occupation the Palestinians would now lead the fight, without any external support or intervention. The foundations for their military bases and recruitment were the Palestinian camps, and the centre of Palestinian operations against Israel was Jordan.

In 1968 some 28 Israeli soldiers were killed by Palestinian resistance fighters in the village of Karamah – meaning 'dignity' in Arabic – and indeed, the fight of the Palestinian commandos lifted the spirit of the Palestinians, not to mention the Arabs, in the aftermath of the 1967 occupation. The Jordanian army had been weakened by the 1967 war, and in the euphoric atmosphere after Karamah even the Jordanian King Hussein declared that he was a 'commando' (Rogan 2009: 347). Palestine Liberation Organization (PLO) attacks against Israel became more and more frequent, peaking at 279 attacks over the first months of 1970. But as the Palestinian refugee camps in Jordan grew to become military headquarters of the PLO and thus outside the authority of the state, the throne of the kingdom became threatened by the Palestinian guerillas, as many wished to create an Arab revolution as part of their liberation project. In September 1970 a boiling point was reached when the Marxist PLO faction Popular Front for the Liberation of Palestine (PFLP) hijacked four airliners and landed three of them in a territory of Jordan that they declared as being 'liberated'. This was the airfield of Zarqa, the town where the supporters of the Amman football teams Faisali and Wihdat were later to be involved in symbolic warfare at the city's football stadium.

The real war, though, happened in the aftermath of the hijackings, as the Jordanian king decided to crush the Palestinian resistance movement in Jordan. For 10 days a battle raged, later to be referred to as Black September. While hundreds of Jordanians were killed, an estimated 3,000 Palestinian civilians and PLO fighters, mainly inside the camps, lost their lives in the fighting (Rogan 2009: 353). When a ceasefire was reached, the PLO left for Lebanon. The camps were in ruins, and worst of all, where most casualties had been suffered and where the military headquarter of the PLO had been located, was the largest and oldest camp in the country, the Wihdat camp, on the outskirts of Amman.

WIHDAT AND PALESTINIAN NATIONALISM

The granting of citizenship to the Palestinians in 1948 by King Abdullah of Jordan, and later King Hussein, had a price tag attached to it: the Jordanization of the Palestinians. To refer to Palestine, or Palestinians, was now forbidden by law. As the West Bank had been annexed into Jordan, the proper terms were West Bank Jordanians (Palestinians) and East Bank Jordanians (Transjordanians). But the Palestinians, as the director of UNRWA reported in 1956, 'bitterly oppose anything which has even the semblance of permanent settlement elsewhere' (quoted in Kimmerling and Migdal 2003: 221).

The Black September event led the Transjordanians to conclude that the Palestinians were not only ungrateful for the hospitality of the Jordanian state, which had granted them refuge and citizenship, but that they were ultimately traitors, the so-called 'enemy within' (Brand 1995: 53). If not before, the Palestinians were now to be considered a security concern, with increased surveillance evident within the camps. A significant change of policy also took place, which surrounded the employment, or lack thereof, of Palestinians from this point onwards. An 'East Bank first' policy was now employed, and Palestinians began to encounter insurmountable problems with Jordanian bureaucracy, like gaining a university scholarship, registering a new business, holding a driving licence and obtaining a passport (Brand 1995). After the 1967 war, a state of emergency had been declared with political organization and indeed Parliament itself was suspended. This continued to be the case until 1989. This in turn would do little to address communal tensions throughout Jordan.

Political opposition in Jordan (as opposed to armed resistance) had been advanced by all parties, including East Bankers and West Bankers alike, rather than being separated by nation affiliations or identities – like the Muslim Brotherhood or the pan-Arab Baath party. With the martial law of 1967 this situation changed irrevocably. And with political organization forbidden, alternative forms of expressing political affiliation began to appear. The most predominant form was in relation to events at the football stadium. The football ground was to become the main arena for political expression, a fact that meant that collective group belonging would become widespread. Thus, while party politics had transcended ethnic belonging, it was ethnonational polarization that would now transpire through the symbolic wars apparent within the football stadiums.

THE ETHNIC BASES OF JORDAN'S BEST FOOTBALL CLUBS

As part of its services for Palestinian youth, UNRWA established different youth centres in the camps. At these centres the main activities undertaken were different forms of sport and physical activity. In 1970 the centres established a variety of different sports leagues, for example within basketball, volleyball, football and boxing, where the various centres would regularly compete against one another (Brand 1988: 183). The absence of meaningful activities for the youth in the camps helped the leagues to become tremendously popular among the refugees. Sport would, for thousands of athletes, represent a focus, even a release, from the apparent hopelessness of daily life, whilst league matches attracted huge, enthusiastic crowds, hungry for action amid the urban slums that the camps came to represent.

In 1975 a further step was taken as the camp teams decided to participate in sports leagues outside their immediate vicinity. They became integrated into the regular Jordanian sports leagues where the Wihdat football team enjoyed tremendous success, which in turn gave rise to feelings of joy and pride among the refugees. That the camp had been the symbol of Palestinian losses during Black September was in no way forgotten or overlooked. The sentiments of the late 1960s, when Palestinian commando raids against Israel, symbolized by the aforementioned confrontation in Karamah in 1968, had created feelings of hope, and a rare sense of victory in spite of the actual military defeat. These sentiments were revived every time Wihdat played. And so when Wihdat played against Jordanian teams thought to promote Transjordanian ethnicity or the army, like Ramtha representing the Bedouin tribes of the north, and Faisali the southern tribes, the crowds chanted as if the civil war was being fought all over again. Indeed, a special horn sound came to be associated with support for the team. And at the matches, the supporters would chant slogans referring to the civil war and their sympathy for the Palestinian resistance.

In 1980 Wihdat went on to win the Jordanian football league. Since then the club has been a symbol for all Palestinians. It represents the very rare phenomenon of Palestinian victory. And so in the minds of its supporters, victory for Wihdat represented a symbolic, if only aspirational, victory for Palestinian resistance. 'All the people of Wihdat sell tomatoes,' Faisali supporters chanted as their club met Wihdat. 'All of us are Palestinians,' the Palestinians answered.

Wihdat was for the Palestinians something to be proud of, a touchstone for identity. As Brand notes (1988: 165), during the first decades after *al nakba* (the catastrophe: the dispersal of the Palestinians), the Palestinians had been degraded, humiliated and politically suppressed, and indeed some were ashamed of being Palestinian. The success of the club removed that stigma. When Wihdat played, their supporters sang, transcending the imaginary scenario of being passive receivers of emergency aid to that of being proud resistance fighters: '*Ma biddna thiin wa la sardin bidna 'anabil*'' – 'we do not want wheat, or sardines, we want bombs.' The supporters explicitly refered to the role of Wihdat in that transformation as they chanted '*suffu al karasi, siffu al karasi. al wihdat al akhdar, biyirda al raasi*' – 'arrange the chairs, the green Wihdat is playing, raising our heads.' The success of the team raised the spirits of the suffering refugee population.

The victories were experienced as national and political victories, providing the Palestinian nation with immense pride. Wihdat was 'something holy, something ... high, it is Palestine', a resident of Wihdat explained,[1] 'when Wihdat lose, Palestine lose (sic).' Because of their many defeats Palestinians were so hungry for victories that the 'portrayal of failure as triumph and defeat as victory was to become almost a stock in trade for the PLO', Khalidi noted (1997: 197). The former deputy director of the club, Sobhi Ibrahim, recalled that an old women had called him once after Wihdat had lost a match,[2] and had cried down the telephone: 'Never play if you are going to lose', she had said. 'We have lost so many times, in 1948, '67, 1970 and '82. When you lose, you remind us of our losses.' But what Wihdat did most often was win, and thus did indeed make the Palestinians 'raise their heads.' 'One day when we had no voice, Wihdat was our voice', the legendary Palestinian leader Yasser Arafat once said. There are four tournaments in Jordan, the domestic league, the FA Cup, the FA Shield and the Super Cup. Since 1990 Wihdat has won the league ten times, and in 2009 and 2011 Wihdat even claimed the quadruple by winning all four competitions in the one season.

The success of Wihdat came at the expense of what used to be the unbeatable, supreme football club in Jordan, Faisali. Faisali has won the Jordanian league a record 31 times, and from 1957 to 1977 had an unblemished league record. But, as a result of the success of Wihdat, since 2003 Faisali has only won the league once – a remarkable transformation.

Since Wihdat first won the league in 1980, its matches against Faisali, and to some extent also against the Ramtha club, have been marked by antagonism and violence. Thus football matches came to represent a display of two contrasting national identies. In fact, as Brand (1988: 184–185) has argued, a certain level of communal tension was good for the Jordanian throne as it would help prevent the possibility of a regime-threatening coalition emerging between the Transjordanian East Bankers and the Palestinian West Bankers, which in the mid-1950s had almost led to the overthrow of the monarchy. By maintaining a manageable level of tension between Palestinians and Transjordanians, the threat of unity to address questions of democratization, unemployment, nepotism and corruption was skilfully avoided.

This is a perspective that gained renewed relevance in 2011 amid the so-called Arab Spring, and the struggle for democracy throughout the Middle East. But against the democracy struggle there remains powerful resistance from political elites and priviliged groups. This has also been true in Jordan. For the monarchy and for Transjordanian nationalists, the democracy struggle represents danger more than freedom. And with it, the symbolic war and violence of the football stadium may suddenly grow and be transposed on society at large.

CASE STUDY: FOOTBALL AND POLITICS

Wihdat–Al Ramtha, 4 April 2011

Every week since the popular uprisings in Tunisia and Egypt began in early 2011, democracy activists have also gathered in Jordan. Each week more and more people joined the protests until progovernment forces eventually attacked the political reform activists. On 24 March 2011, the reform movement established a tent camp at Amman's Jamal Amdel Nasser roundabout, stating that they would continue their campaign until their calls for democratic reforms were addressed. On Friday 25 March 2011, the camp, home to around 2,000 protesters, was attacked by some 200 civilians identified as government supporters and riot police. One of the reform demonstrators was killed and 160 people were injured (AFP 2011).

The reform movement has been desperate to emphasize that their struggle was non-sectarian, not related to the Palestinian–Transjordanian issue, but to a shared political goal of having democratic reform. Nevertheless, the waving of the Jordanian flag became a symbol for the antidemocracy activists as if the reform movement was a Palestinian one.

King Abdullah II went to the southern Jordanian town of Petra to address tribal leaders and comment on the situation. 'The most important thing now is our national unity, which must not be touched,' he told the tribal leaders, 'we need to stay away from any behaviour or attitude that would affect our unity' (AFP 2011). Some would interpret these statements as if the political reform movement, rather than those using violence against it, was what was threatening national unity.

Thus, tensions were high in Amman as the Jordanian football league approached its climax. On Monday 4 April 2011, 10 days after the violence against the demonstrators, Wihdat was to play al-Ramtha, and if they won this game they would, in turn, win the league. When Wihdat won its first title in Jordan in 1980 their supporters had clashed violently with the supporters of al-Ramtha. And, as Jordan had just witnessed political violence, there was a tense atmosphere in Amman during the weekend leading up to the match. But then Faisali failed to win their match on the day before the Wihdat game, meaning the title already belonged to Wihdat before the match against al-Ramtha had even begun.

The match was by no means a sell-out, but in the stand that housed the most enthusiastic Wihdat supporters, the celebrations were simply unstoppable, as they chanted '*Allah, Wihdat, Al-Quds al Arabia*' – 'God, Wihdat, and Arabic Jerusalem' – in order of importance. The name of the director of Wihdat, Tareq Khoury, was also repeatedly chanted as the supporters waited for the match to begin. Khoury had stood up for the supporters the previous December when they had been attacked by police and anti-Palestinian Faisali supporters. However, the Palestinian symbols and chants which had been so dominant during the 1970s and 1980s were now notably absent. 'We are Jordanians, Palestinian Jordanians', said the club director of Wihdat, Muhammad Assaf, as Wihdat stormed to victory. The team had two Palestinians, he said. That meant players being bought from teams in Gaza and the West Bank. Also, there were even Jordanians on the team, he said. '*Allah, Wihdat, Al-Quds al Arabia,*' the supporters continued to chant. As the title was finally theirs, the celebrating supporters unfolded a huge Jordanian flag. Wihdat had won the league, and significantly in the volatile political situation in Jordan, their celebration took place without any violent incidents being recorded.

THE DANGER OF DEMOCRACY

'*Talaqha, ya Abu Hussein,*' the Faisali supporters chant at the matches against Wihdat, 'divorce her, you father of Hussein.' It is the kind of chant that normally makes the royal authorities react with distain. The Jordanian state always lacked national symbols and a national myth (Abu-Odeh 1999: 253). The monuments of the state, in Jeraish and Petra, were not Transjordanian monuments. King Hussein would thus refer to himself as 'Sharif', to emphasize his religious roots as a descendant of the family of the Prophet, as well as a protector of pan-Arab unity (Eickelman and Piscatori 1996: 37). The descent was symbolic capital needed to transcend the separate nations constituting the people of Jordan. As fights between ethnic Transjordanians and Palestinians regularly erupted during football matches, the monarchy would control the violence, and re-establish order. Football matches were therefore reminders of the civil war, of the potential for internal strife and violence, as well as for the need for a transcending symbol which could bring order to the public. Crucially, the symbolic wars at the football stadium were not regime-threatening, they did not attack the king; instead they merely rehearsed the events of the civil war or constituted ways to challenge and belittle the ethnic 'other'.

Ostensibly the '*Talaqha, ya Abu Hussein*' slogan was to break with the code of conduct towards the throne, because it challenged the authority of the King. When Wihdat supporters used antimonarch slogans in 1986, this led to a crackdown on the club, and it was closed for 3 years (Tuastad 1997: 120). But this specific repeated chant of Faisali supporters, according to James Montague (2008: 284), could also be heard in 2007, yet has not led to a reaction against those who utter it, which in turn has made it almost an accepted level of offence. The danger for the throne is that the chant begins to replicate and indeed grow into much more serious political activities.

During the early months of 2011 the Arab Spring also led to calls for democracy in Jordan. In the midst of these, Transjordanian nationalists chose to enter the political scene, fearing democratization as a way in which Jordan could become Palestinized. A letter published in February 2011, as Queen Rania came under attack from 36 tribal leaders, was unprecedented. 'We call upon the King to return lands and farms given to the Yassin family [Rania's family]. The land belongs to the Jordanian people.' By having no less than 36 signatories to a public letter protesting against the actions of the queen, thus breaking a well-established taboo of not criticizing the throne, the dynamics of the situation had changed considerably (Simioni 2011). Queen Rania was accused of 'corruption, stealing money from the Treasury and manipulating in order to promote her public image – against the Jordanian people's will', comparable to the wife of former Tunisian president Leila Ben Ali, who stole from her country's treasury for years, giving her family members vast sums of money and land at the expense of the Tunisian citizens. If the royal family failed to take action, they would suffer the same fate as Tunisia and Egyptian leaders, it was stated in the letter: 'put these corrupt people who stole from the country on trial, regardless of their status'. Queen Rania was 'building centers intended to strengthen her status and serve her interests ... King Abdullah has to stop his wife and her family from taking advantage of their power, otherwise the crown might be in danger' (Simioni 2011).

In Jordan, offending the royal family can lead to 3 years in prison. Ali Habashneh was one of the signatories to the letter. The initative, he said in an interview,[3] was from a new political force emerging in Jordan, the National Committee for Retired Officers. 'We have cells in all the governorates, and small enterprises in every village all over the country,' he said. 'A representative from the intelligence service told us not to form a party. We can send the Muslim Brotherhood to jail, but can we send generals to jail?' The tribal leaders and retired officers are not part of the democracy movement in Jordan. They are in fact a reaction against it. 'We are against a constitutional monarchy,' Habashneh says. Nor does Habashneh want to change the election law. At present the number of seats for each constituency does not reflect the size of the population – and the Jordanian Palestinians, although a majority of the population, could win a maximum of 25 per cent of the seats in the Parliament (Abu-Odeh 1999: 250). 'I will never change anything of it', says Ali Habashneh.

Notably, rather than charging the signatories for attacking the royal family and the national consensus, the King instead listened to their claims, changed the government and replaced government members of Palestinian ancestry with ministers of ethnic Transjordanian origin.

181

Many interpreted this as evidence that 'some are more equal than others' in the Jordanian state. Democracy was as much a threat to well-positioned Jordanians in the buraucracy and army as it was for the monarchy itself. It would mean loss of power and the priviliged status of both. In contrast, for the Jordanian Palestinians a truly democratic state in which each vote counts the same may mean that they could vote for a Palestinian nationalist, a Hamas or Fatah leader, to become prime minister if they so wanted.

With the establishment of a Palestinian state in the West Bank, PLO officials foresee a possible confederation between Jordan and Palestine, a larger Palestine, so to speak.[4] This is a very threatening scenario for both Transjordanian nationalists and the Jordanian monarchy. It largely explains the change of political content expressed by supporters during football matches between ethnic Palestinian-affiliated teams and ethnic Jordanian-affiliated teams. The Wihdat supporters no longer chant commando songs or antiroyal slogans during their matches. And the large flag they unfold on the terraces remains a huge Jordanian one, not a Palestinian flag. Meanwhile the violence that takes place at the matches, and the anti-Rania attacks, continue to prove impossible to ignore in Jordan. A reason why the attacks on Queen Rania have not been suppressed is the fact that she is of Palestinian origin. Anti-Rania slogans are thus anti-Palestinian rather than antimonarchy. It is rather an attempt to purify the monarchy, and preserve it as a unity between the Muslim Sharif and the tribes, as an equation to the first Muslim community led by Prophet Muhammad.

FINAL COMMENTS

After the Israeli–Palestinian peace process was initiated in 1993, a new reality faced the Palestinians in Jordan. Palestinian refugees originating in what became known as Israel in 1948 now perceive that a return to their original homes is beyond the terms of reference within any possible PLO–Israel-negotiated solution to the conflict. They fear becoming victims of another forced migration, to a new established Palestinian state where they do not belong.

This change has also been observed at football matches in Jordan. The 'Palestinianness' expressed by the Wihdat supporters, previously overcommunicated, is currently subdued. The Wihdat supporters no longer use the matches of the Wihdat Football Club as an arena in which their struggle for liberation, communicated through songs and chants. For their supporters, Wihdat instead represents the successful integration of Palestinians in Jordan as true Palestinian Jordanians. But this success has proven too great for some of their Transjordanian adversaries at the football stadium and in fact Jordanian society at large.

In addition to this, the Arab Spring of 2011, which began in Tunisia and Egypt, has brought the question of democracy (or absence thereof) in Jordan to the surface. Democratization may endanger the power of the monarchy as well as the privileged positions of Transjordanians in the Jordanian state. This situation, one of a possible establishment of a Palestinian state west of the Jordan river, and the calls for democratic reforms in Jordan, represents the greatest challenge to the Jordanian monarchy since Black September.

How the Jordanian authorities manage football disturbances is closely followed by different political groups and commentators throughout Jordan. It is alleged by some that it is the Palestinian supporters who have been on the receiving end of violent backlashes, even though it has been Transjordanians who have instigated unrest and antiroyalist chants. Similarly, it has been said that Jordanian riot police have attacked the reform movement rather than those groups that use violence against the peaceful reform demonstrators.

One interpretation of this set of circumstances is that the chants against Queen Rania and her Palestinian origin have forced the King to adjust his policy in favour of his Transjordanian constituency. In spite of Black September, Abdullah II and his father, King Hussein, have to some extent managed to rule Jordan in a non-exclusive, relatively impartial manner. If this equilibrium is disturbed, and the trust of one of the constituencies that go to make up the state of Jordan evaporates, there is a danger, periodically evident at the football matches discussed here, that could spread to the society at large. How ethnically oriented, supporter violence apparent at such games is managed by the authorities is therefore not only a barometer of the political situation in Jordan – it could even serve to determine the future of the Jordanian state.

SUMMARY

In the past domestic football matches that took place in Jordan used to be an arena for the expression of a suppressed Palestinian national identity. Today this has changed. It's true that football remains an arena in which political expression takes place, but now it is Transjordanian nationalists who use it to challenge the presence of Palestinians in Jordan and not the other way round. 'We want the Palestinians out,' they chant during football matches. Recently, even the monarchy has been implicated in an evolving level of unrest amongst the people. Moreover, demands for democratic reforms have emerged in Jordan as they have done elsewhere throughout the Arab world. In this situation the King of Jordan appears to have common interests with Transjordanian nationalists in limiting (as much as possible) the political reforms that others demand with increased vigour.

NOTES

1   Interview with author in Wihdat, September 1995.
2   Interview with author in Wihdat, September 1995.
3   Interview with author in Amman, March 2011.
4   PLO official in interview with author in Amman, March 2011.

REVIEW QUESTIONS

1   How may football be regarded as a barometer of ethnic conflict in Jordan?
2   Why has the expression of Palestinian nationalism at the football stadiums become increasingly subdued during the two last decades?
3   What is the rationale behind the idea that it is in the interest of Jordanian authorities to allow a certain level of supporter violence during football matches, and how convincing do you find this argument?

FURTHER READING

Armstrong, G. and Giulianotti, R. (eds). (1997). *Entering the Field. New Perspectives on World Football.* Oxford: Berg Publishers.

Kuper, S. (2006). *Soccer against the Enemy.* New York: Nation Books.

Lust-Okar, E. and Zerhouni S. (eds). (2008). *Political Participation in the Middle East.* London: Lynne Rienner Publishers.

Robins, P. (2004). *A History of Jordan.* New York: Cambridge University Press.

WEBSITES

CNN Fanzone:

edition.cnn.com/SPORT/football/fanzone/

Middle East Research and Information Project:

www.merip.org

Soccerway:

www.soccerway.com/teams/jordan/al-weehdat/matches

REFERENCES

Abu-Odeh, A. (1999). *Jordanians, Palestinians and the Hashemite Kingdom in the Middle East Peace Process.* Washington, DC: United States Institute of Peace Press.

AFP. (2011). Jordan king urges unity after unrest. *AFP.* http://www.google.com/hostednews/afp/article/ALeqM5i19u8L6xrVqsx8IQNz1WDRkSbZtg?docId=CNG.82fce0d1e069b2865b114176f57c0264.5d1 (accessed 1 June 2011).

Brand, L.A. (1988). *Palestinians in the Arab World. Institution Building and the Search for State.* New York: Colorado University Press.

Brand, L.A. (1995). "Palestinians and Jordanians: A Crisis of Identity." *Journal of Palestine Studies* XXIV: 4.

Cleveland, W.L. (2000). *A History of the Modern Middle East.* Oxford: Westview Press.

Eickelman, D.F. and Piscatori, J. (1996). *Muslim Politics.* Princeton, NJ: Princeton University Press.

Khalidi, R. (1997). *Palestinian Identity. The Construction of Modern National Consciousness.* New York: Colombia University Press.

Kimmerling, B. and Migdal, J. (2003). *The Palestinian People. A History.* London: Harvard University Press.

Montague, J. (2008). *When Friday Comes. Football in the War Zone.* Edinburgh: Mainstream Publishing.

Montague, J. (2011). Soccerleaks: the football files. *CNN.* http://edition.cnn.com/2011/SPORT/football/03/21/soccer.wikileaks.manchester.myanmar/index.html (accessed 1 June 2011).

Omari, R. (2010). "Probe Continues into Friday Football-related Violence." *Jordan Times.* http://jaactomist.wordpress.com/2010/12/12/probe-continues-into-friday-football-related-violence/ (accessed 18 June 2012).

Rogan, E. (2009). *The Arabs. A History.* New York: Basic Books.

Simioni, R. (2011). "Queen Rania is a corrupt thief." *Ynet.news.com.* http://http://www.ynetnews. com/articles/0,7340,L-4028607,00.html (accessed 1 June 2011).

Tuastad, D. (1997). "The Political Role of Football for Palestinians in Jordan," in: Armstrong, G. And Giulanotti, R. (eds) *Entering the Field. New Perspectives on World Football*. Oxford: Berg Publishers.

Wikileaks Updates (2010). Jordanian football game halted amidst anti-regime chants, hooliganism towards Palestinians. http://wikileaksupdates.blogspot.com/2010/12/jordanian-soccer-game-halted-amidst.html (accessed 1 June 2011).

Zahran, M. (2010). Jordanian Police Atrocities Against Palestinians, a Message to Israel? *Qudosi-Chronicles*.http://qudosi.com/2010/12/16/jordanian-police-atrocities-against-palestinians-serves-as-a-warning-to-the-international-community/ (accessed 18 June 2012).

Chapter 11

Managing gender equity in sport

Sally Shaw

TOPICS

Gender equity in sport • Organizational cultures • Feminist approaches to sport management

---

OBJECTIVES

By the end of this chapter you will be able to:

- Have an understanding of gender relations in sport organizations;
- Be aware of the strengths and weaknesses of liberal feminism;
- Appreciate how organizational culture is gendered;
- Reflect on your own sport organizations from a gender perspective.

KEY TERMS

Gender equity – equity within organizational structures and cultures.

Liberal feminism – providing women and girls with the same opportunities as men and boys, without critiquing the structures and cultures of sport.

Neoliberalism – a market-based approach to social policy, for example, focusing on reducing cost as a driver for health reform rather than just improving a population's health.

Organizational culture – the values, beliefs and shared dynamics that help us to make sense of organizations. Often dominated by groups of influential people or ideas.

OVERVIEW

This chapter addresses gender equity within sport organizations: this has been a concern for researchers and practitioners since the 1960s. It is important to address gender equity in sport organizations because, despite massive increases in women's and girls' participation across many sports, their inclusion at higher administrative levels is notably lacking (Acosta and Carpenter 2004). The underrepresentation of women at the higher levels of sport organizations is problematic because it indicates constraints or barriers to women's participation in this essential part of sport, and it also means that sport organizations are missing out on the potential leadership abilities offered by 50 per cent of the population.

This chapter will provide an overview of various attempts to increase the numbers of women in sport administration. The range of theoretical approaches that have informed these attempts will be discussed and examined using practical examples from the New Zealand sports context. The strengths and weaknesses of these approaches will be outlined, indicating where they have been utilized within sport management and their usefulness, or otherwise, to sport managers and students. Finally, a summary of approaches will be provided, with concluding comments regarding the likely future of gender equity within sport management.

CASE STUDY: WOMEN AT HIGH LEVELS OF SPORT ADMINISTRATION

The Secretary General of the New Zealand Olympic Committee (NZOC) is a woman, and there are six women on the board of the NZOC, and only four men (New Zealand Olympic Committee 2001). This gender representation and balance is unusual in sport (Shaw and Cameron 2008) and appears to indicate that, at the highest level of sport administration in New Zealand, gender relations have overcome historical prejudices against women. If we scratch the surface of this picture, and examine other high-level sport organizations in New Zealand, we see that women are underrepresented at the highest administrative levels. For example, Sport and Recreation New Zealand (SPARC)'s High Performance Board comprises one woman and five men (Sport and Recreation New Zealand 2010). SPARC's board represents six men and three women. All nine members of the New Zealand Rugby Union board are men, despite the successes of the Black Ferns (New Zealand women's rugby team) at four successive world cup competitions. These figures more accurately represent the national picture, in which over 80 per cent of sport boards have fewer than 50 per cent female representation (New Zealand Olympic Committee 2011). The underrepresentation of women on boards also flies in the face of research that indicates that diversity in organizations leads to better, balanced strategic decision-making (Fink *et al.* 2003). Some organizations, such as the NZOC, have tried to implement procedures to encourage and support women who want to operate at the highest levels of sport management. Other organizations, such as those in Shaw's (2006) research, hide behind the excuse that 'the best person for the job' will be employed or selected, regardless of what assumptions inform decisions about 'best people'. This chapter will provide insights into both sides of this debate.

THE NEW ZEALAND CONTEXT

The New Zealand sports administration system is very similar to other Commonwealth countries, in particular Australia, Canada and the UK. SPARC is the government-funded agency responsible for distributing funds to national sport organizations (NSOs), such as New Zealand Hockey or New Zealand Rowing, and regional sport organizations (RSOs), such as Sport Otago. These RSOs have responsibility for delivering sport development and participation programmes within the 17 administrative regions into which New Zealand sport is divided. There are two main priorities for government funding: sport participation and health, and high-performance sport (Sport and Recreation New Zealand 2011).

In 1993, Cameron conducted a study, *Gender in New Zealand Sport: A survey of national sport administrators*. In it, she found that 24 per cent of major executive positions in NSOs were held by women. Eighty-one per cent of the positions held by women, however, were either as secretary or as a general board member, while men held the vast majority of leadership positions, such as director, chair or president. In 1994, a wider study of all sport, recreation, fitness and leisure organizations was undertaken, focusing on the level of policy involvement at national level by women in these organizations (Murphy 1994). This study revealed that 27 per cent of people on national boards were women, and that 17 per cent of national boards had no women on their boards. National subcommittees for women were in place in 27 per cent of the organizations.

More recent surveys suggest that these positive signs in the 1990s for women have stagnated or disappeared as we have entered the twenty-first century. According to a report to the NZOC, *Gender Balance in New Zealand Olympic Sports* (Cockburn *et al.* 2007), there has been no change to the gender balance of national boards since Murphy's 1994 study. In 1995, the International Olympic Committee (IOC) undertook a resolution to have 10 per cent of decision-making positions held by women in Olympic sports by 2000, increasing to 20 per cent by 2005. Only half of the New Zealand Olympic sport NSOs have reached this threshold and 22 per cent of the boards had no women. The statistic of boards with no women representatives is an increase on the 1994 data. Informally, an internet search in 2010 reveals that, of SPARC's top-ten funded NSOs, seven chief executive officers (CEOs) are men and three are women, one of which is the CEO of netball, played and administered almost exclusively by women in New Zealand. In the RSOs, 15 CEOs are men, whilst just two women hold that role.

It is problematic to make direct comparisons across these data, as different methodologies were used, different organizations were researched, and it is not possible to say exactly at what levels women worked or volunteered during these timeframes. It is, however, possible to identify a general trend, in which there was a relatively strong representation of women during the 1990s, which did not increase by 100 per cent, as recommended by the IOC in its 1996 resolution. It is also interesting to note that, during the 1990s, New Zealand championed the Winning Women programme through the Hillary Commission, which predated SPARC (Hillary Commission 2001). The Winning Women programme won an international award for its work in 'supporting the development of organisational policies and programmes promoting the involvement of women as leaders and coaches' (Cockburn *et al.* 2007: 9). SPARC, on the other hand, discontinued these policies, promoting physical activity with no focus on gender. Indeed, when the author presented research on gender equity at a pre-Commonwealth Games conference in Melbourne in 2006, she was informed in a conversation that 'SPARC doesn't recognize gender as a problem' by a SPARC employee.

New Zealand's record of gender equity within sport organizations is arguably chequered, with the support of gender equity of the 1990s fading away with the embrace of neoliberal approaches to sport funding that has characterized the end of the twentieth and beginning of the twenty-first centuries. Arguably, because gender had a relatively high profile within sport administration in the 1990s, some managers and policy creators think that gender equity has been achieved, and does not need much attention (Shaw 2006). As such, New Zealand represents a system that is ripe for analysis of how gender equity is (or is not) managed within sport organizations. Over the remainder of this chapter, two of the various approaches to examining gender equity will be outlined, whilst positioning those approaches within the New Zealand context. These approaches are undermined by two types of feminism. The first is liberal feminism, which focuses on providing girls and women with the same opportunities to participate in sport as their male counterparts. The second reflects a more radical approach, in which the culture of sport organizations is challenged to become more aware of gender relations and change accordingly.

LIBERAL FEMINIST APPROACHES TO SPORT MANAGEMENT

Liberal feminism grew out of a critique as early as the seventeenth century regarding the seemingly natural positioning of men in powerful positions (Scraton and Flintoff 2002). Liberal feminists argue that women and girls do not have access to the opportunities afforded to boys and men, so it is inevitable that their path to powerful positions in organizations will be more difficult. For example, in sport, informal networking is considered to be a useful way to gain influence and drive agendas forward. As Shaw (2006) discovered, although women might belong to 'old girls' networks', they are rarely as influential as 'old boys' networks', particularly in sport organizations that administer both women's and men's sports. Liberal feminism argues that if women have the same, or similar, opportunities as men, then they too will achieve success within sport organizations.

In some sport administrations, liberal feminism has led to a proliferation of courses and policies that attempt to provide women with similar, or the same, opportunities as men. For example, Sport England promoted the Active Women campaign in 2009 to encourage more women to participate in sport. This programme funds applications to address constraints to women's participation, such as childcare costs and transport (Sport England 2009). With regard to administrative positions, Cockburn *et al.*'s (2007) report identified the need for mentoring and role modelling and strategies to build the confidence of capable women candidates. As a result of this recommendation, the NZOC is in the process of piloting a mentoring scheme for women who wish to be involved at the highest levels of governance in New Zealand sport.

Liberal feminist approaches have led to other processes within sport organizations. For example, some sport organizations see the equal opportunities suggested by liberal feminism in terms of offering women positions that reflect their perceived strengths. For example, in coaching, Shaw and Allen (2009) found that there were few women in high-performance coaching roles. In part, this was because managers and other influential people in the organizations they volunteered for made assumptions about women's 'natural' caring abilities, which

189

were interpreted as being exclusionary to competition. Consequently, these women were given positions coaching young and less talented teams. In administrative positions, women's perceived caring or nurturing qualities mean that they are often placed in positions as managers or girls' liaison officers or chaperones (Shaw and Allen 2009).

In sport, liberal feminist approaches have opened up some barriers to women's participation in management. This has occurred by offering courses through which women might improve their chances of success, or by identifying areas of strength with which women might have greater affinity. However, this position is tenuous and has been criticized (Shaw and Frisby 2006). In particular, liberal feminism has been criticized for feeding stereotypical views of women, for example, that they will need assistance to succeed at the highest levels of management (Hovden 2000). Similar views about women 'playing to their strengths' have been linked to the proliferation of the view that women will be better suited to the administration of teams or events that involve children and women, which are often lower-profile than men's events (Shaw and Frisby 2006). In the following section, the author will highlight some of these critiques and their implications for sport management.

Liberal feminism and 'fix the women'

Rao et al. (1999) coined the phrase 'fix the women' to describe one way in which women are perceived through the prism of liberal feminism. In this, 'gender equals biological sex. In this view, men and women are assumed to have equal access to opportunities, and they rise and fall on their own merit' (p. 137). When women fail to achieve the levels of managerial or governance responsibility enjoyed by their male counterparts, they are perceived to need 'fixing' through courses or mentoring. The problem of women underachieving lies with women in this situation, not the organizations to which they belong.

In sport organizations, Shaw and Hoeber (2003) found that it was a relatively common practice to expect women to need to be 'fixed' because it was assumed by senior managers that women would come into organizations with less knowledge and political ability than their male peers. Women managers in Shaw and Hoeber's study argued that they had to work harder than men to succeed in their organizations because it was assumed that they would not be as good as the men. These assumptions led to women feeling pressured to go on women's development courses, in order to be 'fixed' and succeed within an unchanging organization.

The current NZOC governance mentoring programme arguably reflects the 'fixing' philosophy. It is intended to assist women who wish to rise up the governance ranks of NSOs. Mentors are assigned to women who are already involved within sport governance to work on issues such as goal setting, communication and access to networks. This approach fits with Rao et al.'s (1999) critique of the assertion that, while a woman may have the technical knowledge to succeed, she 'needs to become political, assertive, and strategic if she is to succeed in the way men have. The problem – and solutions – rests squarely with the individual woman' (p. 137). It is likely that women in New Zealand sport governance will benefit from this programme through networking, career planning and personal skill development. However, using Rao et al.'s analysis, it is certainly aimed at 'fixing' women rather than changing an organization.

Liberal feminism and 'valuing the feminine'

'Valuing the feminine' appears to be an inevitable consequence of liberal feminism, given the gender stereotypes that prevail in sport (McKay 1997). This inevitability stems from the premise within liberal feminism that everyone within sport organizations has equal access to opportunities but rise and fall on their own abilities. The interpretation of liberal feminism that leads to valuing the feminine, again a phrase coined by Rao *et al.* (1999), refers to essentialist views on women's and men's abilities. One interpretation of women's abilities is that they are often perceived to have better listening, supporting and nurturing skills, and greater empathy with people in emotional situations. Within liberal feminism they will rise up the organization as far as they can based on these skills and attributes. Men, on the other hand, are perceived to be better at directing, doing and networking. The skills associated with women have, however, been described by Fletcher (1999) as less influential, private, or 'behind the scenes', skills. Those associated with men are powerful or public skills, valued for 'conquering the global frontiers and exercising the real power in today's multinational corporations' (Ely and Meyerson 2000: 109). Unsurprisingly, then, critics of liberal feminism suggest that the skills associated with men are those that are valued, whereas those associated with women are taken for granted and seen as underpinning support roles.

There are parallels to this argument within the management of sport organizations generally. Research has indicated that coach managers will often assume that women want to work with lower-level development teams or children. While these teams are worthy, and can lead to development of athletes at the highest level, such teams are often not as highly valued in a cultural or financial sense as high-performance, particularly men's, teams (Shaw and Allen 2009). Interestingly, Shaw and Hoeber (2003) found that when athletes with disabilities were not regarded as highly as their able-bodied counterparts and before they received high-performance funding, women were frequently in high-performance coaching roles. However, once high-performance disability sport was more highly valued through the development and recognition of the Paralympics, male coaches began to see coaching as a legitimate career option. Because there is an inherent valuing of male coaches as being better than women, the numbers of female coaches have diminished within high-performance disability sport. More recently, in New Zealand high-performance provincial coaching, Shaw and Allen (2009) found that women only had access to the highest ranked teams when they were acting as managers or chaperones for those teams.

Within sport administration, there are also clear parallels with 'valuing the feminine'. Cameron (1993) noted how most of the women who were in governance positions within New Zealand sport were at the secretary or general board member level. Undoubtedly, these roles are important and necessary in the running of any sport organization. These roles are, however, associated with the private, behind-the-scenes roles identified by Fletcher (1999) as those expected to be held by women because of perceptions regarding their organizational and support skills. In contrast, men held most of the influential public roles, which are likely to have better networking potential and opportunities for the development of personal and organizational agendas.

Valuing women's perceived abilities can open up opportunities for women to participate with management, coaching and governance roles. However, unchallenged stereotypes and taken-for-granted attitudes towards women's strengths and an inability to see beyond traditional nurturing, caring and support roles mean that women are often only 'valued' at levels that hold little financial or cultural credibility within sport organizations. This process reinforces stereotypes about women's abilities, thus making their progression up the ranks to higher governance or coaching levels all the more difficult.

Liberal feminism and structural change

The final liberal feminist approach that will be outlined here is that of structural change. This is most often played out in organizations through organizational policy development, such as diversity policies. Sport organizational policy development may be influenced by national policy, such as the implementation of the Sex Discrimination Act (1975) in the UK or Title IX (1972) in the USA. Sport organizations are not exempt from such legislation and so must act accordingly, usually through the development of some type of gender equity policy. The genesis of gender equity policies within sport organizations has been a problematic one. For example, Acosta and Carpenter (2004), in their extensive longitudinal study of sport organizations since Title IX, have found that, while women's participation in sport has grown exponentially, the number of women administrators of women's sports in the National Collegiate Athletic Association has dropped from 90 per cent to 18.5 per cent. In the UK, Shaw and Penney (2003) argued that the creation of equity policies has been undermined by confusion and disinterest. The creation of equity policies is also often connected to funding for sport organizations. Measuring or assessing the subsequent change in sport organizations is, however, problematic (Shaw 2007), often leading to a lack of commitment to ensure that the policies are meaningful to the organizations. There is, then, a temptation to develop an equity policy but not implement it or follow through on it. Consequently, there is little impetus for change within sport organizations.

Similarly, in New Zealand, Shaw (2006) found that all ten of the Regional Sports Trusts that replied to her survey had gender equity policies. However, she noted that the policies were very similar to each other, suggesting that they may have been copied in order to fulfil an administrative requirement, rather than being created to meet the needs of women within the organizations and regions. Further, when respondents discussed the equity policies, Shaw noted that the language used was arguably dismissive and that the respondents did not engage with the content or intent of the policies. Structural change is very hard to implement and sustain in sport organizations when there is little will to support it, or policy intentions or directions are not clear. Although liberal feminism has led to the development of equity policies, it is very hard to see where these policies have led to successful structural change over the long term.

Liberal feminist approaches to understanding gender relations within sport management have offered opportunities for women to gain access to higher levels of sport management and governance through courses, valuing their contribution, and policies. However, as this section has shown, each of these achievements must also be viewed in a critical light, recognizing that the gains made through the application of liberal feminism have also led to the reiteration of stereotypes and, ironically, undermining some of the goals of liberal feminists. Also, liberal feminism focuses solely on women and their struggles to succeed. It does not have room for men within gender discussions, who may be as constrained by conventional definitions of what it is to be a man as women are by assumptions about females. In the next section, a more radical approach to gender relations and its application within sport organizations will be outlined.

GENDER RELATIONS AS ORGANIZATIONAL CULTURE

The approaches detailed below have evolved out of critiques of liberal feminism. This critique argues that there cannot be equality in gender relations until the gendered nature of sport organizations is recognized and located at the centre of discussions regarding gender equity. Rather than focusing on women or policies, researchers who work in this area argue that all organizational members need to recognize that organizational culture is gendered and address deep cultural considerations.

Organizational culture

Schein's (1991) analysis of organizational culture highlighted the need to understand it as reflecting shared values, concepts, patterns and dynamics that help individuals to develop a sense of collective identity and 'make sense' of organizations. Martin (2001) argued that organizational culture is often manipulated by influential people to reflect the views, values and beliefs of a dominant group. While this may give a feeling of stability and strong organizational culture within organizations, such manipulation, whether intentional or not, can serve to undermine or diminish the views of those who are less powerful.

Organizational culture as gendered

Organizational culture is understood to be gendered (Rao *et al.* 1999). For example, Shaw and Hoeber (2003) found that men who were interested in coaching a sport in which women predominantly participated were routinely described as perverts. This is an example of how an organizational practice can be influenced by an organizational culture that is informed by baseless assumptions. The example shows how cultural influence can be hidden, yet powerful (Hoeber 2008). That is, the dominant perspective of male coaches as perverts was not formally expressed; rather it was part of gossip within the organization. Comments could never be pinned down or challenged with any certainty. It is often hard to pinpoint where organizational cultural beliefs and values have come from, and identify how they could be challenged. Yet, despite this fluidity, the organizational culture and resulting practice are insidious and powerful and were influential enough to ensure that other men who might be interested in coaching this sport were deterred from doing so (Shaw and Hoeber 2003). It is reinforced by organizational members who refuse to acknowledge the gendered nature of organizations, and suppress discussion about it (Shaw 2006).

Organizational culture can be recognized, discussed, critiqued and revisioned through organizational practices in which organizational members take ownership of it. If this occurs,

193

it can be 'unhidden' as gendered within sport organizations; gender cannot be dismissed as 'not a problem' because the points of view of people who perceive gender relations as problematic within organizations would have to be heard (Ely and Meyerson 2000). Individuals would be encouraged to think about their assumptions about gender within sport organizations and how those assumptions frame organizational roles and practices. It is organizational practices like this that make up organizational culture. According to Rao *et al.* (1999), these must be challenged in order to address gender relations in sport organizations. The following sections outline how they propose that this change can be affected.

Critique of organizational culture

In their review of critiquing organizational culture, Shaw and Frisby (2006) identified three areas which are relevant to sport organizations. These areas are: informal practices; symbols of success; and the public face of the organization. Informal practices are an integral part of organizational culture because they influence how people work and also who they have access to. For example, it is not unusual for board meetings to be scheduled in the evenings, outside work hours. For many women, who still have the largest share of childcare responsibilities, finding a child minder might be difficult. For most organizations, it would be unconventional or even frowned upon to take a child to a board meeting. Yet this particular practice can make it very hard for mothers to attend, particularly if they are from lower socioeconomic groups, if they have to pay for childcare.

Symbols of success are important parts of organizational culture because they show what is valued in an organization, and how that value is expressed. Examples of symbols of success in sport organizations include the employment of high-profile retired sports stars who may have no administrative expertise ahead of experienced, yet lower-profile, candidates. The message sent by such actions is that the image associated with high-profile sport is more important than administrative knowledge. This organizational practice most often works in men's favour as, in most sport organizations, they are more likely than women to have enjoyed a higher profile. Other organizational symbols of success are more obviously gendered. For example, Welford (2011) describes how a woman was the first female representative on her regional Football Association board in the UK. As a token of her position, she was solemnly presented with a neck tie, as were the other, male, board members. This gesture showed that men were exclusively expected to be on the board and the administrators had no way of showing that she was valued.

Finally, the public face of the organization is highlighted by Shaw and Frisby (2006) as an essential part of organizational culture. This refers to the ways in which an organization is portrayed to the outside world. As noted above, an organization may be portrayed through a charismatic leader, and the choice of that leader may be gendered. When the leader is a woman, she may have had to work harder than her male counterparts because of assumptions about women's abilities (McKay 1997). Also, when a woman is successful within sport organizations, there may be a feeling that in order to become so, she has been 'a bitch' whereas a man might be described as 'strong' (Shaw and Hoeber 2003). Other examples of the public face of an organization include policies, which state what an organization values. As already described,

194

gender-related policies may be presented to the outside world with great pomp and ceremony, only for them to have little meaning with the organization themselves (Charles 2000).

Organizational practices, such as those identified above, work to reflect and reinforce dominant societal views about gender, who is successful, and why they may be so. Rao *et al.* (1999) and Ely and Meyerson (2000) have outlined ways in which organizations may address organizational culture, in order to look at ways in which organizations may have more equitable gender relations. They call on organizations to engage in narrative revision, in which organizations look at their practices, how they are informed by gendered culture and how they can be changed. There is very little published research from the sport management literature in which such a strategy has been successfully undertaken. However, the following example of the management of coaches in Otago Netball in New Zealand shows how an organization can work towards dispelling myths regarding gender and sport by developing a culture that values women coaches at the highest level, rather than undermining them.

CASE STUDY: MANAGING COACHES IN NETBALL OTAGO

Netball is a very popular sport in New Zealand. It is played by approximately 125,000 people, mainly women (Sport and Recreation New Zealand 2008). Its success is notable from the grassroots, with high levels of school and club participation, to the highest level, with New Zealand winning the World Championships in 2003, and regional New Zealand teams performing admirably in the semiprofessional ANZ Trans-Tasman Netball Competition. Unlike most women's sports, it receives good sponsorship, thoughtful and respectful media coverage, and the high-performance players are admired for their playing skills by adults and children of both genders throughout New Zealand. Administratively, netball is divided into regions. One such region, Otago, is situated at the south of New Zealand's South Island. The regional administration comprises the Netball Otago Board, the members of which are all volunteers, a paid regional development manager (RDM), who has a non-voting position on the board, and a paid administrator. Regional centres are also a feature of netball, that is, North Otago, Clutha, Central Otago and Dunedin centres are all smaller administrative units based around geographical areas within the province of Otago. The centres run their own competitions, which feed into provincial competitions, and have a high level of autonomy in organizing their own affairs. Coaches and officials from the centres are actively encouraged to be part of the development schemes run by Netball Otago, thus encouraging these people to improve their skills and take opportunities to coach or officiate at the highest level possible.

Unsurprisingly, the vast majority of coaches in netball are women. As already noted, women are often relegated to the lower ranks of coaching because of assumptions about their lack of competitiveness (Shaw and Hoeber 2003), insecurity around coaching (Fielding-Lloyd and Meân 2011), childcare and family responsibilities (Dixon and Bruening 2007) and perceived lack of skill at the highest levels (Shaw and Allen 2009). Yet at Netball Otago, there are five provincial coaches and two apprentice coaches, all of whom are women. The predominance of female coaches at these highest levels indicates that women have the ability to coach at the highest levels, are not precluded from doing so because of childcare responsibilities, and are quite secure in their knowledge and ability to instruct. In part, this is because of the culture of Netball Otago, which has been actively developed to ensure that women are coaching at the highest levels.

The first area of this cultural development is evident in the ways that Netball Otago promotes and encourages coaches. In their research, Shaw and Allen (2009) found that there are pathways for coaches that are actively promoted by the RDM and made accessible to all coaches. One coach at Netball Otago described this as 'for a couple of years now and I think we are encouraging a lot of the younger kids to start coaching. High schools really have to rely on those senior students to become coaches'. The RDM outlined the processes as:

> I had a girl yesterday who's a player who wants to start coaching. So I said come to one of our 'starting out on coaching' nights and start off with a school representative team, then maybe become an apprentice coach, and then maybe an age group coach. It's not formalized but take 'Jackie' [who was beginning her high-performance career]. We identified her good qualities, she's keen and motivated. She's coached club level. We had good comments from her senior coach, who's really experienced, and now she's applied to coach [regional] U-19. So if you took an example of a pathway, that's the right thing to do (Shaw and Allen 2009).

This example shows how, when an organizational culture recognizes the ability of women to do something, in this case coaching, and puts the right pathways in place, then women are able to access and benefit from those pathways. In other research, women's commitment to organizational pathways to coaching has been questioned by regional managers (Shaw and Allen 2009). It is likely, however, that if members of an organization create a culture in which women's potential to coach at the highest level is unquestioned, they will go ahead and coach at those levels.

The second area in which organizational culture has been created in a way that counters the conventional views of women as coaches is with attitudes towards motherhood. In many organizations, motherhood is seen as the beginning of the end for coaches, as it is assumed that women will be too busy with childcare to continue, or will not want to bring their children to practices or take them away on tournaments. Netball Otago sets a different cultural assumption for women coaches who have children. The coaches noted this supportive culture. Kath, who had coached for 14 years, noted: 'There's kids on the sideline. The sport is very accommodating with kids, or breastfeeding or whatever has to happen. I like that environment.' Raewyn agreed, saying: 'They are very supportive. Like Jackie's going off to tournament next week and she's taking her wee boy with her.' Pat reminisced that on her first tournament as a representative coach she'd taken her baby with her 'I had to take a support person who looked after her. A lot of coaches I know have little ones' (Shaw and Allen 2009). The RDM described how funding was found to assist a high-level coach to take her new baby to a tournament. As she had coached the team while she was pregnant, it was considered to be too disruptive to change the coaching staff. Rather than refuse to let her have the volunteer coaching position because of her pregnancy and the extra organizational costs of supporting her attendance at the tournament with a newborn, the RDM ensured that there was support for her (Shaw and Allen 2009).

This organizational practice is a feature of an organization whose culture recognizes the value of women as coaches, and is prepared to demonstrate that level of value. Further, it shows that women are able to coach when pregnant and, with support, able to focus on coaching while also childcaring. This cultural belief is at odds with many sport organizations, whose members are quick to dismiss women as potential coaches if they have children, or are unwilling to explore options to assist them in coaching at the highest levels. Such organizations are not only missing out on the experience of these coaches, they are also in danger of losing institutional knowledge that is built up over time.

The two salient features of this case study have shown how organizational culture can be created to be different to convention within sport organizations. Rao *et al.* (1999) suggests that sport managers could create similarly supportive environments that value women coaches as coaches by reflecting on their own organizational practices and the culture that informs those practices.

Critics might suggest that Netball Otago's approach is made easier because it is virtually a women-only organization. Regardless, it is an example of where an organization has challenged traditional views about the management of women coaches. As such, it is an example of how influential people within other organizations could reflect on their own attitudes to women coaches, and change. It is also necessary to note that the activities of Netball Otago are funded by community trusts and other sources of public funding. Giving Netball Otago money to fund childcare indicates a positive societal response or even encouragement for its approach. Organizations like Sport England that tie organizations' funding to equity could reflect on Netball Otago's approach as one that could lead to change regarding high-performance women coaches, without the frippery of expensive social marketing campaigns to get women involved in coaching and participation. Rather, an evaluation and reflection on an organization's culture might lead to real, sustainable change.

SUMMARY

In this chapter, the author has presented two ways in which gender has been viewed within sport organizations. The first was liberal feminism, which has been a powerful tool for recognizing some of the difficulties faced by women in sport organizations. Through liberal feminism, women have been able to attend courses, receive assistance and benefit from equity policies. However, much of this approach is limited because it puts the onus on women to change, rather than the organizations and cultures in which they operate. Moreover, liberal feminist-influenced policies can be met with resistance from some groups of men who feel that they are missing out on the benefits of such policies.

The chapter has also outlined how gender can be viewed as a cultural phenomenon within sport organizations. If influential people within sport organizations choose to reflect on their organization's culture with reference to gender, and make changes, there is the possibility of long-term, sustainable change. Again, this may be met with resistance by some, who may feel threatened by change. However, benefits to the whole organization might be a consequence of this approach, such as more inclusive hiring practices, diverse organizations and, in the end, employing and retaining the best people for jobs or voluntary roles, without the constraints of cultural assumptions about gender.

REVIEW QUESTIONS

1   When considering gender in sport organizations, why is it important to look more deeply than at the numbers of women and men in that organization?
2   What gender equity programmes or policies are you familiar with? Would you say that they follow a liberal feminist framework? Why?

3   Does the Netball Otago model of support for women work because it is dominated by women, or could it work in any sport organization? What are the reasons for your answer?

FURTHER READING

Fielding-Lloyd, B. and Meân, L. (2011). "'I Don't Think I can Catch it': Women, Confidence and Responsibility in Football Coach Education." *Soccer and Society* 12(3): 345–364.

Rao, A. Stuart, R. and Kelleher, D. (eds) (1999). *Gender at Work: Organizational change for equality.* West Hartford, CT: Kumarian Press.

Shaw, S. and Frisby, W. (2006) "Can Gender Equity be More Equitable? Promoting an Alternative Frame for Sport Management Research, Education, and Practice." *Journal of Sport Management* 20(4): 483–509.

WEBSITES

Netball Otago:
    www.netballotago.co.nz
New Zealand Olympic Committee Women in Governance Mentoring Programme:
    www.lumin.co.nz/GovernanceMentoring.htm
    and
    www.olympic.org.nz/nzoc/women-sport
Sport and Recreation New Zealand (SPARC):
    www.sparc.org.nz
Sport England:
    www.sportengland.org/funding/active_women.aspx
Women's Sport and Fitness Foundation (UK):
    wsff.org.uk
Women's Sport Foundation (USA):
    www.womenssportsfoundation.org

REFERENCES

Acosta, R.V. and Carpenter, L.J. (2004). *Women in Intercollegiate Sport. A Longitudinal Study – Twenty Seven Year Update.* West Brookfield, MA: The project on women and social change of Smith College and Brooklyn College of the City University of New York.

Cameron, J. (1993). *Gender in New Zealand Sport: A survey of national sport administrators.* Canterbury, New Zealand: University of Canterbury.

Charles, N. (2000). *Feminism, The State, and Social Policy.* Basingstoke: MacMillan.

Cockburn, R., Gray, K. and Thompson, R. (2007). *Gender Balance in New Zealand Olympic Sports.* Wellington, New Zealand: New Zealand Olympic Committee.

Ely, R.J. and Meyerson, D.E. (2000). "Theories of Gender in Organizations: A New Approach to Organizational Analysis and Change." *Research in Organizational Behaviour* 22: 103–151.

Fielding-Lloyd, B. and Meân, L. (2011). "'I Don't Think I Can Catch it': Women, Confidence and Responsibility in Football Coach Education." *Soccer and Society* 12(3): 345–364.

Fink, J.S., Pastore, D.L. and Riemer, H.A. (2003). "Managing Employee Diversity: Perceived Practices and Organisational Outcomes in NCAA Division III Athletic Departments." *Sport Management Review* 6(2): 147–169.

Fletcher, J.K. (1999). *Disappearing Acts. Gender, Power, and Relational Practice at Work.* Cambridge, MA: MIT Press.

Hillary Commission. (2001). *Winning Women: Women and girls in sport.* Wellington: Hillary Commission.

Hoeber, L. (2008). "Gender Equity for Athletes: Multiple Understandings of an Organizational Value." *Sex Roles* 58: 58–71.

Hovden, J. (2000). "Heavyweight Men and Younger Women? The Gendering of Selection Processes in Norwegian Sport Organizations." *NORA: Nordic Journal of Women's Studies* 1(8): 1–32.

Martin, J. (2001). *Organizational Culture: Mapping the terrain.* Thousand Oaks, CA: Sage.

McKay, J. (1997). *Managing Gender. Affirmative action and organizational power in Australian, Canadian, and New Zealand sport.* New York: State University of New York.

Murphy, M. (1994). *The Level of Policy Involvement by Women in National Sports, Fitness and Leisure Organisations.* Wellington, New Zealand: Hillary Commission for Sport and Leisure.

New Zealand Olympic Committee. (2001). The board. http://www.olympic.org.nz/nzoc/nzoc-board (accessed 9 November 2011).

New Zealand Olympic Committee. (2011). Women in sport. http://www.olympic.org.nz/nzoc/women-sport-new-zealand# (accessed 14 November 2011).

Rao, A., Stuart, R. and Kelleher, D. (eds) (1999). *Gender at Work: Organizational change for equality.* West Hartford, CT: Kumarian Press.

Schein, E.H. (1991). "What is Culture?" in: Frost, P.J., Moore, L.F., Louis, M.R., Lundberg, C.C. and Martin, J. (eds) *Reframing Organizational Culture.* Thousand Oaks, CA: Sage.

Scraton, S. and Flintoff, A. (2002). *Gender and Sport: A reader.* London: Routledge.

Shaw, S. (2006). "Gender Suppression in New Zealand Regional Sports Trusts." *Women in Management Review* 21(7): 554–566.

Shaw, S. (2007). "Touching the Intangible? An Analysis of 'The Equality Standard: A Framework for Sport'." *Equal Opportunities International* 26(5): 420–434.

Shaw, S. and Allen, J.B. (2009). "The Experience of High Performance Women Coaches. A Case Study of two Regional Sport Organisations." *Sport Management Review* 12: 217–228.

Shaw, S. and Cameron, J. (2008). "The Best Person for the Job: Gender Suppression and Homologous Reproduction in Senior Sport Management," in: Obel, C. Bruce, T. and Thompson, S. (eds) *Outstanding: Research about women and sport in New Zealand.* Hamilton: Wilf Malcolm Institute of Educational Research, pp. 211–226.

Shaw, S. and Frisby, W. (2006). "Can Gender Equity be More Equitable? Promoting an Alternative Frame for Sport Management Research, Education, and Practice." *Journal of Sport Management* 20(4): 483–509.

Shaw, S., and Hoeber, L. (2003). "'A Strong Man is Direct and a Direct Woman is a Bitch': Analyzing Discourses of Masculinity and Femininity and their Impact on Employment Roles in Sport Organisations." *Journal of Sport Management* 17(4): 347–376.

Shaw, S. and Penney, D. (2003). "Gender Equity Policies in National Governing Bodies: An Oxymoron or a Vehicle for Change?" *European Sport Management Quarterly* 3: 78–102.

Sport and Recreation New Zealand. (2008). Club membership. http://www.sparc.org.nz/research-policy/club-membership/ (accessed 11 April 2008).

Sport and Recreation New Zealand. (2010). High performance board. http://www.sparc.org.nz/en-nz/About-SPARC/Media/2010-Media-Releases/SPARC-High-Performance-Board/ (accessed 14 November 2011).

Sport and Recreation New Zealand. (2011). About us. http://www.sparc.org.nz/about-sparc (accessed 11 June 2012).

Sport England. (2009). Active women. http://www.sportengland.org/funding/active_women.aspx (accessed 4 August 2010).

Welford, J. (2011). "Tokenism, Ties and Talking too Quietly: Women's Experiences in Non-Playing Football Roles." *Soccer and Society* 12(3): 365–381.

Chapter 12

The role of sport management in the creation of social capital

Richard Tacon

TOPICS

Definitions of social capital • Key issues in social capital research and policy • Theoretical research on sport and social capital • Empirical research on sport and social capital

---

OBJECTIVES

By the end of this chapter, you will be able to:

- Understand the concept of social capital;
- Appreciate how three established theorists in this field defined and used the concept of social capital;
- Identify criticisms of the social capital concept;
- Understand how social capital is relevant to sport management;
- Identify and critique existing theoretical and empirical research on sport and social capital.

KEY TERMS

Bonding – social networks between homogeneous groups.
Bridging – social networks between heterogeneous groups.
Social capital – a multidimensional concept (with multiple interpretations) that refers to the ability to access resources through networks of relationships.
Voluntary sports clubs – local, non-profit organizations in which members play sport.

OVERVIEW

Social capital has become an increasingly important focus for academics, policy-makers and practitioners in a range of areas, including sport. Definitions of social capital vary – this is a recurrent problem – but those employing the concept tend to use it to refer to networks of relationships and various social and cultural aspects of such networks. Social capital has garnered attention because there is evidence that it can facilitate a range of positive social and economic outcomes. However, the concept itself is multidimensional and its effects are difficult to discern or measure directly. Arguably the most pressing question for academics, policy-makers and practitioners is how social capital can be developed and maintained. In sport, the concept of social capital has been enthusiastically embraced, in large part because it accords with many of the social and cultural benefits people have traditionally ascribed to sport. However, as recent research has shown, much more work is needed to understand how the manifold processes of sport engagement might influence wider social processes and how this might vary in different sociocultural contexts and for different groups in society. Such work is important for sport management scholars and practitioners as it may reveal how sports clubs, sport projects and other areas of the sport industry currently contribute to important social and economic outcomes and how they might contribute even more. Social capital is, then, an increasingly influential concept and a crucial area of focus for sport management scholars and practitioners. This chapter seeks to provide an academic overview of social capital and how it has been applied within sport management. The latter part focuses particularly on the critical question of how various forms of engagement in sport might help to create social capital.

INTRODUCTION

Social capital is everywhere. That is to say, it can be found in families, in friendships, in neighbourhoods, at work, in clubs, in the very fabric of social life. It is also to say that the concept of social capital is now everywhere too: in academic books and journals, in policy documents and political speeches, in newspapers, in magazine articles. One recent review declared that 'social capital has taken the social sciences by storm' (Barthkus and Davis 2009: 1). Yet, despite this mushrooming interest, there remains a series of vigorous debates about what social capital is, how it develops, how it can be measured, what effects it has and how it functions to produce any of these effects.

There is also a series of debates around sport and social capital, many of which will be of interest to the sport management scholar and practitioner. How might sport contribute to the development and maintenance of social capital? What aspects of sport participation, sport volunteering or sport spectatorship might be important? Is sport any different to other social and cultural activities in its relationship to social capital? What about traditional forms of exclusion within sport? All these questions provide the background for this chapter, which will analyse important theoretical and empirical research on social capital and sport, paying particular attention to their possible implications for the management of sport. In the foreground, though, will be the pressing question of how social capital develops, what the particular processes are, and what role sport can play in these processes.

THE SOCIAL CAPITAL DEBATE

So, what do people mean when they talk about social capital? In short: different things. At a basic level, definitions of social capital tend to refer to networks of relationships and various aspects of those networks. Beyond this, however, agreement is lacking; further examination is necessary. It used to be common to begin any analysis of social capital by charting the history of the concept and discussing the contributions of the three main social capital theorists: Pierre Bourdieu, James Coleman and Robert Putnam. Now, however, there are many advanced theoretical discussions of social capital, which do this well (Baron *et al.* 2000; Field 2003; Barthkus and Davis 2009) and several which do so in the context of sport (Blackshaw and Long 2005; Coalter 2007; Collins *et al.* 2007; Nicholson and Hoye 2008). As such, this chapter will not dwell long on these issues. Nevertheless, how one understands the term 'social capital' – and how this shapes research, policy and practice in sport and in other areas – remains critical.

Pierre Bourdieu developed his ideas on social capital through his concern with social hierarchy and the creation and reproduction of inequality. In critiquing the prevailing economic orthodoxy, he argued that other forms of capital beyond economic should be considered, most significantly cultural and social capital. He defined social capital as 'the aggregate of the actual or potential resources which are linked to possession of a durable network of more or less institutionalised relationships of mutual acquaintance and recognition' (Bourdieu 1986: 248). In Bourdieu's account, social capital functions to reproduce inequality and remains an asset of the privileged, functioning to maintain their superiority (Field 2003). Like other forms of capital, individuals can deliberately invest in it. In this respect, it is interesting to note, as Field (2003: 14) does, that in *Distinction*, Bourdieu's study of taste among the French middle classes, his sole indicator of social capital was membership of a golf club, which he considered helpful in oiling the wheels of business life (Bourdieu 1984: 291).

James Coleman's work on social capital extended from research on educational attainment and was located within an intellectual framework of rational choice theory. In perhaps his best-known contribution, a paper entitled 'Social Capital in the Creation of Human Capital', he conceptualized social capital as 'a variety of different entities, with two elements in common: they all consist of some aspect of social structures, and they facilitate certain actions of actors – whether persons or corporate actors – within the structure' (Coleman 1988: 98). Social capital is seen here less as a private good and more as a public good, a byproduct that can benefit people other than those whose efforts create it (Field 2003). Coleman (1990: 306–313) identified a number of forms that social capital can take, including obligations and expectations, information potential, norms and effective sanctions, authority relations, appropriable social organization and intentional organization. Coleman raises the possibility that 'constructed' forms of social organization, established for specific purposes, can, in other ways, constitute available social capital. He uses the example of a social club formed by printers in New York, which later became an effective employment referral service (Coleman 1988), but it is possible to see how sports clubs could be considered in this vein, facilitating the flow of information or creating obligations between people.

Robert Putnam is doubtless the best-known proponent of social capital. His initial work on the topic came in his analysis of the performance of regional government administrations in

Italy, entitled *Making Democracy Work*. He argued that the relative success of administrations in the northern regions was due to a higher level of social capital, exemplified by, among other things, a vibrant associational life (Putnam 1993). One of the key indicators used to illustrate social capital in this study was the prevalence of membership in voluntary associations in each region. He later developed his conception of social capital in relation to the USA, defining it, in his best-known contribution, *Bowling Alone*, as 'connections among individuals – social networks and the norms of reciprocity and trustworthiness that arise from them' (Putnam 2000: 19). Here, social capital is more a property of collectives than of individuals and the role of voluntary associations, sports clubs not least among them, is consistently highlighted.

The contributions of Bourdieu, Coleman and Putnam have been described as 'three relatively distinct tributaries of social capital theorizing' (Foley and Edwards 1999: 142). But to infer from this that they have flowed into a single, coherent stream would be a mistake. Halpern (2005) and others have pointed out how wide and scattered the research is that purports to focus on social capital. Nevertheless, it is possible to identify certain commonalities in the way researchers, policy-makers and other commentators have understood and employed the concept. For example, in academic research on social capital, there is now an increasingly accepted distinction between 'network' and 'attitudinal' approaches. Network approaches, influenced largely by Coleman (1990) and Lin (2001), tend to see social capital as various aspects of social structure that facilitate action. So Coleman (1990) argues that, in contrast to other forms of capital, social capital does not inhere in individuals or physical implements of production, but in the structure of relations between and among persons. In certain circumstances and for particular people or groups, these various elements of social structure facilitate certain actions – as and when they do, they can be conceived of as social capital.

The attitudinal approach is somewhat different. Putnam (2000) suggests that, through involvement in voluntary associations and other social networks, people develop values and attitudes, such as trust and reciprocity, which lead to more civic behaviour in society. Consequently, social capital tends to be seen as something like a portable resource that can be developed and then carried around into other areas of life. Yet there are problems with this conceptualization of social capital. Research suggests that values and attitudes like trust and reciprocity are highly sensitive to social context. An aggregate measure of how trusting people are, in general, cannot really be seen as social capital *per se*. Values and attitudes may be considered social capital, but only in so far as they facilitate the actions of people in particular social situations. Moreover, Portes (1998) argues that there needs to be a clear analytical distinction between the sources of social capital, i.e. the mechanisms that create it, social capital itself, and the resources acquired through it. For him, social capital 'stands for the ability of actors to secure benefits by virtue of membership in social networks or other social structures' (Portes 1998: 5). This avoids functional definitions that equate social capital with the resources that can be obtained through it.

At this point, it is also important to acknowledge that several criticisms have been levelled against those using the social capital concept. For example, Fine (2001, 2010) and others have pointed out that, far from being new, social capital is simply a rebranded version of earlier theoretical concepts discussed by Emile Durkheim, Alexis de Tocqueville, Adam Smith, even Aristotle. Field's (2003: 138) adequate rejoinder to such criticism is that this, in itself, is 'no reason for abandoning the concept, any more than we might dump the category of social class just because it existed before Marx came along'. Beyond this, critics have argued that the language used to describe social capital is inappropriate and that its usage is connected with a broad neoliberal outlook. These remain areas of sometimes intense debate.

One particularly significant issue is the lack of understanding of how social capital is created. To date, the majority of empirical research on social capital has concentrated on its effects, but recently a number of academics (Stolle and Hooghe 2003; Krishna 2007) have suggested that the most important question relates to the other side of the equation, namely, how does social capital develop? Stolle and Hooghe (2003) maintain that research on social capital's origins is important for three key reasons. First, and most simply, it addresses a major shortcoming in the literature. Second, it helps us to answer questions concerning direction of cause. Previous researchers have observed relationships between social capital, however defined, and a range of micro- and macro-level outcomes. However, in almost every case there is confusion about the direction of cause. Research that explores the mechanisms through which social capital develops enables us to evaluate more effectively the direction of these relationships.

Third, it allows researchers to explore the 'decline thesis'. Putnam (1995, 2000) argues that overall levels of social capital in the USA are declining and other researchers have assessed these claims in relation to other countries (Hall 1999). But only by understanding what aspects of social capital really matter and the mechanisms through which it develops in various contexts can we draw accurate conclusions about its rise and decline.

There is also a fourth crucial reason for concentrating research efforts on the origins of social capital – it is by far the most pressing concern for politicians, policy-makers and practitioners (Hooghe and Stolle 2003). Understanding the processes through which social capital is created, maintained or destroyed is essential if politicians and policy-makers want to design effective policies that seek to maximize the benefits social capital can bring. And this clearer understanding can also help those responsible for managing sport to identify ways to best promote the growth of social capital, both within and through their organizations.

Early work on social capital also largely ignored its negative consequences. This has been rightly criticized. There is now a general recognition that social capital can have a 'dark side'. Indeed, this has led some social capital scholars to suggest that more differentiated versions of the concept need to be employed in theoretical and empirical work. The clearest example of this is the now quite common distinction between 'bonding' and 'bridging' social capital, terms coined by Gittell and Vidal (1998), but popularized by Putnam (2000). Putnam describes bonding social capital as a kind of 'sociological superglue', reinforcing exclusive identities and homogeneous groups, and bridging social capital as 'sociological WD-40', encompassing people across diverse social cleavages.

While such insights are useful, they need to be handled carefully. In keeping with the more fine-grained conception of social capital described above, these distinctions should perhaps not be thought of as different forms of social capital *per se*, but as different intermediate outcomes. As Portes (1998: 15) notes, the same mechanisms that are appropriable by people as social capital, leading to beneficial outcomes, such as network-mediated benefits, can also produce negative consequences. Coleman makes a similar point. He states: 'a given form of social capital that is valuable in facilitating certain actions may be useless or even harmful for others' (1990: 302). The crucial issue is context. As Foley and Edwards (1999: 148) point out, all distinctions, such as that between bonding and bridging, should be seen as 'extensions of the insight that the value of social capital at any given level depends on the larger context, including the insertion of the individual or group in question into networks of relations at higher levels'. The importance of context is of particular concern for those who 'manage' sport, often in very diverse organizational settings.

One further major issue in social capital research surrounds methodology and the (often unexamined) philosophical assumptions that underpin empirical studies. Empirical research on social capital tends to be dominated by statistical analysis of quantitative data, but there is growing criticism of this type of work. Two lines of criticism can be distinguished. First, there is criticism of some of the technical aspects of quantitative research on social capital, such as the validity and reliability of various statistical indicators, the use of single-item measures and problems of aggregation (de Ulzurrun 2002; Hooghe 2003). This kind of criticism, although it exposes some of the methodological weaknesses inherent to many social capital studies, does not imply a wholesale rejection of variable-oriented analysis. That is, there is no real discussion or critique of the philosophical framework that underpins quantitative research on social capital. Instead, it suggests how such quantitative studies might be improved, for example, through multi-level analysis or multiple-item measures.

The second line of criticism goes further. Several authors have suggested that statistical analysis of quantitative data is inappropriate for investigating a multidimensional phenomenon that must be understood in its specific social context (Schuller *et al.* 2000; Szreter 2000; Devine and Roberts 2003; Johnston and Percy-Smith 2003; Tacon 2010). This constitutes a more fundamental critique of variable-oriented analysis. It has been accompanied by a demand for researchers to explore the underlying mechanisms through which social capital is created. Such research, it is argued, will lead to a better understanding of process, will enable a greater appreciation of context and will allow a clearer view of causal relationships.

SPORT AND SOCIAL CAPITAL

So, where does sport fit into all this? And how might social capital be understood in a sport management context? Even a quick glance at the academic literature on sport shows that interest in social capital is no less evident here than in other disciplines. Indeed, sport academics, policy-makers and practitioners have embraced the social capital concept with a great deal of enthusiasm, if not always with an equal degree of critical reflection. In fact, there are several reasons why a particular interest in the relationship between sport and social capital might have emerged, over and above the general fascination with the concept witnessed elsewhere. First, perhaps superficially, there is the title and image of Robert Putnam's (2000) well-known book, *Bowling Alone*. As Field (2003: 4) points out, 'the picture of bowling lanes peopled by people playing on their own – drawn from Putnam's evidence on the decline of league bowling in the USA – neatly captured the idea of people's steady disengagement from a common public life'. It could be argued, then, as Nicholson and Hoye (2008) do, that this vignette of the lone bowler has coupled sport and social capital in the popular (and academic) consciousness. The resultant decline in participation also has obvious connections with the core concerns of sport management scholars and practitioners.

Second, there is the strong emphasis in much of the social capital literature on membership of voluntary associations and volunteering. This has focused attention on sport simply because a vast number of voluntary associations are sports clubs and – related, of course – sport is one of the most common areas in which volunteering takes place. In England, for example, it has been reliably estimated that around 15 per cent of the adult population volunteer in sport, with 75 per cent of the core, formal volunteering taking place in sports clubs (Taylor *et al.* 2003). Moreover, the same study estimates that voluntary sports clubs in England boast around eight million members. Of course, these figures merely indicate voluntary activity and associational membership within sport and do not themselves constitute evidence of how social capital is created. Nevertheless, the sheer scale of this involvement helps to explain why social capital is increasingly being analysed in the context of sport, and why the concept might be particularly pertinent to the field of sport management.

Third, there is the long tradition of conceptualizing sport as having a series of social benefits, such as tolerance, social cohesion and adherence to moral frameworks (Smith and Waddington 2004). The social capital concept is increasingly being incorporated into this tradition, often adopted as an umbrella term, standing for many of the assumed social benefits of sport. However, as many academic reviews of sport's social (and economic) impacts relate, this tradition is based largely on assertion, rather than on rigorous sociological analysis. Fred Coalter refers to the 'mythopoeic' status of sport: he argues that uncomplicated, positive conceptions of sport are akin to myths that 'contain elements of truth, but elements which become reified and distorted and "represent" rather than reflect reality, standing for supposed, but largely unexamined, impacts and processes' (Coalter 2007: 9). Indeed, research on sport's social and economic impacts has been subjected to a number of criticisms in recent years and, as social capital gets drawn into the wider debate over sport's social role, this has serious implications for academic analysis of the relationship between sport and social capital.

Furthermore, two recent developments in the UK and elsewhere have pushed these concerns from academia into the policy spotlight: first, sport's rise up the political agenda; and second, the increasing emphasis on evidence-based policy-making. Prior to the late 1990s, political interest in sport was really only intermittent (see Chapter 5). In the UK, however, the arrival of a New Labour government in 1997 led to a higher social policy profile for sport. Coalter (2007: 14–19) suggests that this can be explained by the way in which sport fitted with aspects of New Labour's broader agenda – for example, the search for a 'Third Way' between the state and the market and an emphasis on active citizenship and combating social exclusion. New Labour's arrival was also accompanied by a public commitment to evidence-based policy-making. Solesbury (2001) links this to a number of developments: funding bodies increasingly adopting an instrumental view of research; practitioners, responding to better-informed patients or clients, more regularly seeking to ground their practice in evidence; and New Labour politicians being driven predominantly by pragmatism, rather than ideology. The immediate consequence for sport was that a number of policy-related literature reviews were commissioned in order to inform policy and practice (Collins *et al.* 1999; Coalter *et al.* 2000; Department for Culture, Media and Sport/Strategy Unit 2002). However, as described

207

above, shortcomings in much of the literature meant that these reviews tended to reach similar conclusions about the evidence base – mainly, that it was patchy at best.

Drawing broad conclusions, Coalter (2007: 2, emphasis in original) declares:

> There is an emerging view that *the* major methodological limitation on producing evidence for policy-making and practice is the absence of an understanding of processes and mechanisms which either produce, or are assumed to produce, particular impacts and outcomes.

It is interesting to note how closely this methodological discussion parallels the one taking place among social capital researchers. As mentioned earlier in the chapter, many authors (Hooghe and Stolle 2003) have stressed that in order to move social capital research forward, researchers need to carry out work which will develop a deeper understanding of the mechanisms and processes through which social capital is created. One of the reasons for this, as noted there, was that this knowledge is particularly important for policy-makers and sport managers. These twin discussions converge, then, to create a clear research requirement – detailed, policy-relevant research on social capital and sport that focuses on underlying mechanisms and social processes. Researchers must avoid facile claims that involvement in sport 'creates' social capital. Instead, research is needed which seeks to specify what it is about the mechanisms of sport engagement – being a member of a voluntary sports club, for example – that can, in certain circumstances and for certain individuals and groups, lead to the development of social capital. This, in turn, can lead to much better-informed management strategies for sport organizations.

THEORETICAL RESEARCH ON SPORT AND SOCIAL CAPITAL

Academic literature on sport and social capital can be divided into two broad groups: research that employs the concept of social capital directly, and research that engages with aspects of social capital theory without explicitly employing the concept. The first group comprises relatively recent research and can itself be subdivided into two groups: extended theoretical tracts and empirical work.

The second broad group – work on sport that deals implicitly with the social capital concept – is more miscellaneous. Still, it is possible to discern at least four relatively distinct streams of research, all of which offer areas of fruitful reading for sport management scholars and practitioners. First, there is general research on the social impacts of sport. Where this has focused on sport's capacity to promote trust, reciprocity, tolerance, civic engagement and so on, it may be pertinent to the study of social capital. Second, there is research on sports volunteering and the characteristics of voluntary sports organizations (Horch 1998; Heinemann 1999; Cuskelly *et al.* 2006). Third, there is sport management and governance research on the voluntary sector, examining, among other things, interorganizational linkages and relationships between volunteers and paid staff. This could lead to a greater understanding of how social networks are formed and maintained within the context of voluntary sports clubs. Fourth, there is a body of research on social psychology in sport, including studies of the relationship between sport and social integration and prosocial development. Such work may shed light on some of the processes involved in the development of social capital.

Detailed theoretical studies of sport and social capital have tended to incorporate analysis of all three main social capital theorists. While Putnam's dominance has been acknowledged, particularly in relation to sport and social policy, his version of social capital has certainly not been privileged. Indeed, Blackshaw and Long (2005), in one of the most extensive theoretical treatments of social capital in the sport and leisure context, take particular issue with Putnam's work, exposing its communitarian foundations and its structural functionalist perspective. They promote instead a sociological understanding of social capital, arguing that Bourdieu's version permits a clearer analysis of the ways in which marginalized groups act.

Researchers have sought to specify which aspects of sport might be relevant in the processes of social capital formation. Here, Nicholson and Hoye (2008) question the use of participation trends to demonstrate sport's impact, a practice no doubt influenced by Putnam's (2000) famous usage of bowling statistics. As one proxy among many at a macro-level, participation figures may be useful, but in isolated correlations, they are certainly problematic. As the authors point out, 'there are different types of participation and it is likely to be positive, or negative or even neutral given different contexts and circumstances' (Nicholson and Hoye 2008: 9). Indeed, there is a clear difference between participating in sport *per se* and being a playing or even a non-playing member of a sports club. Trends in sports volunteering have also been used as a central plank in arguments about sport and social capital. Yet, as Coalter (2007) and Doherty and Misener (2008) both point out, knowing the total number of sport volunteers or the number of hours contributed is of little use without a deeper understanding of what is involved. Research on the extent and nature of the interactions is required if conclusions about social capital are to be drawn.

Much of the theoretical literature urges researchers to explore empirically the contribution voluntary sports clubs can make to the creation of social capital (Collins 2005; Coalter 2007; Auld 2008). Yet some commentators have expressed doubts about the wisdom of studying this at all. For example, some have suggested sports clubs should be seen as outcomes of social capital, rather than sources. Doherty and Misener (2008) discuss this and direct us to Bourdieu for a way out of the seeming tautology. Bourdieu's argument is simply that 'the profits which accrue from membership in a group are the basis of the solidarity which makes them possible' (Bourdieu 1986: 249). This notion of a virtuous circle is expounded by other social capital theorists, including Putnam (2000), who suggests that sports clubs and other voluntary associations can be analysed as both source and outcome.

Some authors have also questioned whether the member benefit nature of sports clubs renders them unlikely sites for the production or maintenance of social capital (Coalter 2007). Yet, Putnam (2000) emphasizes that social capital refers to networks of social connections, i.e. doing *with*, rather than doing *for*. While the latter is obviously considered laudable and, in Putnam's analysis, is shown to be highly correlated with social capital, it is not part of the definition of social capital. A quick glance back at Coleman's conception would also suggest that the member benefit nature of sports clubs is no impediment to the formation of social capital. In his discussion of appropriate social organization, he uses a residents' association and a social club as exemplars of 'the general point, that organization, once brought into exist-

209

ence for one set of purposes, can also aid others, thus constituting social capital available for use' (Coleman 1988: S108).

It was argued, earlier in the chapter, that perhaps the most pressing questions for social capital researchers are: what are the processes, or mechanisms, through which social capital is developed? and how do these processes function in various contexts to produce different outcomes? Recently, such questions have been taken up in the sport literature. For example, Coalter (2007) stresses the significance of mechanism-based research and draws accordingly on Skidmore et al.'s (2006) work on community participation. Seippel (2006), too, has begun to explore certain mechanisms, both theoretically and empirically, in the sports club context and others are following suit. The next part of this chapter examines some of the recent empirical research on sport and social capital and discusses future research opportunities.

EMPIRICAL RESEARCH ON SPORT AND SOCIAL CAPITAL

Some researchers have followed the attitudinal approach in investigating sport and social capital, conducting quantitative analysis of large-scale survey data. For example, Delaney and Keaney (2005), using the 2002 European Social Survey, found that, after controlling for sociodemographic characteristics, membership of a sports club had a small, but statistically significant, effect on political engagement and trust in civil institutions, a substantial effect on meeting socially with friends, but no effect on social trust. Perks (2007) analysed data from the 2000 National Survey of Giving, Volunteering and Participating, conducted by Statistics Canada, to investigate how playing organized sport during school years contributed to a lifestyle of community participation, as measured by 11 indicators. After controlling for a range of other contributory factors, there remained statistically significant, though weak, relationships between youth sport participation and all measures of community involvement.

Seippel (2006) examined data drawn from a random sample of the Norwegian population and found that membership of a sports organization had a positive effect on generalized trust, but weaker than for membership of other types of organization. Similar significant, but weak, correlations were found for general political interest and voting. It is interesting to note, as Coalter (2007) does, that Seippel (2006) seeks to move beyond 'black-box' correlations. He acknowledges that the indicators used in the survey do not measure social capital directly, but are instead 'social phenomena that might be influenced – increase or decrease – by variations in types and amount of social capital' (Seippel 2006: 171). He also emphasizes the importance of specifying the social mechanisms through which sports clubs may influence social capital. From the literature, he identifies three such mechanisms: provision and facilitation of information; influence of social ties; and reinforcement of identity and recognition.

With all these quantitative studies, it is worth noting once again that the influence of Putnam's work, and the associated 'attitudinal' approach to social capital research, has led to a focus on a relatively narrow range of outcomes, largely associated with political efficacy and democracy. If Putnam's version of social capital remains dominant in policy circles, and many authors have indicated that it is likely to (Coalter 2007), this could have serious repercussions for sport, particularly in the ways that it might be strategically managed in the future. For if sports clubs are found to be less likely than other types of voluntary association to promote these particular political culture attitudes, they might be afforded little significance in policies around social capital. In contrast, earlier sociological conceptions of social capital were much less restricted in their focus and identified a broad range of individual and collective benefits that might arise from membership of voluntary associations. To date, however, these versions of social capital have enjoyed much less political penetration.

There have also been a couple of recent quantitative studies on sports clubs and social capital carried out in the network tradition. Harvey *et al.* (2007), via a postal questionnaire administered to volunteers in two different sports clubs, assessed the social capital effects of sports volunteering, using two particular tools: the position generator, which measures individuals' access to people with different social statuses; and the resources generator, which identifies the resources available to people through their social networks. They found that social capital is unequally distributed among sports volunteers as a function of several social factors, including social class, age, gender and ethnicity. As the authors point out, this 'speaks to the complexity of the distribution, formation, and reproduction of social capital not only within society in general, but also within smaller social worlds such as community sport organizations' (Harvey *et al.* 2007: 220).

Seippel (2008) examined the position, centrality and influence of voluntary sport organizations, by considering networks between categories of organizations in Norway over a period of 20 years. In general, he found that, while sport consistently represented one of the largest categories of voluntary organization (along with trade unions), sport organisztions were quite weakly embedded, although they have gradually become more embedded and centralized. Overall, Seippel (2008) concludes that sports clubs are less influential and less able to promote bridging social capital than other types of voluntary organization.

Exploratory qualitative research on sport and social capital has also been carried out, notably in rural Australia, where Driscoll and Wood (1999), Tonts (2005) and Atherley (2006) have examined the role of sports clubs. These studies identified the capacity of sports clubs to foster both positive and negative aspects of social capital. Driscoll and Wood (1999) suggest that sports clubs have the potential to promote leadership and skill development at an individual level and health and community identity at a collective level. However, as Coalter (2007) rightly points out, their definition of social capital – 'a collective term for the ties that bind us' (Driscoll and Wood 1999: 68) – is vague and has limited analytical value.

Tonts (2005), by means of a questionnaire survey and interviews, found that sports club members perceived social interaction as particularly important. Respondents referred to the capacity of clubs to create 'tight-knit communities', which they associated with community pride, and which Tonts (2005) suggests indicates bonding social capital. In addition, respondents claimed that sports clubs could foster inclusion, transcending class and ethnic and religious barriers, which Tonts (2005) associates with bridging social capital. Both Tonts (2005) and Atherley (2006) stressed the centrality of volunteering to sports clubs' potential contribution, but noted that declining population in rural areas was creating difficulties in this regard. Tonts's (2005) study also revealed certain negative impacts, including class-based exclusion in some sports, such as golf, and exclusionary processes that impacted some Aboriginal residents and those not interested in sport.

211

Some club-level studies have also sought to specify the mechanisms through which social capital might be formed. Burnett's (2006) analysis of the Active Community Club Initiative in the rural village of Tshabo, South Africa, found the following: people who became coaches developed their skills (human capital), which had individual benefits, such as better employment prospects and higher status, and collective benefits, such as the facilitation of opportunities for the rest of the community; reciprocal acts facilitated access to resources at an individual level through the lending of equipment, and at a collective level through community safety when people travelled and played together. Burnett (2006) found that the formation of bonding capital was most common – this was largely restricted to groups of the same age and gender – although the broader operations of the club facilitated linking social capital within the community by providing an umbrella for members of grassroots organizations.

Walseth (2008) looked specifically at how bonding and bridging social capital is formed at sports clubs through interviews with 15 female athletes aged 16–25 belonging to the so-called second generation of immigrants in Norway. Based on Putnam's (2000) theoretical framework, the author found that clubs were often used as arenas to strengthen existing friendships, producing bonding social capital. Respondents tended to focus on similarities between players, in terms of ethnicity and gender, and placed strong emphasis on the social support received. It is interesting to note that team sports were found to be particularly effective in this regard, underlining once more the importance of considering the type of sport involved.

In terms of bridging social capital, Walseth (2008) found that most new ties formed were weak, which supports previous findings. Whereas weak ties have previously been considered beneficial for finding employment (Granovetter 1973), the age of the respondents in this study meant that this was rarely significant; instead, other network-mediated benefits were mentioned, in particular learning about different cultures. The study also highlights the difficulties inherent in the creation of bridging social capital, exemplified by two respondents who joined an 'ethnic majority' club in a richer neighbourhood. Social class was here considered a major barrier by the respondents, not in terms of participation itself, but in terms of trying to build social capital.

It is important, of course, not to generalize too far from one particular study. As Walseth (2008) notes, there are particular structural features that need to be considered when looking at the potential for bridging across immigrant/non-immigrant lines in Oslo: it is an ethnically divided city and the sports clubs tend to be locally embedded with strong historical traditions of participation and volunteering. This local anchoring may also contribute to a degree of 'culture clash' within competitive team sports, a point also raised by Krouwel et al. (2006). A study by Verweel and Anthonissen (2006) called into question the seeming divide between bonding and bridging social capital among 'immigrant' sports club members. Triangulating through participant observation, interviews and survey research in ten Dutch sports clubs, the authors found that immigrants were able to develop both bonding and bridging social capital in monoethnic sports clubs and multicultural clubs. Indeed, the results of the survey, supported by personal interviews, showed that bonding and bridging effects were distributed across clubs and members. Moreover, immigrants did not opt for immigrant sports clubs on the basis of ethnic identity, but, just like native Dutch people, on the basis of personal friendships.

A particularly significant study was carried out in the UK by Crossley (2008). He examined the processes by which informal networks formed in the context of a private health club in Greater Manchester and the mechanisms involved. His ethnographic study identifies a series of key processes and contexts, including 'time–space coincidence', an intimate environment and 'cross-contextual meetings'. Following Coleman (1990), Crossley (2008) analyses the network social capital in terms of its facilitative functions: maximizing physical advantages, through group encouragement to exercise harder; identity and recognition – group members acquired and enacted playful intergroup identities; counselling; provision of information; collective action; and exchange of services.

The study also examined the 'dark side' of social capital, identifying the negative externalities for other gym-goers of the bonding social capital developed. In addition, Crossley (2008) described a brokerage and closure network figuration, where the main group became connected to other groups through key 'brokers'. This is of particular interest because it contradicts Burt's (1992) well-known analysis of the benefits accruing to individuals who bridge structural holes. Here, the brokers experienced tension and other negative externalities, demonstrating, as Crossley (2008) points out, the crucial role of context in seeking to understand the formation and maintenance of social capital.

SUMMARY

In the last two decades, the popularity of social capital as a subject of academic analysis and as a policy concern has grown enormously. This trend shows no signs of abating. Yet social capital remains the locus of fierce debate. In sport, the social capital concept has been taken up enthusiastically, although only recently has it been subjected to close critical scrutiny, while the implications of these debates for the field of sport management are even less developed. Here and elsewhere, it has been argued that researchers, policy-makers and sport managers ought to focus on the pressing question of how social capital is created. A fuller understanding of the processes involved and how such processes operate in different social contexts is paramount if this interest in social capital is to be translated into meaningful social action. For sport management scholars, then, the challenge is to understand and illuminate these sport engagement and social capital processes.

Empirical research on sport and social capital is proliferating, yet the evidence base remains thin. Quantitative analyses have so far been relatively unsophisticated, hampered particularly by the data available. As Seippel (2006: 179) argues, 'we need data designed more explicitly for sports studies, which distinguish more clearly between various aspects of organizational structures and activity, for the many possible networks emerging from a voluntary organization and for the specific topic of sport'. Qualitative research has provided some important insights, but there remains a need for well-conducted, intensive research. Importantly, many sports academics are clamouring for research which examines the social mechanisms and processes through which sports clubs impact social capital (Collins 2005; Seippel 2006; Coalter 2007; Tacon 2010). Although such studies have started to emerge, further research in this area is needed to facilitate greater understanding of the relationship between sport and social capital.

213

REVIEW QUESTIONS

1   What is social capital? (This is not a question with one straightforward answer, but to answer it is to explore the different ways in which it has been understood and employed in research and policy.)
2   How did the three original social capital theorists define social capital?
3   How might sport contribute to the creation of social capital?
4   What are some of the key issues that need to be addressed in future research on sport and social capital?

FURTHER READING

For very good, approachable overviews of social capital, read Field's (2003) *Social Capital* and/or Halpern's (2005) *Social Capital*. These cover the development of the concept and various debates around social capital and review much of the evidence relating to its impact on education, health, crime, the economy, and so on. Hooghe and Stolle's (2003) *Generating Social Capital* looks specifically at the other side of the equation, that is, evidence of how social capital is created. To explore the social capital debate fully, look at social capital criticism in Fine's (2001, 2010) books. In sport, Nicholson and Hoye's (2008) *Sport and Social Capital* is essential reading. It contains a number of chapters dealing with different aspects of the sport–social capital debate. Coalter's (2007) book, *A Wider Social Role for Sport: Who's keeping the score?* also contains a very good chapter on research and policy concerned with sport and social capital.

WEBSITES

Assist Social Capital:
    www.social-capital.net
IPPR:
    www.ippr.org
Sport England:
    www.sportengland.org/research/the_value_of_sport_monitor.aspx

REFERENCES

Atherley, K. (2006). "Sport, Localism and Social Capital in Rural Western Australia." *Geographical Research* 44(4): 348–360.

Auld, C.J. (2008). "Voluntary Sport Clubs: The Potential for the Development of Social Capital," in: Nicholson, M. and Hoye, R. (eds) *Sport and Social Capital.* Oxford: Butterworth-Heinemann.

Baron, S., Field, J. and Schuller, T. (eds) (2000). *Social Capital: Critical perspectives.* Oxford: Oxford University Press.

Barthkus, V.O. and Davis, J.H. (eds) (2009). *Social Capital: Reaching out, reaching in.* Cheltenham: Edward Elgar.

Blackshaw, T. and Long, J. (2005). "What's the Big Idea? A Critical Exploration of the Concept of Social Capital and its Incorporation into Leisure Policy Discourse." *Leisure Studies* 24(3): 239–258.

Bourdieu, P. (1984). *Distinction: A social critique of the judgement of taste.* Cambridge, MA: Harvard University Press.

Bourdieu, P. (1986). "The Forms of Capital," in: Richardson, J. (ed.) *Handbook of Theory and Research for the Sociology of Education.* New York: Greenwood.

Burnett, C. (2006). "Building Social Capital Through an 'Active Community Club'." *International Review for the Sociology of Sport* 31(3–4): 283–294.

Burt, R. (1992). *Structural Holes: The social structure of competition.* Cambridge, MA: Harvard University Press.

Coalter, F. (2007). *A Wider Social Role for Sport: Who's keeping the score?* London: Routledge.

Coalter, F., Allison, M. and Taylor, J. (2000). *The Role of Sport in Regenerating Deprived Areas.* Edinburgh: SECRU.

Coleman, J.S. (1988). "Social Capital in the Creation of Human Capital." *American Journal of Sociology* Supplement 94: S95–S120.

Coleman, J.S. (1990). *Foundations of Social Theory.* Cambridge, MA: Harvard University Press.

Collins, M. (2005). "Voluntary Sports Clubs and Social Capital," in: Nichols, G. and Collins, M. (eds) *Volunteers in Sports Clubs.* Eastbourne: LSA.

Collins, M., Henry, I., Houlihan, B. and Buller, J. (1999). *Sport and Social Exclusion: A report to the Department for Culture, Media and Sport.* Loughborough: Loughborough University/Institute of Sport and Leisure Policy.

Collins, M., Holmes, K. and Slater, A. (eds) (2007). *Sport, Leisure, Culture and Social Capital: Discourse and practice.* Eastbourne: Leisure Studies Association.

Crossley, N. (2008). "(Net)Working out: Social Capital in a Private Health Club." *British Journal of Sociology* 59(3): 475–500.

Cuskelly, G., Hoye, R. and Auld, C. (2006). *Working with Volunteers in Sport: Theory and practice.* London: Routledge.

De Ulzurrun, L.M. (2002). "Associational Membership and Social Capital in Comparative Perspective: A Note on the Problems of Measurement." *Politics and Society* 30(3): 497–523.

Delaney, L. and Keaney, E. (2005). *Sport and Social Capital in the United Kingdom: Statistical evidence from national and international survey data.* Dublin: Economic and Social Research Institute/Institute for Public Policy Research.

Department for Culture, Media and Sport/Strategy Unit (2002). *Game Plan: A strategy for delivering government's sport and physical activity objectives.* London: DCMS/Strategy Unit.

Devine, F. and Roberts, J. (2003). "Alternative Approaches to Measuring Social Capital: A Note on van Deth's 'Measuring Social Capital'," *International Journal of Social Research Methodology* 6(1): 93–100.

Doherty, A. and Misener, K. (2008). "Community Sport Networks," in: Nicholson, M. and Hoye, R. (eds) *Sport and Social Capital.* Oxford: Butterworth-Heinemann.

Driscoll, K. and Wood, E. (1999). *Sporting Capital: Changes and challenges for rural communities in Victoria.* Melbourne: Centre for Applied Social Research.

Field, J. (2003). *Social Capital.* London: Routledge.

Fine, B. (2001). *Social Capital Versus Social Theory: Political economy and social science at the turn of the millennium.* London: Routledge.

Fine, B. (2010). *Theories of Social Capital: Researchers behaving badly.* London: IIPPE/Pluto Book Series.

Foley, M. and Edwards, B. (1999). "Is it Time to Disinvest in Social Capital?" *Journal of Public Policy* 19(2): 141–173.

Gittell, R. and Vidal, A. (1998). *Community Organizing: Building social capital as a development strategy.* Thousand Oaks, CA: Sage.

215

Granovetter, M. (1973). "The Strength of Weak Ties." *American Journal of Sociology* 78(6): 1360–1380.

Hall, P. (1999). "Social Capital in Britain." *British Journal of Political Science* 29(3): 417–461.

Halpern, D. (2005). *Social Capital.* Cambridge: Polity Press.

Harvey, J., Levesque, M. and Donnelly, P. (2007). "Sport Volunteerism and Social Capital." *Sociology of Sport Journal* 24(2): 206–223.

Heinemann, K. (1999). *Sport Clubs in Various European Countries.* Schorndorf: Hofmann.

Hooghe, M. (2003). "Participation in Voluntary Associations and Value Indicators: The Effect of Current and Previous Participation Experiences." *Nonprofit and Voluntary Sector Quarterly* 32(1): 47–69.

Hooghe, M. and Stolle, D. (eds) (2003). *Generating Social Capital/*New York: Palgrave.

Horch, H. (1998). "Self-destroying Processes of Sport Clubs in Germany." *European Journal for Sport Management* 5(1): 46–58.

Johnston, G. and Percy-Smith, J. (2003). "In Search of Social Capital." *Policy and Politics* 31(3): 321–334.

Krishna, A. (2007). "How Does Social Capital Grow? A Seven-year Study of Villages in India." *Journal of Politics* 69: 941–956.

Krouwel, A., Boonstra, N., Duyvendak, J.W. and Veldboer, L. (2006). "A Good Sport? Research into the Capacity of Recreational Sport to Integrate Dutch Minorities." *International Review for the Sociology of Sport* 41(2): 165–180.

Lin, N. (2001). *Social Capital: A theory of social structure and action.* Cambridge: Cambridge University Press.

Nicholson, M. and Hoye, R. (eds) (2008). *Sport and Social Capital.* Oxford: Butterworth-Heinemann.

Perks, T. (2007). "Does Sport Foster Social Capital? The Contribution of Sport to a Lifestyle of Community Participation." *Sociology of Sport Journal* 24(4): 378–401.

Portes, A. (1998). "Social Capital: Its Origins and Applications in Modern Sociology." *Annual Review of Sociology* 24: 1–24.

Putnam, R. (1993). *Making Democracy Work: Civic traditions in modern Italy.* Princeton: Princeton University Press.

Putnam, R. (1995). "Bowling Alone: America's Declining Social Capital." *Journal of Democracy* 6(1): 65–78.

Putnam, R. (2000). *Bowling Alone: The collapse and revival of American community.* New York: Simon & Schuster.

Schuller, T., Baron, S. and Field., J. (2000). "Social Capital: A Review and Critique," in Baron, S., Field, J. and Schuller, T. (eds) *Social Capital: Critical perspectives.* Oxford: Oxford University Press.

Seippel, O. (2006). "Sport and Social Capital." *Acta Sociologica* 49: 169–184.

Seippel, O. (2008). "Sports in Civil Society: Networks, Social Capital and Influence." *European Sociological Review* 24: 69–80.

Skidmore, P., Bound, K. and Lownsbrough, H. (2006). *Community Participation: Who Benefits?* York: JRF.

Smith, A. and Waddington, I. (2004). "Using 'Sport in the Community Schemes' to Tackle Crime and Drug Use Among Young People: Some Policy Issues and Problems." *European Physical Education Review* 10: 279–297.

Solesbury, W. (2001). *Evidence Based Policy: Whence it came and where it's going.* Working paper no 1. London: UK Centre for Evidence Based Policy and Practice, Queen Mary: University of London.

Stolle, D. and Hooghe, M. (2003). "Conflicting Approaches to the Study of Social Capital: Competing Explanations for Causes and Effects of Social Capital." *Ethical Perspectives* 10(1): 22–45.

Szreter, S. (2000). "Social Capital, the Economy, and Education in Historical Perspective," in Baron, S., Field, J. and Schuller, T. (eds) *Social Capital: Critical perspectives.* Oxford: Oxford University Press.

Tacon, R. (2010). *Social Capital in Sport: The processes of social capital formation at voluntary sports clubs.* Leisure Studies Association Newsletter No. 86. Eastbourne: Leisure Studies Association.

Taylor, P., Nichols, G., Holmes, K., James, M., Gratton, C., Garrett, R., Kokolakakis, T., Mulder, C. and Kind, L. (2003). *Sports Volunteering in England.* London: Sport England.

Tonts, M., (2005). "Competitive Sport and Social Capital in Rural Australia." *Journal of Rural Studies* 21: 137–149.

Verweel, P. and Anthonissen, A. (2006). "Ethnic Diversity in Organised Sport: Development of Social Capital by Dutch Immigrants." *The Cyprus Journal of Sciences* 4: 109–128.

Walseth, K. (2008). "Bridging and Bonding Social Capital in Sport: Experiences of Young Women with an Immigrant Background." *Sport, Education and Society* 13(1): 1–17.

Chapter 13

The changing nature of sports volunteering

Modernization, policy and practice

Jimmy O'Gorman

TOPICS

Sports policy and the practice of sports volunteering in the UK • Voluntary sports clubs and policy in the UK • The English Football Association's Charter Standard Scheme

---

OBJECTIVES

By the end of this chapter you will be able to:

- Be aware of the sociopolitical context in which sports volunteering takes place;
- Understand pressures experienced by voluntary sports clubs and sports volunteers;
- Have an awareness of the professional practices affecting sports volunteering.

KEY TERMS

Modernization – a process in which sport organizations have begun to adhere to initiatives proposed and funded by government, which aim to facilitate the delivery of higher-quality, voluntary-led, grassroots sport provision.

Professionalization – the up-skilling of individuals such as sport volunteers to perform the roles expected of them adequately.

Sports volunteers – individuals engaging in all forms of sports voluntary activity (e.g. coaching, secretarial duties), whether formal or informal. It is generally altruistic work, undertaken of a person's own free will, choice and motivation, and is without concern for financial gain.

Voluntary sports clubs (VSCs) – not-for-profit organizations which are organized, administered and operated by sports volunteers. Generally, they are mutual-aid organizations primarily focused on providing sports opportunities.

OVERVIEW

Sports' volunteering is an important aspect of the organization, delivery and sustainability of sports provision in the UK and across other neoliberal countries. Numerous surveys have attempted to measure the scale, impact and economic value of voluntary activity in sport. However, different data collection methods and methodological underpinnings used across surveys (Cuskelly *et al.* 2006: 14; Donnelly and Harvey 2011: PG) make it difficult to compare and interpret data sets on sports volunteer trends with any accuracy. In addition, the definition of volunteering varies from survey to survey. Regardless of the definition followed, the existence and operation of sports systems, particularly in the neoliberal West, both historically and contemporaneously, are reliant on substantial voluntary effort in the form of voluntary sports clubs (VSCs) and sports volunteers. Taylor *et al.* (2003: 6) propose that volunteering is about helping others in sport without receiving any remuneration or expense. Cuskelly *et al.* (2006) adopt Volunteering Australia's more specific definition of volunteering as:

> an activity which takes place through not for profit organisations or projects and is undertaken: to be of benefit to the community and the volunteer; of the volunteer's own free will and without coercion; for no financial payment; and in designated volunteer positions only.
>
> (Volunteering Australia 2005, cited in Cuskelly *et al.* 2006: 5)

Thus, it is extremely difficult to judge the reliability of data, and to draw comparisons, particularly across nations and different sports. Notably, one such caveat relates to studies failing to attempt to understand the complexities of sport volunteering in light of the diverse sociopolitical contexts in which it takes place. A recent report, *Study on Volunteering in the European Union* (European Union 2010), attempts to redress this. In order to understand the demands and needs of the voluntary sector across all 27 EU member states (correct at the time of writing), the report's analysis relied on comparing across a variety of different national surveys supplemented by interviews with volunteers of a variable sample size across the different 27 states of 333 clubs, which is not highly significant or generalizable (European Union 2010: 171).

Volunteering in the UK is equally difficult to determine with any accuracy. Economically, volunteering is estimated as the equivalent of 2 per cent of gross domestic product (European Union 2010), whilst sport is noted as the most engaged-in type of volunteerism, in which 22 per cent of all volunteers were involved with sports and exercise organizations (Low *et al.* 2007). Different surveys have concluded that between 13 and 26 per cent of the population participate in formal volunteering in sport (Davis Smith *et al.* 2002; Attwood *et al.* 2003; Nichols *et al.* 2004; Low *et al.* 2007). Sport England's 2002 National Population Survey estimated that 5.7 million volunteers contributed 1.2 billion hours each year to sport, with a value of over £14 billion and equivalent to 720,000 additional

219

full-time paid workers (Taylor *et al.* 2003). Football, the most commonly engaged-in sport by volunteers across the EU, was found to have 430,000 volunteers contributing 96 million hours in the UK. The Active People Survey conducted by Sport England in 2005–2006 suggested a lower figure – more than 2.7 million (Sport England 2006), whereas Nichols *et al.* (2005) stated that 5.1 per cent of the population formally volunteered in sport, constituting 8.1million club members across over 106,000 clubs. More recently, Taylor *et al.* (2010) suggest that 75 per cent of sports volunteers operate within VSCs, whilst Sport England suggests nearly two million adults (1,972,700) contribute at least 1 hour a week to volunteering in sport – equivalent to a full-time workforce of over 80,000 people (www. sportengland.org/about_us/our_news/volunteers_week.aspx). This anomaly would suggest a downward trend in the number of people volunteering in sport, which requires further investigation. Regardless of these inconsistencies; volunteering in sport is acknowledged as the major sphere of voluntary activity.

Categorizing and breaking down different aspects of volunteering is also difficult. Donnelly and Harvey (2011: 60) present three forms of volunteering: major-event volunteering; volunteering for grassroots and community sport; and volunteering for high-performance sport. The most common and frequently engaged-in form of volunteering in sport in the neoliberal West is directly connected to sports development, at the grassroots (including youth, community) level (Donnelly and Harvey 2011). Despite an emergent body of literature relating to volunteers at this level, relatively little is known regarding how volunteers in sports clubs at the grassroots level operate; how they engage with their national governing body (NGB); and how an emergent body of sports development professionals interact with sports volunteers to implement policies and programmes reliant on voluntary effort. Following an overview of the recent sociopolitical developments pertaining to sports volunteering and VSCs, empirical data gathered from semistructured interviews with volunteers in grassroots football clubs and the football development officers (FDOs) who work with them is drawn on, to present a nuanced account of sports volunteering.

CASE STUDY: MODERNIZING GRASSROOTS FOOTBALL: THE FA'S CHARTER STANDARD

During the past two decades, grassroots football in England has undergone a period of sustained modernization, partly due to government intervention, but also a longstanding appreciation amongst volunteers and some administrators from within the Football Association (FA) itself (Conn 1998; Green 2009) that the provision of grassroots football was in need of urgent attention. A range of reports commissioned by various football bodies were also critical of the condition of the grassroots game (Football Taskforce 1999; Independent Football Commission 2004; Brown *et al.* 2006). High amongst a great many concerns were the state of facilities, quality of coaching and safety and welfare of children playing football. The FA's *Blueprint for the Future of Football* (The Football Association 1991: 63) declared that a strategy and plan for the development of grassroots football was urgently needed. County FAs transformed into limited companies from predominantly voluntary-led organizations, to be run on business principles. In 1997, the FA published *Charter for Quality*, focusing upon the infrastructure for youth and junior football from the grassroots to the elite level. In 2001, the FA's *Football Development Strategy* (The Football Association 2001) highlighted the importance of club development and of the need to develop a more effective club structure at the grassroots level of football in England. It stated that 'The Football Association must support VSCs with the potential to develop a number of teams, providing "football for all" and "football for life"'. The FA Charter Standard Club Programme was established in February 2001 to provide recognition to clubs that are well run, sustainable, with child protection and safety paramount. It also recognizes the club's commitment to coaching, player and coach development and the raising of standards of behaviour in football (Howie 2008).

The Charter Standard currently has three levels of accreditation. Any club can apply for FA Charter Standard status. To apply, clubs must complete an application form and return it to their County FA with the requested supporting evidence. The application is assessed and either approved or returned with an action plan by the County FA-nominated officer. Each advanced level requires additional criteria to be met. Once awarded, FA Charter Standard clubs and leagues are given an annual health check to ensure the standards of provision are maintained. Awards can be withdrawn if a club has a poor disciplinary record, fails to attend in-service FA Charter Standard events or is unable to continue to meet the criteria.

Entry FA Charter Standard clubs

Entry FA Charter Standard clubs (youth, adult accreditations) all feature a trained welfare officer, Criminal Records Bureau (CRB)-checked volunteers, emergency aid-trained volunteers linked to each team, Respect programme sign-up, a level 1 coach for each youth team, appropriate club administration in place and a volunteer coordinator.

Intermediate FA Charter Standard development clubs

Intermediate FA Charter Standard development clubs (youth, youth and adult accreditations) must in addition have at least five teams, a club development plan and a level 2 head coach who has also completed the specialist youth coaching module, and club officials must attend two in-service development events per year.

Advanced FA community clubs

Advanced FA community clubs must have at least ten teams. Community clubs must have male and female football provision, a mini-soccer team, an advanced development plan, and stage at least one workshop per season to improve behaviour. One coach must complete the specialist youth coaching module 2 and one club official needs to have attended an FA mentoring course. The club must have a schools coordinator and volunteer coordinator.

The FA is working towards a target of 75 per cent of all junior grassroots clubs to be Charter Standard-accredited by 2012. By July 2010, over 4,600 clubs had attained the accreditation, with 67 per cent of all mini-soccer and youth football being played in FA Charter Standard clubs (The FA 2010).

VSCS AND VOLUNTEERS IN CONTEXT

A key theme emerging from an expanding body of literature on the contribution of VSCs and sports volunteers to the delivery of organized sport at the grassroots level concerns the ways in which the structure of sports systems in the neoliberal West has transformed over time to present sports volunteers with challenges and opportunities in their practice (Cuskelly *et al.* 2006). Longstanding arrangements between NGBs (traditionally made up of longstanding volunteers themselves) and clubs at the grassroots level, often described as the 'lifeblood' of the sport, have transformed from an administrative and legislative role (for example, NGBs set the rules of affiliation and enforce the laws of play of the International Federations) to one in which VSCs have become important conduits for NGBs to achieve multifaceted goals. Whilst Taylor *et al.* (2003) suggest that, despite its scale and importance, volunteering in sport has traditionally received little recognition or support from government, in comparison to other spheres of volunteering, there has, ostensibly recently, been a sustained period of increasing government intervention in sport (Bloyce and Smith 2010).

As such, sports volunteers and VSCs have, to varying degrees, become units of cross-cutting political aims and objectives in the UK. Indeed, the importance of the sports voluntary sector to stakeholders in other sectors, and increasingly to government, 'underlines the need for good practice in the management of VSOs [voluntary sports organizations] … ensuring that VSOs are governed properly and then supported by best management practice will allow them to be most effective in their delivery of sport,' attest Robinson and Palmer (2011: 257). Whilst such a view makes eminent sense for those involved in sport, it is also symptomatic of some of the challenges the voluntary sport sector faces. In short, several commentators have suggested the sport sector has undergone a period of, and continues to be in the process of, 'modernization' (Green and Houlihan 2006; Adams 2008; Houlihan and Green 2009; Lusted and O'Gorman 2010; Robinson and Palmer 2011). Many suggest that the modernization process for sport occurred in part for a number of overlapping reasons (Adams 2011a; Groeneveld et al. 2010: 1; Robinson and Palmer 2011: 9) in order for government to achieve outcomes for other policy areas: sports contribution to health; political value, for example, national prestige in success and hosting of international events; economics; social inclusion; citizenship and social capital (Auld 2007; Coalter 2007; Hoye *et al.* 2008; Kay and Bradbury 2009; Adams 2011b). To this end, many Western, particularly neoliberal, governments have increasingly adopted interventionist stances with NGBs, and the VSCs under their jurisdiction, in pursuit of such objectives. In the UK, the impetus for professionalization through modernization has arguably been provided by increasing intervention of government, particularly the previous New Labour administration. The modernization of VSCs has involved the mainstreaming of the voluntary sector more generally on to the UK policy agenda, in which voluntary organizations began to experience a new relationship with government and a different policy environment (Kendall 2000: 542). As such, the sociopolitical environment in which sports volunteers operate has changed dramatically, particularly since the mid to late 1990s.

Similar to other neoliberal Western countries (Thibault *et al.* 1991; Cuskelly *et al.* 2003, 2006; Engelberg *et al.* 2007; Taylor *et al.* 2007; SPARC 2008; European Union 2010), research in the UK has suggested that sports volunteers are adopting ever-increasing professional practices. Indeed, the word 'professionalize' is used quite liberally in connection with the modernization process for sport, yet what is quite meant by either term is not particularly defined. General trends which discuss these terms in relation to the changing nature of voluntarism within sport, however, suggest volunteers are experiencing ever-increasing workloads in having to engage with increased bureaucracy, stringent procedures and complex registration overseen by increasing NGB involvement, detailed assessments, technological change, health and safety laws, continuing professional development (CPD), child protection and CRB checking procedures (Taylor *et al.* 2003, 2007; Nichols 2004; Nichols *et al.* 2005; Schulz 2005; Nichols and James 2008; Harris *et al.* 2009; Taylor and Garrett 2010; Adams 2011a, b). VSCs have begun to adopt rationalized approaches to their operations (Schulz *et al.* 2011), in what might be deemed 'professional' practices in managing volunteers, for example, human resource management (Chelladurai 2006; Cuskelly *et al.* 2006). Likewise, volunteers themselves are confronted with increasingly demanding tasks that require specific competencies and skills, creating a tension between, on the one hand, increasing demands placed on volunteers and, on the other hand, the ability (and desire) of volunteers to meet these demands and remain willing to do so in an unpaid fashion (European Union 2010: 171). There has also been a trend towards greater reliance by VSCs on grants from funding bodies which have increased the pressures for professionalism, target setting and development planning in line with government objectives (Garrett 2004; Nichols *et al.* 2005; Schulz 2005).

Several government-influenced reports and strategies have impacted upon volunteer and VSC practice. Game Plan (DCMS 2002) was a response to, and indicative of, New Labour's concern to modernize sport policy processes, addressing the potential for sport policy to be implemented in a more strategic fashion than at any point in the past. The modernization agenda was driven by two key policy documents, *A Sporting Future for All* (DCMS 2000), and *Investing in Change? High level review of the modernization programme for governing bodies of sport* (Deloitte & Touche 2003). It has been continued with the publication of the Department for Culture, Media and Sport's latest vision for sport, *Playing to Win: A new era for sport* (DCMS 2008), and Sport England's 2008–2011 strategy, which states that 'National Governing Bodies are placed at the heart of the strategy as it is their networks of community clubs and other assets that will drive delivery' (Sport England 2008: 10). Clearly, government views VSCs as being potential vehicles with which to achieve policy objectives. Government influences NGBs through sports councils such as Sport England and UK Sport. To drive government objectives through VSCs (for example, increasing the number of people participating in their sport), as part of the Sport England strategy, NGBs have produced 'whole-sport plans' which, among other things, present NGBs with targets to meet across a range of areas. Sport England provides exchequer grants to NGBs, which are conditional on these targets being met. The larger and generally wealthier NGBs have, particularly since 2000, employed specialist professionals in the form of development officers, to work with VSCs and volunteers under their jurisdiction in order to implement such policies and programmes. Following Newman (2001), Green and Houlihan (2006: 53) highlight that these neoliberal reforms empower individuals and organizations, perceived in terms of increased access for controlled government funding, yet, at the same time, are exposed to strongly centralized control through the

223

imposition of rigorous targets and systems of performance measurement. Sanctions are, and have been, enforced on those organizations that fail to meet them[1].

An integral theme of this raft of government policies, directed at the organizations and individuals involved in the sports system, has been the targeting of NGBs to develop a more systematic and structured organization of the clubs under their jurisdiction (DCMS 2000: 40). The development of an accreditation scheme for grassroots clubs to enhance the quality of their delivery, Clubmark, was offered to VSCs. Through Sport England, managed by a private consultancy firm KKP (www.clubmark.org.uk) and overseen by NGBs, professionalization and development of a ''service delivery' philosophy have been encouraged in enticing VSCs to undertake Clubmark accreditation in return for funding or other inducements (Cuskelly *et al.* 2006: 49), such as greater levels of professional assistance from NGB staff and support from other agencies such as local authorities (www.clubmark.org.uk). Clubmark-accredited VSCs achieve minimum operating standards in safeguarding and protecting children, quality coaching, equal opportunities and good management. Volunteering in such clubs, or those that have ambitions of going through the process, becomes more formalized (Robinson and Palmer 2011: 12). An increased focus on professional practice such as CPD requires a greater commitment from volunteers to training and development. Presently, more than 10,000 clubs are Clubmark-accredited across 50 different sports, with more than 4,500 clubs working towards accreditation (www.clubmark.org.uk/faq). In short, driven by VSCs and sports volunteers across all sports, Clubmark is both a product and a process of the modernization of sport. Each sport has a variant of Clubmark which is specifically adapted to meet the requirements of the NGB, but all adhere to the minimum standards appropriated by Clubmark generally. The case study presented earlier outlines the development of the FA's version, the Charter Standard, and its criteria.

The identification (Sport England 2004a) and subsequent positioning (Sport England 2007) of VSCs in England as core components and drivers of participation (Sport England 2004b) of the 'single delivery system' mean VSCs are at the forefront of local sport policy implementation (Adams 2011a). Recently, a range of articles have focused on VSCs and sports volunteers becoming the agents of delivery for government-based sport policy (Nichols *et al.* 2005; Coalter 2007; Nichols and James 2008; Adams and Deane 2009; Harris *et al.* 2009; Adams 2011a; Harris and May 2011; O'Gorman 2011). Generally, these suggest that the disposition of VSCs and sports volunteers, within the modernized context in which they operate, are important factors which need to be accounted for in order to understand the way in which VSCs and sports volunteers engage with, and enact, implementation of policies and programmes.

THE IMPACT OF MODERNIZATION ON SPORT VOLUNTEERING

What do we know of the impact of the drive for modernization within the sport sector on VSCs and their volunteers? Likewise, what is known about the practices of sport development professionals that have emerged as part of the modernization process, in part, to drive it forward?

Modernization has pressured VSCs and volunteers to shift from a traditional mutual-aid outlook (Nichols *et al.* 2005; Adams 2011a), towards a focus on service delivery resonant of more philanthropic mainstream voluntary organizations that provide a service to loosely defined social groups (e.g. Oxfam). Adams (2011a: 29) suggests VSCs' orientation as mutual-aid organizations is counterintuitive to the professional practices they must engage in within this modernization agenda, and presents a dichotomy which has created unresolved tensions. Ostensibly, programmes such as Clubmark potentially alter the expectations of those volunteering within (Harris *et al.* 2009; Adams 2011a), and working with VSCs (Lusted and O'Gorman 2010), which not only threatens the historical and fundamental basis of VSCs' member solidarity (Nichols *et al.* 2005; Adams 2011a), but also questions the suitability of VSCs to deliver government policy objectives (Harris and May 2011).

Likewise, Harris *et al.* (2009; see Chapter 5) question the appropriateness, sensitivity and feasibility of current sport policy, particularly given the emphasis on VSCs as policy implementers. Volunteers' perceptions of government sport policy objectives suggested an apparent lack of, or outdated awareness regarding, the content and aims, which engendered confusion and frustration at the pace of change in the political agenda. Volunteers perceived there to be a top-down approach to policy, with the government and national sport organizations like Sport England and NGBs developing policy with an expectation that VSCs would deliver deferentially (Harris *et al.* 2009: 413). In addition, volunteers either appeared distrustful of government policy or lacked confidence that it could be delivered. Analysis of the responses generated four broad categories of volunteer disposition towards government sport policy: resistant, indifferent, reactive and supportive. Moreover, volunteers within VSCs have differing opinions and perceptions regarding club objectives (Harris *et al.* 2009: 415). Indeed, Nichols *et al.* (2005: 38) note that the pressures on NGBs to modernize and deliver policies and programmes such as club accreditation schemes cascaded into greater pressures on VSCs and volunteers, which was largely interpreted as a challenge to volunteer practice and has generally been met with a degree of ambivalence.

Adams (2011a) found that those VSCs and sports volunteers that are engaged in club accreditation seem to comply willingly with directives, which ensures their presence within the political agenda. However, this is largely predicated upon conditionality. That is, VSCs expect, and indeed are enticed by, the potential of funding for the benefit of their club members and the community. Moreover, the management of VSCs was becoming more business-like, and expectations and impetus were being generated by volunteers wanting clubs to be forward-thinking and dynamic. As such, the disposition of some VSCs was oriented towards the success of the club rather than developing the club structure (Adams 2011a: 34). It is dangerous to assume that because VSCs and sports volunteers are being driven by their NGBs towards accreditation that they will succumb to delivering services and implementing policies such as Clubmark schemes in line with the dominant policy hierarchy (Adams 2011a). Despite differences in VSC motivations for engaging with club accreditation, and the extent to whether clubs have willingly or merely complied, VSCs and volunteers are adapting to a policy core paradigm (Houlihan and White 2002) in that there is an acceptance of, and contribution to, the principles and practice of the modernization agenda for sport.

Schulz *et al.* (2011: 433) generalize that a dominant approach to managing VSCs is the adoption of a rational systems perspective. Rationalism neatly fits with modernization, as in setting the structures within which VSCs operate, that they are formal, and purposely

225

designed for the delivery of sport. Not only is there little evidence to suggest this style of management is appropriate for VSCs, the blanket approach taken by government and its agencies in their treatment and perceptions of VSCs assumes a degree of homogeneity, and rational approaches appear to dominate the thinking about the management of VSCs with few alternative models or ideas (Schulz *et al.* 2011: 435).

Evidently, the complexities of sports' volunteering have been exacerbated by the modernization process. Given the intricacies of such findings, it is a danger to treat all VSCs and all sports volunteers from different sports as homogeneous in their outlook, and important to acknowledge their diversity and autonomy (Nichols *et al.* 1998; Allison 2001; Rochester 2001; Taylor 2004; Taylor *et al.* 2007; Harris *et al.* 2009; Adams 2011a). The available literature tends to overlook such complexities, to reify categories of VSCs and volunteers. Predominantly, there is an adoption of a formal/informal (Taylor *et al.* 2003; Cuskelly *et al.* 2006) classification of VSCs, which implies that sports volunteers within each type adhere to the principles of one or the other. At one end VSCs are informal and traditional, unlikely to seek external assistance and resistant to perceived external 'interference'. At the other end are more contemporary, formal VSCs, managerialist in approach, systematic and more receptive to external assistance (Taylor 2004: 106; Cuskelly *et al.* 2006: 26). Harris and May (2011) have also expanded this typology to include a semiformal category of VSCs, and applied this to the general response of each type of club to the implementation of policies presented to VSCs within the modernization agenda of sport in the UK (Table 13.1).

Table 13.1 *A typology of voluntary sports clubs (VSCs)*

	Informal	*Semiformal*	*Formal*
Aims	Socially orientated, with aims related to mutual enthusiasm	Seeking to develop as VSC and engage in policy. Resource constraints limit commitment	Development oriented with aims consistent with growth and sustainment
Cognition	Majority unaware of specific policy goals for community sport	Some awareness of policy but confusion regarding the specific nature of policy and little, if any, awareness of the expectations on clubs	Majority are aware of broad policy commitment to sport but very few understand the specific policy objective and/or the place of VSCs within this
Direction of response	Resistant and reject role in policy implementation	Potentially responsive to policy, although facility and resource issues constrain full compliance	Responsive to policy and proactively seek external assistance

Source: Harris and May (2011).

Indeed, Harris and May (2011) debate whether there is greater potential for policy implementation amongst those clubs that are towards the more formal end of the spectrum, given that the aims and objectives of such VSCs were consistent with those of the policies led by government, that volunteers within the VSCs were at least aware of the wider policy agenda for sport and were largely responsive to, and proactively sought, external assistance in the form of NGB and local authority development officers.

Investigating the subjective opinions of sports volunteers within the context of modernization, Adams and Deane (2009: 125) argue that this labelling is oversimplistic, prioritizing the characteristics of the VSC at the expense of volunteers' perceptions of their own actions and motivations for being involved in sport. Adams and Deane (2009) argue that the informality or formality of VSCs must be treated separately to the informality or formality of the sports volunteers themselves (Figure 13.1).

Advancing Taylor's (2004) notion of a formal-to-informal continuum in VSC volunteering, informal and formal volunteers may well coexist in the same VSC. Likewise, it may be possible that a sports volunteer maybe inclined to volunteer in a formal manner, for instance, by adopting and expecting managerialist and professional practices, but may be part of a VSC which is informal in its outlook. Four domains of sports volunteering are presented. Generally, there are those volunteers who have similar subjective expectations of not being managed, controlled and directed, i.e. informal volunteering. Then there are those who experience similar expectations of formal training and monitoring, perhaps even with a higher desire to be managed in a particular volunteer role, i.e. formal volunteering.

Whilst these studies build on, and supplement previous studies into the changing nature of VSCs and sports volunteering, less is known about the professional development officers that have emerged over the past 10–15 years with the responsibility of engaging VSCs with the modernization agenda by, amongst other things, enticing or targeting clubs to gain accreditation

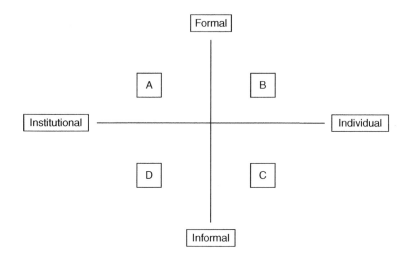

Figure 13.1 *Model of formal and informal sports volunteering*

of Clubmark. In the context of Canadian high-performance sport, Donnelly and Harvey (2011: 59) note a striking similarity across a number of studies investigating the complex and multifaceted relationships between sports volunteers and professional paid sports administrators. First, the increasingly bureaucratized, rationalized and professionalized approach to provision, to varying degrees, placed volunteers in a subservient position in relation to power held by relatively new professional sports administrators. Second, largely contingent on the types of organizations under study, almost counterintuitively, a number of works emphasized difficulties encountered by professional sports administrators in working with organizations dominated by volunteer boards and executive committees (Donnelly and Harvey 2011: 59).

In the UK, Harris *et al.* (2009: 420) hint at sources of tension between professional development staff such as sports development officers working in NGBs or local authorities, in putting VSCs under pressure to professionalize and modernize. Bloyce *et al.* (2008) noted that bureaucratization and working in partnership with other organizations such as VSCs were cited as pressures in relation to the availability of resources and the increasing accountability enforced by a 'target-hitting' culture in prioritizing the achievement of non-sports objectives. They concluded by suggesting that the growing complexity of the networks involved in sports development undermined government's ability to achieve its sporting priorities because SDOs prioritized practice that protected, maintained and advanced their own individual and/or collective interests – an unintended consequence of government policy (Bloyce *et al.* 2008). Given varying motives of VSCs and volunteers, VSCs 'opt in' to modernization and the historically embedded autonomy of VSCs, the suitability of VSCs as conduits by which government should seek to implement policy and achieve a range of social aims and objectives has been questioned (Nichols *et al.* 2005; Coalter 2007; Harris *et al.* 2009; Adams 2011a). Policy-makers are therefore encouraged to acquire a more sophisticated understanding of VSC and volunteer types with regards to their orientation towards implementing policy (Harris *et al.* 2009: 422).

The final section of the chapter provides a brief account of VSCs' reception of a Clubmark scheme, in this case local football clubs' take-up of the FA Charter Standard scheme. This overview draws upon qualitative data collected by the author. This example aims to expand this emerging knowledge on VSCs and their responses to delivering policies and programmes. The data has limitations in that the sample drawn on focuses on grassroots football VSCs and volunteers who have engaged with the modernization process by implementing the Charter Standard, and the observations of the FDOs responsible for enticing and supporting them. As such, it is not the intention to offer new types of VSCs and volunteers, but to build on existing knowledge gained in other work on the nature of volunteering in a rapidly changing sociopolitical context in which VSCs, volunteers and professional administrators find themselves. Unlike the clubs in the works of Taylor *et al.* (2003), Cuskelly *et al.* (2006), Harris *et al.* (2009), Adams (2011a) and Harris and May (2011)and, the focus of investigation was not to understand the receptivity of clubs and volunteers to becoming policy implementers within the modernization agenda, but to understand the views and perceptions of those who had engaged with the modernization agenda by implementing the Charter Standard. The individuals within the sample are representatives of their VSC, and hold a position of authority. As such, the data is limited in terms of Adams and Deane's observations that volunteers within VSCs will have different ideas and motivations regarding their volunteering.

228

A TYPOLOGY OF VSCS AND VOLUNTEERS DISPOSITION IN GAINING CHARTER STANDARD ACCREDITATION

The author's research in this area identified three key types of clubs related to their relationship to the FA's Charter Standard scheme: (1) supportive/proactive; (2) indifferent/reactive; and (3) indifferent/resistant. The clubs discussed below are presented as extreme types, but it must be acknowledged that a club predominantly displaying characteristics of one type may also exhibit some characteristics of the other types, thus conceptualizing them as a spectrum is appropriate.

Supportive/proactive

These tend to be relatively newly formed clubs, or formed from volunteers dissatisfied with their experiences from other clubs that were traditionally reliant on spontaneous, experienced informal volunteers. They generally have a small number of teams. Implementing the Charter Standard is viewed as a means by which to run the club properly along professional and modern guidelines in order to establish the club. There is a particular desire for greater structures, regulations and sustainability, and an improvement in the quality of provision in terms of coaching sessions and child protection awareness.

> instead of just running the club from a piece of paper, things became formalized and got the club in order ... when volunteers and coaches come into the club they know they have to go on a coaching course, a three hours child protection course etc. ... it pushes the club along, and it is something that we can publicize to potential parents, that we are a club that is trying to look out for your kids.
>
> (interviewee A, March 2007)

Engaging with the modernization practices also instilled confidence within volunteers to undertake further training for both their own and the club's development, an acceptance that CPD was desirable, and had enthused volunteers. 'Some have gone on further and taken the level 2 courses and one has done his level 3 and his UEFA 'b' [Union of European Football Associations 'b'] ... so people want to really push themselves, they have the belief' (interviewee A, March 2007). Compliance with FA directives establishes the club as an organization that is in line with the governing body's strategy for the game in 'doing the right things in order to develop football' (interviewee A, March 2007). FA initiatives are viewed as the legitimate way in which to provide grassroots football. There is reliance on and receptivity to the County FDO, and the FA, viewed as legitimate authoritative units from which the club should seek support. An indicative comment from one club states:

> he knows what is required, and has helped us so much in implementing the CS [Charter Standard] and getting our club set up right ... we are happy to do whatever they want ... we are the ones that benefit.
>
> (interviewee A, March 2007)

Although expressing concerns and frustrations with increased bureaucracy in line with the observations in other studies on VSCs as conduits by which to implement policy (Garrett

2004; Nichols *et al.* 2005; Harris *et al.* 2009; Adams 2011a), there is a willing ceding of autonomy. Such observations resonate with those of Donnelly and Harvey (2011), in that professional administrators seem to be in a more powerful, bureaucratic and political position. However, evidence here suggests a willing, rather than forced, compliance by such clubs.

The FDO working with clubs displaying characteristics of this type noted that it was easier to convince those coming to football volunteering new, with no preconceptions, of the merits of the Charter Standard. Indeed, it was possible to shape preferences and influence decisions.

> With the club being fairly new they come on our radar very early in their development as they affiliate to us ... this means it is easy to communicate to them the CS and the benefits of becoming accredited ... I suppose it is easier to guide and support them, as they seem content to be guided by you as they see you as the expert if you like ... you generally find the volunteers come on board fairly quickly.
>
> (FDO 1 interview, January 2007)

The willingness to adopt the Charter Standard and its practices not only shows an acceptance of a 'modernized' approach to running the club and providing football at the grassroots, but also exemplifies a dissatisfaction with the old ways of running football, and the apparent willingness to discard or dilute the old volunteerism. As such, the club and its volunteers adopted a more formal interpretation of their role within the club, which suggests the volunteers within VSCs have undergone a perceptible shift in their outlook. That is, the gaining of Charter Standard accreditation, in this example, set guidelines and altered how the club functioned, not only internally, but also the purpose of its function and for whom it functioned.

Although specific to the Charter Standard, such observations resonate with Harris *et al.*s (2009) observations regarding 'reactive' and 'supportive' volunteers, i.e. those willing to engage with the modernization agenda in willingly implementing policies and programmes such as Charter Standard. More formal in nature (Taylor 2004; Harris and May 2011), in line with the findings of Adams (2011a), these types of club engage in a movement from mutuality to modernization, and adopt a more rationalistic approach to operations in that the VSC were able to ensure volunteers within the club were clear on their roles and responsibilities, reflecting a professional and businesslike approach in becoming deliverers of a service.

Indifferent/reactive

Clubs believe implementing the Charter Standard has made little difference. They tend to be established and have existed for a significant period of time preceding the Charter Standard. Such clubs report that the Charter Standard merely confirms more formally that the activities already present within the club constitute good practice. They invariably had to a lesser or greater extent structures and procedures aligned with Charter Standard, and encouraged CPD among volunteers. One consistent theme in line with more external laws and legislation in general was increased child protection awareness and formalization.

> The club is 11 years old and we have always been proud in the way in which we have been organized ... all the CS has done for us as a football club is to underline where we wanted to be. All the issues that are raised in CS are things that we were already doing. I am so pleased with CS because it reinforced that we were going in the right direction. I can't believe there are people involved in football and still are who don't go through any process of vetting, don't go through any process of interview ... so starting to firm those things up is absolutely brilliant.
>
> (interviewee B, July 2006)

Furthermore, an integral aspect of the motivation to implement the Charter Standard was to improve the club's position to gain funding, ranging from facility development to equipment. Charter Standard is a means to an end for them.

> The County have told us that if we get CS, they will support our application for funding to develop our own facility, which will secure the sustainability of the club into the future, rather than relying on local authority and school pitches.
>
> (interviewee B, July 2006)

Given the sociopolitical context in which FDOs have to meet predetermined targets in the number of clubs that are accredited annually (Bloyce and Smith 2010; Lusted and O'Gorman 2010), such clubs are appealing.

> We target clubs like these a lot ... we convince them of the merits of CS ... they have got the majority of administration, constitution, your codes of conducts ... little needs to be done to get them up to standard and potentially progress through the CS framework ... We have to meet our targets set by the regional development manager ... so targeting these clubs and getting them through the process takes very little work, we always meet our targets.
>
> (FDO 2 interview, June 2006)

Such clubs seem formal in their practice and outlook. There is a coupling of a set of processes, in that clubs of this type have been operating in a manner consistent with modernized practices prior to implementing Charter Standard, dissatisfied with the state of grassroots football and the unstructured, unaccountable longstanding traditions of volunteering. In having their ideals and ambitions met, at the same time such clubs match the profile required for sports development professionals. However, resonating with the findings of Adams (2011a) of clubs looking inwards rather than towards contributing to the policy agenda, the motivation for Charter Standard implementation and adopting more structured and professionalized practices is oriented towards the enhancement of the club *vis-à-vis* other clubs in their locality, and in enhancing the chances of achieving funding and other benefits.

Indifferent/resistant

Clubs suggest the Charter Standard has made no difference whatsoever, and in some cases has been a hindrance. These are in the minority, and tend to be clubs with a large number of teams catering for all junior ages.

231

> I do not see what the club got out of it except to distinguish us even more from our rivals, to say 'look the FA recognise that we are a successful club'. I suppose we can say we're a CS club and that's good but other than that … no.
>
> (interviewee C, May 2006)

They tend to have informal links with established adult clubs in their locality, or within their own club, whereby the success of the club as a whole is judged on the performance of the adult team. They perceive that Chartered Standard benefits should be tangible, for example, guaranteed funding for facility development or football equipment, rather than intrinsic. The Chartered Standard is equated with success on the pitch in terms of winning and producing talent to further the reputation of the club, and will only register children who they believe will enhance their teams' ability. Invariably they have a long history within their community as a recognized club for their relative success in playing at a high standard.

> We've built a reputation over the last three decades … We win all the cups in our area every year, and have actually had five young people sign for professional clubs in the last 18 months … having CS just confirms that we are doing things right to develop our players.
>
> (interviewee C, May 2006)

Such clubs are resistant to the extent that that they see implementing the Chartered Standard as a 'tick box' exercise, and implement because 'it is there, we don't have to like it but if we are seen to be doing the right thing then the FA have got no hold over us' (interviewee C, May 2006). The aims and outlook of accredited clubs did not always match the overarching view of Chartered Standard, and the way in which such clubs were managed from administration to coaching had not measurably altered. It was common practice to align qualified coaches with teams within the club to satisfy the FDO in checking against Chartered Standard criteria. However, in practice, some coaches were not even attached to the club, or were coaching teams other than those listed against their name on the Chartered Standard application. Whilst similar practices exist in all club types on the continuum, the size and scale of these 'resistant' clubs increased the likelihood of such policy slippage occurring within them. Likewise, success on the field of play was the overarching ethos of the VSC and its voluntary members, at the expense, at times, of Chartered Standard guidelines.

> We do have instances where parents are quite difficult at times … this guy was swearing at opposition players and parents … but what do you do? Follow the guidelines and suspend him? The only people suffering then are his kid, and the club, as he is a fantastic player and we don't want to lose him as it would affect our competitiveness.
>
> (interviewee C, May 2006)

Although FDOs are tenuously aware of such practices, there is an appreciation that they are relatively powerless to stop them, as clubs, on paper, meet the required criteria. Given the pressures these sports development professionals are under in terms of meeting targets (Bloyce *et al.* 2008), there is also a temptation to disregard the fact that some clubs (particularly of this type) do not fully meet CS criteria. As such, there is 'a large degree of trust ... a leap of faith that they are doing what they have stated on the form' (FDO 3 interview, May 2006). Given the Chartered Standard is desired by such clubs as more of a status symbol primarily for the ambitions of the club to enhance its reputation and standing in the community, an FDO dealing with a club of this type noted that, rather than targeting them to achieve Chartered Standard, the FDO tended to 'wait for these bigger established clubs to come to us' (FDO 3 interview, May 2006). Given such clubs had longstanding traditions and an embedded ethos, 'they tend to be suspicious of anything we do so it is hard to work with them on any projects or programmes' (FDO 3 interview, May 2006).

Moreover, such clubs are in the minority in implementing the Chartered Standard, given the ethos and practicalities in terms of the size of the club.

> What trips a lot of these bigger and established clubs up is the coaching certificate ... you are looking at a massive volunteer workforce ... they tend not to succeed first time round in putting a CS application in ... and the cost implication puts them off too ... we generally don't hear back from a lot of these bigger clubs as they can't be bothered, it doesn't make a difference to them really ... it is the ones who really want funding that come back to you.
>
> (FDO 3 interview, May 2006)

VSCs and volunteers are 'becoming submerged or continued within the drive to establish the policy architecture around which VSC modernisation can be articulated' (Adams 2011a). Whilst they are engaging with this agenda, it does not necessarily mean the thrust of the organization has moved away from mutual aid or for the benefits of the club and its members at the expense of contributing to a wider political agenda. On the contrary, clubs in the sample across all types exhibited strong views that implementing the Charter Standard was for the benefit of the club in trying to access, amongst other things, NGB support and for a greater chance of being successful in bidding for funding.

SUMMARY

Programmes such as Clubmark are in and of themselves the institutionalization of modernization in sport (Adams 2011a: 32). It is evident that there seems to be some discrepancies between, on the one hand, the aims of policies and programmes such as Chartered Standard, and the actions of VSCs and their volunteers. Following Adams (2011a: 35), there is a tension between the mutual-aid principle of autonomy historically embedded in VSCs, in which members tend to comply with and act in accordance with the best interests of their club, which does not necessarily meet the aims and objectives that government seeks to gain through the implementation of policies and programmes. Moreover, VSCs and volunteers seem to comply with top-down imposed criteria in the Chartered Standard precisely in order to satisfy those desires for autonomy. That is, implementing the Chartered Standard is a means to an end for them, for example, in opening up funding streams.

Coalter (2007) has warned of the dangers that this policy agenda for sport may have on the voluntary sector, and noted that many within sport have expressed concerns regarding the implications of a more directive agenda for sports clubs (Coalter 2007: 551). Specifically, such modernized practices may undermine the nature and strengths of volunteers and VSCs, particularly their autonomy. This leads some authors to question the suitability of VSCs and sports volunteers as suitable conduits by which government can seek to achieve policy objectives (Garrett 2004; Nichols *et al.* 2005; Harris *et al.* 2009; Adams 2011a).

It may also be that the approach by government towards sport in this modernization agenda has assumed that sport as an institution is homogeneous. That is, given the appropriate structural conditions, such as programmes like Clubmark, VSCs will provide outputs commensurate with government policy aims and objectives. Evidence from the data presented here and other authors into VSCs and the modernization agenda, have intricately shown there to be a wide variety of VSCs and volunteers involved in sport, who interpret, implement and operationalize policies and programmes such as the Chartered Standard in a multifaceted and complex way.

Alternatively, others have pointed out the resilience of VSCs and volunteers in the face of relatively rapid change and intervention. Adams (2011a) argues that, despite concerns over the fragmentation, fractiousness and ineffectiveness of sports organizations (Houlihan and Green 2009: 678), and the concerns regarding the predominance of the small, single-team club type (particularly in football) (Collins 2010), VSCs have proven to be relatively durable in the face of rapid change, despite elements of their practice being altered. This could, as is highlighted above, be due to the club types and motivations of volunteers to engage with policies and programmes such as the Chartered Standard as part of the modernization agenda.

Indeed, Byers (2009) notes that research on voluntary sport organizations is a field of study which has a substantial, and expanding, literary base, but which requires greater synthesis and comparative research, as well as consideration of how work in this sector may contribute to knowledge of volunteering, volunteer management and organizations more widely, in order to advance the knowledge base and to increase further the quality of research outputs. This is more important in the UK given the political landscape for sport has recently changed again, with cuts in budgets for deliverers of sports services such as local authorities and NGBs through reduced Sport England funding, and the wider political aims of the coalition government in promoting the 'Big Society'. Likewise, the EU report (European Union 2010: 6) stated a desire to 'determine the scope of possible future policies and actions which could be more effectively implemented at the European level rather than at national or regional/local level'. It may be that VSCs and sports volunteers may be subjected to greater degrees of change and uncertainty given, on the one hand, an ever-increasing intervention in the future, from even greater layers of political administration, and on the other hand, a reduction in the resources and support mechanism available given a potential drawing back of the UK state. The impact of this on VSCs, volunteers and professional development officers remains to be seen, and is an area that warrants attention and investigation.

NOTE

1 Sport England and UK Sport have reviewed and curtailed the funding arrangements of some NGBs that have failed to meet targets for grassroots (participation, for instance) and elite sport (medals at international championships, for example) respectively, UK Athletics being a prime example (Grix 2009).

234

REVIEW QUESTIONS

1   Explain some of the ways in which volunteering, including sports volunteering, has become embedded within wider political and social agendas of serving governments.
2   Outline some of the primary ways in which a process of modernization has impacted upon volunteerism in sport.
3   Consider the future for sports volunteerism in your country – how might the management of volunteers have an important role to play for sport in the years ahead?

FURTHER READING

Adams, A. (2011). "Sports Development and Social Capital," in: Houlihan, B. and Green, M. (eds) *Handbook of Sports Development.* London: Routledge.
Bloyce, D. and Smith, A. (2010). *Sport Policy and Development: An introduction.* London: Routledge.
Hoye, R., Cuskelly, G., Taylor, T. and Darcy, S. (2008). "Volunteer Motives and Retention in Community Sport Organizations." *Australian Journal on Volunteering* 13(2): 40–48.

WEBSITES

Clubmark:
www.clubmark.org.uk/ has a database of all accredited clubs
Running Sports:
www.runningsports.org/ is designed to help sports clubs and sports volunteers run their clubs.
The FA Charter Standard:
www.thefa.com/charterstandard
Volunteering England:
hwww.volunteering.org.uk/resources/goodpracticebank/specialist+themes/ Sport+volunteering/ has some useful information and case studies on sports volunteering

REFERENCES

Adams, A. (2008). "Building Organisational/management Capacity for the Delivery of Sports Development," in: Girginov, V, (ed.) *Management of Sports Development.* Oxford: Butterworth-Heinemann.
Adams, A. (2011a). "Between Modernization and Mutual Aid: The Changing Perceptions of Voluntary Sports Clubs in England." *International Journal of Sport Policy and Politics* 3(1): 23–43.
Adams, A. (2011b). "Sports Development and Social Capital," in: Houlihan, B. and Green, M. (eds) *Handbook of Sports Development.* London: Routledge.

Adams, A. and Deane, J. (2009). "Exploring Formal and Informal Dimensions of Sports Volunteering in England." *European Sport Management Quarterly* 9(2): 119–140.

Allison, M. (2001). *Sports Clubs in Scotland Summary*. Research digest no. 59. Edinburgh: SportScotland.

Attwood, C., Singh, G., Prime, D., and Creasey, R. (2003). *2001 Home Office Citizenship Survey: People, families and communities*. Home Office Research Study 270. London: Home Office.

Bloyce, D. and Smith, A. (2010). *Sport Policy and Development: An introduction*. London: Routledge.

Bloyce, D., Smith, A., Mead, R. and Morris, J. (2008). "'Playing the Game (Plan)': A Figurational Analysis of Organizational Change in Sports Development in England." *European Sport Management Quarterly* 8(4): 359–378.

Brown, A., Crabbe, T., Mellor, G., Blackshaw, T. and Stone, C. (2006). *Football and its Communities: Final Report*. Manchester: Football Foundation.

Byers, T. (2009). "Research on Voluntary Sport Organisations: Established Themes and Emerging Opportunities." *International Journal of Sport Management and Marketing* 6(2): 215–228.

Chelladurai, P. (2006). *Human Resource Management in Sport and Recreation*. Champaign, IL: Human Kinetics.

Coalter, F. (2007). "Sports Clubs, Social Capital and Social Regeneration: Ill Defined Interventions with Hard to Follow Outcomes." *Sport in Society* 10(4): 537–559.

Collins, M. (2010). "From 'Sport for Good' to 'Sport for Sport's Sake' – Not a Good Move for Sports Development in England?" *International Journal of Sport Policy and Politics* 2(3): 367–379.

Conn, D. (1998). *The Football Business: Fair Game in the 90s*. London: Mainstream.

Cuskelly, G., Harrington, M. and Stebbins, R.A. (2003). "Changing Levels of Organizational Commitment Amongst Sport Volunteers: A Serious Leisure Approach." *Loisir/Leisure Special Issue: Volunteerism and Leisure* 27(3–4): 191–212.

Cuskelly, G., Hoye, R. and Auld, C. (2006). *Working with Volunteers in Sport: Theory and practice*. London: Routledge

Davis Smith, J., Ellis, A. and Howlett, S. (2002). *UK-Wide Evaluation of the Millennium Volunteers Programme*. DfES Research Report 357. London: DFE.

DCMS (2000). *A Sporting Future for All*. London: Department of Culture, Media and Sport.

DCMS (2002). *Game Plan: A strategy for delivering governments sport and physical activity objectives*. London: Department of Culture, Media and Sport.

DCMS (2008). *Playing to Win: A new era for sport*. London: DCMS.

Deloitte & Touche (2003). *Investing in Change? High level review of the modernization programmes for governing bodies of sport*. London: UK Sport.

Donnelly, P. and Harvey, J. (2011). "Volunteering and Sport," in: Houlihan, B. and Green, M. (eds) *Handbook of Sports Development*. London: Routledge.

Engelberg, T., Zakus, D. and Skinner, J. (2007). "Organisational Commitment: Implications for Voluntary Sport Organisations." *Australian Journal on Volunteering* 12(1): 24–36.

European Union. (2010). *Study on Volunteering in the European Union: Final Report*. Brussels: European Commission.

Football Taskforce. (1999). *Investing in the Community*. London: Football Taskforce.

Garrett, R. (2004). "The Response of Voluntary Sports Clubs to Sport England's Lottery Funding: Cases of Compliance, Change and Resistance." *Managing Leisure* 9: 13–29.

Green, C. (2009). *Every Boy's Dream: England's Football Future on the Line*. London: A&C Black.

Green, M. and Houlihan, B. (2006). "Governmentality, Modernization, and the 'Disciplining' of National Sporting Organizations: Athletics in Australia and the United Kingdom." *Sociology of Sport Journal* 23(1): 47–71.

Grix, J. (2009). "The Impact of UK Sport Policy on the Governance of Athletics." *International Journal of Sport Policy* 1(1): 31–49.

Groeneveld, M., Houlihan, B. and Ohel, F. (2010). *Social Capital and Sport Governance in Europe.* Oxford: Routledge.

Harris, S. and May, T. (2011). Growing sport through clubs: understanding and respecting the heterogeneity of club types. Presentation at PSA sport study group conference, University of Birmingham, 18 March, 2011. http://www.sportandrecreation.org.uk/sites/sportandrecreation.org.uk/files/web/documents/pdf/SVRN%202011%20Spencer%20Harris%20University%20of%20Hertfordshire.pdf (accessed 28 June 2012).

Harris, S., Mori, K. and Collins, M. (2009). "Great Expectations: Voluntary Sports Clubs and Their Role in Delivering National Policy for English Sport." *Voluntas* 20(4): 405–423.

Houlihan, B. and Green, M. (2009). "Modernization and Sport: The Reform of Sport England and UK Sport." *Public Administration* 87(3): 678–698.

Houlihan, B. and White, A. (2002). *The Politics of Sport Development: Development of sport or development through sport.* London: Routledge.

Howie, L. (2008). The FA Charter Standard Club Programme. http://www.thefa.com/GetIntoFootball/CharterStandard/Club/~/media/Files/PDF/Get%20into%20Football/Charter_Standard_2009/charter_standard_overview.ashx/charter_standard_overview.pdf (accessed 7 January 2011).

Hoye, R., Cuskelly, G., Taylor, T. and Darcy, S. (2008). "Volunteer Motives and Retention in Community Sport Organizations." *Australian Journal on Volunteering* 13(2): 40–48.

Independent Football Commission. (2004). *Report on Child Protection in Football.* Teesside: University of Teesside.

Kay, T. and Bradbury, S. (2009). "Youth Sport Volunteering: Developing Social Capital?" *Sport, Education and Society* 14(1): 121–140.

Kendall, J. (2000). "The Mainstreaming of the Third Sector into Public Policy in England in the Late 1990s: Whys and Wherefores." *Policy and Politics* 28(4): 541–546.

Low, N., Butt, S., Ellis Paine, A. and Davis Smith, J. (2007). *Helping Out: A national survey of volunteering and charitable giving.* London: Cabinet Office.

Lusted, J. and O'Gorman, J. (2010). "The Impact of New Labour's Modernisation Agenda on the English Grass-roots Football Workforce." *Managing Leisure* 15(1): 140-154

Newman, J. (2001). *Modern Governance: New Labour, policy and society.* London: Sage.

Nichols, G. (2004). "Pressures on Volunteers in the UK," In: Stebbins, R.A. and Graham, M. (eds) *Volunteering as Leisure/Leisure as Volunteering: An international assessment.* Wallingford, Oxford: CABI Publishing.

Nichols, G. and James, M. (2008). "One Size Does not Fit All: Implications of Sports Club Diversity for their Effectiveness as a Policy Tool and for Government Support." *Managing Leisure* 13(2): 104–114.

Nichols, G., Shibli, S. and Taylor, P. (1998). "Pressures that Contribute to a Change in the Nature of the Voluntary Sector in British Sport." *Vrijetijdstudies* 16(2): 34–46.

Nichols, G., Taylor, P., James, M., Garrett, R., Holmes, K., King, L., Gratton, C. and Kokolakakis, T. (2004). "Voluntary Activity in UK sport." *Voluntary Action* 6(2): 31–54.

Nichols, G., Taylor, P., James, M., Holmes, K., King, L. and Garrett, R. (2005). "Pressures on the UK Voluntary Sports Sector." *Voluntas* 16(1): 33–50.

O'Gorman, J. (2011). "Where is the Implementation in Sport Policy and Programme Analysis? The English Football Association's Charter Standard as an Illustration." *International Journal of Sport Policy and Politics* 3(1): 85–108.

Robinson, L. and Palmer, D. (2011). *Managing Voluntary Sports Organisations.* London: Routledge.

Rochester, C. (2001). "Regulation: The Impact on Local Voluntary Action," in: Harris, M. and Rochester, C. (eds) *Voluntary Organisations and Social Policy: Perspectives on change and choice.* Basingstoke: Palgrave.

Schulz, J. (2005). "Paid Staff in Voluntary Sporting Organisations: Do they Help or Hinder?" in: Nichols, G. and Collins, M. (eds) *Volunteers in Sports Clubs*. Eastbourne: Leisure Studies Association.

Schulz, J., Nichols, G. and Auld, C. (2011). "Issues in the Management of Voluntary Sports Organisations and Volunteers," in: Houlihan, B. and Green, M. (eds) *Handbook of Sports Development*. London: Routledge.

Sport England. (2004a). *The Framework for Sport in England. Making England an Active and Successful Sporting Nation: A vision for 2020*. London: Sport England.

Sport England. (2004b). *Driving up Participation: The challenge for sport*. London: Sport England.

Sport England. (2006). *Active People Survey Headline Results*. London: Sport England.

Sport England. (2007). *Sport England Policy Statement: The delivery system for sport in England*. London: Sport England.

Sport England. (2008). *Sport England Strategy 2008–2011*. London: Sport England.

SPARC. (2008). *Volunteers: The Heart of Sport – The Experiences and Motivations of Sports Volunteers*. Wellington: SPARC.

Taylor, B. and Garratt, D. (2010). "The Professionalisation of Sports Coaching: Relations of Power, Resistance and Compliance." *Sport, Education and Society* 15(1): 121–139

Taylor, P. (2004) "Driving Up Participation: Sport and Volunteering," in: *Sport England. Driving up participation: the challenge for sport*. London: Sport England.

Taylor, P., Nichols, G., Holmes, K., James, M., Gratton, C., Garret, R., Kokolakadikis, T., Mulder, C. and King, L. (2003). *Sports Volunteering in England 2002*. London: Sport England.

Taylor, P., James, M., Nichols, G., Holmes, K., King, L. and Garrett, R. (2007). "Facilitating Organisational Effectiveness Among Volunteers in Sport." *Voluntary Action* 8(3): 61–67.

Taylor, P., Barrett, D. and Nichols, G. (2010). Volunteers and Members in Sports Clubs. Voluntary Action Conference 1–2 March. http://www.ivr.org.uk/NR/rdonlyres/1AC56ED8-BFE9-4D86-8CA2-AD43899EB89F/0/GeoffNicholsVolunteersandmembersinsportsclubs.pdf (accessed 14 March 2011).

The Football Association. (1991). *Blueprint for the Future of Football*. London: The FA.

The Football Association. (1997). *Charter for Quality*. London, The FA.

The Football Association. (2001). *The Football Development Strategy 2001–2006*. London: The FA.

The FA. (2010). *FA Charter Standard Clubs: Annual health check guidance*. London: The FA.

Thibault, L., Slack, T. and Hinings, B. (1991). "Professionalism, Structures and Systems: The Impact of Professional Staff on Voluntary Sport Organizations." *International Review for the Sociology of Sport* 26(2): 83–98.

Chapter 14

Sporting preferences in the Arab world

Examining consumerism in the United Arab Emirates

Sean O'Connor and David Hassan

TOPICS

Sport in the Middle East • The preferences of consumers in the Middle East • Sport in the United Arab Emirates • Motorsport

---

OBJECTIVES

By the end of this chapter, you will be able to:

■ Detail the nuanced nature of Middle East identities;

■ Demonstrate a firm understanding concerning the use of sport in a range of Middle East countries;

■ Offer a particular knowledge of sport in the United Arab Emirates (UAE);

■ Retain a detailed appreciation of the demographic and socioeconomic profile of motorsport fans in the UAE.

KEY TERMS

Emerging market profiles – a term that recognizes that certain nation-states, in this case countries such as the UAE and Qatar, have begun to emerge on the international sporting landscape in a manner that would have been considered unlikely only a decade earlier.

Middle East sport – a term that refers to the sporting profile of consumers and the industry at large across the Middle East, a working definition of which typically includes certain, predominantly Muslim, countries in North Africa.

Motorsport – a term that refers to an array of motorized sporting disciplines, albeit often deemed coterminous with its leading disciplines, i.e. Formula One and the World Rally Championships.

Sport consumer demographics – the age, gender, geographic location and, occasionally, social class of consumers of sport, and sports entertainment in particular.

Sport in the UAE – Sporting participation and entertainment preferences demonstrated by residents, including the indigenous Emirati community, of the UAE.

OVERVIEW

Sport in the Middle East is an important vehicle for social, economic and political change. Indeed, by deploying certain modernization agendas and with personal and political support offered at the highest levels of government, increasingly it is used as an indicator of regime stability and prestige (Amara 2005). It is also relatively diverse in regard to what sports citizens choose to engage with, either as participants or spectators. Moreover, from the perspective of potential sponsors, the Middle East constitutes something of a 'green-field site', possessing unrivalled opportunities for expansion and growth. Later in this chapter, by drawing upon a critical use of marketing data collected by the research company TGI Arabia/PARC, some initial appreciation of the Middle East market in terms of consumer preference and demographic profiling will be offered. As relatively little is known about the region, its sporting preferences or even the strategic use of sport, an appropriate place to begin any comprehensive analysis of sport in Middle East is by identifying those pursuits that already command a level of popular support and, additionally, to examine areas of potential expansion in this regard. With this in mind, a particular focus is accorded to motorsport in the UAE. Through the success of the Formula One Etihad Airways Grand Prix, staged at the futuristic Yas Marina circuit, Abu Dhabi, the UAE has very quickly established its place amongst the pantheon of world motorsport. This development however increasingly needs to be a sustainable one and so a proper appreciation of the sport's current market demographics, and those who may potentially become part of these in the future, is central to its continued viability and growth. It is a important process for sports bodies to undertake, not least by those seeking to expand into emerging markets, and thereby not only define their arrival but to underpin this by remaining fully aware of their ongoing, latent market potential.

Indeed, from the aforementioned, extant data, it is possible to construct a particularly informative profile of motorsport consumers in the UAE and across the Gulf States. This reveals such enthusiasts as being largely young males, principally employed within the private sector, holding at least a first degree and having sizeable and available levels of disposable income. Such consumers are more likely than not to follow regional and international news and religious debates but are also very likely to be non-natives of the UAE and in fact typically emerge from outside the Middle East region altogether. Not-

240

withstanding this prominent, non-native involvement in motorsport, interestingly, UAE nationals are more likely than not to have attended a motorsport event in comparison to most other similarly sized events. This is because motorsport – primarily Formula One racing – is interpreted as a modern and evolving pastime, one that is in receipt of government support and sponsorship and thereby contributing towards national and regional pride.

CASE STUDY: QATAR BRINGS THE FIFA WORLD CUP TO THE MIDDLE EAST

On 2 December 2010 Qatar won the right to host the 2022 FIFA World Cup and in so doing became the first Middle East nation to be accorded this prestigious honour. Strategically it provides a raft of potentially new supporters, participants and consumers for the sport, a phenomenon that extends throughout the region as Qatar received backing from across the Arab world when tabling its successful bid. Moreover the Communications Director for the Qatari delegation, Nasser Al-Khater, described the effects of staging the 2022 tournament as going 'a long way in bridging cultural divides between East and West that are often inhabited by ignorance, suspicion, politics and war' (www.qatar2022bid.com).

The management consultancy firm Grant Thornton undertook research in 2010, commissioned by the Qatar 2022 bid team, which confirmed 'that football is the number one sport in the Middle East, that the region has massive untapped football development potential, and that Qatar will act as the catalyst to help drive the growth of football across the Middle East' (www.prnewswire.com). The Chairman of the Qatar bid, Sheikh Mohammed bin Hamad Al-Thani, argued persuasively that the 2022 World Cup would allow millions of new fans to participate in the sport; indeed, the Grant Thornton report estimated that awarding the tournament to Qatar 'would grow the value of football in the region by some $14 billion by 2022 [up 52 per cent on 2010 figures] and by a further $10 billion [46 per cent] by 2042; while increasing football match attendances across the region in 2022 by 13.4% – an additional 4.2 million spectators [this excludes World Cup attendances]' (www.prnewswire.com).

With regard to the potential impact of tourism following the Qatari World Cup, the 2010 hosts South Africa reported very promising figures following what was the first ever tournament staged on the continent of Africa. They suggested that there were '1,401,725 foreign tourist arrivals in June and July 2010; with 309,554 of the foreign tourists indicating that their primary purpose was to attend the 2010 FIFA World Cup' (www.southafricantourism.com). Qatar's 'proximity to European and Asian markets is likely to enhance the commercial value of hospitality rights compared to South Africa 2010' whilst, in addition, it should also 'help drive interest in football across an Indian population of over 1.1 billion' (www.prnewswire.com).

The television coverage of the 2010 FIFA World Cup in South Africa established a new viewing record for a sporting tournament 'with an unaudited total number of cumulative viewers close to 30 billion people ... whilst a television audience of 700 million people tuned in to watch the Netherlands vs. Spain World Cup Final match' (www.prnewswire.com). As '82% of the world's time zones will receive Qatar 2022 games "live" in prime time, with a potential match day peak audience of 3.2 billion viewers; this has the potential to create an enhanced rights value for FIFA' (www.prnewswire.com). Each match that takes place in the 2022 tournament will allow Qatar the opportunity to profile and promote its country, and indeed the Middle East as a whole, throughout the world and thereby intensify the long-term commercial benefits of hosting the event for its key stakeholders. In addition further advancements in social media may push the boundaries of interactive TV by generating additional discussions about the region through internet traffic. This in turn will grow the economic and commercial impact for the Middle East far beyond current, established profit margins whilst also presenting additional merchandising and sponsorship opportunities for FIFA, again within a relatively untapped marketplace, thereby fully globalizing the appeal of association football around the world.

MIDDLE EAST

Use of the term 'Middle East' embraces a diverse range of nation-states, each with its own distinct and unique histories (Goldschmidt and Davidson 2006). Interestingly, as a means of promoting a sense of regional identity, one particular sporting event, the Pan-Arab Games, has emerged as both a promotional tool and a barometer of international coherence for the region (Henry *et al.* 2003). Clearly sport has a very important role to play within a number of countries throughout the Middle East. In fact, locating international sporting events in that part of the world conveys prestige upon existing administrations and offers unparalleled regional and international marketing opportunities for many countries. This was particularly apparent in the case of the 2006 Qatar Asian Games (Amara 2005).

However, for the purposes of this chapter the use of the term 'Middle East' will be interpreted as comprising the UAE, Saudi Arabia (KSA), Kuwait, Lebanon, Egypt, Jordan, Syria, Qatar and Algeria. Together these countries constitute a diverse range of hereditary, autocratic and democratically elected governments alongside quasisecular and fundamentalist configurations of Islam. Some are geographically coherent, such as UAE, whilst other states, self-defining as being part of the Middle East (e.g. Algeria), are geographically more attenuated.

How can sport be marketed across such a diverse hinterland where, in addition to these intraregional differences, demographic factors and income levels predetermine the numbers of available participants and spectators? What is the relationship between traditional sporting activities and those which have been incorporated into the region through colonialism and, laterally, arising from ever-increasing and unregulated global flows (Jagdish 2004; Moore and Lewis 2009)? Finally, what impact, if any, might regional and global recessions have upon sport consumer incomes and the level of investment that stakeholders are willing to confer upon sport when considering the long-term viability of these same investments (Hosking and Robertson 2009; Pradhan 2009)? These are questions this chapter will consider and attempt to respond to, albeit in a limited way in some cases due to the absence of reliable supporting data, throughout the course of the ensuing discussion.

The demographic profile of almost all the countries of the Middle East may be considered youthful whilst also reflective of exponential growth in overall population size. In total some 50–65% of the region's resident population is under 24 years of age, supporting an often volatile sport consumer market (Fuller 2003). However, participation in the full gambit of sporting opportunities remains largely dependent upon one's gender and level of disposable income. Whilst participation and spectatorship of sport globally remain essentially, if by no means exclusively, the preserve of men (Messner 1994), in the Middle East (albeit differentially within societies in the region) women's involvement in sport either as participants or spectators remains significantly less than that of their male counterparts.

The disadvantage experienced by women is a factor of both Islamic teachings and the influence of patriarchy more broadly; within fundamentalist societies women may be proscribed from involvement in sport through received beliefs as to their moral and physiological frailty (Ahmed 1992) and in secularist Islamic states, such as Egypt, through the unwillingness of a sport patriarchy to permit gender-specific arenas in which Muslim women may compete (Walseth and Fasting 2003).

Whilst participation or spectatorship as generic activities is not necessarily income-dependent for some sports, this remains a major consideration. Whereas the oil-rich Gulf States, including KSA, enjoy a high per capita income level, this is not true across the entire region and in some cases spectatorship is contingent upon factors including distance from, and transport to, certain sporting events or, in terms of remote viewership, simply by having access to the requisite terrestrial and/or digital media to follow a preferred sport or league.

Sporting patronage is also dependent upon the presence of appropriate infrastructure, for example race tracks and football stadia, and again whether the consumer's preferred access is actual or virtual. Thus, understood in its entirety, sport has become an established marker of regime status, nation-state stability and prestige within the Middle East. It is not possible for the reader to overestimate the level of importance many state administrations now attach to sport, which it is believed conveys positive influences in both an expedient and highly desirable fashion. Particularly in the so-called 'oil states', sport has also become a means of promoting a mode of economic diversification, whilst foreign investments in sport franchises, including English Premier League clubs and throughout Europe, complete a symbiotic investment relationship that is somewhat atypical amid harsh economic times (Eason 2009).

TGI/PARC SURVEY DATA

Initial surveys concerning the sporting preferences of the people of the Middle East undertaken by TGI Arabia focused upon UAE, Kuwait, Lebanon and Egypt but have now extended to comprise the geographical and self-defining Middle East in its entirety. The purpose of TGI/PARC-initiated research lies in identifying consumer trends across a broad spectrum, which includes 16 product-marketing categories deploying indices that include media usage (including newspapers), terrestrial and digital media, product choice and brands, together with social attitudes and other reference points through the use of standardized demographic indices. Such indices include education, income and home ownership, all factors indicating levels of disposable income and which in turn allow the respondent to be classified, amongst other outcomes, as a sport consumer.

The data is derived from a quantitative and randomized survey using a structured questionnaire (Curwin and Slater 2004). It draws its findings from a sample of over 4,000 respondents within each nation-state, regardless of overall population size (Arber 2001). The survey is conducted with individuals rather than households and a points mechanism is used to achieve a potential score of 100, with education (university degree) and car and computer ownership accorded the single largest weightings (17, 17 and 10 respectively). Other points are awarded for ownership of a range of consumer goods, access to air travel and use of the internet. Although the data collection processes and indices are common across all research sites, socioeconomic stratification is applied internally within each nation-state rather than across the region.

In each research site (each country) the sample population is preselected into four socio-economic level (SEL) groups: group 1, at the apex, with 10 per cent; group 2 with 20 per cent; group 3 with 30 per cent; and finally group 4, with 40 per cent. Although the units of analysis used by TGI/PARC are only tangentially income-related, potential indicators of earnings, including education level and disposable income predictors (including the purchasing of consumer durables), are used.

The limitations of the TGI sampling technique from an academic perspective lie in its standardization, which is both its strength and a potential source of weakness given the variable population sizes of the nation-states surveyed. This is also a demographic profile that is informed solely by the financial nexus around income levels and lifestyle choice presumptions; its purpose is applied marketing research rather than pure academic research but nevertheless it makes an excellent source of data when applied to sport consumption and patronage. Thus the data critiqued latterly in this chapter is derived principally from the TGI/PARC Motorsports UAE 2009 survey whilst initially focusing upon results generated from a region-wide survey undertaken by the same research agency (TGI/PARC 2010). In both cases expressed permission to draw upon this data has been sought by the authors and granted by the rights' holder.

SPORT CONSUMPTION IN THE MIDDLE EAST

In its widest sense academic interest in the consumption of sport, especially in developing global markets, is an emerging field of enquiry, drawing upon (but by no means exclusively so) the disciplines of anthropology, sociology and political science and remaining dependent upon the peculiarities of the sporting event in question, the political environment in which it takes place and the economic vibrancy of its host country. Marketing to sport consumers is the business corollary of sport consumption but, as has been inferred, the drive to socialize individuals, members of social or ethnic groups, into sport may be informed by factors beyond those offered by the financial nexus.

Sport consumption in the Middle East perfectly exemplifies this phenomenon. Again across the region sport performs a role in promoting emergent nationalism, is regarded as a means of breaking down traditional antipathies (Sorek 2007; Younes 2010) – although this role is not peculiar to this region (Hassan and O'Connor 2007) – and is used as a means of defining and renegotiating often divergent and contested identities (Stevenson and Alaug 2010) whilst simultaneously offering an important platform for the further engagement of marginalized groupings, including, as has been noted, women, who may not participate in formalized sport for religious or social reasons (Walseth and Fasting 2003; Matuska 2010).

Interest in sport across the region is also quite diverse and somewhat unpredictable. Although association football (soccer) is the most popular sport within all nation-states, with the highest ratings in Egypt (56.53 per cent), Bahrain (52.37 per cent) and Kuwait (51.27 per cent), the second most popular sports are possibly as interesting to the outside observer. For example, in the UAE and Kuwait the sport of choice is cricket, reflective of the significant non-Arab, ex-pat population resident within these two countries. In Lebanon, Jordan, Bahrain and Syria the sport in question is, again somewhat surprisingly, basketball whilst in KSA aquatics, principally swimming, is one of the highest-ranking disciplines in terms of overall popularity. In Qatar athletics records the second highest popularity level, whilst boxing rates equally highly for sport consumers in Egypt. Local and national identities deliver certain, perhaps somewhat atypical, sports, including billiards, patronized by 11.13 per cent of respondents in Jordan and 18.92 per cent in KSA. The sport of volleyball is popular in Bahrain and Qatar, as is horse riding in Jordan and KSA, the latter a legacy of that country's national heritage, with table tennis considered to be comparatively popular in Qatar. Aerobics, jogging and keep fit are all cited as commanding relatively significant levels of interest across all of the countries in the region and can again be interpreted as an aspect of the gendered nature of sport consumption there (Walseth and Fasting 2003).

In all of the countries of the Middle East car racing is identified as a sport commanding considerable levels of interest. Some 19.28 per cent of those surveyed in the UAE had a strong interest in it, whilst 17.21 per cent (Lebanon), 23.24 per cent (KSA), 15.91 per cent (Jordan), 15.81 per cent (Syria), 23.55 per cent (Qatar), 6.55 per cent (Egypt), 26.40 per cent (Bahrain), 17.35 per cent (Algeria) and 26.22 per cent (Kuwait) confirm the pan-regional standing of the sport. The highest levels of interest in motorsport are across the Gulf States, which enjoy a comparatively higher per capita income, with Egypt located at the opposite end of this particular spectrum. Finally, whilst Algeria demonstrates, on the face of it, a high interest level in motorsport, this remains particularly noteworthy as such support is largely divorced from proportionate levels of car ownership.

Motorsport has become a high-profile spectator sport through the televized media and, increasingly in the region, through participation by residents as volunteers acting as marshals and stewards and in so doing broadening the level of participative engagement in what is otherwise a driver and team-only sport. An additional benefit for such volunteers is their association, as in the case of the Abu Dhabi Grand Prix, with a novel and highly prestigious event. The motives for volunteering are beyond the scope of this chapter but are nevertheless well documented (Caldwell and Andereck 1994; Farrell *et al.* 1998; Green and Chalip 1998; Strigas and Jackson 2003; Downward *et al.* 2005). However findings from the aforementioned Abu Dhabi Grand Prix (2009) indicate sports' consumers find volunteering to be a worthwhile use of their time (ATCUAE 2010). In addition to participation through this medium, consumers of motorsport are spectators through actual attendance at events as well, in some cases, virtually through television and the internet.

UAE results

The TGI/PARC UAE 2009 sample size was 4,956 out of an estimated population of 3,914,000 (TGI/PARC 2010). From this sample 54 per cent were males, 46 per cent females and this balance is a factor of both population and income/education demographics. The fluidity of the occupational and nation-state boundaries is reflected in the fact that only 22 per cent of

245

the surveyed sample were UAE citizens, with 30 per cent self-designating as Arab ex-pats but also as many as 46 per cent as non-Arab ex-pats, indicating the heavy dependence of the UAE economy upon national and regional 'outsiders'.

Of the overall sample, some 912 respondents (19–28 per cent) expressed an interest in motorsport on the basis of 'engaging or taking part regularly,' 'occasionally' or 'like to watch on TV,' 'read about it in the papers,' and, finally, 'paid to attend a sports event'. This indicates that motorsport has an already creditable constituency, based upon the chosen sample (almost one-fifth), and provides the basis for further expansion. That said, at present this figure remains substantially below the sport consumer level of association football (soccer), which stands at 45.20 per cent.

This can, in part, be attributed to the globalization of football but also reflects the legacy of coverage of the FIFA 2006 World Cup in Germany (Amara 2007). This is because 59 per cent of nationals and an even higher number of Arab ex-pats (64 per cent) cite football as a preferred sport, yet only 27 per cent of non-Arab ex-pats do so. There appears to be a 'temporary' and perhaps disproportionate interest amongst the former in football. However it is impossible to state with conviction whether this represents a sustained or in fact temporary engagement with the game. Cricket was cited by 35.23 per cent of respondents as their sport of choice and can be anticipated as reflecting the high non-Arab ex-pats composition of the SEL 1 sample, including respondents from the UK, Australia, India and Pakistan, because 57 per cent of non-Arab ex-pats cite cricket as their preferred sport, yet only 17 per cent and 3 per cent of Arab ex-pats and nationals, respectively, did so (TGI/PARC 2010).

In total some 912 respondents of the TGI SEL 1–4 respondents self-define on the basis of gender, nationality, age group and income. More men self-define as consumers of motorsport than women (64 per cent males, 36 per cent females) and this gender profile is consistent with findings for this and other sports elsewhere, including throughout the Middle East region. Because the UAE is a nationality-permeable nation-state, owing to its heavy dependence upon foreign labour, more respondents emerge as nationals of other states in the region than might be otherwise expected (133/912) and likewise amongst those from beyond the region (71/912). When combined, these two population categories outnumber UAE respondents (118/912), delivering in percentage terms Arab ex-pats 40 per cent, non-Arab ex-pats 34 per cent and UAE nationals 26 per cent. The fact that UAE natives constitute the lowest category of residents in the country is telling but also presents the nation-state as an interesting case study for students of sport management and marketing.

The age profile of respondents is similar to that found in other demographic research into spectator attendances at motorsport events (Hassan and O'Connor 2007);

Age (years)	%
15–24	27%
25–34	38%
35–44	25%
45–54	27%
55+	8%

However, when compared with association football, we find both an age-related inversion (52 per cent at 15–24 years) commensurate with active participation in the sport as well as a consistent plateau of interest above 40 per cent, which peaks at age 55+ at 49 per cent, this being only 3 percentile points below that in the youngest age group. Once again this may be a factor of national and pan-Arab identity (Amara 2007), but also indicates a contrasting feature of motorsport, where the peak of interest is in early middle age, declining to an almost negligible level upon retirement, or it may be simply a factor of the lower sample size.

The age factor as reinforcement does become valid when considered alongside income and social class (SEL), given there is normally a positive correlation between age and income or career status. Motorsport correlates positively with SELs 1 and 2 (145 and 125 respectively) but less so – 101 (SEL 3) and 73 (SEL 4) – amongst other demographic groups.

The inference drawn is that in the lowest income band, car ownership, which is taken as an important but not mandatory criterion for interest in motorsport, is limited. The largest section of car owners is in the lower- to middle-income categories, delivering a total of 46 per cent for both bands with the 7,001–10,000 Dhs per annum band (27 per cent) as the largest-income/interest grouping of all. This may correlate directly with age but no data is currently available for the age/income variable, which is regrettable as this may reasonably be assumed to be a dependent variable. One may deduce from the age and gender profiles offered that the premium audience is located amongst upwardly mobile young men progressing apace within their chosen careers (65 per cent below 35 years of age).

Of all respondents, more than half (51 per cent) are employed in the private sector with 32 per cent in government employment, whilst a further 11 per cent are self-employed. When social class and interest levels for sport are compared it is apparent that the higher the socioeconomic grouping, the higher the interest level for all sports, except cricket (21 per cent social class A; 33 per cent social class B) and yoga (14 per cent social class A; 19 per cent social class B), which may also be a factor of gender and class. Engagement in sport activities is largely a factor of leisure time, education and the use of exercise as a healthy lifestyle choice alongside the obvious ability to participate in the chosen activity.

There is no correlation in the data between mode of employment, income level and age but, in common with other public/private economies in the region, higher salaries are usually evident in the private sector. In 2007, before the onset of the worldwide economic downturn of September 2008 and beyond, salaries in the private sector throughout the UAE rose by 10.7 per cent per annum, only exceeded in the Gulf States by Oman, but this was largely a factor of high inflation rates in UAE and Qatar and consequently increased living costs. It does not in itself indicate a level of effective disposable income (Gulf Talent 2007). Motorsport from a consumer perspective does not necessarily demand large financial outlay in terms of associated products, in comparison with sports such as football, and the direct participation rate is lower, whilst spectatorship can be conducted through terrestrial and digital media except where sport consumers elect to attend regional events in person.

Motorsport events are amongst the most high-profile sports gatherings in UAE and indeed throughout the Middle East. In fact, the Fédération Internationale de l'Automobile (FIA)strategy document (2009) envisages a coalescence of interested parties, from government to the media, the automotive industry and sponsors, to continue to emerge within the region in the time

247

ahead. Moreover the report recommends a classic consumer focus to develop additional growth. Yet only 1 per cent of all respondents had made the financial commitment of paying to attend a motorsport event, albeit UAE nationals were twice as likely to have attended an event in person (2 per cent). This indicates not only geographic propinquity but also the value of national and regional events and competitors in galvanizing and sustaining interest (FIA 2009).

Regular active participation in motorsport is highest amongst non-Arab ex-pats but the disparity is not wide enough to be statistically significant, whereas UAE nationals are three times as likely to engage in occasional active participation compared to the total sample (3–1 per cent). All nationalities watch motorsport on television (14 per cent) but the most avid consumers are Arab ex-pats (17 per cent) and the least, non-Arab ex-pats (10 per cent). The use of newspapers to follow motorsport is also differentiated but the low rating by non-Arab ex-pats is assumed to be a factor of language access or preference for English-language international titles such as the *New York Herald Tribune*.

Further relevant demographic data from the TGI/PARC study relates to marital status and level of formal education amongst motorsport consumers. Marital status, especially if the respondent has children, might arguably indicate a less direct participative involvement in the sport, although it would have negligible impact upon television viewing habits or access to information and engagement through newspapers, for instance. Some 44 per cent of respondents were married with children, 12 per cent were married but had no children whilst 42 per cent were single; the remaining 2 per cent were divorced or widowed. There is no correlation in the data calibrating this to age or to nationality.

Formal education is seen as a factor in income generation and arguably is also an indicator in choice of leisure activities (Becker 1996). In the TGI/PARC UAE 2009 data, 34 per cent of the cohort possessed a university first or higher degree and 25 per cent a university diploma, whilst 30 per cent have completed secondary schooling. The data does not indicate the balance of formal education amongst the constituent national identities or age groups. The high percentage of formally educated and qualified respondents is a factor of social class and SEL (TGI/PARC 2010) but is also related to the ex-pat nature of the UAE working environment, where education and professional qualifications are related to employment.

The TGI/PARC UAE 2009 survey also provides data about lifestyle and product choices, including banking. Banks originating outside the UAE, such as HSBC, Citibank and Standard Chartered, are less regularly patronized than by the whole sample but overall 62 per cent of motorsport consumers hold accounts in banks, 53 per cent with a current account and 28 per cent a savings account. In terms of credit cards, 53 per cent hold a bank-based card whilst 45 per cent have a personal loan and indeed 44 per cent have taken out a bank loan to buy a car.

Motorsport consumers diverge from the total sample in their banking choices but three of the major banks in Dubai and Abu Dhabi predominate: Dubai Islamic Bank, Abu Dhabi Islamic Bank and the Abu Dhabi Commercial Bank and 42 per cent of respondents agreed that a bank's reputation was an important factor in deciding where to place one's money. Motorsport consumers were more likely to shop at non-UAE-owned department stores, such as Marks & Spencer (58 per cent; total sample 64 per cent), Paris Gallery (18 per cent; 27 per cent), Debenhams (27 per cent; 27 per cent) and BHS (14 per cent; 18 per cent). This finding is anticipated to be a factor in the strong non-Arab ex-pat profile of the total cohort.

Developing sport consumer profiles, as TGI/PARC has done, is essential in the ongoing marketing of motorsport (and indeed sport more generally); demographic and financial analysis is demanded by companies in their placement of products, whilst at the same time motorsport is becoming more consumer-oriented, according to the FIA (2009). The number of people who follow motorsport obviously far exceeds those who actually participate in it. The action of volunteering as a steward or marshal offers a range of benefits, whilst recent ATCUAE research (2010) highlights the transition within the sport in the Middle East from an elitist, professional perspective to one in which 'the ... volunteer should become the focus of the club's attention' (p. 14). From an overall perspective, including the long-term sustainability of the sport in the region, this development is to be encouraged and should be leveraged through sponsorship portfolios that celebrate the inclusivity of the sport rather than perpetuate its perceived elitism.

SUMMARY

The TGI/PARC data, covered extensively throughout the second half of this chapter, offers a starting point for further research into the field of sport consumerism across the Middle East. Motorsport in the UAE offers insight into this process whilst growing interest in the sport is fuelled by government backing and high-profile sponsorship. People who follow motorsport are arguably more internationally oriented and more reflective in their world view, listen to more international news (39 per cent; average for sample 35 per cent), Arab news (32 per cent; 29 per cent) and religious debates (42 per cent; 31 per cent) than others. They are aspiring to greater success, relative to their age group, for higher SEL membership and further education. As a consumer group well informed about cars, motorsport and the world they inhabit, motorsport consumers offer a rich marketing potential for a wide range of products.

However, the relationship must be reciprocal and there is growing evidence that the sport's ruling body, the FIA, is aware of this fact. At the pan-regional level the stress upon volunteering indicates that this is being seen as the way forward in aggregating consumer involvement and translating a latent interest into a passionate engagement with the sport. Thus motorsport is arguably becoming more conscious of its consumer base and research, such as that detailed here, is valuable in helping sponsors identify cohort parameters and characteristics but also in enabling them to become more receptive to the demands of consumers. There is opportunity for further detailed research into the marketing of sport and its diversity of patronage within the region and of motorsport in particular, as the TGI/PARC UAE 2009 survey confirms. In future years this is precisely the type of research that those who wish to leverage additional value from sport will require and draw upon and thus, for students of sport management and marketing, appreciating its value and employing appropriate methodologies in an atypical social and cultural setting to generate it is a must.

REVIEW QUESTIONS

■ Based on the evidence provided in this chapter, provide a broad overview of the sporting preferences, in terms of their consumption, throughout the Middle East region.

- What do some of the major sporting developments, primarily the awarding of the 2022 FIFA World Cup to Qatar, potentially mean for the region in terms of its future development?
- What are some of the particular sporting preferences for Emirati nationals living in the UAE?

FURTHER READING

Amara, M. and Theodoraki, E. (2010). "Transnational Network Formation Through Sports Related Regional Development Projects in the Arabian Peninsula." *International Journal of Sport Policy* 2(2): 135–158.

Hassan, D. and O'Connor, S. (2007). "The Socio-economic Impact of the FIA World Rally Championship 2007." *Sport in Society* 12(6): 709–724.

Strigas, A. and Jackson, N. (2003). "Motivating Volunteers to Serve and Succeed: Design and Results of a Pilot Study that Explores Demographics and Motivational Factors in Sport Volunteerism." *International Sports Journal* 7(1): 111–121.

WEBSITES

Abu Dhabi Touring Car Club of the United Arab Emirates (ATCUAE):
www.atcuae.ae
PR Newswire:
www.prnewswire.com
Qatar bid 2022:
www.whyQatar2022.com

REFERENCES

Ahmed, L. (1992). *Women and Sport in Islamic Society.* Alexandria, Egypt: Alexandria University.

Amara, M. (2005). "2006 Qatar Asian Games: A 'Modernization' Project from Above?" *Sport in Society* 8(3): 493–514.

Amara, M. (2007). "When the Arab World was Mobilised Around the FIFA 2006 World Cup." *Journal of North African Studies* 12(4): 417–438.

Arber, S. (2001). "Designing Samples," in: Gilbert, N. (ed.) *Researching Social Life,* 2nd edn. London: Sage.

ATCUAE. (2010). *Motorsport Volunteerism in the UAE: Research findings from 2009 Ethiad Airways Abu Dhabi Grand Prix.* Dubai, UAE: FIA/Indiana State University: Abu Dhabi Men's College.

Becker, G.S. (1996). *Accounting for Tastes: Part 1 Personal Capital, Part 2 Social Capital.* Cambridge, MA: Harvard University Press.

Caldwell, L.L. and Andereck, K.L. (1994). "Motives for Initiating and Continuing Membership in a Recreation-related Voluntary Association." *Leisure Studies* 16: 33–44.

250

Curwin, J. and Slater, R. (2004). *Quantitative Methods for Business Decisions,* 5th edn. London: Thomson Learning.

Downward, P., Lumsden, L. and Ralston, R. (2005). "Gender Differences in Sport Event Volunteering: Insights from Crew 2002 at the XVII Commonwealth Games." *Managing Leisure* 10: 219–236.

Eason, K. (2009). Show me the money: Gulf states secure place on world stage. *The Times.* http://www.timesonline.co.uk/tol/sport/more_sport/article6917970.ece (accessed 7 November 2010).

Farrell, J.M., Johnston, M.E. and Twynam, D.G. (1998). "Volunteer Motivation, Satisfaction and Management at an Elite Sporting Competition." *Journal of Sport Management* 12: 288–300.

FIA. (2009). *Driving Motorsport Together: FIA Middle East Strategy 2010–2014.* Dubai: FIA.

Fuller, G.E. (2003). The youth factor: the new demographics of the Middle East and the implications for US policy. *Brookings.* http://www.brookings.ed/papers/2003/06middleeast_fuller.aspx (accessed 6 November 2010).

Goldschmidt, A. Jr. and Davidson, L. (2006). *A Concise History of the Middle East,* 8th edn. Boulder, CO: Westview.

Green, B.C. and Chalip, L. (1998). "Sport Volunteers: Research Agenda and Application." *Sport Marketing Quarterly* 7(2): 14–23.

Gulf Talent. (2007). Gulf salaries rise by 9.0%. *Gulf Talent.* http://www.gulftalent.com/home/Gulf-salaries-rise-by-90-Article-25,html (accessed November 2010).

Hassan, D. and O'Connor, S. (2007). "The Socio-economic Impact of the FIA World Rally Championship 2007." *Sport in Society* 12(6): 709–724.

Henry, I.P., Amara, M. and Al-Tauqi, M. (2003). "Sport, Arab Nationalism and the Pan-Arab Games." *International Review for the Sociology of Sport* 38: 295–310.

Hosking, P. and Robertson, D. (2009). Dubai in deep water as ripples from debt crisis spread *The Times.* http://business.timesonline.co.uk/tol/business/markets/the_gulf/article6934261.ecce?pri (accessed 6 November 2010).

Jagdish, B. (2004). *In Defence of Globalization.* New York: Oxford University Press.

Matuska, N. (2010). "The Development of Women's Football in Morocco." *Middle East Viewpoints: Sports and the Middle East*: 25–37.

Messner, M.A. (1994). "Sport and Male Domination: The Female Athlete as Contested Ideological Terrain," in Birell, S. and Cole, C.L. (eds) *Women, Sport and Culture.* Champaign, ILL: Human Kinetics.

Moore, K. and Lewis, D. (2009). *Origins of Globalization.* New York: Routledge.

Pradhan, S. (2009). *Economic Recession and the Middle East's World Trade: Recent policy trends and implications.* Dubai: Dubai Gulf Research Centre.

Sorek, T. (2007). *Arab Soccer in a Jewish State: The integrative enclave.* Cambridge, UK: Cambridge University Press.

Stevenson, T.B. and Alaug, A.K. (2010). "Yemeni Football and Identity Politics." *Middle East Viewpoints: Sports and the Middle East* 16–19.

Strigas, A. and Jackson, N. (2003). "Motivating Volunteers to Serve and Succeed: Design and Results of a Pilot Study that Explores Demographics and Motivational Factors in Sport Volunteerism." *International Sports Journal* 7(1): 111–121.

TGI/PARC. (2010). *Motorsports TGI UAE 09.* Dubai: PARC.

Walseth, K. and Fasting, K. (2003). "Islam's View on Physical Activity and Sport: Egyptian Women Interpreting Islam." *International Review for the Sociology of Sport* 38(1): 45–60.

Younes, J. (2010). "A Step on the Path to Peace: How Basketball is United Arab and Jewish Youth in Jerusalem." *Middle East Viewpoints: Sports and the Middle East* 38–41.

Chapter 15

The methodology of mega-events

The culture of vanity and measuring real benefit

Kamilla Swart and Urmilla Bob

TOPICS

Mega-events, overestimations and a fixation on the positives • Current approaches to mega-event research • Future mega-event research challenges

---

OBJECTIVES

By the end of this chapter, you will be able to:

- Describe the types of sport mega-events research that are most common and understand why such research is undertaken;
- Identify the methodological approaches typically adopted for mega-event research and articulate the main limitations associated with these current approaches;
- Articulate the main areas of mega-event research that are often neglected and understand the implications of these omissions when assessing mega-event impacts and inform future planning efforts;
- Demonstrate an understanding of the challenges and constraints experienced in relation to mega-event research through relevant case study analyses.

KEY TERMS

Economic impact – the 'net change in a host economy directly attributed to a sporting event or operation' (Turco *et al.* 2002: 53).

Environmental impact assessment – 'a process to predict the environmental effects of a proposed project throughout its lifecycle and to recommend ways to eliminate, minimize or mitigate those impacts' (Vancouver 2010 and International Academy of Sport Science and Technology (AISTS)2009: 9).

Legacy – all the intended and unintended, positive and negative, tangible and intangible structures or societal relations that develop in the context of an event and that continue for a significant period of time after the event has ended (Preuss 2007).

Mega-events – large-scale cultural (including commercial and sporting) events possessing dramatic character, mass popular appeal and international significance (Roche 2000), such as the Olympic Games, FIFA World Cup, Commonwealth Games and International Rugby Board Rugby and International Cricket Council Cricket World Cups.

Stakeholder – a person or organization that has a legitimate interest in a project or entity and could be affected by an organization's economic, social and environmental performance (Vancouver 2010 and AISTS 2009).

OVERVIEW

Developed and developing countries are increasingly bidding to host mega-events such as the Olympics Games and the FIFA World Cup. Mega-events are viewed as key drivers to enable and promote a range of developmental agendas, especially in relation to economic and social benefits, and longer-term legacies. However, the benefits often championed by governments to justify significant expenditure required by these mega-events are generally understood to be overestimated and, in keeping with this, long-term legacies are rarely achieved or sustained.

Consequently, there is significant debate about what the impacts of mega-events are and how best to conduct research to ascertain impacts and their implications. This chapter critically examines current research in relation to mega-events and benefits, focusing mainly on the fixation with positive outcomes that tend to ignore negative impacts and long-term legacy assessments. The next section provides an overview of current approaches to mega-event research. This is followed by an examination of mega-event research challenges and finally, concluding remarks are made in order to bring the chapter to a close.

CASE STUDY: OLYMPIC GAMES IMPACT STUDY

The subject of sustainable development has increasingly centred on identifying appropriate and effective tools and specific indicators to monitor impacts and assist in centralizing sustainability considerations in mega-event planning and design.

The International Olympic Committee (IOC) has centralized the importance of sustainable development and social responsibility in the bidding and hosting of the Olympic and Paralympic Games. It developed the Olympic Games Impact (OGI) programme in 2003, which measures the long-term impact of the Games through a consistent and comparable reporting system across all future Games. The OGI programme includes 126 indicators that measure the status of a range of environmental, sociocultural and economic dimensions of the host city, region and nation. The findings are presented in a series of four reports across a period of 12 years. The first report provides the baseline against which indicator data in future reports will be compared and analysed (prepared 3 years prior to the Games). This baseline report is followed by a pre-games report, which analyses updated contextual data. The games-time report is produced next to examine Olympic-event data. Finally, a post-games report concludes the OGI study. It includes updated data and summaries of previous reports and presents the conclusions regarding the actual impacts of the Games.

The purposes of OGI are to enhance the sustainability of the Games, to promote positive Games' legacies, and to create a knowledge base for future hosts. The Vancouver 2010 OGI study, conducted by the University of British Columbia (UBC) is the first full OGI study ever to be attempted in accordance with the IOC requirements and is intended to present trends over a 12-year period, including legacy-type impacts that may occur after the Games (VANOC 2007; Bob 2010; OGI-UBC 2010).

INTRODUCTION

Mega-events are increasingly viewed as catalysts to drive and advance an array of developmental agendas, especially with respect to economic and social benefits. This is particularly noticeable in developing contexts or emerging markets where the opportunity to host a mega-event is deemed to promote economic opportunity, destination profiling, social benefits and sporting legacies. Additionally, there is a focus on environmental issues and links to broader global aspects, such as promoting diversity and understanding. There is a significant body of literature that has examined the negative and positive impacts of hosting mega-events, with many cautioning that the costs often outweigh the benefits and that long-term legacies are rarely attained or sustained (Crompton 1995; Baade and Matheson 2002, 2004; Bohlmann and van Heerden 2005; Cashman 2006; Preuss 2007; Allmers and Maennig 2008; Matheson 2008; Higham and Hinch 2009). Furthermore, the bidding for and hosting of mega-events are associated with massive investments, often from publicly funded bodies. Thus, there is also the aspect of public accountability to be considered in this regard.

There is significant debate about what the impacts of mega-events (both positive and negative) are and how best to conduct research to ascertain impacts and their implications. The magnitude of the event, together with the inherent complexity of hosting the world's largest spectacle, raises several issues in relation to undertaking research in a consistent manner and deciding on appropriate methodological approaches. As described in the following section, much of the research tends to be dominated by the economic impact, albeit that there is a growing body of knowledge concerning a broader range of impacts. Moreover, the research tends to fixate on the positive impacts of hosting events, as elaborated upon over the course of the next section.

MEGA-EVENTS AND FIXATING ON THE POSITIVES

Cornelissen *et al.* (2011) assert that, thus far, much of the research on sport mega-event legacies has been very selective in its focus, centring on events' economic and infrastructural impacts while their social, political and environmental legacies have generally been neglected. However, they do indicate that, increasingly a broad spectrum of impacts that traverse a wide range of markers (such as social, economic, environmental and political) are being integrated into assessing events. Furthermore, they assert that there are intended and unintended consequences of hosting mega-events. Research tends to focus on the intended consequences or direct impacts that are easier to identify and assess. As such, mega-events research tends to prioritize the measurement of economic, infrastructural and social impacts, as discussed next.

Economic impacts, which are the key justification for hosting mega-events, are associated with problematic projects, especially in *ex ante* (pre-event) studies that tend to overinflate economic benefits and underestimate economic costs. For example, Table 15.1 illustrates two forecast studies that were conducted by Grant Thornton in relation to the World Cup. While increases are noted for contribution to gross domestic product (GDP), it is underscored that this was mainly related to significant increases in government expenditure on stadia and infrastructure. Moreover, while the tourist projections increased, a study by South African Tourism (2010) reported the number of foreign arrivals (including tourists from the rest of Africa) to be much lower than forecasted – 309,554 foreign arrivals as a result of the World Cup. Consequently, tourism receipts were also less; South African Tourism notes a figure of R3.64 billion, in comparison to the Grant Thornton (2008) forecast of R8.9bn. It is further evident that massive cost escalations are often associated with the hosting of mega-events. As underscored by Tolsi (2010), the 2010 bid book was not in the public domain until recently and 'is a curious mélange of hyperbole and underestimation' and argues that the

Table 15.1. *Economic impact projections of the 2010 FIFA World Cup (2003 and 2008)*

	Grant Thornton 2003	Grant Thornton 2008
Direct expenditure	R12.7 billion	R14.75 billion
Contribution to gross domestic product	R21.3 billion	R66.75 billion
Generate annual job equivalents	159,000	415,000
Additional government taxes generated	R7.2 billion	R19 billion
Upgrade of stadia and infrastructure	R2.3 billion	R33 billion
Foreign tourist projections	235,000	480,000
African tourists	45,300	150,000

Source: Grant Thornton (2003, 2008).

figures represent gross miscalculations of taxpayers' money on infrastructure such as stadia. It should also be acknowledged that the early indicators of the World Cup's economic impacts are mixed; however long-term impacts have yet to be determined.

In certain cases, as Cornelissen *et al.* (2011) indicate, events may leave hosts with escalating public debt, which was the case for the city of Montreal, host to the 1976 Summer Olympics. It took the city three decades to pay off the debt generated by the Games. Additionally, the researchers assert that there is scant evidence for the popular claim that events can lead to immediate tourism and investment gains for hosts, arguing that, typically, there is a time lag of several years before a host's tourism sector may display growth. Furthermore, it is possible that the host's tourism market may actually contract during the year of the event, as was the case during South Korea's co-hosting of the 2002 FIFA World Cup (Lee and Taylor 2005).

Job creation and reduction in unemployment rates also emerge as an important economic benefit associated with mega-events. However, jobs associated with mega-events are either parttime or contract-bound and there is little evidence that permanent jobs are created over the long term. There is a significant body of literature that critically examines the widely held assumption among mega-event hopefuls that positive economic benefits are associated with mega-events (Crompton 1995; Baade and Matheson 2002, 2004; Cashman 2006; Preuss 2007; Allmers and Maennig 2008; Matheson 2008; Higham and Hinch 2009; Tingli and Chengqing 2010). These studies indicate that there are several negative economic impacts, including debt burdens, profiling the destination as a high-cost tourist attraction (prices increase significantly during the hosting of a mega-event), increase in corruption and remaining infrastructure that are not used or cannot be sustained. It is important to underscore that these negative impacts are rarely mentioned during the bidding process, again reinforcing the assertion that mega-event bidders tend to focus on positive economic impacts and ignore negative impacts that can have long-term consequences for the hosts.

Infrastructural benefits are deemed to be critically important, especially in developing contexts where often infrastructure is inadequate but seen as a key driver for improved economic growth. There are two main types of infrastructural investment: transport and communication systems and sporting facilities. Chappelet and Junod (2006) assert that sporting legacy refers to sporting facilities newly built or renovated for an event and which will serve some purpose after the event has concluded. They further indicate that these sporting infrastructures often become 'emblematic symbols' for the host city and depict its link with sports. But, as indicated earlier, the viability and sustainability of this infrastructure remain areas of concern, with many mega-event infrastructural projects becoming 'white elephants' following the event.

Transport and communication systems, according to Chappelet and Junod (2006), refer to the different types of networks, ranging from transport to telecommunications, which are renovated or developed for a mega-event and maintained after the event is complete. This includes new access routes by air, water, road or rail. Chappelet and Junod (2006) also argue that an event can provide the trigger for promoting modernization of basic services, such as water, electricity and waste treatment. In terms of South Africa's hosting of the 2010 FIFA World Cup, infrastructural development emerged as a key component, with government asserting that the event triggered the development of infrastructure that was already earmarked as part of broader development efforts.

256

Very few studies on mega-events examine local business perceptions, despite the almost exclusive spotlight on economic impacts. However, one such study was McKenna and Bob's (2010) examination of the local business perceptions of the 2010 FIFA World Cup in Durban, one of the tournament's host cities. The main focus was on whether local businesses benefited from the event, especially in relation to the massive infrastructural investments that occurred. The focus on local business perceptions provided insights into the concerns and attitudes of a key, yet neglected, stakeholder. The study revealed that, although there were local businesses that supported the hosting of the event, they experienced significant constraints that prevented them from leveraging direct financial benefits from the tournament, which included FIFA regulations and restrictions, limited participation in event planning and an inability to market products directly to visitors.

The social impacts often relate to the intangible, subjective experiences associated with the event, the 'collective memory' (Chappelet and Junod 2006: 85). These experiences are viewed as benefiting both locals and visitors. The studies often focus on visitor surveys and resident perception studies. Poynter (2006) also suggests that mega-events effects could include intangible aspects such as enhanced city/host country images, more efficient local governance practices or improved communal wellbeing. Cornelissen and Maennig (2010) illustrate that there is a growing body of research that shows that the 'feel-good' factors linked to a once-in-a-lifetime experience and nation building are the key benefits associated with hosting mega-events. Cornelissen and Maennig (2010) in particular focus on this intangible/immeasurable aspect of hosting the FIFA World Cups in Germany 2006 and South Africa 2010. By drawing on the two experiences of the FIFA World Cups, they examine this sense of communal wellbeing and reveal how mega-events induce the 'feel-good factor'. They also examine how political and sociocultural processes influence a sense of national pride and promote nation building. They illustrate that, while the main research and media focus was on economic and related tourism impacts, the feel-good effect appeared to be the largest and most obvious consequence of the World Cups. They also examine the impacts of these feel-good effects on the longer-term political implications for host locations. Social impacts also include the skills and development opportunities to which locals are exposed through voluntarism and other projects associated with the mega-event.

Bob and Swart's (2009), Bassa and Jaggernath's (2010) and Chain and Swart's (2010) studies of resident perceptions in Cape Town and Durban of the 2010 FIFA World Cup in South Africa illustrate that residents in both locations supported South Africa and their respective cities hosting the event. Additionally, most residents had high expectations regarding the social and economic impacts of the tournament, especially in terms of local economic development and job creation. The focus on economic impacts reinforces the discussion outlined earlier that mega-events are mostly associated with economic benefits, although often not realized to the extent anticipated. It is important to note that, although residents supported the event and associated it with economic benefits, most realized that these benefits would be unevenly distributed and that most South Africans were unlikely to benefit directly economically from South Africa hosting the event. Residents in these studies also felt that the mega-event would develop national pride and nation building. This supports Cornelissen and Maennig's (2010) assertion that the social experience related to the 'feel-good effect' is likely to be the most widespread benefit among locals.

257

Research also shows that mega-events can have negative social impacts. Resident studies, such as those by Bassa and Jaggernath (2010) and Chain and Swart (2010), show that the main negative social impacts relate to disruptions experienced by locals, concerns related to crime, increase in the cost of living, and increases in rates and taxes after the event to pay off debts that have been incurred. Other aspects include social exclusion as a result of limited participation in event planning and activities as well as restricted access to services and facilities, such as stadia and public transport infrastructure. In terms of the latter, a key issue is the cost of accessing these services and facilities, which are often out of reach for ordinary citizens. This is of particular concern in developing countries where the gap between the rich and the poor is significant. The Centre on Housing Rights and Evictions (COHRE 2007) also shows that in some instances the hosting of mega-events results in the forced removal of residents, especially more vulnerable and poor households. They show that often the benefits of mega-events are not reaped by all and the negative impacts experienced by many people are in direct violation of human rights laws. Specifically, COHRE (2007: 29) illustrates that FIFA's attempts to embrace socially responsible ideals and its commitment 'to protecting and promoting human, social and economic development' is often not realized since these events have had a significant negative impact upon housing rights. 'Clean-up' programmes in particular associated with World Cup events have led to the displacement of homeless people, especially near stadium venues.

Increasingly, there is a body of literature that examines the environmental impacts associated with hosting mega and large-scale sport events (Gossling 2002; Wood 2005; Schmied *et al.* 2007; Ahmed and Pretorius 2010; Bob 2010). These studies reveal the importance of increased awareness on sustainability imperatives in relation specifically to minimizing and mitigating against negative environmental impacts associated with hosting mega-events. Furthermore, they indicate that, although a global activity of this scale can be assumed to have a substantial negative impact on the environment, its consequences have seldom been reviewed, evaluated or quantified. The 'greening of events' and promoting carbon neutral events are gaining in prominence and are becoming key components of assessing whether mega-events can be considered viable and/or sustainable. The sport events industry and related activities often attract significant numbers of people (the bigger the event, the larger the impact) and interact with the natural resource base and the environment generally in numerous ways. However, in the past environmental concerns have been largely ignored in relation to event planning and design as well as impact studies. Davenport and Davenport (2006) show that that the greatest ecological threats that any form of mass tourism creates, such as mega sport events, indisputably lie in the infrastructure and transport arrangements required to support it (such as the physical development of resorts, consumption of fuel by buildings, aircraft, trains, buses, taxis and cars, overuse of water resources, pollution by vehicle emissions, sewage and litter), which accrue into substantial, often irreversible, environmental degradation as well as social consequences. The 2010 FIFA World Cup's Green Goal programme is used by Ahmed and Pretorius (2010) as an illustrative example to examine environmental issues pertaining to the hosting of mega-events. Additionally, strategies and approaches to integrate environmental considerations in the planning and design of events are considered. While these studies examine the magnitude of environmental impacts given the size of the event,

258

most of these studies highlight that mega-events provide an ideal opportunity for environmental education.

Mega-events are deemed to have different impacts in developing and developed contexts. Since developed countries tend to have established and state-of-the art infrastructure, the hosting of mega-events is often seen as prestigious and key to promoting a destination. Additionally, countries (such as Germany's hosting of the 2006 FIFA World Cup) use the event to change the image of the host and promote national pride and nation building. In developing countries the agenda is significantly more developmental. Cornelissen (2010) illustrates that developing nations such as China, South Africa and Brazil have become significant players in the sport mega-event industry, through, respectively, China's hosting of the 2008 Beijing Summer Olympic Games, South Africa's hosting of the 2010 FIFA World Cup and Brazil's upcoming hosting of the 2014 football finals and the 2016 Olympic Games. These countries hope that the hosting of the event will promote long-term legacies in relation to economic and social benefits. Pre-event consultancy research tends to focus on the positive benefits in developing countries, especially in relation to economic, infrastructural and investment impacts. However, a significant body of academic research, cited earlier, cautions about whether benefits will be accrued, who is most likely to benefit and what will be the likely long-term burdens on the country. In terms of this last factor, this is a particular concern given that many host cities and countries are still paying off debts incurred as a result of hosting a mega-event.

CURRENT APPROACHES TO MEGA-EVENT RESEARCH

As per the OGI case study above, there is a move towards triple-bottom-line (economic, social and environmental) event research in addition to media impact assessments, albeit that the economic impacts still dominate. Economic impact measurement is a powerful tool to demonstrate the financial benefits that can result from hosting a mega-event (www.eventimpacts. com). Visitor spend is the biggest factor in generating economic impacts. There are generally two approaches to economic impact assessments: top-down and bottom-up approaches. The top-down approach uses national economic data and is thus likely to be less costly. In addition, it uses aggregated data and only identifies additional visitor nights, which are statistically counted (Preuss and Kursheidt 2009). The bottom-up approach is used to address this limitation and includes the administration of questionnaire surveys to spectators during the event. Preuss (2005) argues that the consumption patterns of these tourists are not often precisely evaluated and concludes that the accurate determination of money streams from event-affected persons is the basis for reliable assessments of economic impacts of events. Challenges associated with mega-event research are discussed further in the next section.

Social impacts generally refer to the effect that the event has on people's lives. It is therefore necessary to understand how the event impacts on the perceptions and behaviour of people, directly or indirectly (www.eventimpacts.com). Most social impact research focuses on visitors' and residents' perceptions of the event. Satisfaction with respect to various aspects of the event and the broader destination are generally included in event attendee surveys. This can be targeted at both residents and visitors. Enhancing destination image and/

or changing perceptions of destination image, as in the case of the 2010 FIFA World Cup in South Africa, fall within the ambit of social impact research. Similarly, nation building and social cohesion are two other social factors that can be considered in relation to a mega-event. Depending on the objectives of a mega-event, participation in the sport, i.e. creating more awareness of the sport, increasing interest in the sport and/or increasing recreational and competitive participation in the sport, can also be considered. Mega-events generally require a huge volunteer force and can thus be important settings for training opportunities and skills development. Volunteer surveys are implemented to understand the quality of the volunteer experience that can assist in the operational planning for future events. Social impact research also includes targeting specific groups such as women and youth in order to understand their experiences and participation levels.

Several approaches can be used to examine the environmental impacts of mega-events. These include environmental impact assessments (EIAs), carbon footprint analysis, ecological modelling and 'green' surveys to examine perceptions of residents, visitors and other stakeholders. Collins *et al.* (2009) specifically illustrate how ecological footprint analysis and environmental input–output modelling can be used to assess the environmental impacts of mega sporting events.

It is important to note that environmental impacts are complex. As Bob (2010) indicates, event environmental impacts may be direct or indirect, immediate or cumulative, short-term or long-term, and while some impacts may only impact the vicinity in which the event is held, others could have impacts on entire ecosystems. Particular concerns relate to land degradation associated with infrastructural development, waste generation and energy use. These aspects require assessment prior to the hosting of the event (preferably during the bidding stage) and therefore necessitate that mega-events should undergo EIAs. Bob (2010) further states that EIAs are generally undertaken to modify and improve the design of an event, ensure efficient resource use, enhance social aspects (often social impact assessments are part of EIAs), identify measures for monitoring and managing impacts and informing decision-making processes. Additionally, EIAs should include research aimed at measuring direct impacts on the natural environment as well as pollution and carbon emissions attributed to the event. Care should be taken to establish the carrying capacity, which Mathieson and Wall (1982, cited in *Garrigos et al.* 2004: 277) define as 'the maximum number of people who can use a place without an unacceptable alteration in the physical environment and an unacceptable decline in the quality of the recreational experience'. Research should be undertaken to establish the carrying capacity of an individual event and examine whether this is exceeded.

In addition to triple-bottom-line impact assessments, assessing media impacts of a mega-event is critically important given the role that a mega-event can play in profiling a destination. Basic media impact assessments include evaluating the fit between the messages and the mega-event objectives to be achieved, the type of coverage, the reach in terms of target markets and the tone and themes of the coverage. Media impact assessments can range from pre-, during and post-event coverage to track any changes or shifts in the kind of coverage received. It is also important to understand what matters and, more significantly, what may be missing from the coverage the destination had or is receiving in relation to hosting the mega-event.

Some of the challenges experienced when conducting mega-event research are addressed in the following section.

ADDRESSING MEGA-EVENT RESEARCH CHALLENGES

It appears as if countries catch the mega-event 'bug', as there is a fixation around hosting more large-scale and mega-events once one has been successfully hosted.

A key issue in the literature that impacts on mega-event research is the clarification of key terms and concepts. For example, Cornelissen *et al.* (2011) assert that it is striking that, despite the focus of several studies on the legacy impacts of sport mega-events, there is little consensus within the research community about what the term 'legacy' entails in relation to mega-events or how it should be defined. Furthermore, large-scale, hallmark, major and mega-events are often used interchangeably, although they refer to significantly different types of events. Another key concept that is debated pertains to differentiating between direct and indirect benefits.

Preuss (2011) contends that a more refined measurement model is required to assess economic impacts based on tourism. He adds that different studies found varying economic effects on South Africa's GDP as a result of the World Cup, thus creating an uncertainty of the potential positive legacy of the 2010 World Cup. Factors contributing to these differential effects include the use of different frameworks, many challenges and complexities associated with assessing the economic impacts of mega-event research (Preuss 2011). The case of the 2010 FIFA World is provided to illustrate this point.

Preuss (2011) reports that one of the many challenges in assessing the economic impact of the World Cup is a lack of knowledge of consumption patterns by visitors and the number of people visiting (and not visiting) South Africa. In addition, the quality and accessibility of South African data are important to consider. Spronk and Fourie (2010) note that there is lack of consistency in the data collected for expenditure by tourists. A key concept to be considered in economic impact studies is crowding out – the reduction in private consumption as a result of increased demand; however these studies are often criticized when crowding out is not considered (Matheson 2008; Barclay 2009; Preuss 2011). The differential impacts on the World Cup mentioned previously all employed top-down approaches and hence Preuss' contention that a bottom-up approach would allow for more precise measurement of the primary tourism impact, with the addition that reliable official statistics can assist in evaluating crowding out. However, the cost and complexity of the empirical research required need to be borne in mind.

Given that the impacts of mega-events are wide-ranging, more recent impact research has tended to undertake a more integrative approach incorporating all components (tangible and intangible aspects) of events in appraisals of their impacts, as well as including different sets of stakeholders, i.e. the visitors, residents, local business and sport organizations. For example, for the UEFA Euro 2008 Championship finals, a team of researchers focused on identifying the most important short-term and long-term effects on the economy, society and the environment, in addition to media and infrastructure impacts (Moesch and Muller 2008). Attempts have also been made to use a single tool to implement a more holistic evaluation as well as to compare impacts across a range of events. For example, the City of Cape Town used the Sport Event Impact Model (SEIM), developed by the national department of sport, Sport and Recreation South Africa (SRSA), to assess the impacts of the FIFA 2010 World Cup. SEIM was developed with the primary aim of providing a standard model for measuring and determining the social, economic and sport-related impacts of sport events (Urban-Econ and SRSA 2010).

Attempts have also been made to use the same methodology across several editions of the mega-event. For example, a group of South African researchers has been working with international researchers to assess the economic impacts of the 2010 World Cup using the same methodology used for the 2006 World Cup. It is anticipated that the study will be continued to assess the economic impacts of the 2014 edition in Brazil.

The planning of mega-event research is often not integrated into the overall planning of the event and is generally planned as an add-on, thus limiting the value, and can also be hampered by time constraints. In addition, given that many of the impact studies consider only the short-term impacts, there is a need for more longitudinal research. However, a key concern is the limited resources (especially financial) that are made available for mega-event impact research, despite the huge public investments used to fund these events. Thus, longitudinal research is hardly ever considered and therefore it remains unclear whether long-lasting legacies can be associated with sport mega-events.

CASE STUDY: 2010 FIFA WORLD CUP SOUTH AFRICA RESEARCH AGENDA

The 2010 research framework was developed in consultation with several academics and stakeholders during two workshops focused around maximizing benefits to key stakeholders in terms of World Cup legacies. In both workshops attendees reinforced the importance of systematically undertaking research in relation to the 2010 FIFA World Cup. This was recognized as being especially important given the unique opportunities and challenges faced in relation to Africa hosting its first mega-event. The 2010 FIFA World Cup provided an opportunity to unpack whether trends and patterns emerging from research on previous mega-events (specifically the FIFA World Cup) would be discernible in 2010 and how these related to development efforts in South Africa particularly and Africa more generally. However, given the timeframes and the lack of political will to allocate the resources necessary to implement a coordinated research agenda that emanated from the first workshop, the participants at the subsequent workshop focused on highlighting key research priority areas for 2010.

The two main research thrusts related to the economic and social/political impacts. The workshops underscored the relevance of the research agenda in order to maximize limited resources and engender collaboration. Lessons from the 2010 FIFA World Cup research agenda illustrate that the research required for mega-events of this nature research necessitates partnerships and interdisciplinary capacity from a range of stakeholders. Furthermore, the mobilization of the necessary resources to undertake the research required and attempts to leverage buy-in at a national level and among host cities to ensure consistency in the research approaches and data collected are necessary (Swart and Bob 2010).

SUMMARY

This chapter clearly shows that mega-event research remains largely fixated on economic aspects, more recently embedded in the broader ambit of developmental impacts. While social development is a part of developmental agendas, research tends to focus on direct economic impacts in relation to return on investments. This is often also mainly associated with tourism benefits, including destination profiling and marketing in terms of media coverage. Indirect economic impacts relate mainly to infrastructural investments.

This chapter also reveals that very often these impacts are overestimated and rely on *ex ante* (pre-event) projections emanating from commissioned research undertaken by consultancy companies on behalf of the host destination. *Ex post* (post-event) research is often undertaken by academics and a more critical stance is adopted. It is unsurprising that *ex post* studies have more realistic economic impact figures and are almost always lower than *ex ante* studies. Additionally, bottom-up and top-down economic impact assessments have significantly different results. This suggests that, in terms of economic assessments, there needs to be a critical examination of current methodological approaches.

Social mega-event research is also increasing, particularly resident perception surveys. The main issues emerging in relation to this research are a focus on experiences during the event, challenges experienced and expectations in relation to hosting a mega-event, as well as 'feel-good' aspects linked to nation building and national pride. The aspects under investigation should be expanded to include impacts on sport development and the promotion of healthier lifestyles (or are mega-events encouraging a more sedentary, spectatorship lifestyle?), media assessments and analysis, given the importance of the media in profiling the destination and the event, impacts on disadvantaged groups such as women and the poor (the focus on women is important given that mega-sport events are male-oriented), infrastructural assessments and environmental considerations.

In terms of specific methods, it will be useful for generic survey instruments to be developed that can be adapted to specific geographic contexts and types of mega-events. The commonality in terms of key aspects will permit comparative analyses that so far have been limited due to methodological differences and inconsistencies. Furthermore, a stakeholder perspective should be adopted and therefore assessments should include an examination of the experiences and perceptions of a range of groups rather than focusing largely on visitors and residents. Key stakeholders who should be considered include local businesses, sponsors, event organizers, government agencies and non-governmental organizations/civic organizations. Additionally, a holistic evaluation of mega-event impacts should be considered as well as longitudinal research.

The chapter highlights that there are considerable debates about the range of impacts to be considered and prioritized, how they interrelate with each other and the methodological approaches to be adopted to monitor and assess mega-event impacts. The significance of undertaking event impact research is underscored. It is also highlighted that the issues are complex and it is not always possible to discern impacts directly attributable to the mega-event. Moreover, as the size of the mega-event increases, so do the impacts and the challenges associated with assessing the intended and unintended consequences.

REVIEW QUESTIONS

1 You have been appointed as a consultant to evaluate the impacts of the 2014 FIFA World Cup. Identify which methodological approaches you will adopt and the challenges that may need to be mitigated given that the event spans several host cities.
2 Review the current OGI studies and advise how they can be adopted to assess the impacts of the FIFA World Cup given that there is no such requirement for the World Cup.
3. Develop a research plan for evaluating the impacts of the 2014 Commonwealth Games. Identify the research partners and the resources required to implement a coordinated mega-event research plan.

FURTHER READING

Cornelissen, S., Swart, K. and Bob, U. (2011). "Towards Redefining the Concept of Legacy in Relation to Sport Mega-events: Insight from the 2010 FIFA World Cup." *Development Southern Africa*, 28(3): 307–318.

Maennig, W. and Zimbalist, A. (eds). (2012). *Economics of Mega-sporting Events*. Cheltenham: Edward Elgar.

Pillay, U., Tomlinson, R. and Bass, O. (eds) (2009). *Development and Dreams: The urban legacy of the 2010 FIFA World Cup*. Pretoria: HSRC.

WEBSITES

FIFA:
www.fifa.com
International Olympic Committee:
www.olympic.org
OGI-UBC Olympic Games Impact Study:
www.ogi-ubc.ca/home.asp
Sheffield Hallam University Sport Industry Research Centre Major Events:
www.shu.ac.uk/research/sirc/rc_majorevents.html
Sustainable Sport and Event Toolkit:
www.sset-platform.org

REFERENCES

Ahmed, F. and Pretorius, L. (2010). "Mega-events and Environmental Impacts: The 2010 FIFA World Cup in South Africa." *Alternation* 17(2): 274–296.

Allmers, S. and Maennig, W. (2008). "South Africa 2010: Economic Scope and Limits." *Hamburg Contemporary Economic Discussions* 21: 1–33.

Baade, R. and Matheson, V.A. (2002). "Bidding for the Olympics: Fool's gold?" in: Barros, C.,

Ibrahimo, M. and Szymanski, S. (eds). *Transatlantic Sport: The comparative economics of North American and European sports.* Cheltenham: Edward Elgar.

Baade, R. and Matheson, V.A. (2004). "The Quest for the Cup: Assessing the Economic Impact of the World Cup." *Regional Studies* 38(4): 343–354.

Barclay, J. (2009). "Predicting the Costs and Benefits of Mega-sporting Events: Misjudgement of Olympic Proportions?" *Institute of Economic Affairs* 29(2): 62–66.

Bassa, Z. and Jaggernath, J. (2010). "Living Close to 2010 Stadiums: Residents' Perceptions of the 2010 FIFA World Cup and Stadium Development in Durban, South Africa." *Alternation* 17(2): 121–145.

Bob, U. (2010). "Sustainability and Events Design," in: Tassiopoulos, D. (ed.) *Events Management: A development and managerial approach.* Cape Town: Juta.

Bob, U. and Swart, K. (2009). "Residents' Perceptions of the FIFA 2010 FIFA Soccer World Cup Stadia Development in Cape Town." *Urban Forum* 20: 47–59.

Bohlmann, H.R. and van Heerden, J.H. (2005). *The Impact of Hosting a Major Sport Event on the South African Economy. University of Pretoria, Department of Economics Working Paper Series.* Paper number 2005–09. Pretoria: University of Pretoria.

Cashman, R. (2006). *The Bitter-sweet Awakening: The legacy of the Sydney 2000 Olympic Games.* Petersham: Walla Walla Press.

Centre on Housing Rights and Evictions (COHRE). (2007). *Fair Play for Housing Rights: mega-events, Olympic Games and housing rights – opportunities for the Olympic movement and others.* Geneva: COHRE.

Chain, D. and Swart, K. (2010). "Residents' Perceptions of the 2010 FIFA World Cup: A Case Study of a Suburb in Cape Town, South Africa." *Alternation* 17(2): 146–172.

Chappelet, J. and Junod, T. (2006). "A Tale of 3 Olympic Cities: What can Turin Learn from the Olympic legacy of other Alpine Cities?" in: Torres, D. (ed.) *Major Sport Events as Opportunity for Development,* 14–16 June, Valencia, Spain.

Collins, A., Jones, C. and Munday, M. (2009). "Assessing the Environmental Impacts of Mega Sporting Events: Two Options?" *Tourism Management* 30: 828–837.

Cornelissen, S. (2010). "The Geopolitics of Global Aspiration: Sport Mega-events and Emerging Powers." *International Journal of the History of Sport* 27(16–17): 1–18.

Cornelissen, S. and Maennig, W. (2010). "On the Political Economy of 'Feel-good' Effects at Sport Mega-events: Experiences from FIFA Germany 3006 and Prospects for South Africa 2010." *Alternation* 17(2): 96–120.

Cornelissen, S., Swart, K. and Bob, U. (2011). "Towards Redefining the Concept of Legacy in Relation to Sport Mega-events: Insight from the 2010 FIFA World Cup." *Development Southern Africa,* 28(3): 307–318.

Crompton, J. (1995). "Economic Impact Analysis of Sports Facilities and Events: Eleven Sources of Misapplication." *Journal of Sport Management* 9: 14–35.

Davenport, J. and Davenport, J.L. (2006). "The Impact of Tourism and Personal Leisure Transport on Coastal Environments: A Review." *Estuaries Coastal and Shelf Science* 67: 280–292.

Garrigos, S.F.J., Narangajavanab, Y. and Marques, D.P. (2004). "Carrying Capacity in the Tourism Industry: A Case Study of Hengistbury Head." *Tourism Management* 25(2): 275–283.

Gossling, S.G. (2002). "Global Environmental Consequences of Tourism." *Global Environmental Change* 12: 283–302.

Grant Thornton. (2003). South Africa 2010 Soccer World Cup Bid Executive Summary. http://wiredspace.wits.ac.za/bitstream/handle/10539/5950/Appendix.pdf?sequence=2 (accessed 15 June 2011).

Grant Thornton. (2008). 2010 World Cup set to contribute R55bn to SA's GDP. *Africa the Good News.* http://www.africagoodnews.com/brand-africa/2010-fifa-world-cup/231-2010-world-cup-set-to-contribute-r55bn-to-sas-gdp-.html (accessed 15 June 2011).

Higham, J. and Hinch, T. (2009). *Sport and Tourism: Globalization, mobility and identity.* Oxford: Butterworth Heinemann.

Lee, C. and Taylor, T. (2005). "Critical Reflections on the Economic Impact Assessment of a Mega-event: The Case of the 2002 FIFA World Cup." *Tourism Management* 26(4): 595–603.

Matheson, V.A. (2006). *Mega-events: The effect of the world's biggest sporting events on local, regional and national economies. Research Series* No. 06–10, College of the Holy Cross. Worcester, MA: Department of Economics, College of the Holy Cross.

Matheson, V. (2008). "Mega-events: The Effect of the World's Biggest Sporting Events on Local, Regional and National Economies," In Howard, D. and Humphreys, B. (eds). *The Business of Sports.* Westport, CT: Praeger.

McKenna, F. and Bob, U. (2010). "Business Perceptions of the 2010 FIFA World Cup and Related Infrastructural Development: A Case Study of the Moses Mabhida Stadium and the Durban Beachfront Developments." *Alternation* 17(2): 200–224.

Moesch, C. and Muller, H. (2008). "UEFA Euro 2008 Evaluation and Impacts on Sustainable Development," in: *Challenges Facing Football in the 21st Century*, 15–17 May. University of Berne, Switzerland.

OGI-UBC. (2010). Olympic Games Impact Study – A Backgrounder. http://www.ogi-ubc.ca/about. asp (accessed 15 June 2011).

Poynter, G. (2006). *From Beijing to Bow Creek: Measuring the Olympics effect.* East Research Institute Working Papers in Urban Studies. London: University of East London.

Preuss, H. (2005). "The Economic Impact of Visitors at Major Multi-sport Events." *European Sport Management Quarterly* 5(3): 281–301.

Preuss, H. (2007). "The Conceptualisation and Measurements of Mega Sport Event Legacies." *Journal of Sport and Tourism* 12(3–4): 207–227.

Preuss, H. (2011). "Crowding-out Impact Calculation for Mega-events: The 2010 FIFA World Cup Case." *Development Southern Africa*, (in press).

Preuss, H. and Kursheidt, M. (2009). "How Crowding-out Affects Tourism Legacy," in: *Sport Mega-events and Their Legacies Conference*, 2–4 December 2009, Stellenbosch: South Africa.

Roche, M. (2000). *Mega-events and Modernity: Olympics and Expos in the growth of global culture.* London: Routledge.

Schmied, M., Hochfeld, C., Stahl, H., Roth, R., Armbruster, F., Türk, S. and Friedl, C. (2007). *Green Champions in Sport and Environment: Guide to environmentally-sound large sporting events.* Frankfurt: Federal Ministry for the Environment, Nature Conservation and Nuclear Safety (BMU), Berlin and German Olympic Sports Confederation (DOSB), Division Development of Sports.

South African Tourism. (2010). *Impact of the 2010 FIFA World Cup.* Johannesburg: SA Tourism.

Spronk, K. and Fourie, J. (2010). South African mega-events and their impact on tourism. *Stellenbosch Economic Working Papers*: 03/10. http://ideas.repec.org/p/sza/wpaper/wpapers102. html (accessed 25 March 2011).

Swart, K. and Bob, U. (2010). Assessing the economic impact of the 2010 FIFA World Cup – lessons for developing countries. http://www.icsspe.org/bulletin/drucken.php?No=60 (accessed 20 February 2011).

Tingli, L. and Chengqing, W. (2010). *Empirical Research on Economic Impact of Mega-event: Based on the case of the 2008 Olympic Games.* Paper funded by the China Postdoctoral Science Foundation. 4th International Conference on Management and Service Science, 24–26 August 2010. Wuhan, China. http://www.massconf.org/2011/Proceeding2010.aspx (accessed 2 July 2012).

Tolsi, N. (2010). The World Cup bid book fiasco. *Mail & Guardian Online.* http://www.mg.co.za/article/2010-06-13-the-completely-miscalculated-world-cup-bid-book-that-cost-us-a-bundle (accessed 25 June 2010).

Turco, D.M., Riley, R. and Swart, K. (2002). *Sport Tourism.* Morgantown, WV: Fitness Information Technologies.

Urban-Econ and SRSA. (2010). *Sport Event Impact Model Research Report.* Pretoria: Sport and Recreation South Africa.

VANOC. (2007). Vancouver 2010 Olympic Games impact program baseline report. http://www.vancouver2010.com/dl/00/35/13/-/35136/prop=data/tzomid/35136.pdf (accessed 20 May 2009).

Vancouver 2010 and International Academy of Sport Science and Technology. (2009). Sustainable sport event toolkit. http://sustainable-sport.org/files/SSET_v1.4%20A4_LowRes_ENGLISH.pdf (accessed 15 June 2011).

Wood, E.H. (2005). "Measuring the Economic and Social Impacts of Local Authority Events." *International Journal of Public Sector Management* 18(1): 37–53.

Chapter 16

Corporate social responsibility in the sports industry

Michelle Brassell

TOPICS

Corporate social responsibility (CSR) in sport • Effective strategies for promoting CSR within sporting organizations • Reporting/marketing of CSR activities and their impact • Future developments in the field of CSR

OBJECTIVES

By the end of this chapter, you will be able to:

■ Provide a background to CSR and its application within the sports sector;
■ Offer an understanding of how clubs and other sporting bodies engage with CSR;
■ Highlight the challenges faced by the sports industry in this area;
■ Define the characteristics of best practice within CSR management;
■ Detail the future trends and innovations in CSR in the sports sector.

KEY TERMS

Cause-related marketing – a marketing partnership between a for-profit and not-for-profit organization for mutual gain.

Community investment – how businesses support communities and manage their positive impact for corporate and social benefits.

Gifts-in-kind – the resources that businesses donate to community initiatives or charities free of charge. In the sports sector this typically refers to shirts, footballs and other sports equipment, office space or the use of sports facilities.

Living roof – a roof that is partially or fully covered in vegetation. Also known as a green roof, it provides insulation and a habitat for wildlife and helps to reduce negative environmental impacts.

Philanthropic – the act of altruistic giving.

OVERVIEW

Corporate social responsibility (CSR) is an increasingly common term in the sports sector in the UK and elsewhere and typically relates to the community engagement activities in which clubs and sports organizations are involved. As with other businesses, clubs across the UK and Europe are at various stages of their CSR journeys. Recruiting a talented and diverse workforce, the impact of their product or service on vulnerable groups or the impact of their company on the environment are typical CSR considerations. There is a high level of scrutiny in this field and companies are expected to communicate their CSR activities in the public domain. Companies publicly report on their CSR activities through a number of reporting tools, such as the Global Responsibility Index or the Corporate Responsibility Index in the UK and will produce CSR reports that set out their strategy, targets, impact and progress against established goals, as well as future plans across all of the identified social and environmental issues that are central to their business. This helps to drive transparency and the continuous development towards achieving 'responsible businesses'. The question remains: How far along the CSR journey are sports clubs? This chapter will seek to establish what sports clubs and other bodies are doing with respect to CSR, the motivations for CSR in sports and how this area is expected to develop in the time ahead.

AN INTRODUCTION TO CORPORATE SOCIAL RESPONSIBILITY

CSR is one of the commonest terms used to describe how a business manages its social and environmental impacts, with the objective of maximizing its positive impact and minimizing its negative effect on its identified stakeholders. Stakeholders typically include employees, customers, suppliers, shareholders, communities and the environment. It is a voluntary practice that encourages businesses to go beyond regulation and legislation. Other terms used to describe this concept include corporate responsibility, corporate citizenship, sustainability, ethical business or responsible business practice.

CSR is a dynamic and often debated concept that became widely used in the 1970s, having become nomenclature in the 1950s with Bowen's classic book, *Social Responsibilities of the Businessman* (1953). In 1979 Carroll introduced a four-part framework which recognized a company's responsibilities as being ethical, discretionary (philanthropic), economic and legal. Over the years, CSR has evolved from a philanthropic model which typifies the practice of businesses simply donating money to charitable causes to a focus on a strategic approach that is embedded into core business operations and provides corporate benefits, as well as those to wider society (Holme and Watts 2000; Porter and Kramer 2006). This 'win–win' approach to CSR is promoted by one of the largest and oldest business-led coalitions working in this field in the UK, Business in the Community (BITC). Established by business leaders in 1982 against a backdrop

269

of high unemployment and social unrest, these business leaders recognized that it made good business sense for businesses to play a role in addressing the social challenges faced by society at that time (Grayson 2007: 16). Today, BITC boasts a membership of over 800 businesses ranging from FTSE 100 companies to small and medium enterprises, including some sports organizations. It aims to 'mobilize business for good' across four areas of impact – community, environment, marketplace and workplace (Figure 16.1 and Box 16.1). BITC, along with scores of other CSR practitioners and agencies, advocates that embedding CSR policy and principles into core operations can have a positive impact on a company's brand and reputation, ability to attract and retain talented employees, ability to innovate and its bottom line.

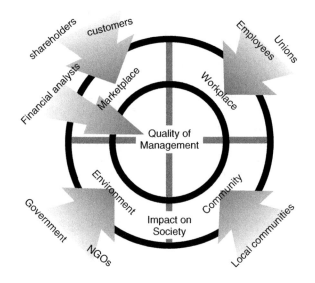

Figure 16.1 *A model for corporate social responsibility. NGOs, non-governmental organizations.*

Box 16.1: A framework for corporate social responsibility
BITC sets out responsible business as

- Having clear leadership, governance and values
- Helping to develop employees and the future workforce
- Influencing behaviour through products and services
- Managing social, environmental and economic impacts in supply chains
- Investing in the communities in which businesses operate and those communities in greatest need
- Taking action to reduce climate change and prepare for a low-carbon economy
- Working with others to promote action and greater change

Source: Adapted from www.bitc.org.uk/issues/
what_is_responsible_business (accessed 13 November 2010).
BITC, Business in the Community.

SPORT AND CSR

Smith and Westerbeek (2007) suggest that 'nothing distinguishes sports organisations from corporations when it comes to CSR' (p. 6). It follows that professional sports clubs are businesses in their own right and therefore are expected to apply CSR to their business operations in the same way as other companies. The rationale for the development of BITC's Clubs that Count initiative was also based on this principle and the desire of the clubs and sports organizations involved in the development of the programme to be judged alongside businesses from other sectors.

In 2005, BITC worked with clubs and sports organizations that were considered to be leaders in the field of CSR in the sports industry (including Charlton Athletic FC, Everton FC, Burnley FC, Leyton Orient FC and the FA Premier League) to develop the Clubs that Count programme, which aimed to support professional sports clubs to apply and develop CSR policy and practice. It identifies the following benefits for the sports sector to engage with the CSR agenda (2008a: 5), which will be discussed in more detail later:

- Attract and retain sponsors.
- Secure investment and planning for developing stadia.
- Grow fan bases.
- Build local partnerships, reputation and brand awareness.

The programme provided a framework for clubs' CSR activity, supporting them to communicate this activity both within the club as well as externally, and to develop it. Clubs were invited to take part in the Clubs that Count Tracker on an annual basis: this was an online confidential benchmarking tool that asked clubs questions about their management and practice of CSR. (Box 16.2 outlines some examples of the material issues in sport.) From 2005 to 2008, BITC worked with over 60 professional sports clubs and organizations

Box 16.2: A key to corporate social responsibility issues in sport

Community	Marketplace
Understanding community needs (local; national; international)	Local, national and international considerations
Dialogue and engagement with fans and local-community stakeholders	Supply chain
Social issues (e.g. education, employability, homelessness, health)	Responsible sponsorship and cause-related sponsorship/marketing
Support for charities	Vulnerable or underrepresented groups
	Fan safety

Environment	Workplace
Stadium waste management	Health and safety
Transport and travel	Equality and diversity
Heating and lighting	Players and non-playing staff
Water use	

271

from the UK and Europe on their CSR activities. These represented a wide range of sports, including football, rugby, cricket and horse racing, demonstrating the growing interest in CSR in sport.

PERCEPTIONS OF CSR

It is important to note that CSR definitions and practices often vary, as perceptions of CSR differ from one country to another and from one business to another. Research conducted by the World Business Council for Sustainable Development across seven countries (2000) to test its definition of CSR demonstrates the different perceptions of CSR from societies across the globe (Holme and Watts 2000: 6). Companies will also face different societal challenges depending upon where they operate. HIV and AIDS will be a serious issue for those operating in parts of Africa, for example, as their employees and their employees' families will often be affected by the epidemic. For companies operating in the UK, education and employability are important issues, whilst poverty and workers' rights will be key considerations for those operating in India, for example. It is therefore not a 'one-size-fits-all' model and when setting out on its CSR journey a business should prioritize the issues that are most relevant to its core products and services. When comparing CSR activity across different sports leagues and in different countries, it will be important to take these points into account.

The reality of course is that businesses of all sizes and types are at different stages in their knowledge of, and approach to, CSR. Whilst larger multinational companies will more often than not have CSR departments dedicated to CSR policy, practice and reporting, smaller and medium-sized businesses may argue they are too focused on surviving to think about CSR or will focus on a particular area of CSR such as community investment. This is also often the case with sports clubs.

Globalization, firing increased expectations and scrutiny of businesses from employees, customers, government and non-governmental organizations (NGOs), has driven interest in CSR (Grayson 2007). In turn, this has created significant and increasing interest in CSR activity in the sports sector. It has long been argued that sport is uniquely placed to tackle social challenges. Nelson Mandela famously said:

> Sport has the power to change the world. It has the power to unite in a way that little else does. It speaks to youth in a language they understand. Sport can create hope where once there was only despair. It is more powerful than governments in breaking down racial barriers. It laughs in the face of all types of discrimination.

Some argue that, due to the unique characteristics of sport, CSR in the sports industry can have a greater impact than in other sectors (Smith and Westerbeek 2007; Sheth and Babiak 2009). The fact that clubs are often already interwoven into communities, coupled with the mass appeal and global reach of sport, alongside its inherent positive health benefits, gives the sports sector an advantage in having a positive impact on society, over other industries such as tobacco, oil and gas or finance.

A FOCUS ON COMMUNITY

In the UK, a significant number of professional football and rugby clubs are located within deprived neighbourhoods. They are part of the social fabric and history of the local community and are often the largest brand within them. They therefore have a major role to play in addressing inequalities. UK sports clubs are addressing some of society's most pressing issues through a wide range of community and charity programmes and have been for many years. In football, the roots of many clubs' community programmes can be traced back to Football in the Community schemes established in the 1980s to help clubs develop links with their communities and, in turn, to develop a new generation of fans.

A number of Football in the Community schemes have evolved over the years, from the traditional youth football coaching model towards more complex community and education programmes that address a wide range of issues. It is common for clubs to set up a separate charitable trust or foundation to enable them to deliver a broader range of programmes. This enables them to develop partnerships, attract further funding and ring-fence finance for charitable or community engagement activities. Increasingly clubs are working internationally, representing their wider marketplace and overseas support.

Charlton Athletic FC set up the Charlton Athletic Community Trust (CACT) in 2004. It built on the work of its Football in the Community programme, which was instigated in 1992 when the club moved back to its home stadium, 'the Valley', in south-east London, following a period sharing stadia with firstly Crystal Palace and then West Ham United football clubs. One of the main objectives of setting up the trust was to bring all of the club's community outreach work under one umbrella and provide a framework for increased activity. The club's community outreach work helped the club integrate itself back into its home ground, grow its fan base and attract and retain sponsors, who saw the benefits of being involved in their community outreach work. Axis Europe, a small and medium enterprise, has been a long-standing sponsor of Charlton's community work. Their partnership supports CACT's social inclusion work that works with young people excluded from education and provides estates leagues, helping to reduce crime and antisocial behaviour within local communities.

Charlton Athletic FC was in the Premier League from 2000 to 2007. The club is now in League two of the English Championship, which has significantly reduced the club's income. As Steve Sutherland, CACT's Women's and Girl's Football Committee member and former Commercial Director at the club states, 'having a separate trust has enabled CACT's extensive community activities to continue to grow despite the club's misfortunes on the pitch'. Sutherland believes that cutbacks in club-funded CSR activities (e.g. charitable donations, gifts-in-kind) are inevitable when a club is fighting for survival.

The Charlton model has been the focus of many case studies of best practice and has claimed numerous awards (e.g. 2009 Home Office Tilley Award for crime reduction initiatives, Football League Championship Community Club of the Year 2009 and BITC Jubilee Big Tick for long-term investment in communities 2008). It has also been recognized as one of the largest community programmes in sport, with a turnover of £2,739,000 and engaging 7,000 young people on a weekly basis.

273

WORKING ACROSS THE GLOBE

Owing to the success of their work in the south-east of England, in 2002, CACT were asked to develop a community cohesion programme in the township of Alexandra in Johannesburg. The aim of the initiative was to help break down barriers between police in South Africa and young people. Working with British Airways, the Metropolitan Police and the Foreign and Commonwealth Office, the programme has now successfully expanded to Durban and Cape Town and engages teachers, local police, community workers and the unemployed to help coach young people.

Some of Europe's bigger brands are also working internationally. FC Internazionale's Project InterCampus[1] was set up in 1997 with the aim of using football as an educational tool for development. Working in some of the most deprived communities across the globe, the programme consists of a number of sports activities aimed at strengthening existing initiatives within the 21 countries in which they currently work. Academy Award-winning film director Gabriele Salvatores has produced a film of their work (BITC and G-14 2008: 12).

NATIONAL INITIATIVES

Many UK clubs and sports are also involved in national programmes such as Playing for Success (PfS) – an initiative that develops study support centres in sports clubs to provide innovative learning environments for young people who are at risk of underachieving.[2] The PfS curriculum uses the appeal of sport to develop young people's numeracy, literacy and ICT skills. Some clubs have expanded the programme to include other subjects such as languages (e.g. Arsenal FC's Languages Double Club), sciences and media (Blackburn Rovers FC). PfS is a partnership between the Department for Education, local authorities and a range of sports. The Premier League and the Football Foundation are founding partners of the initiative, which was launched in 1997.

Over 10 years on, the programme boasts partners from across 19 sports, including the Football Leagues, Rugby League and Union and the England and Wales Cricket Board and works with over 160 clubs. It has also provided an attractive programme for business sponsors to invest in as part of their own CSR activity – Experian, for example, support the Nottingham Forest Study Support Centre. PfS has also recently expanded to the Netherlands where centres have been established at clubs across the country, including at PSV Eindhoven, FC Zwolle, Vitesse Arnhem and ADO Den Haag.

DEVELOPMENTS ACROSS EUROPE

In 2007 BITC worked with the G-14,[3] the then-representative body of 18 of the most influential clubs in Europe to review the CSR activities of G-14 members, including AC Milan (Italy), Borussia Dortmund (Germany), FC Barcelona (Spain), FC Porto (Portugal), Manchester United (UK), Olympique Lyonnais (France) and PSV (the Netherlands). It involved interviews with over 30 representatives from clubs' marketing, communications, commercial, finance, public relations and community departments and was thought to be the first pan-European study of its kind. The final report aimed to demonstrate to policy-makers how clubs can be involved in the issues raised by the first European Union White Paper on Sports (2007). The paper sets out the EU's ambitions to utilize the full potential of sport to achieve its social, economic and integration ambitions and to reach out better to EU citizens. The BITC/G-14 report highlights the important role the clubs play in their local, national and international communities. It refers to the wide range of partners from across government, charities and the private sector with which these clubs work to 'improve social cohesion, health and environmental performance'. A further and more comprehensive study of CSR in European football is currently being carried out by Dr Geoff Walters of Birkbeck University, who was successful in being awarded a grant as part of the first edition of the Union des Associations Européennes de Football (UEFA) research grant programme (forthcoming at the time of writing).

SPORTS REPRESENTATIVE BODIES AND LEAGUES: PROVIDING A FRAMEWORK FOR CSR

There has also been a move from the European and national leagues or associations to provide a framework for their clubs' CSR activities and a platform to communicate these activities. UEFA adheres to 11 values, including those that aim to protect young people, grassroots sport and promote fairness and transparency in the game, and launched its first Social Responsibility Strategy in October 2007. It has a number of core social responsibility partnerships, including charities and organizations that address racism, reconciliation and peace, football for all, health, violence and humanitarian aid. UEFA has also committed to donating 0.7% of its average revenues to football and social responsibility activities (Tacon and Walters 2010).

The Premier League's Creating Chances programme has been established as an overarching brand to represent and promote the community and charitable activities of the 20 premier league clubs and the Premier League itself. Similarly, the Football League Trust was set up to broaden the relationship between professional Football League clubs and their communities. It has established a gold, silver and bronze framework for its funding criteria which aims to improve clubs' strategic investment in their communities.

SPONSOR-LED INITIATIVES

It is important for leagues and governing bodies to recognize the value of their sports' community activities and provide a framework for this activity as it can facilitate collaborative action with sponsors. Barclays are the main sponsors of England's Premier League. As part of this relationship, Barclays has invested £37 million – the largest ever investment in grassroots sports by a private-sector company – into the Barclays Spaces for Sports programme.[4] The programme develops wasteland into community sports sites and regenerates sports facilities to bring communities together through sports. Working with a range of partners, including the Football Foundation, environmental charity Groundworks, and various clubs across different leagues and sports as well as local government, the programme has developed over 200 sustainable community sports sites in the UK. The programme is a key aspect of Barclays'

275

community investment strategy and has now expanded to other countries in which Barclays works, including China, South Africa and Spain.

PREMIERSHIP RUGBY: EMBEDDING CSR PRINCIPLES AND PRACTICES

In rugby, Premiership Rugby's business strategy 'cements clubs as hubs in their communities', explains their Head of Community, Wayne Morris. In order to enter the league, for example, clubs have to adhere to standards, which include a section on community that stipulates clubs have to deliver national community programmes as well as meet agreed standards on facilities and child safety, for example. Added to this, all Premiership Rugby players are contracted to participate in community activities through player appearances at events, for example. Around half of their clubs have separate foundations or trusts to deliver their community work but community/trust managers will always sit on the senior leadership team within the club. This is considered good practice and can help embed community activity into the running of the club and ensure senior management are aware of the value of the community activity.

This strategic approach adopted by Premiership Rugby ensures the integrity of the game and that it maximizes its opportunity to create social change. This brings benefits to the game in terms of added value for sponsors who increasingly want to support grassroots sports through their own marketing and CSR strategies. The example from Premiership Rugby, which sees the commercial and community managers working closely together, ensures that potential sponsors are aware of their CSR work. Morris explains that he has seen an increased role for the community team in the sponsorship negotiation process over the last 5 years or so. He states that 'sponsors want to partner with Premiership Rugby and its clubs on community engagement activities and that the commercial directors work closely with the community team to develop programmes that meet the needs of the sponsor, the community and the game'. The MBNA Tackling Numbers programme, for example, helps to develop young people's numeracy skills through tag rugby and the Aviva Schools Programme aims to improve health, fitness and team skills.

CAUSE-RELATED MARKETING

Perhaps the most famous example of a 'cause-related marketing' sponsorship deal is FC Barcelona's partnership with UNICEF. FC Barcelona's strategy to be 'more than a club' is committed to supporting the world's most vulnerable children (FC Barcelona 2010). In 2006, UNICEF became the first logo to appear on the club's shirt in over 100 years. As part of the 5-year agreement, the club donates €1.5 million per year to help fund projects aimed at combating HIV and AIDS in Africa and Latin America (UNICEF 2006). This ground-breaking partnership demonstrates how a club can use its iconic brand to raise public awareness of a cause. Aston Villa FC was the first club in the Premier League to develop its partnership with local charity partner Acorns Children's Hospice by sporting the charity's name on players' shirts in 2008–2009 and 2009–2010. In doing so Aston Villa agreed to forgo an annual commercial shirt sponsorship, which was reported to be worth £2 million (*The Times* 2008).

OTHER SPORTS

In 2009, the British Horse Racing Authority published *Racing Together,* a first step towards the development of a community investment strategy to capture, reflect and build upon racing's contributions to communities across the country. In 2009 an independent review was carried out to establish the extent and impact of horse racing's community activities (Business in the Community Clubs that count). The review demonstrated that over half of race courses have a community programme tackling issues such as enterprise education, life skills development and health, and that over 180 charity race days are run by the 60 racecourses across the UK each year.

A FOCUS ON ENVIRONMENT

As we have seen, the broader definition of CSR expects businesses to take action to reduce their impact in the environment. Environmental or ecological considerations were considered the lowest priority for the clubs involved in a study carried out by Sheth and Babiak (2009). The study reviewed perceptions of CSR across the team owners and community relations managers in four major leagues in the USA (Major League Baseball, National Hockey League, National Basketball Association and National Football League). All of the clubs involved held the view that their CSR activities were philanthropic or community-based with community activities having strategic objectives such as developing fan bases (p. 442). This tends to be consistent with European clubs in that most clubs will refer to the work the carry out in their communities when asked about CSR activities. However, there are some examples from European sports clubs which have specific environmental policies, including Arsenal FC, FC Barcelona, Liverpool FC and Olympique de Marseille (BITC and G-14 2008: 14). There are also examples of clubs taking steps to reduce their own carbon footprint and that of their fans, for example at Borussia Dortmund, FC Bayern München, Real Madrid CF (BITC and G-14: 14) and Liverpool FC's Sweeper Zone project (BITC 2008: 22). Non-league Dartford, in the south-east of England, is thought to be leading in the environmental game with its ecostadium (Ethical Consumer 2008/2009; *The Guardian* 2010). It boasts two rainwater lakes for the 20,000 litres of water a day it takes to maintain a football pitch, as well as solar panels, sustainably sourced timber framework and a grassed living roof.

SPORTING EVENTS AND THE ENVIRONMENT

Sporting events such as the Olympics, Paralympics and Formula One are also taking steps to reduce carbon emissions and the environmental impact of their events. A recent study, commissioned by Formula One Teams Association, was carried out by independent experts in environmental performance assessment Trucost.[5] The study set out to measure greenhouse gas emissions associated with Formula One racing, demonstrating the industry's commitment to developing innovations to improve efficiency across the automotive industry. The United Nations Environment Programme, set up in 1994, supports and challenges the sports sector to embed environmental considerations into its operations, and to use the power of its appeal to raise awareness of environmental issues amongst the public. It states that the Olympic

277

Movement has integrated the environment into its charter, has a Sport and Environment Commission to advise it on environment-related policy, and has developed its Agenda 21 for sport and the environment to encourage its members to play an active part in sustainable development (United Nations Environment Programme, Sport and the Environment, 2012). The Sydney Games in 2000 are considered to be the first-ever green Olympic Games.

CSR REPORTING

Manchester City provides a good example of a club that goes beyond community in its approach to CSR and aims to tackle its environmental impact. It is one of the few clubs that have produced a CSR report (2009–2010 season) and that has a person responsible for its wider social and environmental responsibilities as opposed to a community manager. Chelsea FC (2005–2006, 2006–2007 and 2007-2008) and Aston Villa (2009–2010 season) appear to be the only other two clubs that have also produced CSR reports (Aston Villa Football Club 2010; Chelsea FC). Elsewhere in Europe, Olympique Lyonnais has also recently produced an annual report on the work of its foundation (2008–2009).

CSR-reporting experts have been critical in social media networks (Cohen 2010; Connor 2010) of the community focus of the reports and the lack of information on material issues such as environmental impact and supply chain issues surrounding sourcing of sporting apparel, for example. However, Aston Villa FC's Sustainability report has been commended for going beyond a community focus to address issues such as environment, staff health and wellbeing and equality and diversity issues (Csr-reporting 2010). It also sets out some key performance indicators against which to track progress. A common challenge for clubs is to communicate the positive work they are doing both internally across the club, and externally. CSR reporting in the sports sector is a step forward and is one way of increasing awareness of the work clubs are doing in this area as well as driving improvement.

BEST PRACTICE IN CLUBS' CSR MANAGEMENT

BITC's Clubs that Count framework suggested that clubs that performed well in CSR demonstrated that they:

- integrate community/environmental programmes into the management and ethos of the club;
- have policies in place around community, environment, workplace and marketplace issues;
- engage stakeholders (community and fans) in decision-making;
- work in partnership with sponsors and other organizations on joint initiatives that benefit society;
- have internal leadership for corporate responsibility at board level;
- measure and monitor impact and investment;
- communicate on their activity internally and externally;
- engage employees: players and non-playing staff.

Those clubs that are successful see many rewards in terms of increased profile and reputation, opportunities to partner with sponsors on joint initiatives that benefit the community as well as to develop and grow fan bases. Having board-level representation for a club's community or CSR activities ensures leadership and recognition of the importance of this activity to the club's business strategy.

CRITICISM OF CSR

Unsurprisingly, increased scrutiny and expectations of business and sports clubs have given rise to criticism of CSR. Critics argue that CSR is often used for public relations purposes and is often a bolt-on, not built-in, to business practice. In his chapter 'The Evolution and Revolution of CSR' (Visser 2010), Wayne Visser calls for a CSR revolution. Visser argues that the 'continuous improvement' approach to CSR that sees companies working towards CSR standards and benchmarks is not sufficient to address the sustainability crises that we currently face. He also argues that CSR is still too often viewed as peripheral to a company's core business and that there continues to be a lack of senior-level support for CSR and cites shareholder obsession with short-term financial gain as a barrier to 'high-impact CSR'. This, he says, requires a long-term approach to stakeholder engagement.

These challenges and criticisms are also valid in the sports world. CSR activities are still all too often viewed as the responsibility of the 'community arm' of the club. Steve Sutherland believes that commercial directors and sports' sponsorship agencies are too often not aware of the added value that clubs' community activity can leverage for sponsors and how this might develop into a partnership for mutual benefit. He would like to see this model become more embedded across sports. As an advisor to amateur boxing, Sutherland also sees opportunities for community-led sponsorship initiatives expanding into boxing and other less high-profile sports.

Clubs' CSR activities are, for the most part, limited to community engagement. There is evidence that clubs are beginning to recognize their wider impacts on the environment (Aston Villa) and some have been addressing their carbon footprint for many years (Manchester City). In a high-profile sport, there is still significant progress to be made on the wider gamut of CSR issues. Workplace issues such as equality and fair pay for non-playing staff were raised in a report by the Institute of Public Policy Research and the Fair Pay Network in August 2008. The report uncovered examples of Premier League clubs paying their non-playing staff (e.g. catering staff, receptionists and kiosk cashiers) rates below the minimum wage, and it calls on clubs to sign up to a Hatrick Gold Standard. This standard sets ethical employment conditions (Institute for Public Policy Research 2008).

SUMMARY

In a high-profile and highly scrutinized sector, there are many demands on clubs to take action to tackle social problems and support charities as well as to reduce their impact on the environment and to operate as responsible businesses. There are therefore many stakeholders in the sports sector that can, and do, have an influence on CSR in sports. These range from the national and international leagues and regulatory bodies, through to fans, NGOs, charities, national and local governments, sponsors as well as the general public. Sporting events such as the Olympics, major competitions and Formula One also have an important role to play in challenging and supporting members and participants to embed social and environmental considerations into business operations.

There have been major developments in recent years that have seen some sports move towards a more systematic approach to managing their impact on society. There has been an increase in the number of clubs which have set up foundations or charitable trusts, and there have been moves from national and international sporting bodies to establish the extent and nature of CSR activity in their respective sports (e.g. Formula One, British Horse Racing Authority, UEFA). These frameworks can support and promote existing activity as well as challenge members to improve by sharing best practice.

Sports clubs and sports events are using their brand, influence, facilities, players and athletes to address some of the world's most challenging problems. By working in partnership with others, clubs can improve their brand and reputation as well as develop new income streams. Communicating and reporting on community activities and impact as well as broader CSR issues help to drive improvement and inspire others. Football's weekly television review programme in the UK, Match of the Day, has included a community section as a regular feature. This has helped to raise awareness of the positive work in the football industry. Clubs have also been seen to be promoting their charitable partnerships on match days on advertising hoardings around the stadium.

National initiatives such as Playing for Success are successful examples of how sharing best practice across leagues and sports and across other countries can inspire action in others.

Clubs however face similar challenges to other businesses in terms of embedding CSR into the heart of their business operations. It is important that senior management within clubs as well as sporting bodies recognize the value of community engagement activity to maximize opportunities for this work and for the club. Sponsors increasingly see added value in supporting joint initiatives with clubs that have a positive impact on society (MBNA Tackling Numbers, Barclays Spaces for Sports).

However, clubs are also being challenged to look at other areas of CSR such as the environment, workplace issues and issues surrounding supply chain and responsible sponsorships. It is essential that all employees working within clubs and sporting bodies recognize their role in the CSR agenda. Community teams need to monitor and evaluate the impact of sports' community and environmental programmes to demonstrate to funders and other stakeholders that their initiatives are making a difference. Commercial managers should be aware of the CSR priorities of potential sponsors as well as the value of a club's community activity. PR teams should spot opportunities to communicate the positive work of clubs and sporting events, and facilities and operations managers play an important role in managing environmental impacts. Finally, leadership is key to the success of an integrated approach to CSR. Without this, the full potential of what sport can achieve in this area will not be realized.

Sport has a unique ability to deliver social change. There is a growing body of academic research in the area of CSR and sport. A heightened interest from the CSR community and academics, prompting detailed debate, will lead to more progress in this area. Trends towards sharing best practice between sports and leagues across countries as well as with other businesses that are considered to be leaders in the field are positive steps for the sports industry.

NOTES

1   http://intercampus.inter.it/aas/ic2010?L=en (accessed 2 July 2012).
2   www.rexhallassociates.com/our-work/pfscentres (accessed 2 July 2012).
3   The G-14 was disbanded in 2008 and is now incorporated into the European Clubs Association.
4   See http://group.barclays.com/about-barclays/citizenship/our-programmes/community-programmes/barclays-spaces-for-sports (accessed 2 July 2012).
5   See www.teamsassociation.org/press-release/2010-06-30/formula-one-unveils-ground-breaking-carbon-emissions-reduction-programme for further details.

REVIEW QUESTIONS

1   Detail some of the typical practices that sports clubs are involved in to publicize and promote their CSR activities.
2   What are some of the common motivations for clubs and other sports organizations when deciding to get involved in CSR as part of their portfolio of industrial practices?
3   In your opinion, what is the future direction for CSR and sport? What new initiatives are likely to come to fruition and what motivating factors may accelerate this in the time ahead?

FURTHER READING

Porter, M. and Kramer, M.R. (2006). *Strategy and Society: The link between competitive advantage and corporate social responsibility*. Harvard Business Review.
Sheth, H. and Babiak, K. (2009). "Beyond the Game: Perceptions and Practices of Corporate Social Responsibility in the Professional Sport Industry." *Journal of Business Ethics* 91(3): 433–450.
Tacon, R. and Walters, G. (2010). "Corporate Social Responsibility in Sport: Stakeholder Management in the UK Football Industry." *Journal of Management and Organization* 16(4).

WEBSITES

Businesslink:
   www.businesslink.gov.uk
CSR Europe:
   www.csreurope.org
Nike:
   nikeinc.com/pages/responsibility

REFERENCES

Aston Villa Football Club. (2010). Sustainability report. http://www.corporateregister.com/a10723/30728-10Co-6483608Q2710424696T-UK.pdf (subscribe to access).

Bowen, H.R. (1953). *Social Responsibilities of the Businessman.* New York: Harper.

British Horse Racing Authority. (2009). Racing together. http://www.britishhorseracing.com/racingtogether/ (accessed 13 November 2010).

Business in the Community. Clubs that count. http://www.bitc.org.uk/community/community_investment/measuring_and_reporting/working_with_sport/clubs_that_count.html (downloaded 17 November 2010).

Business in the Community. (2008). A spotlight on partnerships. http://www.bitc.org.uk/resources/publications/spotlight_ctc.html (accessed 13 November 2010).

Business in the Community and G-14. (2008). Community engagement – insights into the contribution of European club football.http://www.bitc.org.uk/resources/publications/community_engagement.html (accessed 13 November 2010).

Carroll, A.B. (1979). "A Three-dimensional Conceptual Model of Corporate Performance." *Academy of Management Review* 4(4): 497–505.

Chelsea FC. CSR reports. http://www.chelseafc.com/page/Social_Responsibility_Details/0,,10268~2066047,00.html (accessed 17 November 2010).

Cohen, E. (2010). CSR is not a sport. http://csr-reporting.blogspot.com/2010/11/csr-is-not-sport.html (accessed 17 November 2010).

Connor, D. (2010). Not a Premier League CSR report. http://davidcoethica.wordpress.com/2010/10/28/not-a-premier-league-csr-report/ (accessed 17 November 2010).

Csr-reporting (2010). What they said at the CSR conference. http://csr-reporting.blogspot.co.uk/2010_11_01_archive.html (accessed 2 July 2012).

Ethical Consumer Guide to Football (2008/2009). http://www.ethicalconsumer.org/buyersguides/miscellaneous/premiershipfootballclubs.aspx (accessed 1 July 2012).

European Union. (2007). White Paper on sports. http://ec.europa.eu/sport/white-paper/white-paper_en.htm#1 (accessed 2 July 2012).

FC Barcelona. http://foundation.fcbarcelona.com/ (accessed 2 July 2012).

FC Internazionale, Project InterCampus. http://intercampus.inter.it/aas/ic2010?L=en (accessed on 2 July 2012).

Grayson, D. (2007). Business-led corporate responsibility coalitions: learning from the example of Business in the Community in the UK – an insider's perspective – Business in the Community, Doughty Centre for Corporate Responsibility and the Kennedy School of Government, Harvard. http://www.hks.harvard.edu/m-rcbg/CSRI/publications/report_26_GraysonBus-LedCRCoalitions.pdf (accessed 13 November 2010).

Holme, R. and Watts, P. (2000). Making good business sense. The World Business Council for Sustainable Development. http://www.wbcsd.org/plugins/DocSearch/details.asp?txtDocTitle=making good business sense&txtDocText=making good business sense&DocTypeId=-1&ObjectId=Mjg 1&URLBack=result%2Easp%3FtxtDocTitle%3Dmaking+good+business+sense%26txtDocT ext%3Dmaking+good+business+sense%26DocTypeId%3D%2D1%26SortOrder%3D%26Cur Page%3D2 (accessed 13 November 2010).

Institute for Public Policy Research. (2008). Premiership clubs should become ethical employers and pay fair wages to everyone working off the pitch. http://www.ippr.org/press-releases/111/2629/premiership-clubs-should-become-ethical-employers-and-pay-fair-wages-to-everyone-working-off-the-pitch (accessed 2 July 2012).

Manchester City. (2009/10). CSR report. http://csr.mcfc.co.uk/# (accessed 13 November 2010).

Olympique Lyonnais. Rapport annuel OL fondation saison 2008/09. http://www.olweb.fr/fr/Accueil/100007/Article/52666/Rapport-annuel-OL-Fondation-saison-2008-2009.

Playing for Success. http://www.rexhallassociates.com/our-work/pfscentres (accessed 2 July 2012).

Porter, M. and Kramer, M.R. (2006). "Strategy and Society: The Link Between Competitive Advantage and Corporate Social Responsibility." *Harvard Business Review*, 78–92.

Sheth, H. and Babiak, K. (2009). "Beyond the Game: Perceptions and Practices of Corporate Social Responsibility in the Professional Sport Industry." *Journal of Business Ethics* 91(3): 433–450.

Smith, A.C.T. and Westerbeek, H.W. (2007). "Sport as a Vehicle for Deploying Corporate Social Responsibility." *Journal of Corporate Citizenship* 25(Spring): 43–54.

Tacon, R. and Walters, G. (2010). "Corporate Social Responsibility in Sport: Stakeholder Management in the UK Football Industry." *Journal of Management and Organization* 16(4).

The Guardian (2010). Which football club is the greenest? http://www.guardian.co.uk/football/2010/jan/06/football-clubs-environmentally-friendly (accessed 17 November 2010).

The Times. (2008). Aston Villa forgoes £2 million sponsorship to support charity. http://www.thetimes.co.uk/tto/public/sitesearch.do?querystring=Aston+Villa+forgoes+%C2%A32+million+sponsorship+to+support+charity&p=tto&pf=all&bl=on (accessed 2 July 2012).

UNICEF. (2006). Sport for development. Football Club Barcelona. http://www.unicef.org/sports/index_40934.html (accessed 17 November 2010).

United Nations Environment Programme, Sport and the Envrionment (2012). http://www.unep.org/sport_env/about.aspx (accessed 1 July 2012).

Visser, W. (2010). http://waynevisser.blogspot.co.uk/2010/03/csr-20-evolution-revolution-of.htm (accessed 2 July 2012).

Chapter 17

The dark sides of sport governance

*Dino Numerato, Simone Baglioni
and H. Thomas R. Persson*

TOPICS

Sport governance • Politics and power in sport • The influence of the mass media in sport • Sport and social exclusion

OBJECTIVES

By the end of this chapter you will be able to:
- Be aware of sociocultural factors and mechanisms influencing decision-making processes in sport governance;
- Develop a critical perspective towards the functioning of sport governing bodies;
- Have a knowledge of the existing body of literature dealing with questions of power, ideology and internal disputes and struggles in sport governance;
- Become familiar with different forms of sport governance-related struggles;
- Become familiar with the notion of good governance as a tool to prevent and overcome the dark sides of sport governance.

KEY TERMS

International Federation of Association Football (FIFA) – international governing body of football.

International Olympic Committee (IOC) – international non-governmental sport association primarily focused on organizing and promoting the modern Olympic Games.

Power – the capacity of an individual or a group of actors to exert their will over others and have control over material and symbolic resources and decision-making process.

Social exclusion – a social process whereby individuals or specific social groups (e.g. women, disabled people or ethnic minorities) are marginalized and therefore excluded from participation in common activities of social life, e.g. sport governance.

Sport governing body (SGB) – an association comprising a complex system of both formal and informal relationships, that organizes and governs a sport at both elite and amateur levels through decision-making processes and a regulatory framework.

OVERVIEW

Conflicts of interest, financial irregularities, misuse of power, lack of transparency, manipulation of trust, ideological struggles, social exclusion; these are different examples of the dark sides challenging contemporary sport governance. Although the emergence of various dark sides has been inherent to sports associations since their origins, recent literature on sport management has argued that their frequency has increased, hand in hand with the growing encroachment of sport with politics, mass media, sponsorship and business. Notwithstanding the relatively high importance of the dark sides in contemporary sport governance, academic attention on this phenomenon has been rather limited (Petroczi 2009).

To reduce this gap in the literature, this chapter summarizes existing scholarship about the phenomenon and considers potential future developments within SGBs in relation to their dark sides. We define as the dark sides of sport governance those behaviours that are detrimental for sport, sports associations and their civil and democratic nature (Seippel 2006), or those behaviours violating legal or organizational norms, or those that are deliberately harmful for sporting people, specific social groups or even for the whole society (Numerato and Baglioni forthcoming). Frequently, the dark sides of sport governance are expressed through power games, allegiances or various forms of corruption. On the other hand, the dark sides of sport governance shall not be confused with any form of struggle and conflict, which can be an inherent part of sport governance and democratic discussion among members and governance boards (Kerwin *et al.* 2011).

Throughout this chapter we emphasize also that an emergence of the dark sides in sport governance cannot be grasped solely in terms of mere personal and isolated scandals as it is frequently represented in the media portrayal of single scandals and affairs related to sport management. Additionally, the dark sides of sport governance must be viewed as a product of structural and systematic developments of contemporary sport, governance and overall society. In other words, the dark sides of sport governance must not be perceived exclusively as particular conflicts, struggles or plots organized by single persons or small groups, but rather as the results of more general social processes and developments, the increasing interconnection of sport with business, media and sponsorship and encroachments with politics. This happens not only at a global level of sport governance and management related to professional and elite sport, but also at national levels of sport governance and management of amateur sport.

285

The chapter addresses the following questions: What are the main elements of the dark sides of sport governance? What are their antecedents? How might a future scenario of the dark sides of sport governance look in terms of the key actors involved, the nature of struggles and the factors influencing them? We make use of a number of examples from contemporary sport governance at global and at national level to illustrate our answers to these questions.

The chapter is structured as follows. Firstly, we provide an introduction to the concept of sport governance, with a particular focus on those aspects of sport governance enhancing the occurrence of the dark sides. Secondly, three specific elements of the dark sides of sport governance are discussed: the politicization of sport governance and its negative impacts on sport; the commercialization of sport governance and the detrimental effect of the symbiotic relationship between sport, media and sponsorship; and the persisting exclusionary practices alongside the categories of gender and ethnicity. Finally, the chapter discusses some potential future developments in sport governance in relation to the dark sides.

CASE STUDY: VOLLEYGATE

The term 'Volleygate' has been used in sporting circles to refer to processes such as misuse of power, falsification of documents, financial mismanagement and accusations of bribes in the International Volleyball Federation (FIVB) during the presidency of Mexican Ruben Acosta. The term was coined in November 2002 by the former President of the Argentinean Volleyball Federation, Mario Goijman. Goijman accused, before a Swiss court, Acosta and Jean-Pierre Seppey (the President and the General Manager of FIVB respectively) of having falsified the FIVB financial report prepared by Pricewaterhouse Coopers in view of the Federation World Congress in 2002. In particular, Goijman accused Acosta of having deleted a note about a series of royalties amounting to 8.32 million Swiss francs he received in exchange for the assignment of broadcasting rights (Canton de Vaud 2006).

In March 2003, Goijman then also submitted a complaint to the Ethics Commission of the International Olympic Committee (IOC), of which Acosta was a member. Considering that a decision related to Goijman's accusation was pending in front of the Swiss court, the IOC formulated a statement that 'the money from sport must go to sport' (IOC 2003), through which it expressed its disappointment about the high amount of royalties Acosta received for negotiating broadcasting rights for FIVB events (Chappelet and Kübler-Mabbott 2008). Acosta resigned from the IOC in May 2004 as he would have been ineligible for a new mandate the following year due to his age limit: the case was never discussed further by the IOC Ethics Commission.

Although the falsification of the report was acknowledged by the Swiss court, Acosta was acquitted of all the charges as the act itself did not have to be considered a crime according to the Swiss legal system (Bureš 2008). However, despite the discovery of such irregularities, and the related IOC recommendations and court decision, there has not been a change in the association's presidency. Acosta managed to strengthen his position and to undermine democratic principles in the association by adopting further norms and rulings. Over the years he managed to approve particular conditions for the election of the presidency, summarized in 11 'Legal prerequisites for new candidates to the FIVB presidency' (Sparre 2006). As a consequence of these rulings, Acosta's position in the presidency became *de facto* unchallengeable.

That the FIVB was not governed according to democratic principles becomes evident also by considering its code of conduct, according to which the President could expel any official or player who publicly criticized the organization. Following these rules, and due to financial irregularities, his major opponent Goijman and the Argentinean Volleyball Federation, which openly supported Goijman's action, were expelled from the FIVB. Ruben Acosta decided to step down from his presidency after 24 years in place, soon after the Beejing Olympics in 2008 (Sparre 2008).

SPORT GOVERNANCE

Sport governance can be defined in more than one way. It is commonly accepted as making a distinction between systematic governance, corporate/good organizational governance or simply good governance, and political governance (Henry and Lee 2004). In short, systematic governance refers to competition, cooperation and mutual adjustment between organizations. Good governance refers to the accepted norms and values that contribute to a fair allocation of resources and profits or losses (financial or other) as well to the general good management of organizations involved in the sports business. Political governance refers to:

> the processes by which governments or governing bodies seek to steer the sports system to achieve desired outcomes by moral pressure, use of financial or other incentives, or by licensing, regulation and control to influence other parties to act in ways consistent with desired outcomes.
>
> (Henry and Lee 2004: 25–26)

Governance could be described as network-based. In line with Hoye and Cuskelly (2003), we would argue that any conceptualization of governance ought to have its primary focus on the distribution of power, the way it is exercised, and how those in power are controlled.

Recent changes in sport governance, such as the increased influence of funding agencies and associated politicians, broadcasters, sponsors, stadia management and event organizations, have to some extent favoured the development of the dark sides of governance (Hoye and Cuskelly 2007). Whilst these interconnections may provide financial as well as other gains for SGBs, the same networks may generate 'power struggles, loss of autonomy of organizations, asymmetrical relationships, different levels of commitment in the relationship, conflicting loyalties, changes in resource allocation, resource imbalances, goal displacement and resistance to change.' (Thibault and Harvey 1997: 60). Even if it might be hard to prove whether dark sides of governance are given a silent approval in organizations, or the extent to which it stems from individuals acting on their own, the distance between SGBs and their membership can make it even harder for the constituencies involved to assess if their organization is run in a fair and responsible way (Aguilera and Cuervo-Cazurra 2004).

287

STRUCTURAL AND DISCURSIVE FACETS OF THE
DARK SIDES OF SPORT GOVERNANCE

There are two levels at which one can understand the functioning and development of the dark sides of sport governance, and in particular of SGBs. One level focuses on the structural dimensions of sport governance: its network-shaped form and related functionalities. The other level focuses on the discursive dimension, in other words on the cognitive and symbolic devices on which SGBs frame their action and legitimacy.

At the first level of analysis, it is possible to ascertain how the structure of sport governance *per se* may generate external relationships that can lead to dark sides. Sport governance, in fact, builds on the capacities of both individuals and organizations to develop networks, ties and relationships that serve the purpose of keeping the sport sector and its governance system together. Sport governance depends on interactions among athletes, club activists, sport managers, sponsors, local authorities and supranational sport organizations. At the centre of this governance system there are powerful individuals in top management roles, like sport federation presidents and chief executive officers (CEOs). SGBs are power arenas (Sugden and Tomlinson 1997, 1998; Hoye and Cuskelly 2003; Moreau 2004; Porro 2006): they decide how funds are allocated among clubs and local branches; they decide where to host an international sport event in a specific country (e.g. an international regatta) with all the economic and reputational implications that come with such a decision. But SGBs also decide who will be appointed in key positions in the organization's overall management, as well as who might be part of the Olympic delegation for a specific discipline.

Hence, the top management of SGBs are at the centre of a wide net of interests, both economic and symbolic, and as such they are in a position of power. Ordinary power games and techniques also apply to the functioning of sport governance. Firstly, the leaders of SGBs may wish to keep their power for a certain time, no matter how ultimately beneficial this may be for a specific SGB or even sport discipline. To maintain such a powerful position, SGBs leadership may be ready to misuse rules and governance methods. A common misuse is one affecting the ordinary democratic decision-making processes of sport. SGBs, like all democratic organizations, are guided by formal procedures for the appointment of their governance bodies: leaders are elected by a legitimate assembly through a competitive recruitment procedure. However, the way votes are sought and gained does not always follow a fair and transparent procedure.

For example, a recent research project entitled *Sport and Social Capital in the European Union* (Numerato and Baglioni forthcoming), comparing SGB governance systems across Europe, has unveiled that sport federations' presidents and boards are ready to bargain with local branches and clubs to secure their support at board/presidential elections in return for federation resources (Baglioni 2010). It is a *do ut des* (I give you something to have something back from you) strategy, where presidents and boards wishing to be confirmed or elected are ready to use federation – that is collective – resources for their own goal (being elected or re-elected). This may seem a normal and acceptable strategy unless we consider that, through this dark-side process, resources will be allocated not on the basis of needs or performances, but rather on the basis of personal interest of those in positions of power in sport.

288

For instance, the decision to use funding for sport infrastructure development may not follow a rational path: resources might reasonably be expected to go to those areas or clubs having shown a particular effort in the recruitment of new participants or having shown a potential for development if their sport infrastructure is improved. Instead, resources will be sent to clubs/branches assuring their vote to the president/board willing to be re-elected or elected, disregarding their performances and merits. Hand in hand with increasing commercialization of sport, economic resources become a tool for personal power development plans rather than a tool for sport practice development (Slack and Amis 2004; Numerato and Baglioni forthcoming).

In the long term, this policy will be detrimental to sport development not only because it is unjust (not rewarding those who deserve it) but also because this system of sports governance that is subject to such power games does not allow any real challenge or 'voice' of opposition, interpreted through the lens of Hirschmann's (1970) 'exit, voice and loyalty' perspective. In this sense, leadership turnover is rare, with a consequent sclerotic degeneration of decision-making mechanisms. 'Exit strategies' become often the only solution left to virtuous individuals opposing the way SGBs are run, with the result of a substantial impoverishment of sport governance and practice. The authors of this study observed these strategies during their ethnographic fieldworks in SGBs in Italy and in the Czech Republic during 2007 of the aforementioned research project *Sport and Social Capital in the European Union* (Numerato and Baglioni forthcoming).

The second level of observation of dark sides in sport governance deals with the use of cognitive resources in SGBs. This form of the dark side is connected to communication processes, information disclosure and manipulation of information and trust. Sport governance leaders act as gate-keepers of information going in and out of their federation or organization. The management of information becomes a critical tool when such leaders aim to remain in power. For instance, access to, and management of, information plays a relevant role in neutralizing potential internal challengers. Critical voices or bellicose intentions by challengers will be deliberately hidden by the leadership that maintains a gate-keeper role in internal communication flows. The authors of this chapter have met with cases where challengers were not purposively invited to attend a board (or with cases where the legal composition of an assembly during which the leadership would have been attacked was questioned because of a calculated lack of sufficient votes guaranteeing legal value to decisions: Numerato and Persson 2010, Numerato and Baglioni forthcoming).

Information can not only be hidden or denied, but it can also be manipulated. For example, the leadership may keep for itself an amendment to a previously collectively adopted decision: it has happened that the president of a sport federation had personally changed a decision taken by the board, presumably trusting that no one would have checked and that no one would have complained. This latter action suggests that trust in the leadership of SGBs is often abused (Numerato and Baglioni forthcoming).

ANTECEDENTS OF THE DARK SIDES OF SPORT GOVERNANCE

Both structural and cognitive forms of the dark sides of sport governance can occur as a consequence of the increasingly close relationship between sport and politics, broadcasters and sponsors. The dark sides of governance are also informed by the ways in which decision-making processes within SGBs often mirror wider societal processes, including those around social exclusion. Further examples of these antecedents of the dark sides of sport governance will be provided in the following three sections.

SGBs under political pressure

History shows that sport and politics are strictly intertwined, in relation to both democratic and non-democratic governments. The twentieth century has witnessed the development of a symbiotic relationship between political projects such as Nazism, Fascism or Communism and sport. In these cases, sport provided opportunities for strengthening national cohesion and developing spirit of competition ready to be used well beyond the sport sphere; it represented the ideal realm to enroot myths of race supremacy – in Nazism and Fascism – but also myths of class and class organization supremacy in Communist regimes (Fisher 2002; Guttmann 2003; Girginov 2004; Bolz 2007; Wagg and Andrews 2007). Sport officials were usually nominated by political parties and were loyal to the totalitarian ideologies and SGBs were instrumentally used by non-democratic regimes to implement their policies aggressively. Sport has provided spatial, figurative and material opportunities for non-democratic regimes to strengthen their political programmes while simultaneously increasing social and political consensus around their elites.

In contemporary democratic societies, sport is used by politicians for various reasons. For potential political leaders, sport is helpful to gain consensus and increase popularity and as such, sport may ease a shift from a career in commercial activities into a political career: for example, football team ownership by entrepreneurs having then become politicians, like Silvio Berlusconi in Italy and Bernard Tapie in France. In both cases, success in football was used as a stepping stone for success in other spheres like politics (Eastham 1999; Porro and Russo 2001). Success in sport was to be a predictor of success in other spheres, including politics. The intertwining of politics and sport is crystal clear in the case of Mr Berlusconi, the owner of Milan FC and the Italian Prime Minister for almost two decades, starting from the early 1990s. As pointed out by Diamanti (2005), MrBerlusconi adapted a football organizational model, symbols and identity issues to politics at the point that it has been difficult to distinguish between one and the other. He called his party Forza Italia (Go Italy!), evoking a well-known chant to support the Italian football team or other Italian national sports representatives. His party's colour is blue, the same colour chosen for the Italian sport teams' shirts. Moreover, the Forza Italia organizational structure replicates football organization: the party is organized around a network of local clubs, with a 'low degree of ideology and a high degree of personal identification' (Diamanti 2005: 8).

There are, however, also cases when a political career is built starting from a peak position in an SGB like a federation. In this case what counts is the web of ties and contacts sport provides: the scope of a federation president's network, for example, spans from contacts in the sport sector and other civil society spheres, to contacts in the economy-commerce (sponsors and the use of their economic capital to fund a political campaign), up to the various levels of political governance (Slack and Amis 2004; Booth 2011). Sometimes the interests represented by such a vast system of relations coincide. For example, when a federation board decides to host a relevant international sport event in a city, there are economic and reputational benefits for the city. Hence, special relationships will be established between the federation board, especially its president, and the city ruling economic, cultural and political elite. Allegiances of national football association leaders with political or cultural elites with a potentially detrimental effect for sport governance have recently been documented through an ethnographic inquiry in the Czech Republic and Italy (Numerato 2009b; Numerato and Baglioni forthcoming). This social capital of contacts will be mobilized as necessary by the federation president and may also translate into important support to aid a successful future career as a politician. Sport, in this case, may have been used instrumentally for individual political purposes, which may not lead to an improvement of the sport governance and sport practice in the society.

In countries where SGBs have a hybrid nature and are thus 'quasi-public' organizations, as they depend on government for funding or their legal status puts them under governmental direct or indirect responsibility, the proximity with political/governmental elites puts SGB leaders at risk of permeability to politics-driven interests or requests. Numerato (2009a) provides vivid evidence of this risk in his analysis of regional sport policies in the Czech Republic. He uses the term 'political clientelist' to describe the ways in which sport policy decisions are made in areas where there is a lack of accountability and meritocracy in the distribution of resources. On the one hand, politicians use the arena of sport governance as a tool of public relations to increase their visibility and power. On the other hand, sports managers aim to bring in resources for their specific sport club, sport discipline or even a specific preferred individual in sport. In their study of political clientelism in Greece, Henry and Nassis (1999) demonstrated how loyalty and commitment from sport officials to politicians can facilitate easier access to valuable and rare resources for sport.

In sum, the intertwinement of politics and sport that is so diffused in current societies offers multiple opportunities for the development of dark sides of sport governance. SGBs – both in the form of their leaders and their constituencies – should be better aware of the potentially negative consequences that being closely aligned to politics and politicians can bring in sport governance.

The dark sides of sport governance and the sporting triangle

In a quite similar way to politics, the mass media plays a significant role in contemporary sport governance. Garry Whannel describes how the transformation of SGBs occurred simultaneously with the rise of television in the 1960s:

> The new revenues available from television advertising endorsement and sponsorship placed amateurism under growing strain. Governing bodies that refused to compromise found themselves under threat of losing their power to new entrepreneurially oriented organizations. ... By the mid-1980s, amateurism was all but dead, and most governing bodies had been forced to come to terms with the new world of sport agents, sponsorship brokers, and television deals. Sport was reshaped to meet the needs of television and the promotional industry.
>
> (Whannel 2009: 214)

291

The existence of the so-called sporting triangle between sport, sponsors and the media (Boyle and Haynes 2000), often deconstructed through the approaches of critical management studies and the political economy of sport, can easily nourish the development of the dark sides of sport governance. Due to the complexity of relations between sport federation officials, the media, sponsors and marketing companies, the networks of sport governance can be easily configured to favour the specific interests of both media and sponsors. Symbiotically, the 'loyalty' and commitment of sport officials in that regard are often rewarded.

The functioning of these mechanisms can be illustrated by the classical example of the success of Horst Dassler, the former CEO of Adidas and the so-called 'puppet master of the sporting world' (Slack and Amis 2004: 274). In the 1950s and 1960s he managed to promote the Adidas brand through sponsoring Olympic teams globally. Not only did this strategy open up markets to him in many countries, but it also helped him accumulate politically valuable networks, in particular in countries from Africa and Asia with less developed but more potentially lucrative markets. The huge amount of contacts he established became an efficient tool to control the decision-making processes at the global governance level. The IOC decision to assign the marketing rights for the 1988 Olympic Games to ISL Marketing, a company controlled by Adidas, has been interpreted as a result of the ties Horst Dassler accumulated over the years (Slack and Amis 2004; Tomlinson 2005).

Another symptom of existing allegiances between sponsor and sport governance framed by the logic of media promotion comes from the example of the commercialization of the Olympic movement. Magdalinski and Nauright (2004), in their analysis of different aspects of commercialization of the Olympic movement, argue, by reviewing relevant literature, how different technical educational courses in classrooms are coupled with corporate objectives to promote products and brands of key Olympic sponsors.

On the other hand, the role of sponsors is not limited to facilitating the development of the dark sides of sport governance. As a reaction to some negative aspects connected to sport governance, sponsors can decide to step down from sports' support, considering the negative impacts that these developments might have on their brand. This situation recently happened in relation to the cash-for-votes scandal around the last presidential FIFA election. In May 2011, the disclosure of corruption allegations led to the suspension of two executive committee members, the Qatari president of the Asian Football Confederation Mohamed bin Hammam and Trinidad and Tobago FIFA former vice-president Jack Warner.[1] Whereas the traditional FIFA sponsors Coca-Cola and Adidas 'limited' their public reactions to expressing their concerns (Press Association 2011), the Gulf Arab airline Emirates declared that it would consider whether to renew its partnership agreement with FIFA beyond 2014. According to Emirates Airlines representatives, the final decision will be verified by a commissioned research assessing the impact of Emirates' association with FIFA (Reuters 2011).

The dark sides of SGBs are connected with the media not only in terms of allegiances between sponsors and sport federations officials. Media content and media production processes can facilitate occurrence of the dark sides, in particular by sport journalism that is rather uncritical in nature, and through the marginalization of problematic issues (Schultz-Jorgensen 2005; Horky and Nieland 2011). The fact that journalists seldom investigate the negative aspects of sport governance often stems from the fact that questioning suspicious and detrimental behaviour of sport officials can lead to an alienation of their sources. In other words, journalists' access to sport federation officials and to sport clubs can be limited or denied once they portray critically sport governance processes. For example, journalists may not be invited to press conferences, their access to a general assembly can be forbidden and they can find themselves banned in sport governance corridors (Smith 1976; Rowe 2007; Numerato 2009a).

The media can also contribute to dark sides in sport governance through their work on symbolic aspects of sport: at this level, media can help by hiding or strategically reinterpreting the dark sides of sport governance. This can be done, for example, by instrumentally using issues of transparency or accountability. Jennings (2011), one of the journalists who has often been banned from sport federations due to his critical investigative approach, has documented throughout his experience with the FIFA a discrepancy between the way in which the issue of transparency is publicly presented and promoted and the manner in which it is (not) actually practised. Sports officials can also strategically manipulate a media portrayal of decision-making processes and electoral campaigns in SGBs due to their allegiances with selected sport journalists or by providing them with only partial and biased information (Numerato 2008; Numerato and Persson 2010).

When sport governance reflects social exclusion

SGBs are often in a position to determine policies on inclusion and exclusion. This may relate to all types of potentially uneven and unequal relationships in our societies, including old and young, disabled and able-bodied people, men and women, and divisions associated with ethnicity. Therefore, topics of social inclusion and exclusion (ethnic relations, gender and age equality, disability politics) should be integral parts of contemporary sport governance (Persson 2008, 2010; Bradbury et al. 2011). While claims are being made for sport as a vehicle for promoting social integration and a tool for peace-making and conflict resolution (Henry 2005; Giulianotti 2011), it is also an arena to which not everyone has the same access, where separatist ideas and ethnic tensions are expressed (Warren 2002) and where discursive constructions of minorities are normalized and legitimized (Knoppers 2011).

The FRA (European Union Agency for Fundamental Rights 2010) concluded, in its report on racism, ethnic discrimination and exclusion of migrants and minorities in sport, that most European and international umbrella SGBs have now adopted antiracism or antidiscrimination clauses. Amongst these, UEFA is highlighted in the report as an example of good practice, with racism and ethnic discrimination on its corporate social responsibility agenda since the beginning of the twenty-first century. Nevertheless, despite the fact that both UEFA and FIFA have documented their awareness of racist and discriminatory action in football (FIFA n.d.; UEFA 2005, 2011), little has been done against the underrepresentation of people with ethnic minority backgrounds and specifically women (see Chapters 6 and 11). Incidents of racism, as well as antisemitism and anti-Gypsyism,[2] are being identified, in particular in Italy and Germany, expressed by right-wing extremists becoming active, particularly in amateur leagues (European Union Agency for Fundamental Rights 2010).

Showing little awareness of the reality of the sport and the governing policies of his own organization, FIFA President Sepp Blatter expressed his view on the topic, stating that there

293

'is no racism [on the pitch], but maybe there is a word or gesture that is not correct. The one affected by this should say this is a game and shake hands' (CNN 2011). Not surprisingly, Blatter's statement resulted in several high-profile debates, discussion and much criticism across old as well as new media channels.

Statements such as this may be hard to understand if read separated from the wider sport governance scene, from the international level to national, regional and local levels. That men from the ethnic majority group in society are in the driving seat in terms of power distribution worldwide on a societal level, specifically in terms of institutional power, is hard to refute (Pfister 2010). This masculine hegemony can take several forms, such as gender and ethnic skewedness on SGBs marked by homosocial networks (Fasting and Knorre 2005; Claringbould and Knoppers 2008; Fundberg 2009; Hovden 2010). Gender (and ethnic, age, disability) blindness represented by sport policy, showing little awareness of structural gender (and ethnic, age, disability) inequalities, and the use of a gender prefix to make feminine (e.g. Women's Champions League) or disabled versions (e.g. Paralympic archery) of the unquestioned male and able-bodied sport norm are two examples of the prolonged problem sport has had with handling diversity (see Chapter 11; Talbot 2002, The FA n.d.). A darker side of the fragile and therefore often protected bastion of male hegemony is the growing number of reported cases of sexual harassment and sexual assault against minors by male coaches. In Sweden, for example, this has been brought to light on several occasions during 2011 and functioned as a serious wake-up call for the Swedish sport movement (Sydsvenskan 2011; Sand *et al.* 2011).

It is also expressed through sexism, such as when FIVB changed the dress code for women, less and tighter, leading up to the 1998 World Championships in volleyball in Japan (Jönsson 2007: 136) and it implicitly justifies ethnically determined barriers and avenues to representation in the English Premier League as well as international teams (Agergaard and Sørensen 2009). Furthermore, dominant ideas of ethnicity and gender can affect the possibilities of becoming English Premier League coaches (Cashmore and Cleland 2011), and can inform the ways in which SGBs and clubs relate to parents from ethnic minority groups by uncritically accepting preconceived and hegemonic norms in terms of how things are done, always have been done and always should be done (Persson 2010: 71).

SUMMARY: BETTER GOVERNANCE OR FURTHER DARK SIDES ON THE HORIZON?

Contemporary sport management has to struggle with different forms of dark sides in sport governance that might challenge the achievement of primary objectives of sport as contributing to societal, physical, psychological, economic and relational wellbeing. In contrast, the dark sides can have strong detrimental effects on sport that can permeate into wider society.

The dark sides of sports governance can be understood through both their structural and discursive dimensions. The structural dimension is connected to the network nature of sport governance, the discursive dimension to the ways of communication of, and in, SGBs. In addition to internal factors like struggles over leadership or the allocation of material resources, the emergence of the dark sides in sport governance is facilitated by three external causes: the linkage with politics; the symbiosis of sport with the spheres of mass media, sponsoring and marketing; and last but not least, social exclusion principles in regard to diversity (ethnic, gender or disabilities), often reproduced within the SGBs.

There are strategies that SGBs or sport associations can develop to challenge these dark sides. For example, the recent establishment of FIFA's Independent Governance Committee (Pieth 2011) or initiatives external to sport governance bodies, such as numerous series of activities promoted by the playthegame.org platform or by Transparency International (Schenk 2011), a transnational NGO that recently questioned the level of independence of the aforementioned Committee within FIFA. These initiatives called for structural changes in sport governance, strengthening transparency and accountability mechanisms. There is at least some evidence of action aimed at promoting good governance in sport. In the context of this chapter, good governance is seen as the antidote to the dark sides of governance. In other words, it is seen as expressions of the imperfections in the system (Zattoni and Cuomo 2008) and as attempts to rectify, for example, corruption, nepotism, bureaucracy and mismanagement (Nanda 2006) in an efficient, open and responsible way (Leftwich 1993, cited in Rhodes 2000). Hence, good governance is an example of best practice, i.e. recommendations of how best to achieve a social as well as professional legitimization, internally but with related external benefits (Zattoni and Cuomo 2008). Without the support of the different stakeholders, such as the membership, there is no legitimacy for SGBs' current policies and methods of working (Persson 2011).

In this context, the role of critical management studies and sociocultural analysis of sport governance should not be limited to understanding the traditional power games and to uncovering different network configurations leading to the dark sides of sport governance. There is a necessity to analyse the ways in which sport governance is influenced by pressures towards good governance but also the ways in which the inner malaise of sport organizations might cope with emerging calls for transparency, accountability or good governance. In this context sport sociology and sport management scholars are likely to put more emphasis on strategic adoption and discursive strategies of the actors involved in the dark sides of sport governance in order to unveil 'discursive manipulation or surface rhetoric' (Palmer 2000: 376) of SGB officials. New mechanisms are being implemented. However, one needs to ask: are the calls for good governance synonymous with a path towards better governance, or do the contemporary signals of strategic adaptation and instrumentalization of good governance represent new signs of dark sides of sport governance? Consequently, one should continue to adopt a critical approach to making sense of these early attempts by sports governance organizations to challenge the dark sides outlined in this chapter.

NOTES

1   After this decision from May 2011, the FIFA ban was extended to other officials involved in the scandal, in mid-October 2011 (BBC 2011).
2   The term 'anti-Gypsyism' is used in the European Union Agency for Fundamental Rights' report and is seen as a derogatory term referring to Roma, but also directed towards any fans of opposing teams (European Union Agency for Fundamental Rights 2010: 33).

295

REVIEW QUESTIONS

1   Explain the reasons behind Horst Dassler's commercial success outlined in the chapter. What characteristics of contemporary sport facilitated these developments?
2   How could politics and sport develop a 'healthier' relationship? Which cultural, political and legal solutions could avoid such a relationship producing dark sides of sport governance?
3   Your local, regional and national SGBs are likely to have policies that aim to tackle discrimination based on ethnicity, sex, age and disability. Try to find one of these policies and identify how they plan to implement their objectives into sport.

FURTHER READING

Baglioni, S. (2010). "The Social Capital of Sport: The Case of Italy," in: Groeneveld, M., Houlihan, B. and Ohl, F. (eds) *Social Capital and Sport Governance in Europe*. London: Routledge, pp. 146–162.
Hoye, R. and Cuskelly, G. (2003). "Board–Executive Relationships within Voluntary Organisations." *Sport Management Review* 6: 53–74.
Hoye, R. and Cuskelly, G. (2007). *Sport Governance.* London: Elsevier.

WEBSITES

Play the game:
    www.playthegame.org
Transparency International:
    mideastsoccer.blogspot.se
Transparency in Sport:
    www.transparencyinsport.org

REFERENCES

Agergaard, S. and Sørensen, J.K. (2009). "The Dream of Social Mobility: Ethnic Minority Players in Danish Football Clubs." *Soccer and Society* 10(6): 766–780.
Aguilera, R. V. and Cuervo-Cazurra, A. (2004). "Codes of Good Governance Worldwide: What is the Trigger?" *Organization Studies*, 25(3): 415–443.
Baglioni, S. (2010). "The Social Capital of Sport: The Case of Italy," in: Groeneveld, M., Houlihan, B. and Ohl, F. (eds) *Social Capital and Sport Governance in Europe*. London: Routledge, pp. 146–162.
BBC. (2011). FIFA bans four Caribbean officials after cash-for-votes inquiry. http://news.bbc.co.uk/sport2/hi/football/15315021.stm (accessed 19 November 2011).
Bolz, D. (2007). "Le Sport dans l'entre-deux-guerres, ou outil politique universel? Architecture

sportive et action politique en Italie fasciste et en Angleterre," in: Kratzmuller, B., Marschik, M., Müllner, R., Szemethy, H. D. and Trink, E. (eds) *Sport and the Construction of Identities.* Vienna: Verlag Turia+Kant, pp. 307–314.

Booth, D. (2011). "Olympic City Bidding: An Exegesis of Power." *International Review for the Sociology of Sport* 46(4): 367–386.

Boyle, R. and Haynes, R. (2000). *Power Play: Sport, media and popular culture.* Harlow: Longman.

Bradbury, S., Amara, M., García, B. and Bairner, A. (2011). *Representation and Structural Discrimination in Football in Europe: The case of ethnic minorities and women. Summary report of key findings.* Loughborough: Loughborough University: Institute of Youth Sport, School of Sport, Exercise and Health Sciences.

Bureš, R. (2008). Why sport is not immune to corruption. http://www.coe.int/t/dg4/epas/Source/Ressources/EPAS_INFO_Bures_en.pdf (accessed 30 June 2012).

Canton de Vaud (2006). Ordonnance. http://www.playthegame.org/upload//Indictment.pdf (accessed 6 November 2011).

Cashmore, E. and Cleland, J. (2011). "Why Aren't There More Black Football Managers?" *Ethnic and Racial Studies* 34(9): 1594–1607.

Chappelet, J.-L. and Kübler-Mabbott, B. (2008). *The International Olympic Committee and the Olympic System: The governance of world sport.* London: Routledge.

Claringbould, I. and Knoppers, A. (2008). "Doing and Undoing Gender in Sport Governance." *Sex Roles* 58(1–2): 81–92.

CNN. (2011). Blatter: "There is no racism" on pitch. http://edition.cnn.com/video/#/video/sports/2011/11/16/fifa-sepp-blatter.cnn (accessed 16 November 2011).

Diamanti, I. (2005). "Foot Politics: Tifo dunque voto." *Limes* 2: 7–10.

Eastham, J. (1999). "The Organisation of French Football Today," in: Dauncey, H. and Hare, G.(eds) *France and the 1998 World Cup: The national impact of a world sporting event.* London: Frank Cass, pp. 58–78.

European Union Agency for Fundamental Rights. (2010). Racism, ethnic discrimination and exclusion of migrants and minorities in sport: A comparative overview of the situation in the European Union – October 2010. http://fra.europa.eu/fraWebsite/attachments/Report-racism-sport_EN.pdf (accessed 6 December 2011).

Fadnes, J.K. (2007). Volleygate – an ongoing battle. playthegame.org. http://www.thepulse2007.org/?p=11 (accessed 6 December 2011).

Fasting, K. and Knorre, N. (2005). *Women in Sport in the Czech Republic: The experiences of female athletes.* Prague, Oslo: Norwegian School of Sport Sciences and Czech Olympic Committee.

FIFA. (n.d.). Anti-racism – FIFA against discrimination. http://www.fifa.com/aboutfifa/socialresponsibility/antiracism/index.html (accessed 7 December 2010).

Fisher, P. (2002). "Creating a Marxist-Leninist Cultural Identity: Women's Memories of the German Democratic Republic's Friedensfhart." *Culture, Sport and Society* 5: 39–52.

Fundberg, J. (2009). Vilka är idrottens valda makthavare? Om rekrytering till styrelser inom svensk idrott FoU-rapport 2009:6 (Who are the chosen board members in Swedish sport? A research report to the Swedish sports confederation.) http://www.rf.se/ImageVault/Images/id_2928/ImageVaultHandler.aspx (accessed 6 December 2011).

Girginov, V. (2004). "Totalitarian Sport: Towards an Understanding of its Logic, Practice and Legacy." *Totalitarian Movements and Political Religions* 5(1): 25–58.

Giulianotti, R. (2011). "Sport, Peacemaking and Conflict Resolution: A Contextual Analysis and Modelling of the Sport Development and Peace Sector." *Ethnic and Racial Studies* 34(2): 207–228.

Guttmann, A. (2003). "Sport, Politics and the Engaged Historian." *Journal of Contemporary History* 38(3): 363–375.

Henry, I.P. (2005). Sport and multiculturalism: a European perspective. http://olympicstudies.uab.es/pdf/wp102_eng.pdf (accessed 6 December 2011).

Henry, I. and Lee, P.C. (2004). "Governance and Ethics in Sport," in: Beech, J. and Chadwick, S. (eds) *The Business of Sport Management*. Harlow: Pearson Education, pp. 25–42.

Henry, I.P. and Nassis, P. (1999). "Political Clientelism and Sports Policy in Greece." *International Review for the Sociology of Sport* 34(1): 43–58.

Hirschmann, A.O. (1970). *Exit, Voice, and Loyalty: Responses to decline in firms, organizations, and states*. Cambridge, MA: Harvard University Press.

Horky, T. and Nieland, J.-U. (2011). *ISPS 2011: First Results of the International Sports Press Survey 2011*. Play the Game 2011 Conference. Cologne.

Hovden, J. (2010). "Female Top Leaders – Prisoners of Gender? The Gendering of Leadership Discourses in Norwegian Sports Organizations." *International Journal of Sport Policy and Politics* 2(2): 189–203.

Hoye, R. and Cuskelly, G. (2003). "Board–Executive Relationships within Voluntary Organisations." *Sport Management Review* 6: 53–74.

Hoye, R. and Cuskelly, G. (2007). *Sport Governance*. London: Elsevier.

IOC. (2003). Ethics Commission decision of notification to the parties. http://www.olympic.org/Documents/Reports/EN/en_report_879.pdf (accessed 5 November 2011).

Jennings, A. (2011). "Investigating Corruption in Corporate Sport: The IOC and FIFA." *International Review for the Sociology of Sport* 46(4): 387–398.

Jönsson, K. (2007). *Feminism, Maskulinitet och Jämställdhet*. [Feminism, masculinity and equality.] Malmö: Idrottsforum.org.

Kerwin, S., Doherty, A. and Harman, A. (2011). "'It's Not Conflict, It's Differences of Opinion': An In-Depth Examination of Conflict in Nonprofit Boards." *Small Group Research* 42(5): 562–594.

Knoppers, A. (2011). "Giving Meaning to Sport Involvement in Managerial Work." *Gender, Work and Organization* 18(S1): e1–e22.

Leftwich, A. (1993). "Governance, Democracy and Development in the Third World." *Third World Quarterly* 14(3): 605–624.

Magdalinski, T. and Nauright, J. (2004). "Commercialisation of the Modern Olympics," in: Slack, T. (ed.) *The Commercialisation of Sport*. New York: Routledge, pp. 185–204.

Moreau, D.B. (2004). *Sociologie des fédérations sportives: la professionnalisation des dirigeants bénévoles*. Paris: L'Harmattan.

Nanda, V.P. (2006). "The 'Good Governance' Concept Revisited." *Annals of the American Academy of Political and Social Science* 603(1): 269–283.

Numerato, D. (2008). "Media Activities and Reflexivity: The Case of Czech Sports Actors." *Media Studies* 3(3): 257–277.

Numerato, D. (2009a). "The Media and Sports Corruption: An Outline of Sociological Understanding." *International Journal of Sport Communication* 2(3): 261–273.

Numerato, D. (2009b). "The Institutionalisation of Regional Public Sport Policy in the Czech Republic." *International Journal of Sport Policy* 1(1): 13–30.

Numerato, D. and Baglioni, S. (forthcoming). "The Dark Side of Social Capital: An Ethnography of Sport Governance." *International Review for the Sociology of Sport*.

Numerato, D. and Persson, H.T.R. (2010). "To Govern or to Dispute? Remarks on Sport Governance in the Czech Republic and Denmark." *Entertainment and Sports Law Journal* 7/2.

Palmer, C. (2000). "Spin Doctors and Sportsbrokers: Researching Elites in Contemporary Sport – A Research Note on the Tour de France." *International Review for the Sociology of Sport* 35(3): 364–377.

Persson, H.T.R. (2008). "Social Capital and Social Responsibility in Denmark – More than Gaining Public Trust." *International Review for the Sociology of Sport* 43(1): 35–51.

Persson, H.T.R. (2010). "Danish Sport Governance – Tradition in Transition," in: Groeneveld, M., Houlihan, B. and Ohl, F. (eds) *Social Capital and Sport Governance in Europe*. London: Routledge, pp. 63–84.

Persson, H.T.R. (2011). "Good Governance and the Danish Football Association: Between Inter-national and Domestic Sport Governance." *International Journal of Sport Policy and Politics* 3(3): 373–384.

Petroczi, A. (2009). "The Dark Side of Sport: Challenges for Managers in the Twenty-first Cen-tury." *European Sport Management Quarterly* 9(4): 349–352.

Pfister, G. (2010). "Are the Women or the Organisations to Blame? Gender Hierarchies in Danish Sports Organisations." *International Journal of Sport Policy* 2(1): 1–23.

Pieth, M. (2011). Governing FIFA: concept paper and report. http://www.fifa.com/mm/docu-ment/affederation/footballgovernance/01/54/99/69/fifagutachten-en.pdf (accessed 1 December 2011).

Porro, N. (2006). *L'Attore sportivo. Azione collettiva, sport e cittadinanza*. Molfetta: La Meridiana.

Porro, N. and Russo, P. (2001). "Berlusconi and Other Matters: the Era of 'Football-Politics'". *Journal of Modern Italian Studies* 5(3): 348–370.

Press Association (2011). Coca-Cola joins Adidas in expressing concern about FIFA shenani-gans. *The Guardian*. http://www.guardian.co.uk/football/2011/may/30/coca-cola-adidas-fifa (accessed 19 November 2011).

Reuters (2011). Dubai's Emirates reconsidering FIFA sponsorship-report. *The Guardian*. http://www.guardian.co.uk/football/feedarticle/9926360 (accessed 19 November 2011).

Rhodes, R.A.W. (2000). "Governance and public administration," in: Pierre, J. (ed.) *Debating Governance*. Oxford: Oxford University Press, pp. 54–90.

Rowe, D. (2007). "Apollo Undone: The Sports Scandal." in: Lull, J. and Hinerman, S. (eds) *Media Scandals. Morality and desire in the popular culture marketplace*. Cambridge: Polity Press, pp. 203–221.

Sand, T.S., Fasting, K., Chroni, S. and Knorre, N. (2011). "Coaching Behaviour: Any Conse-quences for the Prevalence of Sexual Harassment." *International Journal of Sport Science and Coaching* 6(2): 229–242.

Schenk, S. (2011). Safe hands: building integrity and transparency at FIFA. http://www.transpar-ency.org/content/download/62590/1002688 (accessed 1 December 2011).

Schultz-Jorgensen, S. (2005). "The World's Best Advertising Agency: The Sports Press." *Mandag Morgen* 37: 1–7.

Seippel, O. (2006). "Sport and Social Capital." *Acta Sociologica* 49(2): 169–183.

Slack, T. and Amis, J. (2004). "Money for Nothing and your Cheques for Free? A Critical Perspec-tive on Sport Sponsorship," in: Slack, T. (ed.) *The Commercialisation of Sport*. New York: Routledge, pp. 269–286.

Smith, G.J. (1976). "A Study of a Sports Journalist." *International Review for the Sociology of Sport* 11(3): 5–26.

Sparre, K. (2006). FIVB rules make it impossible to challenge president. http://www.playthegame.org/news/detailed/fivb-rules-make-it-impossible-to-challenge-president-1247.html (accessed 5 November 2011).

Sparre, K. (2008). Acosta voluntarily gives up presidency of the FIVB. http://www.playthegame.org/news/detailed/acosta-voluntarily-gives-up-presidency-of-the-fivb-1121.html (accessed 5 November 2011).

Sugden, J. and Tomlinson, A. (1997). "Global Power Struggles in World Football: FIFA and UEFA, 1954–74, and their Legacy." *International Journal of the History of Sport* 14(2): 1–25.

Sugden, J. and Tomlinson, A. (1998). *FIFA and the Contest for World Football: Who rules the people's game?* Cambridge, UK: Polity Press.

Sydsvenskan. (2011). Nytt sexövergrepp i friidrotten. (New sexual assault in track and field.) http://www.sydsvenskan.se/sverige/article1467904/Nytt-sexovergrepp-inom-friidrotten.html (accessed 14 December 2011).

Talbot, M. (2002). "Playing with Patriarchy: The Gendered Dynamics of Sports Organizations," in: Scraton, S. and Flintoff, A. (eds) *Gender and Sport: A reader*. London, Routledge, pp. 277–291.

The FA (n.d.). Get into football – disability football. http://www.thefa.com/GetIntoFootball/GetInto-FootballPages/Disability%20Football (accessed 6 December 2011).

Thibault, L. and Harvey, J. (1997). Fostering interorganizational linkages in the Canadian sport delivery system. *Journal of Sport Management*, 11(1): 45–68.

Tomlinson, A. (2005). "The Making of the Global Sports Economy: ISL, Adidas and the Rise of the Corporate Player in World Sport," in: Silk, M.L., Andrews, D.L. and Cole, C.L. (eds) *Sport and Corporate Nationalisms*. Oxford: Berg, pp. 35–65.

UEFA. (2005). UEFA executive committee declaration against racism. http://www.uefa.org (accessed 7 December 2011).

UEFA. (2011). UEFA and FARE: Ten years of fighting racism. http://www.uefa.org(accessed 7 December 2011).

Wagg, S. and Andrews, D.L. (eds) (2007). *East Plays West: Sport and the Cold War*. London: Routledge.

Warren, I. (2002). "Governance, Protest and Sport: An Australian Perspective." *Entertainment Law* 1 (1): 67–94.

Whannel, G. (2009). "Television and the Transformation of Sport." *Annals of the American Academy of Political and Social Science* 625(1): 205–218.

Zattoni, A. and Cuomo, F. (2008). "Why Adopt Codes of Good Governance? A Comparison of Institutional and Efficiency Perspectives." *Journal of Compilation* 16(1): 1–15.

Chapter 18

The evolution of sport management in the twenty-first century

David Hassan

TOPICS

Emerging trends in sport management • Volunteerism: the future of sport? • Sport and regulation

---

OBJECTIVES

By the end of this chapter you will be able to:

- Appreciate the emerging themes within the social and cultural management of sport;
- Understand that the management of sport cannot be regarded as a homogenized profession but must respond to constraints present at a national and local level;
- Identify where the focal points for the successful management of sport will emerge from, and the skills necessary to respond to these.

KEY TERMS

Regulatory framework – in the future the need for sport managers to become sufficiently aware of the constraints placed upon their decisions and actions by a legal imperative will become ever more apparent. Thus proving conscious of the regulatory framework in which sport takes places will be of paramount importance for those seeking employment in this field.

Urban space – one of the challenges for sport is the declining capacity within inner-city settings to facilitate continued involvement in organized participation in physical activity. This urban space, which is simply adequate scope to allow for the practice of sport, is instead typically dominated by retail outlets and housing.

> **Volunteers** – the willingness of individuals to give freely of their time without expectation of material or in-kind return, that is, the act of volunteerism, will represent the most significant challenge for sport managers of the future.

OVERVIEW

The purpose of this final, concluding chapter is to draw together the key themes that have emerged during the course of what has proven to be a detailed and wide-ranging anthology. It aims to reveal these factors in a manner that confirms a view that the successful sport manager of the future will not simply be one who can capture the core elements of finance, organizational behaviour, marketing and resource management but crucially also one who can set these issues in their proper context. Thus, being aware of the social and cultural factors that inform management practice within a variable and unpredictable sporting environment will be at the heart of effective sport management in the years to come.

THE EVOLUTION OF SPORT MANAGEMENT

Much of the sport management literature that emerged during the latter part of the twentieth century adopted a very functional, almost abstract approach to the management process. The profession was conceived of in largely generic terms with little account of the varying social and cultural contexts in which sport was taking place or being governed. In latter times a more comprehensive assessment of these variables, from gender, to ethnicity, the specific needs of special populations and the challenges presented by emerging markets, has consequently led to a more sophisticated response to the management of sport, which is informed and impacted by these and other factors (Roberts 2009; Ming *et al.* 2011).

A number of important themes emerge from this anthology, which serves to condition the thinking of the reader, who is in turn conscious of the challenges that lie ahead in the field of sport management. O'Boyle's insightful analysis (Chapter 1) of the need to establish defined and appropriate performance management structures and systems points towards the efficient deployment of scarce resources, their maximization and management in the new management environment of the early twenty-first century. It appears this is more salient than ever due to the examples of poor governance of sporting organizations, their underperformance and even cases of malpractice on the part of certain personnel that occasionally defined the latter part of the twentieth century and sadly continues in part to do so to this day. The latter may be due to the high degree of liquidity present, endemic many sporting bodies, or it may be the inappropriate deployment (or election to office) of individuals to positions of responsibility that their capabilities, euphemistically referred to as their 'skills set', are unable to address. In any event, O'Boyle's timely contribution reminds the reader that, notwithstanding the flexible and evolving nature of applied sport management, there remains a need for proper structures to be implemented to quantify the efficiency of organizations regarding the management of their often limited resources (Sillitoe 1969).

302

The management of one key resource, urban space, remains a principal concern of many inner-city agencies. With the pressures of housing, retail and infrastructure competing for the same piece of land, amid increasingly congested cities, it is often recreational space that becomes the first casualty of rationalization. Matuska (Chapter 2) reveals the situation in the city of Casablanca, Morocco, where the lack of urban space to engage in physical activity is most acutely experienced by the disadvantaged, the poor and other minority groups. It is a perfect example of the requirement to manage sport according to the social needs of a target population and of how a failure to do so has a knock-on effect in terms of personal well-being, health and social exclusion for the marginalized. It is where the emerging field of health economics reminds the reader of how investing in a novel and innovative response to longstanding and intensive demands upon public finances can prove to be a strategically responsible act. In all of this, the need for appropriate public policy responses, followed by their implementation at a local level by socially responsive sport managers, becomes manifest (Rigg 1986).

REGULATORY FRAMEWORK

One of the recurring themes within professional sport over recent years has been the need for an enhanced regulatory framework to safeguard participants, officials and the general public (Greenfield and Osborn 2000). It is an argument at the heart of two separate chapters contained within this collection, penned by Reid and Kitchin, on doping in sport (Chapter 3), and by Anderson (Chapter 4), who examined the relationship between criminal law and a number of separate activities within the sports arena. In the case of the latter, Anderson's contribution contains a salutary reminder that sport does not operate in some benign utopia but is as subject to the rigours of the law as any other aspect of modern life. Where this issue becomes problematic is when one reflects upon the inherent physicality of certain sporting activities and the very strong possibility that participants may be injured as a result of this engagement. The challenge for managers therefore is to protect one of the most important features of sport – its combative nature – whilst remaining conscious that overstepping these boundaries may result in criminal prosecution, especially where it can be proven that this behaviour was premeditated on the part of the aggressor and thus designed to inflict pain and injury.

Evidently, where this latter point has particular relevance is in the ongoing battle against the scourge of doping in sport (Coakley and Hughes 1994). Those who intentionally decide to cheat the system and their fellow athletes by ingesting performance-enhancing drugs arguably represent the most immediate challenge to the integrity of sport and, consequently, embody the need for managers to remain socially responsive to the changing nature of the multi-million-dollar doping industry (Chambers 2009). It is Reid and Kitchin's detailed analysis of this field (Chapter 3) and of the culture of compliance and sympathy offered by those who wish to excuse illegal and unethical practices that strikes at the core of the modern dilemmas facing the sport manager. In some parts of the world, for instance, the presence of a sympathetic media that retains a vested interest in preserving a wholesome image of its athletes and their success does little to make the job of the sport manager any more straightforward.

One of the settings during which the issue of illegal drug-taking in sport receives most attention is the Summer Olympic Games, including at the recent Olympiad help in London in August 2012 (Roche 2000). Spencer Harris' analysis of the UK government's attitude towards the community sport element of the London Games (Chapter 5) is of interest to the global sport manager because both the 'ripple' and much-vaunted 'legacy' effect of major tournaments appear to point to a wider remit regarding mega sports events than has certainly been the case heretofore. There is an onus on sport scholars and students alike to consider properly the full extent of the legacy concept, which needs to be more than simply a study of economics, and include social and political impacts as well (Coakley and Hughes 1994). One of the key aspirations of hosting any major event should be the momentum it creates among the indigenous population in encouraging them to participate in sport, yet successive initiatives, promoted by a host of state administrations, appear to have had only a limited impact in persuading people to engage in physical activity and improve their health and well-being. The future of sport management is likely to be defined by its capacity to encourage greater involvement in sport and physical fitness by the majority of us who choose not to engage in regular healthy activity at present.

The access to resources often considered necessary to participate in regular exercise is further complicated if one is subject to marginalization and discrimination in society. It is a theme developed by Lusted (Chapter 6) in his analysis of sport and 'race' and specifically the needs of governing bodies to develop policies designed to facilitate and encourage greater participation in their activities by members of ethnic minorities. All too often, however, the upper echelons of many governing bodies of sport are dominated by white, ageing males and there remains a responsibility upon those in positions of influence, and indeed the sport in general, to ensure that their organizations are truly representative of the population at large (Roberts 2009). Of course, when the opportunity arises to make public one's opposition to racism, be that at institutional, organizational or participatory level, then any equivocation or unreasonable qualification on the part of key personnel should be highlighted and roundly condemned. This is where the insightful and progressive sport managers of the future require the cultural sensitivity that has been the core thesis of this collection in its most opaque form.

Indeed, it is entirely probable that the future of sport management will be about addressing the twin agendas of access and equality. It is an argument at the heart of Dowling et al.'s comprehensive coverage of the Special Olympics' Youth Unified Sports initiative, which pairs athletes (young people with intellectual disabilities) and partners (contemporaries without a disability) on the same sports team (Chapter 7). It is an example of the purest form of integration of otherwise marginalized minorities with the ultimate intention of achieving full inclusion within society. It is a reminder that the most effective response to longstanding issues is often the most simple. This, alongside the remarkable reach of the Special Olympics organization, with over three million members worldwide as of 2012 and counting, suggests that collaboration between national governing bodies of sport, including those that explicitly promote a socially responsible agenda, can constitute a progressive and impactful way forward in the time to come.

Of course, for a whole host of reasons – financial, utility maximization, supporter demands and one's own personal expectations – it appears a growing body of academic and popular literature has emerged over recent years glorifying a 'culture of risk' within sport. The propensity of those who either willingly subject themselves to risk or continue to perform in sport when injured is understandable at some level but the long-term impacts of this, especially upon professional athletes, can often be profound. The argument contained within the excellent work of Killick *et al.* (Chapter 8) is that the input of significant others, from owners to team coaches, must be closely examined to consider if their actions are in the very best interests of players with whom they come into contact. There can emerge a conspiracy of expectation upon participants to engage in a sport even when they are injured and clearly unable to perform to their optimum. Sport managers, working now and in the future, would do well to reflect upon the short-term folly of this practice and, if anything, properly consider and implement strategies designed to ensure the very best playing talent is available for as long as is conceivably possible.

Nowhere is this more important, it seems, that in the developing world, which has also had to deal with the ill effects of sports labour migration over recent decades. It is an issue adopted by Schroeder (Chapter 9), who points to the impact of globalization upon the transfer of athletic talent as part of a process that has not always had the best interests of the individual sportsman or woman at heart. The management of such prodigious talent, from identifying it, to considering it as a viable investment, to its ongoing development and, eventually, its retirement from active engagement in sport, highlights the very important role played by the sport manager in this career management process. In particular it points to the range of skills required by someone wishing to pursue a career in this field but is also suggestive of the value in developing these through internships, other forms of work experience as well as engagement in real-life, practical settings alongside a course of academic study. It appears the future of sport management will belong to those willing to embrace a broad range of opportunities to develop their professional experience, which may include openings overseas and in different cultural settings throughout the world.

One of the emerging regions of interest to those working in sport management is the Middle East. It is because of the remarkable presence it now retains within world sport, primarily through the hosting of mega sports events, but also because of the diverse social and cultural mores and values of the region, that it retains such fascination (Stevenson and Alaug 2010). Understanding these cultural practices is at the heart of effective sport management as in its absence no meaningful progress can be achieved. It is timely therefore that within this anthology two chapters highlight this apparent dichotomy: the work of Tuastad (Chapter 10) examining sport in a divided Jordan and the detailed analysis of the sporting preferences of the people of the UAE undertaken by O Connor and Hassan (Chapter 14). The latter is particularly interesting on two counts: firstly, because it is remarkably difficult to secure access to factual information concerning the sporting choices of the people of the Middle East and secondly, because it reveals the diverse nature of this interest and a setting in which local idiosyncracies appear to assume precedence over global sports. Together the two chapters suggest a need for the prospective sports manager initially to become sufficiently aware of the cultural setting in which s/he is employed and, from this, to appreciate the role that sport can perform in ameliorating discord in many of the world's divided societies.

In a global sense, however, it appears the future of sport management will cohere around the proper recruitment, retention and development of volunteers as there exist insufficient resources to service the expanding needs of event organizers adequately or even the everyday requirements of sporting federations (Stolle and Hooghe 2003; Strigas and Jackson 2003). It is an issue dealt with at length by O Gorman (Chapter 13), and yet his analysis has relevancy to almost all managers of sport as properly understanding and responding to the needs of one's volunteer base will, it seems, be fundamental to the future survival and success of sport as a whole. Yet O Gorman is sufficiently adept in his analysis to recognize that the ethos of volunteerism varies according to the social and cultural context in which one finds oneself. In certain parts of the world it is extremely difficult to recruit adequate numbers of volunteers because the act of volunteering carries with it certain negative connotations, which convey a demeaning ideology. In contrast, within other parts of the world, volunteering is if anything on the rise and certainly in a small number of individual governing bodies of sport remains absolutely central to their ongoing prosperity. This of course is an emerging theme of the contribution to this collection made by Swart and Bob (Chapter 15), who perhaps capture the essence of modern-day sport – the hosting of mega sport events. Notwithstanding the growth and development of grassroots sport, it appears the future of sport management will be largely informed by major sports events, which serve a host of agendas not least for developing and aspirational nation states (Roche 2000).

SUMMARY

This final chapter has sought to crystallize the key aspects of modern sport management. It has brought to the fore questions of volunteer recruitment and retention, the emerging policy responses to a variety of public agendas in which sport and physical activity remain central and the increasing spectre of a legal framework around sport. Moreover as the growth of sport in parts of the world that hitherto has been limited becomes substantial, the ability to respond to particular mores and values surrounding ethnicity, religious and cultural expectations appears ever more prominent. In short, sport managers must be more aware than ever of the social context in which they are employed and prove capable of responding to this in order to develop and prosper.

REVIEW QUESTIONS

1   Detail what you consider to be the three most important and emerging factors in the management of sport from a social and cultural perspective in the next decade.
2   What skills and attributes might you, as a prospective sport manager, seek to develop alongside your academic qualifications as you seek future employment in this profession?

FURTHER READING

Ming, L., MacIntosh, E. and Bravo, G. (2011). *International Sport Management*. Champaign, IL: Human Kinetics.
Slack, T. and Parent, M. (eds) (2007). *International Perspectives on the Management of Sport*. London: Butterworth-Heinemann.

Trenberth, L. and Hassan, D. (eds). (2011). *Managing Sport Business: An introduction*. Routledge: London.

WEBSITES

European Association for Sport Management:

www.easm.net

International Sport Management:

sportism.net

Sport Management:

www.sportsmanagement.co.uk

REFERENCES

Chambers, D. (2009). *Race Against Me, My Story*. Madrid: Libros International.

Coakley, R. and Hughes, J. (1994). *Deviance in Sports, Sport in Society, Issues and Controversies*, 5th edn. St Louis, MO: St Louis University Press.

Greenfield, S. and Osborn, G. (eds) (2000). *Law and Sport in Contemporary Society*. London: Frank Cass.

Ming, L., MacIntosh, E. and Bravo, G. (2011). *International Sport Management*. Champaign, IL: Human Kinetics.

Rigg, M. (1986). *Action Sport: Community sports leadership in the inner cities*. London: Sports Council.

Roberts, K. (2009) *Key Concepts in Sociology*. Basingstoke: Palgrave Macmillan.

Roche, M. (2000). *Mega-events and Modernity: Olympics and expos in the growth of global culture*. London: Routledge.

Sillitoe, K. (1969). *Planning Leisure*. London: HMSO.

Stevenson, T.B. and Alaug, A.K. (2010). "Yemeni Football and Identity Politics." In *Middle East Viewpoints: Sports and the Middle East*. Washington, DC: Middle East Institute, pp. 16–19.

Stolle, D. and Hooghe, M. (2003). "Conflicting Approaches to the Study of Social Capital: Competing Explanations for Causes and Effects of Social Capital." *Ethical Perspectives* 10(1): 22–45.

Strigas, A. and Jackson, N. (2003). "Motivating Volunteers to Serve and Succeed: Design and Results of a Pilot Study that Explores Demographics and Motivational Factors in Sport Volunteerism." *International Sports Journal* 7(1): 111–121.

Index